UNCOMMON UNDERSTANDING

UNCOMMON UNDERSTANDING

DEVELOPMENT AND DISORDERS OF LANGUAGE COMPREHENSION IN CHILDREN

D.V.M. Bishop

*Senior Scientist, MRC Applied Psychology Unit,
Cambridge, UK*

Psychology Press
a member of the Taylor & Francis group

Copyright © 1997 by Psychology Press Limited
a member of the Taylor & Francis Group

Psychology Press, Publishers
27 Church Road
Hove
East Sussex, BN3 2FA
UK

British Library Cataloguing in Publication Data
A catalogue record for this title is available from the British Library

ISBN 0-86377-260-9 (Hbk)
ISBN 0-86377-501-2 (Pbk)

Printed and bound in the United Kingdom by Bookcraft Ltd., Bath

Contents

Foreword

When I embarked on postgraduate research, a wise friend warned me to choose my thesis topic carefully, as I would be likely to be engrossed with the same problem for the rest of my academic career. I now realise the truth of those words. My thesis title was "Language comprehension: Normal and abnormal development"; now, 20 years later, I have written a book on exactly the same topic. This might imply that I have become increasingly specialised as time has gone by, developing a rich understanding of a highly specific area. Nothing could be further from the truth. What seemed like a simple question: "Do language-impaired children have comprehension problems?" has grown like yeast in warm water. The more understanding one gains of the issues, the more one realises just how much there is still to discover. A major reason for this is that "comprehension" is not a unitary skill; to understand spoken language, one needs the ability to classify incoming speech sounds, to relate them to a "mental lexicon", to interpret the propositions encoded by word order and grammatical inflections, and to use information from the environmental and social context to select, from a wide range of possible interpretations, the one that was intended by the speaker. There is no way that one can summarise a child's "receptive language level" in terms of a score on a single test: comprehension is multifaceted. My aim here is to integrate research in language acquisition, psycholinguistics and neuropsychology to give a comprehensive picture of the process we call "comprehension", right from the reception of an acoustic stimulus at the ear, up to the point where we interpret the message the speaker intended to convey by the utterance.

The emphasis of this book is very much on specific language impairment (SLI); other conditions that affect language development, such as hearing loss, or autistic disorder, are given only a passing mention. Furthermore, the focus is on research and theory, rather than practical matters of assessment and intervention. Nevertheless, while this book is not intended as a clinical guide to assessment, it does aim to provide a theoretical framework that can help clinicians develop a clearer understanding of what comprehension involves, and how different types of difficulty may be pinpointed. I hope also that practitioners will also find the contents provide a stimulus for developing new methods to tackle comprehension problems. Many researchers justify their theoretical studies with the statement "if we understand the nature of the disorder better, we will be able to devise more effective interventions", but all too often this is a hollow promise, because the research is buried in scientific journals that are not accessible to the typical speech-language therapist or teacher working in a busy school or clinic. One of my aims was to synthesise a sprawling and complex literature in a form that was readable without being over-simplistic.

I would like to acknowledge the support of the Medical Research Council, who have funded all my work on specific language impairment, and Freda Newcombe, my thesis supervisor, who first aroused my interest in the topic. Much of this book was written in the tranquillity and sunshine of the University of Western Australia, and I would like to thank the Psychology Department for their hospitality, and the Reid Library, whose staff were always patient and helpful in tracking down material. The APU support staff, Jackie Harper and Daphne Hanson, who helped with checking of references and inordinate quantities of photo-copying, made all the difference at the final stages of producing the book. Thanks also to Wen-Tao Song for providing information about Chinese ideograms, and Gary Job for artwork.

I must not forget to mention the staff and pupils of special schools and language units in the UK who so generously gave of their time to help with my research, and offered many an insightful comment that influenced my thinking. Staff at the three schools where I started my doctoral studies, and where I continue to find a welcome, deserve an especially warm thanks: John Horniman School, Worthing; Moor House School, Oxted; and Dawn House School, Mansfield.

The book has benefited greatly from comments by expert reviewers, Elizabeth Bates, Robin Chapman, Jane Oakhill, and Maggie Snowling. I am grateful to them for sharing their expertise and preventing me from many a statement that was unclear, clumsy, or just plain wrong (but with the usual disclaimer that the things that are still unclear, clumsy, and just plain wrong are entirely my responsibility). Additional thanks are due to Sarah Hawkins and Geoff Potter, who helped me in the production of spectrograms. Ramin Nakisa, Ted Briscoe, Heather van der Lely, Gina Conti-Ramsden, Sally Butterfield, Karen Croot, Alex Shepherd, Linda Clare, Peter Bright, Sophie Scott, and Rik Henson read drafts of parts of the book, and offered invaluable feedback from both expert and novice perspectives. I must record my special gratitude to two stalwart APU post-graduates, Elisabeth Hill and Hilary Green, who read the entire book in draft form and offered invaluable suggestions and criticisms. Finally, thanks to my husband, Pat Rabbitt, who understands like nobody else.

DOROTHY BISHOP
Cambridge, December 1996

1

From sound to meaning— A framework for analysing comprehension

Language is so readily acquired and so universal in human affairs that it is easy to forget what a complex phenomenon it is. Despite years of research, we still understand remarkably little about how language works. Consider the problems there have been in developing computers that can process human language. What an advantage it would be to have an automatic system that could listen to a person talking and translate their speech into a written form—a combined Dictaphone and word processor that did all the work of an audio-typist. Technology is now advancing to the stage where this kind of machine is possible, but it has taken more than 30 years of intensive research to achieve this goal, and the best contemporary speech recognition devices are less good than a four-year-old child at recognising a stream of continuous speech spoken by an unfamiliar speaker. Suppose, though, we try to crack a different problem: rather than getting a machine to recognise spoken words, let us present it with

ready-typed sentences, and see if it can decode meaning well enough to translate from one language to another. Here too, enormous effort has been expended in trying to achieve a solution, yet the results so far are unimpressive (see *Machine translation*, overleaf). One thing that makes language comprehension such an intriguing topic is that it is something that computers are relatively bad at, despite their enormous power and speed of operation. Against this background, it is all the more remarkable that nearly all children soak up language in the first few years of life, apparently requiring only a modest amount of linguistic stimulation in order to develop, by the age of four years or so, into language users who are far more competent than the most sophisticated computer.

This chapter will set the scene for the rest of the book by giving a preliminary overview of the different stages involved in comprehension. In Chapter 2, we turn to consider what is known about

Machine translation

In the 1950s, there was optimism that computers would readily be able to tackle the task of translating between languages. All that would be required would be knowledge of vocabulary and grammar of source and target languages and rules for converting one to another. It was only when computer scientists began to tackle this task that we started to appreciate just how much understanding of meaning depends on general knowledge as well as the words in a sentence. A high proportion of the words in a language are ambiguous, as was illustrated in a famous example by the philosopher Bar-Hillel (cited in Arnold, Balkan, Humphreys, Meijer, & Sadler, 1994), who noted the problems that would be encountered by a machine translation system confronted with a sequence such as:

> Little Peter was looking for his toy box. The box was in the pen.

To interpret this correctly, one needs to have knowledge of the relative size of typical pens and boxes, to recognise that it would be well nigh impossible to put a box in a pen, as in Fig. 1.1, below, and to appreciate that in the context of a small child, "pen" can refer to a playpen. Bar-Hillel's view was that computers could never be given sufficient knowledge to deal with this kind of problem, and so machine translation was doomed.

Ambiguity is also found in the grammar of a language. For instance, computer programs designed to translate technical manuals can have difficulty with a sentence such as:

> Put the paper in the printer and then switch it on.

Humans have sufficient knowledge of paper and printers to realise that "it" must be the printer, but for a program equipped with only vocabulary and grammatical rules, this would be ambiguous.

Despite these difficulties, machine translation systems have been developed to do a reasonable "first pass" translation in a specific domain, such as weather reports or timetable enquiries. However, they cope poorly when presented with material outside the subject area for which they have been adapted. Cheap, nonspecialised translation devices that are on the market for use with personal computers may produce output that gives the gist of a meaning, but they have a long way to go before they can match a human translator, as illustrated by this example from Arnold et al. (1994).

Source text (German Teletext travel news)
Summerurlauber an den Küsten Südeuropas oder der Ost- und Nordsee müssen vereinzelt mit Beeinträchtigungen des Badespasses rechnen.
    An der Adria wird bei Eraclea Mare und Caorle wegen bakterieller Belastungen vom Baden abgeraten.

Computer translation
Summer vacationers at the coasts of South Europe or the east- and North Sea must calculate isolated with impairments of the bath joke.
    At the Adria Mare and Caorle is dissuaded at Eraclea because of bacterial burdens from the bath.

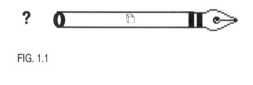

FIG. 1.1

---

children with a specific language impairment (SLI), many of whom have difficulty in learning to understand as well as to produce language. The later chapters explore individual processes in more detail and ask how far a deficit at a specific level might be the root of the language difficulties seen in children with SLI. Although the emphasis is on understanding, abnormalities of children's expressive language will also be discussed, insofar as these help illuminate the types of linguistic representations that might be affected in SLI.

STAGES AND REPRESENTATIONS

Figure 1.2 depicts a simplified model of the stages involved in processing a spoken message from acoustic waveform to meaning. This kind of model conceptualises comprehension as a process whereby information is successfully transformed from one kind of representation to another. Initially, the information is available in the form of a complex acoustic signal. This is encoded into a phonological representation which retains all the linguistically salient detail, but ignores other information, dramatically reducing the amount of information to be processed. Phonological representations then make contact with long-term representations in a mental lexicon, enabling one to associate a given sound pattern with meaning. As we proceed down the information-processing chain, our representation becomes increasingly abstract and remote from the surface characteristics in the original signal. This type of information-

processing model became popular in the 1960s and, although it has limitations which will become apparent as we proceed, it is still widely used in neuropsychology, where it provides a useful framework for distinguishing the different levels at which a cognitive process may be disrupted. We shall illustrate the model by tracing through the mental representations that are generated by the listener on hearing the utterance "The fish is on the table".

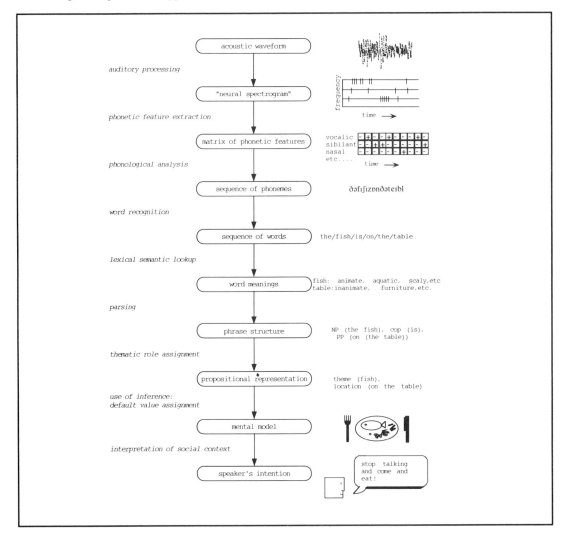

FIG. 1.2   Model of the stages of processing involved in transforming a sound wave into meaning when comprehending the utterance "the fish is on the table". In this model, comprehension is depicted as a purely "bottom-up" process, with incoming information being subject to successive transformations in sequential order. As we shall see, this is a gross oversimplification.

Speech recognition

Someone speaks, and a sound wave is generated. This is converted in the ear into a neural signal which then is processed by the brain and interpreted by the listener as a meaningful message. Chapter 3 is concerned with the first three stages of information processing shown in Fig. 1.2, from "auditory processing", through to "phonological analysis".

Figure 1.3 shows a simplified representation of the stages involved in converting an acoustic signal (i.e. a sound waveform) into an auditory form (i.e. a neural representation). A mechanical transformation of the signal is carried out in the middle ear, with neural encoding achieved in the inner ear. Vibrations of the basilar membrane in the cochlea stimulate the hair cells, which feed impulses into the auditory nerve. A neurally encoded representation of the frequency and intensity characteristics of the sound is conveyed via the auditory nerve and subcortical systems to the auditory cortex of the brain. In the auditory cortex there are brain cells that fire selectively in response to sounds of specific frequencies, as well as others that respond to changes in frequency over a given range or direction (Kay & Matthews, 1972). The brain thus maps sound into a neural representation that contains crucial information about the amount of energy in different frequency bands and its rate of change, a so-called "neural spectrogram".

The usual use of the term "spectrogram" is to describe a visual representation of frequency and intensity of an acoustic signal over time (see *Spectrograms*, next page). Figure 1.5 shows a spectrogram of the utterance "the fish is on the table". The first thing that is apparent is that the signal is not neatly chunked into words: gaps are as likely to occur within a word as at a word boundary. The perceptual experience of a sequence of individual words is achieved by the brain's interpretative processes which convert a continuous stream into discrete units. (We become all too aware of this when listening to an unfamiliar language; when we can't identify the words, speech is perceived as both rapid and continuous.) There are other problems that the listener has to contend with in interpreting a speech signal. The characteristics of the acoustic signal will vary from speaker to speaker, and will vary for the same speaker depending on such factors as speech rate or emotional state. Furthermore, speech typically occurs against background noise: the listener has to extract the critical speech material from a welter of acoustic information. Cocktail parties are well-loved by psychologists, not just for their social and alcoholic possibilities, but because they demonstrate so convincingly the human capacity to attend to a single speech stream against a babble of background chatter.

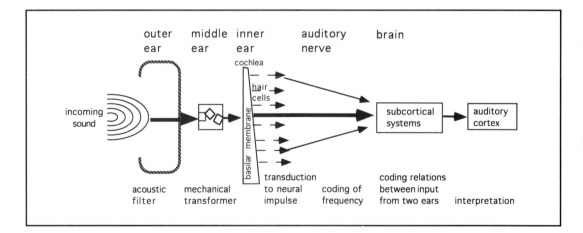

FIG .1.3   Schematic diagram of initial stages of auditory processing of incoming speech. For a more detailed account see Evans (1992).

Spectrograms

The spectrograph is a device that converts speech signals into a three-dimensional visual representation, the spectrogram. Variations in intensity (which are perceived as changes in loudness) are represented by the darkness of the trace, with the most intense being the blackest. Variations in frequency are represented on the y-axis, and time is shown on the x-axis.

The spectrograms in Fig. 1.4 show the sound patterns corresponding to syllables differing by a single vowel.

In the 1950s, a "pattern playback" was devised, which converted spectrograms back to an auditory form. This enabled researchers to modify the spectrogram, or even create hand-painted spectrograms, to investigate the auditory perceptual correlates of particular changes in the signal (Cooper, Liberman, & Borst, 1951).

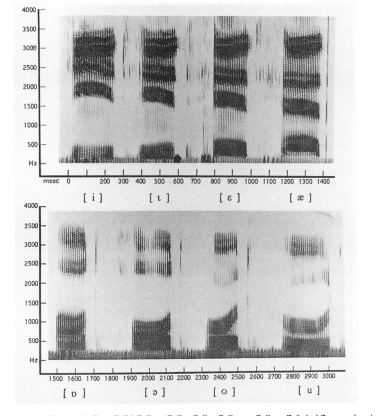

FIG. 1.4   A spectrogram of the words "heed", "hid", "head", "had", "hod", "hawed", "hood", "who'd" as spoken in a British accent. (Reproduced from Ladefoged, 1993.)

How do we extract the systematic information from such variable input? For many years it was assumed that children must first learn to recognise the phonemes from which all words are composed (see *Phones and phonemes*, overleaf). The phonemes of English are shown on the table on the inside of the front cover. The argument for a level of representation between the acoustic signal and the word is strengthened by the evidence that people have no difficulty in operating with unfamiliar stimuli at this level. Even young children can repeat back unfamiliar strings of

Phones and phonemes

In using symbols to represent speech sounds, a distinction is made between the phonetic level of representation, which classifies speech sounds in terms of how they are produced, and the phonemic level, which classifies sounds in terms of how they are used to convey meaning. The two are related but not equivalent. At the phonetic level, symbols are used to denote elements that are defined in physical terms. At the phonemic level, the elements are abstract linguistic units that may have variable articulatory correlates, but which are functionally equivalent in how they signal meaning.

Phonetic symbols, transcribed in square brackets, are used to represent phones, i.e. particular speech sounds corresponding to specific articulatory configurations. For instance, [p^h] denotes the sound made by forcing air pressure to build up behind the closed lips and then releasing this abruptly with an audible expulsion of breath (aspiration), while holding the vocal cords (in the larynx) apart, so they do not vibrate. The symbol [p] denotes the sound that results from the same articulatory gestures when the opening of the lips is not accompanied by aspiration. To appreciate the difference, try saying "pit" and "spit" while holding your hand in front of your mouth. You should be able to feel a puff of air for "pit" but not "spit". In English, words such as "rip" may be said with the final consonant either aspirated or unaspirated: this has no effect on the meaning we perceive—we still hear "rip". However, if the same articulatory gestures are made while holding the vocal cords together causing vibration in the larynx (voicing) before the release of air through the lips, then the phone [b] is produced, and we identify a word with a different meaning, "rib".

When individual phones are used contrastively in the language to convey differences in meaning, they correspond to phonemes. Phonemes are transcribed between slashes. In English, [p] and [p^h] are not contrastive, but rather function as alternative forms of the same phoneme, /p/. However, [b] and [p] are contrastive, and so different phonemic symbols are used to denote them, /b/ and /p/ respectively.

Different languages vary not just in terms of the phonetic inventory of sounds that they use, but also in how they partition phones into contrastive phonemes. Thus, in Hindi, as in English, stops may be aspirated or unaspirated. However, in Hindi, aspiration distinguishes a phonemic contrast, and words produced with [p] and [p^h] will differ in meaning. For instance, [pal] means "take care of", whereas [p^{h}al] means "edge of knife".

In the course of learning a language, we develop a sensitive perceptual ability to discriminate between phonemes, but find it hard to hear, or produce, phonetic differences that are not contrastive. Thus, native Japanese speakers will have much greater difficulty than English speakers in both perceiving and producing the distinction between [r] and [l], because this contrast is not used to signal different meanings in Japanese. In English, we do not have the vowel sound [y]*, and so when we try to learn French, we have difficulty learning how to distinguish words such as "tout" [tu] and "tu" [ty]. In a similar vein, English speakers will have much more difficulty than Hindi speakers in making a perceptual discrimination between [p] vs. [p^h], even though English speakers regularly produce both phones. These examples illustrate that correct production and perception of speech sounds is not simply a function of auditory and articulatory competence; our ears and articulators may be perfectly adequate, but we will still make mistakes if we have not learned to classify speech sounds in the right way for the language we are trying to speak.

*To produce the vowel [y], try to say "eeee" with your lips rounded.

speech sounds, provided these are reasonably short and do not overload their memory capacity (Gathercole & Adams, 1993). If I say "prindle" and you repeat it accurately, this must mean that you are able to perform some analysis that enables you to extract the articulatory correlates of the signal. Thus a level of representation between a relatively unprocessed auditory stimulus and the word, as shown in Fig. 1.2, is motivated both on the grounds of efficiency and because it would explain our ability to analyse and reproduce novel sequences of speech sounds with such facility.

The spectrograph was developed in the 1940s with the expectation that if we could convert the speech signal into an appropriate visual display, it would be a relatively simple matter to identify the crucial features that were used to distinguish phonemes. And it certainly is the case that a skilled speech scientist can look at a spectrogram and identify fairly readily certain salient features that make it possible to distinguish vowels from consonants, plosives from fricatives, nasals from non-nasals, and so on (see *Acoustic cues in speech perception*, p.8). An important point to note is that

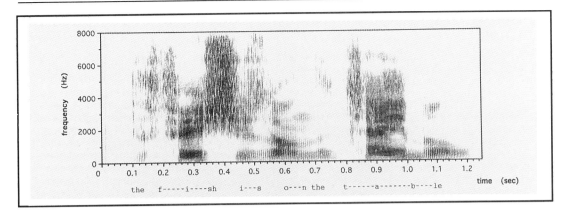

FIG. 1.5   Spectrogram of the utterance "the fish is on the table" spoken by a British male.

some of this critical information occurs in a very brief space of time. For instance, the place of articulation of a consonant is reflected in a rapid change in formant frequency over an interval of less than 40 msec. A difference of 20 msec in "voice onset time" differentiates stimuli labelled as voiced consonants from unvoiced. An influential theory of SLI, first put forward by Tallal and Piercy (1973a), maintains that difficulties in identifying brief or rapid auditory events are at the root of the language learning difficulties of these children. Such a deficit would lead to great difficulties in discriminating between certain speech sounds, especially those differing in terms of voicing or place of articulation, and so the theory provides a plausible account of SLI as a perceptual disorder. This theory will be thoroughly evaluated in Chapter 3.

Although the ability to distinguish between brief and rapid auditory events is necessary for adequate speech perception, it is not sufficient. One of the more perplexing findings from the early spectrographic studies was that there is no constancy between the acoustic signal and the phoneme. Despite the general features shown in *Acoustic cues in speech perception*, overleaf, there is no specific pattern that we can identify as the hallmark of the phoneme /d/, for instance (see Fig. 1.6, below, and examples shown in *Spectrograms*, p.5): the same phoneme will have different acoustic correlates, depending which phonemes preceded and followed it (see Liberman, Cooper, Shankweiler, & Studdert-Kennedy, 1967, for a review).

Indeed, the same acoustic waveform could be perceived as a different phoneme, depending on the word in which it occurred. Because our alphabet represents the phonemic structure of words (albeit imperfectly), most people assume that speech is simply a sequence of distinct speech sounds, so that

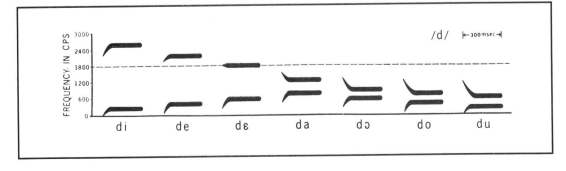

FIG. 1.6   Spectrographic patterns sufficient for the synthesis of /d/ before vowels. (Reproduced from Liberman et al., 1967.)

Acoustic cues in speech perception

Look again at Fig. 1.5 (p.7) and notice the areas of the spectrogram where the signal contains dark horizontal bands. These areas of increased energy at a given frequency are known as formants. Vowels are characterised by steady-state formants, i.e. those regions where the formant remains at one frequency. Specific vowels differ in terms of the patterning and frequencies of the formants, as can be seen from the portions of the spectrogram corresponding to the vowels in "fish", "is", "on", and "table".

Nasal consonants, such as the initial sound in "man" and "neck" and the final sound in "ring", are characterised by a weakening in the intensity of the upper formant of the preceding vowel, together with an additional low frequency resonance. This can be seen in Fig. 1.5 for the "n" sound of "on".

Stops are consonants produced by a sudden constriction of the airway (formed by lips, or contact of tongue against the soft or hard palate) followed by a release. One can see a brief attenuation of sound before a stop (see the "t" and "b" of "table") followed by a transient burst of noise (i.e. areas with no formant structure, where energy is spread across a wide range of frequencies with no patterning). This is followed by a rapid change in the formant frequencies.

Fricatives are produced by forcing air across the partially closed articulators, as in the initial and final sounds of "fish". They can be seen on the spectrogram as an extended period of noise. Fricatives such as /s/, /z/, and /ʃ/ (i.e. the final sound of "fish") have particularly large amounts of acoustic energy at high frequency and are known as "sibilants".

Another feature that can be seen on the spectrogram are patterns of vertical bands which correspond to glottal pulses, made when the vocal cords are held close together to produce "voicing". This is particularly evident in the final syllable of "table". Whispering is a form of speech with no voicing. Many consonants have phonemically contrastive forms that are distinguished only by "voice onset time", i.e. the interval between the onset of the consonant and the onset of glottal pulsing. For so-called "voiced" consonants, such as /b/, /d/, and /g/, the onset of voicing is early, whereas in their "unvoiced" analogues, /p/, /t/, and /k/, the vocal cords are initially held apart, and the onset of voicing occurs later. Using synthesised speech, where voice onset time is systematically varied, researchers have shown that there is a fairly abrupt shift in perception from voiced to unvoiced forms. Another acoustic cue to voicing is length of a preceding vowel: voiced consonants are preceded by longer vowels than unvoiced.

Another dimension on which phonemes differ is place of articulation. For instance, the consonants /p/, /t/, and /k/ are all unvoiced stops, but for /p/ the closure is at the lips, for /t/ between tongue and alveolar ridge, and for /k/ between back of the tongue and the velum. A strong correlate of place of articulation is the direction and slope of the formant transition from adjacent steady-state vowels. A further cue is provided by the frequency of the noise component.

For more detailed treatment of acoustic cues to speech perception see Borden, Harris, and Raphael (1994).

when we hear "cat", we perceive, in rapid sequence, the auditory equivalents of /k/, /a/, and /t/, and that by dissecting the acoustic signal at the right points and reassembling it, we would be able to create the sound "tack". Not so. Phonemes do have common articulatory characteristics in different contexts; when I produce the consonant [k], I do so by making contact between the back of the tongue and the velum and releasing this with an explosive burst of air, while holding the vocal cords apart. However, the precise location of the velar contact will vary depending what comes next: it will be further forward when the following vowel is made in the front of the mouth, as in "key" than when the next vowel is a back vowel, as in "coo". Other features, such as lip position will also be

affected by the phonetic context: contrast the shape of the lips when saying "key" or "coo". This overlapping of adjacent articulations is known as "co-articulation". The acoustic correlates of a given phoneme are highly variable. In short, what one sees at a given point in time in the speech signal is the composite effect of a sequence of phonemes, and unravelling this to isolate the contributing articulations is a major problem for speech recognition.

Lack of acoustic invariance for phonemes created such difficulties for attempts to build computerised speech recognition systems that people began to consider using different units of analysis. Klatt (1980) proposed the diphone (i.e. pairs of phonemes) as providing a more workable level of analysis, on the grounds that it enabled one to take phonetic context into account. Stevens and Blumstein (1981) went in the other direction, decomposing phonemes into bundles of subphonemic features and looking for acoustic correlates of these. Our interest here, however, is not so much in the relative merits of different approaches used by speech recognition systems, as in what such developments tell us about the problems confronting the human listener. The point that emerges clearly is that the phoneme is by no means a natural or obvious unit of perception.

This insight is particularly pertinent when we consider the young child who is learning to make sense of an incoming speech stream. The fact that speech perception might not be a straightforward business of matching phonemes to learned auditory "templates" was emphasised when researchers started studying the role of "phonological aware-ness" in literacy acquisition. It was not uncommon to find children who at the age of five or six years seemed quite unable to match or identify individual phonemes (and who hence had great difficulty in learning letter–sound correspondences), and yet who had no obvious or gross difficulties in speech production or understanding. Somehow, they seemed to succeed in word recognition and production without apparently using the phoneme as a perceptual unit. Liberman, Shankweiler, and Liberman (1989) argued that their difficulty had to do with the lack of one-to-one correspondence between segments of the acoustic signal and phonemes. Early investigators tended to assume that speech sounds were represented in the acoustic signal like beads on a string; a better analogy might be that they are like jelly-babies that are threaded on a string and then heated in an oven, so that adjacent items merge. One cannot chop off a segment of speech corresponding to /d/: rather the /d/ characteristics are "smeared" across the whole syllable.

If children have such difficulty in identifying phonemes, is there evidence they use other units in speech perception? In a review of research, Walley (1993) concluded that early phonological development involves a progression from larger to more fine-grained units of analysis. Initially, the child may operate with whole words or even short phrases, simply encoding these in terms of certain salient features, such as number of syllables, stress, and presence of phonetic features such as nasality or sibilance somewhere in the input (without any specification of exactly where) (Waterson, 1971). Such a child might not be able to distinguish between different syllables that contain the same features in different combinations, but would nevertheless be able to store templates of words with incomplete representations of phonetic information. As Walley noted (p. 317): "Although seldom considered, the fact that children produce a certain contrast does not necessarily imply the presence of that contrast in their perceptual representations for words, which might instead be stored and retrieved as unsegmented wholes." By the age of three or four years, most children appear to be aware of the subsyllabic units of onset and rime (see *Units of phonological analysis*, overleaf), but only later, perhaps as a consequence of exposure to print, do they recognise the smaller phonemic elements. One theory that will be reviewed in Chapter 3 maintains that many of the problems of children with SLI can be accounted for by assuming that they persist much longer than other children in analysing speech at the level of gross syllabic units, without awareness of phonemes.

Thus although Fig. 1.2 (p.3) shows a level of representation corresponding to a sequence of phonemes, it is important to appreciate that this is just one possible form of representation. Most researchers would agree that there is at least one intermediate level of representation between the "neural spectrogram" and word recognition, but there are several different forms this could take (see, e.g. Marslen-Wilson & Warren, 1994). Developmental studies suggest the form of representation may change in the course of a child's development.

In Chapter 3, we will consider how far comprehension problems in children with SLI can be explained in terms of defective speech perception.

Lexical semantics

Chapter 4 is concerned with the processes shown in Fig. 1.2 (p.3) as "word recognition" and "lexical semantic lookup".

Units of phonological analysis

Interest in children's awareness of different phonological units was stimulated by studies of reading development which showed that "phonological awareness" was an important predictor of success in literacy. Most nonexperts assume that young children can readily detect that "cat" has three sounds. However, studies in which children are asked to judge which sounds are alike or different, or to add, delete, or count speech elements, indicate that by three to four years of age, most children are readily able to analyse syllables into onset (initial consonant(s)) and rime (vowel and any subsequent consonants) (see Table 1.1, below). However, awareness of phonemes often comes only after the child learns to read (Treiman & Zukowski, 1991). Thus, the preschooler would be able to pick out "cat" and "rat" as being similar to one another, and different from "back", but might be unable to judge that "cat" and "moat" ended with the same sound.

TABLE 1.1

Different Levels at Which Words Can Be Decomposed into Smaller Units

	Orthographic		Phonemic	
word	SANDWICH		sandwɪʧ	
syllable	SAND	WICH	sand	wɪʧ
onset + rime	S + AND	W + ICH	s + and	w + ɪʧ
phoneme	S + A + N + D	W + I + CH	/s/ /a/ /n/ /d/	/w/ /ɪ/ /ʧ/

Word learning. The child who is learning language must identify recurring meaningful patterns from the stream of incoming speech and store these in long-term memory, so that they are recognised as familiar words when encountered again. Mental representations of words contain information both about the phonological form of the word, and a representation of its meaning. Vocabulary acquisition may be seen as the process of storing representations of familiar sequences of speech sounds in a mental dictionary or "lexicon", and associating these with specific meanings. One can see that, in principle, there are several types of impairment that could make it difficult to form new long-term representations of words: (1) the child might have problems retaining in memory sequences of speech sounds corresponding to words; (2) there might be an inadequate or abnormal representation of meaning (to take a simple example, the child may know the word "dog" but treat it as referring to all four-legged animals, a case of "overgeneralisation" of meaning); or (3) the child may have a normal representation of meaning and a normal ability to form phonological representations in the lexicon, but have difficulty in forming links between the two. The first of these possibilities has attracted particular interest with regard to SLI, where it has been demonstrated that children do have unusual difficulty in repeating novel sequences of sounds (Gathercole & Baddeley, 1990b), leading to the proposal that it is limitation of phonological short-term memory that restricts new vocabulary learning. This theory will be evaluated in Chapter 4.

Word recognition (lexical access). Once the child has a store of familiar words (mental lexicon), then the problem of word comprehension is not solved. There is still the task of matching items in the store with sequences of sounds in the incoming speech signal. There are at least two major problems that a psycholinguistic model must address. First, as described earlier, the acoustic signal is not physically segmented into words, so how is the listener to know where each word begins and ends? The second problem is how to find a match for a spoken word from the huge number of representations stored in long-term memory. The speed of word recognition makes it implausible that we search rapidly through all the words that we know until a match is found. In Chapter 4, we will consider how far an impairment in lexical access can explain comprehension problems seen in some children.

Sentence interpretation

Chapter 5 moves on to deal with the use of grammatical knowledge in language understanding.

Syntactic rules and relationships Understanding involves more than simply identifying the meanings of individual words. The same words convey different meanings depending on how they are organised: "the man chases a big dog", "the big man chases a dog", and "the dog chases a big man" and "the dogs chase a big man" all mean different things. The incoming sentence must be parsed into phrases corresponding to units of meaning, and the relationships between these decoded. Certain parts of speech, notably verbs and prepositions, serve the function of denoting relationships between properties, things, places, and actions, in contrast to concrete nouns, which serve to refer to objects.

Within a phrase, inflectional endings may be used to convey meaning (e.g. noun plural "-s" as in "dog" vs. "dogs") and also to denote meaningful relationships between different phrase elements, (e.g. possessive "-s", as in "man's dog"). The so-called "function words", a small set of words with a primarily grammatical function, can also serve to modify meaning of words they occur with, e.g. "not black", "I will go", "this dog".

An individual who had poor mastery of grammar but reasonable understanding of word meaning might manage to achieve a fair degree of understanding of spoken language by combining knowledge of vocabulary with common-sense inference about what is likely to have been said. Thus if one only understood that a speaker had referred to "fish" and "table", it might, in many circumstances be sufficient to deduce the intended

meaning. Indeed, you may have experienced this kind of situation when attempting to follow a conversation in a language in which you are barely proficient. Appreciation of one or two cue words and some intelligent deduction can take one a long way. However, it is all too easy to lose the thread or to make the wrong deduction, especially if the conversation is not following an expected course. Comprehension problems due to grammatical deficits may, therefore, be less obvious than difficulties at earlier stages of processing, but they are easy enough to demonstrate in test situations when one can devise materials so as to make grammar critical, as in the example in Fig. 1.7 (overleaf).

In Chapter 5, we will consider in detail how children learn the grammatical regularities of their language. This is a topic that is critical for linguists working in the Chomskyan tradition, who regard children's remarkable ability to learn whatever ambient language they are exposed to as evidence for considerable innate structuring of knowledge in the brain. Children with SLI have generated enormous interest from linguists because they raise the possibility that there might be some individuals in whom this innate substrate for language is deficient.

Understanding sentences in real time

Understanding of sentences not only requires knowledge of grammar, but also the ability to deploy that knowledge in real time. There is ample evidence that we do not wait until the end of a sentence in order to assign it an interpretation. Rather, this is gradually built up by stages as we perceive each new segment of the input utterance. Sentence understanding is harder than single word interpretation not just because it involves grammatical relationships, but also because it places heavy processing demands on an interpretative system that must build sentence interpretations "on line", and which will run into trouble if the rate of new input exceeds the system's processing speed. Furthermore, the system must be able to deal with the ambiguity that characterises spoken language, which is often most marked when we have only part of a sentence available. Suppose we hear the first three syllables of our

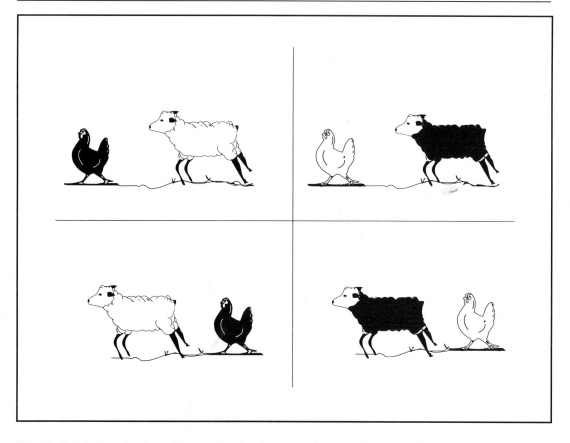

FIG. 1.7 Multiple choice item for testing comprehension of grammatical structure: "the chicken follows the sheep that is black". The child's task is to point to the picture that matches the spoken sentence.

sentence "the fish is on the table"; we do not know whether this should be interpreted as "the fish is" or "the fishes" until we listen on , and realise that only the first reading gives a complete sentence.

Chapter 6 contrasts processing accounts of SLI, which maintain that the operations involved in on-line computation of sentence meaning are impaired, with the representational accounts of Chapter 5, which assume that underlying grammatical knowledge is defective.

Beyond the sentence: Context and discourse

Integrating sentence meaning with general knowledge: Comprehension as selection.   Chapter 7 deals with the next step shown in Fig. 1.2, that of using inference to go beyond what has been literally stated to infer meaning. Most

comprehension tests assess the ability to extract the literal meaning of a word or sentence, either by acting out a described sequence of events (e.g. demonstrating with small toys "the tiger chases the elephant") or by selecting a picture from an array to match a spoken sentence (as in Fig. 1.7, above). Yet there is far more to comprehension than this. Most sentences are open to numerous alternative interpretations (see *Language ambiguity,* opposite). Comprehension involves selecting a meaning from a range of possibilities, rather than simply decoding *the* meaning. We continually and unconsciously disambiguate highly ambiguous material by using general knowledge to infer what is meant in a given context. For instance, consider the sentence "the fish is on the table". If one hears this uttered in the context of a dinner party, then one will assume that the fish is dead, on a plate, and

---

Language ambiguity

The following example comes from Pinker (1994), who uses it to illustrate the problems experienced when humans try to build a computer that will understand language. The problem is not that the computer is unfamiliar with the words or grammar: it has been programmed to store prodigious amounts of language. The difficulty is that, unlike a human being, it cannot use contextual cues to home in automatically on the single correct meaning.

Thus, presented with the sentence "Time flies like an arrow", the computer (a Harvard model from the 1960s) generated no less than five alternative readings:

- Time proceeds as quickly as an arrow proceeds
- Measure the speed of flies in the same way that you measure the speed of an arrow
- Measure the speed of flies in the same way that an arrow measures the speed of flies
- Measure the speed of flies that resemble an arrow
- Flies of a particular kind, time-flies, are fond of an arrow

---

(unless one is enjoying Japanese cuisine) cooked. One can, however, envisage an alternative context which would lead to very different expectations. For instance, a child has just finished planting waterweed in a new tank for the family's tropical fish collection and is intending to return the prize Siamese fighting fish to its refurbished home. Meanwhile, mother wanders in with a hungry cat at her heels. The child says, in alarm, "the fish is on the table!". In this context, the listener would certainly not expect the fish to be dead, cooked, or on a plate. It is precisely this aspect of comprehension that is so intractable in the field of machine translation (see *Machine translation,* p.2).

The evidence for contextual effects on comprehension that is reviewed in Chapter 7 does more than elaborate the model shown in Fig. 1.2 (p.3). It begins to challenge the kind of model that regards comprehension as involving a uni-directional flow of information from the peripheral sense organ (the ear) to the centre (cortex). Figure 1.2 (p.3) shows comprehension as progressing through speech perception, lexical access and sentence decoding to a point where an abstract propositional representation of the sentence is formed, implying that this representation of the literal meaning of an utterance is then combined with contextual information and general know-ledge to yield an interpretation. Although this kind of model has been influential, there is mounting evidence from both developmental and psycho-linguistic research to indicate that context and prior knowledge guide all aspects of sentence interpretation as each word is encountered. Consider, for instance, the stage at which an incoming speech stream is segmented into words. There is often considerable ambiguity in the possible ways that segmentation can be achieved, but we use our contextual knowledge to overcome this. This is apparent to anyone who has asked an audio-typist to transcribe material on an unfamiliar topic. For example, a typist who was transcribing notes I had made on a book concerned with the evolution of language typed:

This book considers the question of how language is a rose.

A colleague who was concerned with studies on the Beck Depression Inventory found his words typed as:

Forty patients were administered the beady eye.

Clearly, the segmentation of a speech stream cannot be a simple bottom-up process, driven solely by perceptual input; the listener uses prior knowledge, context, and expectations, to achieve this task, and to select a meaning from a range of possibilities.

A more realistic diagram that illustrates top-down as well as bottom-up influences on interpretation is shown in Fig. 1.8, overleaf.

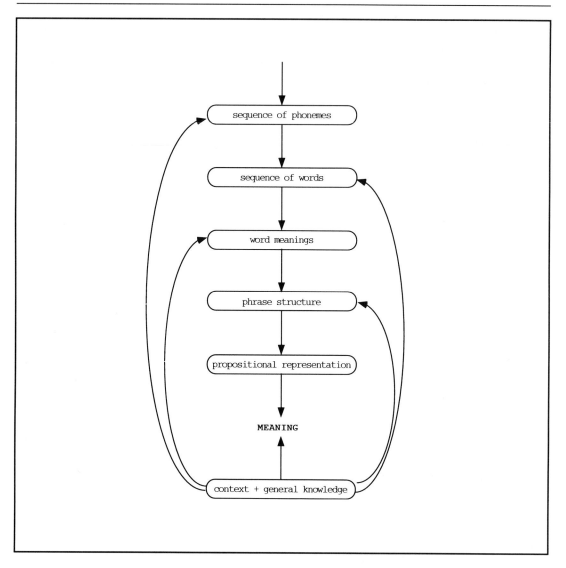

FIG. 1.8   Modified model of stages in comprehension from phonological representation to meaning, showing top-down effects of context and general knowledge on earlier stages of processing.

Comprehension of discourse.   To conduct a coherent conversation, or to follow the plot in a story, it is not sufficient to understand isolated sentences. The need to integrate general knowledge with linguistic information becomes even more critical when we move from understanding single sentences to comprehension of longer stretches of talk, i.e. discourse. One must be able to form links between one utterance and another to build up what has been termed a "mental model". The notion of a mental model has been criticised as vague, but is necessary to capture the fact that understanding involves integrating information into a coherent conceptual structure, which encodes links between pieces of information, and which incorporates general knowledge in addition to what has been directly stated. To form such a structure, one must do more than decode the words one hears: it is necessary to make heavy use of inference. Consider the following brief story:

1. Jane went to the sweetshop with her mother.
2. While her back was turned, a man took her money.
3. They had to go to the police station.

The pronouns "her", and "they" pose no problems for the listener, although they are potentially ambiguous ("her" in sentence 2 could refer to Jane or her mother; "they" in sentence 3 could include the man). We are not puzzled by the transition from the sweetshop to the police station, although no explicit mention is made of a theft. Consider how different the story would sound if sentence 2 had read "She asked for some jelly-babies and the man took her money". One would then assume that "the man" was the storekeeper, who took money as payment, and the listener would be waiting to be given a reason for the visit to the police station.

Understanding of discourse is an area which has only recently attracted the attention of researchers in the field of SLI, yet there is mounting evidence that for at least some children, ability to comprehend discourse is worse than would be expected on the basis of understanding of isolated sentences. This issue will be reviewed in Chapter 7.

Social cognition and interpretation of a speaker's intention

In Chapter 8 we move on to consider the final process shown in Fig. 1.2 (p.3), where social understanding is integrated with meaning conveyed by language to interpret another person's intention. So far, the process of language comprehension has been described as if the main task for a listener is to decode a message by matching a descriptive statement to a state of affairs in the real world. Such an analysis ignores the fact that language is used for a wide range of communicative functions that go far beyond simply informing the listener of a state of affairs. People use language to influence one another: to instruct, command, complain, persuade, express feelings, and so on. Communication is only achieved when the listener goes beyond understanding the propositional meaning of an utterance to appreciate the speaker's intention in

making a particular utterance. In fact, the surface form of an utterance may give a very inaccurate indication of the underlying meaning. Consider the following utterances:

1. Would you mind opening the window?
2. I don't suppose you would like to come to dinner tonight.
3. You must be so sad at leaving this lovely weather behind. (Addressed to British person about to go to Australia for Christmas.)

Utterance 1 is a command with the grammatical form of a question, whereas utterance 2 is an invitation with the grammatical form of a statement. In both cases, politeness constrains the form of the utterance, so the command seems less abrupt than "open the window" and the invitation less pressing than "come to dinner tonight". The speaker of utterance 3 is being ironic and means the opposite of what he says. Consider the utterance in Fig. 1.2 (p.3): "The fish is on the table". If one was enjoying pre-dinner drinks and the host had entered and made this statement, he would not be pleased if his guests merely nodded with interest at being informed of this state of affairs. In this context, the speaker would expect the listeners to infer his intention was to persuade them to come to the table to eat. In the alternative context suggested earlier, where a child had temporarily removed a tropical fish from its tank, and her mother let the cat in the room, the statement "the fish is on the table!" would be a warning to keep the cat away.

Ability to comprehend utterances such as these necessitates that the listener not only understands the words that are uttered, but also has the ability to infer the other person's likely intentions in making such an utterance. This calls for a sophisticated level of understanding of other people's cognitive states. Impairment in this domain of social cognition is a core feature of autistic disorder, and it has been suggested that this deficit can account for pragmatic abnormalities in the language of children with autism (Frith, 1989). In Chapter 8, we review some of the evidence and consider how far similar problems can account for comprehension problems in some children with SLI.

MODULARITY AND INTERACTION IN LANGUAGE COMPREHENSION

In Chapter 9 we look more critically at the kind of bottom-up information processing model depicted in Fig. 1.2 (p.3), and conclude that, while it does provide a helpful framework for thinking about the different levels of comprehension that may be impaired, it fails to elucidate the developmental aspects of SLI. A conceptualisation of language in terms of modular processes has been something of a straitjacket, focusing attention on representational deficits, leading to a neglect of processing accounts of comprehension problems.

The publication of Fodor's (1983) book *The Modularity of Mind* had a profound impact on the study of language, with its claim that many of the processes involved in comprehension were undertaken by special brain systems termed modules. According to Fodor, a module is a domain specific and informationally encapsulated brain system responsible for handling a particular type of mental representation, which has the properties listed in Table 1.2, below. These properties may be illustrated by considering how the brain handles speech perception. Domain specificity refers to the fact that the mechanisms involved in speech perception appear to be distinct from those used for other kinds of auditory analysis, and operate only on acoustic signals that are taken to be utterances. Information encapsulation refers to the fact that modular processing cannot be influenced by higher cognitive operations. This results in mandatory processing: one cannot easily ignore incoming speech; even if attention is switched away from interpreting utterances, one will immediately respond on hearing a salient signal such as one's

TABLE 1.2

Fodor's Characterisation of Properties of a Module

Domain specificity
System constrained in terms of the range of information it can access

Mandatory processing
No voluntary control over whether relevant input is processed

Limited central access to intermediate representations
Information is not available to conscious awareness (e.g. auditory characteristics of speech sounds, or precise syntactic form of an utterance are difficult or impossible to report, even though the utterance containing these was understood)

Speed
Complex information processing takes place remarkably quickly

Information encapsulation
Information from higher levels is not fed back to lower ones (i.e. no top-down processing occurs)

Shallow output
Computes only a very limited range of representations

Fixed neural architecture
Handled by a circumscribed and dedicated brain region

Characteristic breakdown patterns
Associated with selective deficits in one area of functioning that cannot be explained in terms of some general loss of capacity

Characteristic pace and sequencing in development
Developmental course of a modular function is highly dependent on maturation of endogenous systems, and insensitive to environmental influences

own name. Processing in a modular system is fast and automatic, in contrast to central processes concerned with long-term memory and reasoning, which are typically slow, optional, and general purpose, able to combine information from a variety of sources. In Fodor's scheme, processing of language up to the stage where a propositional representation is generated is modular. Later stages of understanding, i.e. incorporating general and social knowledge to interpret the utterance, are seen as central processes, and do not have the characteristics of modules.

One important source of evidence for modularity comes from the study of adults with acquired brain injuries. Demonstration that brain injury causes cognitive impairment is often theoretically uninformative, but Milner and Teuber (1968) pointed out that if one group of patients are impaired in function X but not Y, whereas another group are impaired in Y but not X, we have a double dissociation which demonstrates that X and Y are logically independent of one another. This line of reasoning forms the cornerstone for the enterprise of cognitive neuropsychology, where the aim is to develop models of the cognitive processes involved in particular mental operations by analysing patterns of deficits in brain-damaged individuals. Coltheart (1987) and Shallice (1988) give excellent reviews of the field. The emphasis is largely on case studies of individuals who show highly selective patterns of cognitive deficit and who can inform theory by demonstrating the relative independence of different cognitive processes. A great deal of evidence has accumulated to support the view that, not only is language processing largely independent of other cognitive functions, but within the language system there are independent stages which may be selectively disrupted. For instance, one may see patients who lose the ability to understand spoken language while retaining the ability to repeat (e.g. Berndt, Basili, & Caramazza, 1987), or who are able to read content words but not function words (Gardner & Zurif, 1975). Others may have particular difficulty in understanding sentences where word order is critical (Schwartz, Saffran, & Marin, 1980). In yet other cases, there may be loss of the ability to name or comprehend items of a given semantic class (e.g. Warrington & McCarthy, 1987). Evidence such as this has been taken as supporting the view that the early stages of processing depicted in a model such as Fig. 1.2 (p.3) may each be regarded as depending on one or more independent modules.

Neuropsychological studies can also provide evidence for the mediation of modular processes by particular brain regions. According to Fodor, information processing systems that have the characteristics of modularity are typically "hard-wired", rather than being learned. Fodor uses evolutionary arguments to support the idea that a complex processor that rapidly performs a dedicated function is likely to be preprogrammed, and the finding that damage to a particular brain region can lead to a highly specific impairment in a particular stage of language processing has been taken as evidence for this view.

The claim that modules are innate is important, because it implies that the cognitive neuropsychology approach can be applied to developmental as well as acquired disorders. If we have specific brain regions that are already specialised for language processing at birth, then it seems reasonable to suppose that a child who is impaired in a modular process must have suffered damage to, or maldevelopment of, such a system. Enthusiasm for modularity has led to mounting interest from those studying developmental disorders, with a new discipline of developmental cognitive neuropsychology being spawned, and models of cognitive architecture derived from adult studies used as a basis for investigating children's difficulties (Temple, 1997).

However, we need to be very careful about assuming that there is a neat parallel between adult neuropsychology and developmental disorders. As will be argued in Chapter 9, the tendency to identify modularity with innateness has led some authors to assume that impairment of a language process that is usually autonomous must mean that there is a defect in the hard-wired module for handling that process. Other explanations need to be considered. An alternative view is that modularity is an emergent property of a developing system, rather than a pre-existing constraint on development (see, e.g. Bates, Bretherton, & Snyder, 1988;

Karmiloff-Smith, 1992). If this is the case, then the interpretation of dissociations and associations between different deficits is not straightforward, because we will expect considerable interaction between different levels of processing. One cannot simply knock out one stage of language processing and expect the other components of the system to develop normally. As we shall see, most children with SLI show a complex constellation of difficulties with many different stages of processing, rather than the cleancut dissociations seen in some adult acquired disorders.

This does not mean that cognitive neuropsychology has no relevance for the study of developmental disorders. Case studies of adults with acquired lesions can provide important insights into the types of processes that are implicated in different stages of comprehension, and the study of such cases has led to the development of ingenious approaches disentangling the different contributions to defective language performance. However, the simplicity of the double dissociation logic is deceptive, and not always appropriate for throwing light on SLI, where children with highly selective problems are the exception rather than the rule. To understand SLI, we need to focus not so much on demonstrating double dissociations, as on interpreting complex patterns of impairment. For instance, if a child has problems both with understanding inflectional endings, and with distinguishing between speech sounds, can we conclude that a fundamental auditory perceptual problem is the root of the difficulties, or that the child is less likely to attend to and analyse speech sounds whose syntactic significance is not appreciated? Or do both deficits reflect some more general limitation of processing capacity in working memory? If we are interested in understanding associations between deficits, rather

than dissociations, then the single case approach is singularly inappropriate, because we cannot tell whether the co-occurrence of impairments is a chance occurrence or a systematic pattern. We need to study groups of individuals in order to look at correlations between impairments in different processes.

It cannot be emphasised enough that a focus on group studies does not preclude an interest in individual differences. The deficits in children with SLI are not just complex, they are also heterogeneous, and so a critical question is how to interpret variation in language profiles. Variation from child to child could mean that we are in fact dealing with a group of different disorders, in which case it is important to find ways of cleanly distinguishing them. However, we must remember that some variation may just be meaningless noise; tests are never perfect indicators of underlying cognitive processes and may be subject to influences of attention, motivation, and other random fluctuations. Furthermore, some variation in test performance might reflect individual differences in cognitive profile similar to those seen in the normal population; after all, if we tested any class of children on a battery of language measures, we would expect to find different profiles of strength and weakness from one to the next. Furthermore, the pattern of impairment that we see may change over the course of development. Clearly, there is no sense in reducing group data to a composite mean, when this is not representative of any individual in the group. However, the answer is not to restrict attention to the study of individual cases, but rather to look for patterns of impairment across children; only by studying groups of individuals can we begin to disentangle what is systematic signal and what is noise from the complex patterns of impairment that are seen in SLI.

2

Specific language impairment

In general, language acquisition is a stubbornly robust process; from what we can tell there is virtually no way to prevent it from happening short of raising a child in a barrel.

Pinker (1984, p.29)

OVERVIEW

1. The question "why do some children have difficulty learning language?" can be answered at several different levels: in terms of neurobiology, etiology, and underlying cognitive processes. Although this book is primarily concerned with the last of these, this chapter reviews neurobiological and etiological aspects.

2. Before looking at causal issues, the chapter considers the definition of specific language impairment (SLI), which is the term applied to a child whose language development is substantially below age level, for no apparent cause. The diagnosis raises numerous conceptual problems. We need to consider how language should be assessed, which conditions should be excluded, whether IQ is important, and how to take into account age-related changes. Traditional notions, such as the use of statistical cut-offs to identify language impairment, and the importance of establishing a mismatch between language and nonverbal IQ, will be challenged in this chapter.

3. Although most authorities agree that SLI is heterogeneous, there is little consensus about how it should be subclassified. The traditional distinction between expressive and receptive subtypes is unsatisfactory, for two reasons: first, the boundary between the two subtypes is hard to draw because most children with SLI have comprehension problems when properly assessed, and, second, there are many different forms that a comprehension problem can take. Linguistically based classifications seem more promising but await proper validation.

4. At the neurobiological level, SLI does not seem to be the consequence of acquired focal brain damage. Rather, the evidence suggests some abnormality in early neurological development, probably before the child is born.

5. Genetic factors have been strongly implicated in the etiology, and seem more important than the home language environment in determining which children are at risk for SLI.

INTRODUCTION

Chapter 1 reflected on the amazing task that a child achieves when learning to comprehend and produce language. By the age of four years, the average child will have mastery over subtle and sophisticated skills in phonological analysis, grammar, semantics, and pragmatics. Yet there are exceptions. There are children who are physically and emotionally intact, who have been raised in homes with articulate, loving, communicative parents (and kept well away from barrels), and whose development is following a normal course in all other areas, but for whom language learning poses major problems.[1] The burning question is "why?"

There are, in fact, several different levels at which this question can be interpreted. First, there is neurobiology: here the issue is whether there is structural damage or abnormality in the brain of a child with language difficulties, or whether the problem is only to do with how the brain functions. Related to this, there is the question of etiology, i.e. underlying causes. For instance, we may consider whether language development is put at risk by premature birth, neurological disease, defective genes, abnormality of the communicative environment, or by conditions that interfere with hearing early in life. Finally, we can consider the question in terms of psycholinguistic processes, i.e. ask what it is about language that gives a small minority of children such difficulty. Possible answers to this question might be that there is some fundamental defect in perception, in memory, or in abstracting grammatical rules. The primary focus of this book is this final level of explanation, but this chapter will include a brief review of what is known about neurobiology and etiology. The important thing is to recognise that these levels of explanation are distinct. For instance, as we shall see, there is good evidence that language impairment can be caused by genetic factors, but this is not a complete answer to the "why?" question—genes do not cause behaviour. Genes control the manufacture of proteins, and act as an important influence on neurological development. However, behaviour of the organism, including language learning by the child, will always be influenced by the interaction between the brain and the specific environmental experiences it is exposed to (see Michel & Moore, 1995).

The study of underlying psycholinguistic processes is important for several reasons. First, progress in areas such as molecular genetics depends critically on an adequate conceptualisation of the disorder in question; if we group together children with diverse disorders, biological studies are unlikely to obtain coherent results. The more we understand the cognitive and linguistic bases of impairment, the easier it is to devise tests that pinpoint homogeneous subgroups of children with a common underlying deficit, and so get a clearer picture of the relationships between brain and behaviour. Second, research on psycholinguistic mechanisms is, at least in the immediate future, more likely than genetic or biological studies to lead to new interventions for children with language impairment. Third, children with language impairment can sharpen our awareness of what is involved in normal language acquisition. By studying children who fail to master this immensely complex skill, we can gain a clearer perspective on exactly what it is that most children learn so effortlessly, and what the cognitive prerequisites for such learning are.

This chapter will provide some background on language impairment in children, covering aspects of definition, diagnosis, subtypes, associated characteristics, neurobiology, and etiology. These topics could easily fill a book on their own, and the coverage here has to be selective and partial, but I hope will be sufficient to give the reader a feel both for what is known about the nature and causes of SLI, and for the problems that confront those who study children with this condition. The next six chapters will consider different levels of processing in turn to see how each is affected in language-impaired children. The final chapter will reflect on the kinds of models and research strategies that are most suited to furthering our understanding of SLI.

DEFINITIONS

It is generally the case that the less well we understand a condition, the more varied and inconsistent is the terminology that we use to refer to it. Children with unexplained difficulties in language acquisition have been variously referred to as having "developmental aphasia", "developmental dysphasia", "delayed language", "specific developmental language disorder", and, most recently, "specific language impairment". Although each term is used to refer to cases where language fails to follow a normal developmental course for no apparent reason, choice of terminology is not neutral. "Aphasia" and "dysphasia" literally mean "loss of speech" and "disorder of speech" respectively, but in contemporary neurology they are used synonymously to refer to language disorder resulting from brain injury. It is this neurological connotation that has led to these terms falling into disfavour when referring to developmental disorders, where brain damage is seldom implicated. "Delayed language" implies that the only abnormality is in the timing of language development, and that the child is progressing through the normal stages but at a slowed rate. The problem with this term is that we simply don't know whether it is an accurate conceptualisation of the problem. Indeed, the question of whether children with language difficulties are simply slower in acquiring language than other children, or whether they have some selective disorder has been much debated. The term that is usually preferred in contemporary research, "specific language impairment", remains neutral with regard to the delay/disorder question—"impair" is defined by the *American Heritage Dictionary* as "to diminish in strength, value, quality, or quantity". The word "specific" is intended to denote that the language impairment is seen in the context of otherwise normal development. "Specific language impairment", usually abbreviated to SLI, will be the preferred terminology in this book.

DIAGNOSTIC CRITERIA

Zangwill (1978) provided a definition of "developmental dysphasia" (i.e. SLI) as referring to slow, limited, or otherwise faulty development of language in children who do not otherwise give evidence of gross neurological or psychiatric disability, and where the language difficulty is not secondary to deafness. The extract of narrative speech shown in Table 2.1 is taken from an eight-year-old boy who fits this definition. He came from an unremarkable home background, obtained average scores on nonverbal measures of ability (see *Assessment of nonverbal ability*, pp.24–25), had normal hearing and no evidence of any neurological impairment. One does not need expertise in developmental psycholinguistics to note that his language is less complex and contains more grammatical errors than one would expect to see in a child of this age.

However, what about a child of three who is talking in two-word utterances, when most of his peer group are producing complex sentences? Or the eight-year-old who is highly verbal and articulate but who frequently gropes for a word? Should we diagnose SLI in a five-year-old child with a nonverbal IQ of 75 who speaks in one-word utterances? Or in a child who has a history of chronic conductive hearing loss and now has limited vocabulary but whose hearing has recovered to normal levels? These less clear-cut cases raise a number of questions that one has to grapple with when trying to formulate criteria for diagnosing SLI, namely:

1. How severe does a language problem have to be? Also, should we assess severity purely in terms of statistical abnormality or in terms of the extent to which the child has communicative difficulties in everyday life?
2. What aspects of language should be taken into account in defining SLI?
3. How do we identify children whose problem is "specific"? Most diagnostic definitions state that there should be a substantial discrepancy

TABLE 2.1

Transcript of Story Being Retold by Eight-year-old Child with SLI

Original story	Child's version
Bernard walked down the steps and into the garden.	one day Bernard went down the steps, and into his 'garden.
When he got there, he was very surprised by what he saw.	and he- and he wa-
In the garden there was a purple monster, with big teeth and little horns.	and he 'shock to see a 'monster in his 'garden,
What are you doing in my garden, said Bernard.	and him say, … what are 'you doing.
I'm a monster, and I like eating little children and I'm going to eat you up said the monster.	n the 'monster said, … I like to 'eat little boys. n I 'eat you. plus that he s a little bit 'bigger than Be:rnard.
Before Bernard could say another word, the monster ate him up.	then he ate Bernard 'up before he could say any- any other 'word,
Only one of his trainers was left.	n leave Bernards 'trainer behind.
The monster went inside and bit dad's leg while he was reading the paper, but dad didn't take any notice.	and, when 'dad was reading the newspaper, Bernard bite- the 'monster bite … … that dad 'leg. but the- but dad never took any 'notice.
The monster thought that if he made lots of noise they might notice him, so he jumped up and down on the TV and broke one of Bernard's toys against the wall.	… and thought … if I make too much 'noi:se, … then- then- … then will 'recognise Bernards mum and dad. his m- he 'jump on the 'telly, and he smash one of Bernards 'toy.
But still they didn't notice him.	but they 'never heard him.
It's time to go to bed now Bernard, said mum.	n his mum said, … 'time to bed Bernard
The monster walked upstairs carrying Bernard's teddy in his paw.	… n Bernard went slowly up the stair holding … … the 'monster went up the stairs with his 'teddy bear. up s- slow, up the 'stairs.
When he got into his bed, he said, I'm not Bernard, I'm a monster.	and the 'monster say, … I m a 'monster.
"Not now, Bernard" said mum, and she switched off the light.	his mum s- his 'mum switch off the 'light and say, not 'now, Bernard.

Symbols: ' stressed word; … pause of approximately 0.5 sec; - broken off speech; : lengthened sound; conventional punctuation is omitted.

The story used the basic plot and picture book from a commercially available picture book for children, *Not Now Bernard* (McKee, 1980). The child is not required to give a verbatim recall of the story, but rather to retell it while looking at the pictures. The sample story shown here is well below the level of a typical eight-year-old, in terms of grammatical errors, grammatical complexity, and amount of information from the original story.

with nonverbal ability, but, as we shall see, the validity of this criterion is not universally accepted.

4. Should children with a history of potential causal factors, such as hearing loss or neurological disease, be excluded from the category of SLI?

5. If a child who meets criteria for SLI at five years of age no longer does so at eight years of age, does this mean that the child no longer has SLI, or does it mean that we should revise our criteria?

1. Assessing language impairment: Statistical abnormality or interference with everyday life?

Because language skills develop throughout childhood, one cannot define SLI in terms of some absolute criterion. For instance, it would not make sense to say that any child who speaks in two-word utterances has a language impairment, because this would include the majority of two-year-old children. Clearly, one has to take into account the child's language abilities in relation to those of other children of the same age. In order to do so, one must have good normative data on language development, so that one has a reasonable idea not just of the average level of language ability at different ages, but also of the range of ability. Provided this information is available (and for many languages it is not), the usual approach is to take some statistical criterion, such that a language impairment is recognised if the child's score is in the bottom 3% or 10% for children of that age. For instance, the research diagnostic criteria specified

by the World Health Organization (*International Classification of Diseases, ICD-10*, 1993; see Table 2.2, below) specify that the child score at least two standard deviations below age level on a language assessment (i.e. in the lowest 3% of the population). There is, however, one problem with this approach, namely that it entails that the prevalence of SLI will be a constant and entirely arbitrary figure irrespective of the age of the children, the country they live in, and the time in history—if you define a language impairment as a score in the lowest 3%, then 3% of children will be language-impaired. The language level of the entire population might improve or decline dramatically, but you would still have a prevalence rate of 3%. The inherent circularity of statistical definitions is all too often overlooked by those who debate the prevalence of SLI, without apparently realising that it can be anything you want it to be if your criterion is purely statistical.

How can we escape this circularity? One answer would be to define disorder, not in terms of statistical abnormality, but in terms of disability, i.e. the extent to which there are difficulties in carrying out everyday activities, and/or handicap, i.e. whether the impairment places the child at a disadvantage in society. The American Psychiatric Association's *Diagnostic and Statistical Manual* (*DSM-IV*; 1994) has diagnostic criteria for "developmental language disorder" that are closely similar to those of *ICD-10* but they do include an additional requirement, namely that the language

---

TABLE 2.2

ICD-10 Research Diagnostic Criteria for Specific Developmental Language Disorders

- Language skills, as assessed on standardised tests, are below the 2 standard deviations limit for the child's age

- Language skills are at least one standard deviation below nonverbal IQ as assessed on standardised tests

- There are no neurological, sensory, or physical impairments that directly affect use of spoken language, nor is there a pervasive developmental disorder

- A distinction is made between *receptive* language disorder, where comprehension is more than 2 *SD* below age level, and *expressive* language disorder, where only expressive language is this severely affected, and where understanding and use of nonverbal communication and imaginative language functions are within the normal range

Assessment of nonverbal ability

Intelligence is usually assessed by sampling a range of verbal and nonverbal behaviours, to generate a composite index that reflects in statistical terms how far the overall level of performance is in keeping with scores obtained by a representative group of children of the same age. For instance, in the widely used Wechsler Intelligence Scale for Children (Wechsler, 1992), scores on five verbal and five nonverbal ("performance") subtests are combined to give a full scale IQ, on a scale where the mean is 100 and the standard deviation (*SD*) is 15. Thus an IQ of 85 is 1 *SD* below the mean and an IQ of 70 is 2 *SD* below the mean. In a random sample of 50 children, we would expect to find about 8 children with an IQ of 85 or less, and 1 or 2 with an IQ of 70 or less.

In the general population, scores on verbal and nonverbal ability tests tend to be correlated, and so it makes sense to combine them to arrive at a composite measure of overall ability, full scale IQ. However, in many developmental disorders, children have specific impairments in one area of ability, and to get a clear picture of the profile of scores one needs to have separate measures of different areas of functioning. When a child has evident language difficulties, it is useful to assess nonverbal functioning using tests that minimise the role of language. In many children, one finds a discrepancy between scores on verbal IQ tests and those on nonverbal, or performance, IQ tests.

The content of nonverbal tests is variable. Illustrative examples from Wechsler subtests are given in Figs. 2.1, 2.2, and 2.3 below, and in Figs. 2.4 and 2.5 opposite.* In some cases, such as Coding or Picture Arrangement subtests, it can be argued that although the test requires no overt language on the part of the child, covert verbal mediation will facilitate task performance, and so a child with a language deficit may be penalised.

Coding.   The correct code must be written as quickly as possible in the box below each symbol, according to the key printed at the top.

Picture Completion.   Child's task is to indicate (by verbal or nonverbal means) the part that is missing in a picture.

FIG. 2.2   Picture completion.

Block Design.   The task is to assemble a set of blocks to make a specific design as quickly as possible. Each block has some faces that are red or white, and others that are half red and half white.

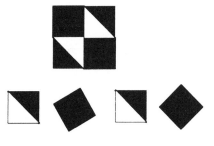

FIG. 2.3   Block design.

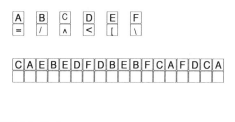

FIG. 2.1   Coding.

*Examples are made up rather than taken from actual test material, but they illustrate the kinds of task that children are presented with.

Assessment of nonverbal ability (continued)

Picture Arrangement. The child is shown a set of three to six pictures that must be arranged into a sequence to tell a story. Credit is given for fast performance.

Object Assembly. A composite figure must be assembled from elements as quickly as possible.

Other Assessments. Other nonverbal assessments that are often used with children with SLI include Raven's Progressive Matrices (Raven, Court,

& Raven, 1986), and selected subtests of the McCarthy Scales of Children's Abilities (McCarthy, 1972) or British Ability Scales (Elliott, Murray, & Pearson, 1983). Some psychologists prefer tests devised for deaf children, where verbal instructions are minimised, such as the Non-Verbal Intelligence Test (Snijders & Snijders Ooman, 1959) or Leiter International Performance Scale (Leiter & Arthur, 1955). However, norms do become outdated, and the older tests are likely to overestimate nonverbal IQ. For more detailed treatment of assessment issues, see Yule (1987).

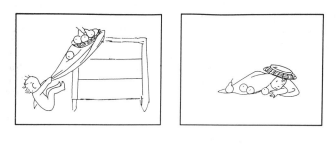

FIG. 2.4   Picture arrangement.

FIG. 2.5   Object assembly.

difficulties interfere with academic or occupational achievement or with social communication. In clinical practice, this criterion will almost always be met, since a child is unlikely to be referred for a professional opinion unless a parent or teacher is concerned about language. However, in research contexts where children with SLI might be identified by population screening, the *ICD-10* and *DSM-IV* criteria would be likely to select overlapping but not identical subgroups of children. There are both pros and cons to incorporating the notion of disability into a definition of SLI. On the one hand, it grounds the diagnosis in clinical concern and avoids the arbitrariness of purely statistical definitions. But on the other hand, people's opinions about what constitutes a communicative disability may vary considerably, depending on the social environment, the demands placed on the child, and parental readiness to seek professional help. Two children with exactly the same level of language ability may be diagnosed as affected or unaffected, solely on the basis of whether the adults who know them are concerned about their language. Some language disorders may go unrecognised altogether, especially if they occur in children who have behaviour problems (Cohen, Davine, & Meloche-Kelly, 1989). To my knowledge, nobody has tried to relate statistical test-based diagnoses of SLI to ratings by parents, teachers, peers, or even children themselves, of how far communication problems affect everyday life, but it would be a worthwhile exercise to carry out. My impression is that parents and teachers readily detect

TABLE 2.3

Stark and Tallal's (1981b) Criteria for Specific Language Impairment

- normal hearing on pure tone screening

- no known history of recurrent otitis media

- no emotional or behavioural problems sufficiently severe to merit intervention

- performance IQ of 85 or above

- normal neurological status (i.e. no frank neurological signs, no history of head trauma or epilepsy)

- no peripheral oral motor or sensory deficits

- articulation age (assessed on Templin-Darley's 1960 Test) no more than six months below expressive language age

- in children aged seven years or above, reading age no more than six months below language age

- language age (mean of receptive language age and expressive language age) at least 12 months lower than chronological age or performance mental age, whichever was the lower

- receptive language age at least six months lower than chronological age or performance mental age, whichever was the lower

- expressive language age at least 12 months lower than chronological age or performance mental age, whichever was the lower

Note: Receptive language age was defined as average of age-equivalent scores on Test of Auditory Comprehension of Language (Carrow, 1975), the Token Test (De Renzi & Vignolo, 1962), and the Auditory Reception and Auditory Association subtests of the Illinois Test of Psycholinguistic Abilities (Kirk, McCarthy, & Kirk, 1968).
Expressive language age was defined as average of age-equivalent scores on the Expressive Portion of the Northwestern Syntax Screening Test (Lee, 1971), Vocabulary subtest of Wechsler IQ, Grammatic Closure subtest of Illinois Test of Psycholinguistic Abilities, and the Developmental Syntax Screening Test (Lee, 1974).

communication problems that lead to reduced intelligibility or immature-sounding sentence structures, but they are much less sensitive to language problems that affect comprehension, vocabulary size, or verbal memory.

There is an alternative approach that is sometimes used in the definition of SLI, which involves translating a child's score into an "age equivalent" score, and regarding the child as language-impaired if the gap between chronological age and language test age exceeds a certain amount, say 12 months or so. This is the approach used in criteria published by Stark and Tallal (1981b), which have been widely adopted (see Table 2.3, opposite). This method does have the potential to escape from the circularity of statistical definitions, but it brings with it new problems of its own (see *Age equivalent scores*, p.28).

In sum, there is no simple answer to this first question. In practice, most children who are seen clinically and recruited for research studies will meet the dual criterion that (1) a parent or teacher is concerned about language functioning and (2) scores on a language measure are statistically abnormal, probably at least one *SD* below the mean. However, it is important to recognise that a rather different subset of children will be identified in studies that adopt an epidemiological approach and rely solely on statistical criteria. In these cases, there may be inclusion of children whose language is poor for their age, but who are not giving any cause for concern to parents or teachers. Finally, it is important to appreciate that gaps between "language age" and chronological age can mean very different things in terms of severity of impairment, depending on the age of the child and the language measure.

2. What aspects of language should be taken into account in defining SLI?

As later chapters will emphasise, language is not a unitary skill. Comprehension involves a host of different subskills, ranging from the ability to discriminate between speech sounds, to recognise vocabulary, to decode complex sentences, to reason verbally, to remember strings of words, to understand what another person's intention is in making an utterance, and so on. In *Receptive language assessments* (pp.29–30), some common receptive language tests are described: a similar range of measures exists for expressive language. It is not a trivial issue to decide which language abilities should be taken into account in defining disorder. There is no consensus in this area, although it is generally agreed that it is important to use tests with good psychometric properties (see *What makes a good psychological assessment?*, p.31), and to use a battery that samples a range of expressive and receptive language functions, avoiding reliance exclusively on verbal IQ tests that tend to assess acquired knowledge and reasoning rather than language functions such as grammatical ability. One then has the option of taking a composite index of language ability by averaging language test scores, or adopting the kind of approach favoured by Bishop and Edmundson (1987a), who diagnosed SLI if there was a severe deficit (e.g. 2 *SD* or more below the mean) on any language measure, or moderate levels of deficit (e.g. 1.5 *SD* or more below the mean) on two or more measures. The disadvantage of this approach is that it places a lot of weight on a single test, so there is a real risk of over-identifying children on the basis of temporary lapses of attention, etc. On the other hand, it has the advantage that it has the potential to identify the child who has selective difficulties in one area, such as word-finding, where the average score would not be a sensitive indicator of the severity of impairment (see Bishop, 1989c).

The fact that researchers and clinicians tend to use different batteries of language tests when defining SLI may be one reason for the inconsistency of findings in this field, although it must be said that, in our current state of knowledge, it is difficult to give good reasons for preferring one set of measures to another. Once we gain a better understanding of the underlying nature of SLI, we will be able to devise measures that pinpoint the problem and which can be used to define a more coherent group (or groups) of children with SLI.

3. Nonverbal IQ as a criterion

Implicit in the concept of SLI is the notion that there is a difference between the child whose

Age equivalent scores

Can you see anything odd in the following statement?

> In 1994, Government Ministers in the UK were alarmed to discover that 30% of primary school children had a reading age below their chronological age.

The answer is that, since "reading age" is computed by finding the average reading level for a group of children of a given age, the expectation is that, after excluding those whose reading score is precisely at age level, then 50% or the remainder will read below age level and 50% above. For instance, if the average score on a given reading test for a group of nine-year-olds is 40, then any child who obtains a score of 40 will be given a reading age of nine years. However, for 40 to be the average, there must be equivalent numbers of children scoring above and below this level. This example illustrates one problem with "age equivalent" scores; they convey the impression that any child who scores below age level has a problem, when in fact, a certain proportion of children must score below average, by definition.

There are further problems for age equivalent scores. Suppose you hear that a child has a "language age" that is two years below chronological age. Most people would conclude that this is a serious problem; after all, two years seems like a lot of ground to make up. In fact, the problem might be serious or trivial: it all depends on two things; first, how the average score on the test changes with age, and second, how much variation in test scores is typically found at a given age. The clinical significance of a given discrepancy between chronological age and language age is completely uninterpretable without further information about test variance, and, most importantly, it is likely to vary substantially from one test to another.

Figure 2.6 shows fictitious results from three language tests to illustrate this point. For test A, the mean score changes only gradually with age and there is a large amount of individual variation at a given age. For test B, age accounts for a substantial amount of test variance; thus at a given age, the distribution of children's scores is packed tightly around the mean, and the mean score increases markedly with age. For test A, a score that is two years below age level is well within normal limits; for test B it is much more abnormal.

In practice, relationships between age and test means and variances are seldom constant. In Chapter 4, when we look at vocabulary learning, we find that variance as well as mean vocabulary level increases with age (see *Estimating vocabulary size*, p.84). In contrast, on many language tests, a period of rapid growth in the early years is followed by slower improvement through middle childhood, as illustrated in test C. In these cases, we cannot have a stable interpretation of the significance of a given mismatch between chronological age and language age even within the same test. A two-year lag might be highly unusual in a young child, and well within normal limits in an older child.

In general, use of age equivalent scores is strongly discouraged by experts in psychometrics because they are so dependent on normative distributions of test scores as to be uninterpretable at best and positively misleading at worst.

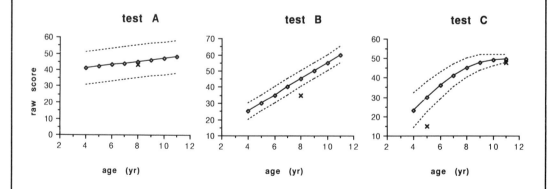

FIG. 2.6 Fictitious results from three language tests. The central line shows the mean score at each age, with the surrounding lines defining ± 1 *SD*. The crosses indicate scores that, in "age equivalent" terms, are two years below average.

Receptive language assessments

The aim here is not to give a comprehensive review of receptive language tests, but rather to introduce some of those that are widely used for children aged 4 years and over, together with some examples to familiarise the reader with the kind of tasks they employ.*

General tests of understanding

Reynell Developmental Language Scales, Comprehension Scale (Reynell, 1985)
The earliest items involve asking parents about the kinds of words the child responds to. In later stages, the child is asked to first pick out a named item from an array, and then to act out commands of increasing complexity (e.g. "put the cow between the pigs", or to identify items on the basis their properties (e.g. from an array of toy animals, identify "which one sings"). (Age range: one to seven years.)

Speech discrimination

Auditory Discrimination Test (Wepman, 1973)
The child hears a pair of single syllable words differing in a single sound (e.g. rail/whale) and must judge if they are the same or different. (Age range: five years and over.)

Goldman–Fristoe–Woodcock Test of Auditory Discrimination (Goldman, Fristoe, & Woodcock, 1970)
The task is to select the picture that matches a spoken word from an array that includes distractors with similar-sounding names, e.g. man/pan/van/can. (Age range: two years to adult.)

Word recognition

Peabody Picture Vocabulary Test—Revised (US) (Dunn & Dunn, 1981) and British Picture Vocabulary Scale (UK) (Dunn, Dunn, Whetton, & Pintilie, 1982)
Both tests involve selecting from an array the picture that matches a spoken word. A sample item is shown in *Testing children's understanding of words (receptive vocabulary)*, (p.86). The vocabulary becomes increasingly more difficult, and includes rare and abstract words such as "foliage" or "glutinous". (Age range: two to eighteen years.)

Concepts

Boehm Test of Basic Concepts (Boehm, 1971)
Tests understanding of words used to express concepts such as space, location, time, etc., by asking children to mark a worksheet using instructions such as "mark the squirrel that is next to the elephant", or "mark the box that is above the chair". (Age range: three to seven years.)

Sentence understanding

Token Test (de Renzi & Vignolo, 1962; DiSimoni, 1978) and *Clinical Evaluation of Language Fundamentals —Revised, Oral Directions subtest (Semel, Wiig & Secord, 1980)*
The Token Test involves carrying out commands with respect to an array of coloured squares and circles, starting with easy commands such as "pick up the red circle", to more complex commands such as "pick up the small green circle and the big red square". In the final section, grammatically complex commands are used, such as "If there is a red circle, pick up the white square". (Age range: three years to adult.) The CELF-R oral directions subtest has a similar format.

Comprehension of grammatical contrasts

Test for Reception of Grammar (TROG) (Bishop, 1989b) and *Test of Auditory Comprehension of Language: Revised edition (Carrow-Woolfolk, 1985)*
The format of these tests is that for each item the testee must select from an array the picture that matches a spoken sentence. Distractors depict sentences differing in terms of word order or grammatical inflections (see Fig. 1.7 (p.12) for a sample item). (Age range: TROG, 4 to 12 years; TACL-R, 3 to 9 years.)

(continued overleaf)

*As with the examples from nonverbal assessments, the examples given here are analogous to, rather than instances of, real test items.

Receptive language assessments (continued)

"Common-sense" verbal reasoning

The Wechsler Intelligence Scale for Children (Wechsler, 1992)
This includes a subtest named "Comprehension", in which the child has to use common sense, general knowledge and social understanding to work out answers to questions such as "what should you do if you found a child much smaller than you alone and crying in the street?" Note that a low score could reflect problems in formulating a response (e.g. finding the correct words and putting them together coherently), or difficulty in understanding the test sentence, as well as poor verbal reasoning. (Age range: six to sixteen years.)

Informal clinical assessment

There are many aspects of comprehension that are not covered by standardised tests. See Miller and Paul (1995) for suggestions for informal nonstandardised approaches to comprehension assessment.

Understanding of narrative

Clinical Evaluation of Language Fundamentals —Revised, Listening to Paragraphs subtest (Semel, Wiig, & Secord, 1980), Wechsler Objective Language Dimensions, (WOLD), Listening Comprehension subtest (Rust, 1996), and Wechsler Objective Reading Dimensions (WORD: Rust, Golombok, & Trickey, 1993)
In the CELF-R Listening to Paragraphs subtest, the child is read a short story and must then answer questions about it. The WOLD adopts a similar format. These are not "pure" comprehension tests because they involve the child in formulating a spoken response, and they tax memory as well as understanding. The WORD includes a reading comprehension subtest in which the child must answer questions that involve drawing inferences from a written text, rather than simply remembering details that were explicitly mentioned in the passage. (Age range: CELF-R, five to sixteen years; WOLD and WORD, six to sixteen years.)

---

development is slow across the board, and one who has a selective impairment of language. There are many conditions that cause global developmental delay, and in such cases language development will typically keep pace with other domains, such as nonverbal ability, self-help skills, and motor skills. Such nonspecific developmental delays are usually seen as qualitatively different from SLI, and likely to have different causes and prognoses.

There are two ways in which one can define SLI to exclude cases of global developmental delay. The more stringent approach, which is adopted in the criteria proposed in both *ICD-10* and *DSM-IV* (World Health Organization, 1993; American Psychiatric Association, 1994), is to require that there be a substantial discrepancy between language ability and score on a test of nonverbal intelligence. If one attempts to implement this definition, one is immediately confronted with the problems of which language test(s) to use, which nonverbal test to use, and how to define a "substantial" discrepancy. In *ICD-10*, a gap of 1 *SD* between language ability

and nonverbal IQ is recommended, but this is an ad hoc criterion which has come under increasing attack. Cole, Dale, and Mills (1992) have pointed out that discrepancy scores are typically not very reliable, and the same child may have wildly different verbal–nonverbal discrepancies when assessed on different occasions, especially if different tests are used.

Furthermore, as Stark and Tallal (1981b) found when they attempted to apply discrepancy criteria to clinically referred cases, there are many children who have all the linguistic characteristics of SLI, but who don't have a large mismatch between verbal and nonverbal ability. In a similar vein, Vargha-Khadem, Watkins, Alcock, Fletcher, and Passingham (1995) found that in a family with many members affected by serious syntactic and phonological problems, several of the affected individuals also had rather low nonverbal IQ. In a twin study of SLI, Bishop (1994b) reported that it was not uncommon to find identical twins where one met a stringent definition of SLI with a large verbal–nonverbal discrepancy, and the other had

What makes a good psychological assessment?

The three major factors to be taken into account when evaluating a new assessment tool are:

- is it valid?
- is it adequately standardised?
- is it reliable?

Validity

Validity has to do with the question of whether the test measures what it purports to measure. For instance, if I were to devise a test in which the child was asked to find the picture to match a spoken word, but the pictures were poor illustrations of the concepts they were supposed to depict, then a low score could arise because the child did not interpret the pictures as intended, rather than because of real failure to understand the vocabulary. On the other hand, if the correct picture in a multiple choice test is inherently more attractive and attention-grabbing than the distractor items, then the child's score could give an inflated estimate of understanding. In both cases, the validity of the test would be put into question. A quantitative approach to assessing validity is to consider how far a test correlates with some "gold standard" that is used to assess the construct being measured. Although true "gold standards" do not exist in psychological assessment, it can be reassuring to find that a test shows moderate correlations with other tests assessing related constructs, and it can also help validate a test if we can show that results from a formal assessment agree with assessments obtained in different contexts (e.g. naturalistic observations or teacher reports).

Standardisation

In many assessment situations, we need to establish how far a child's performance is in line with that of other children of the same age. We therefore need to have the test standardised on a sample of children that is (1) representative of the population that the test will be used with (in terms of such factors as range of social backgrounds), and (2) large enough to enable us to get an accurate estimate of the variance and mean of scores at each age. This is important because the usual method of expressing a test result is in terms of number of standard deviations from the normative sample mean, i.e. as a standard score. If the estimate of the population average score or *SD* is imprecise, then standard scores will reflect this imprecision. Particular caution is needed in interpreting results from tests where the normative sample contains fewer than 50 individuals.

Reliability

A child's performance on a language assessment can be influenced by many factors that have little to do with the ability that the test purports to assess. The child's emotional state, distractibility, and tiredness can all affect performance, and scores on some items may be influenced by guessing. In some cases, prior experience of similar materials may lead to improved performance. A reliable test is one in which these sources of variation are minimised, and most of the variance in scores from one child to the next is associated with fairly stable characteristics of the individual. One way of assessing reliability is to administer the test to the same sample of children on two occasions separated by an interval of a couple of weeks or so. The correlation between scores obtained on the two occasions gives a measure of test-retest reliability. If it is low, we would question whether the test is useful for assessing stable language characteristics. Another index of reliability is the test's internal consistency, i.e. the extent to which different items in the test are correlated with the overall score.

Developing and standardising a psychological test is a time-consuming and expensive business. As McCauley and Swisher (1984a,b) have pointed out, many popular language tests have weak psychometric credentials. Often they are poorly standardised, and lack evidence of reliability.

equally poor language ability, but did not meet the definition of SLI because the nonverbal score was also somewhat depressed. Bishop's study suggested that the discrepancy definition may be over-restrictive. Others have made this point motivated more by clinical concerns. There are cases where nonverbal IQ is within broadly normal limits (i.e. over 70) and there are evident language deficits that interfere with everyday life, but without a large verbal–nonverbal discrepancy the child is left in a diagnostic limbo, denied therapeutic attention because criteria for SLI are not met. Many researchers do adopt a less restrictive definition, diagnosing SLI if language scores are impaired and nonverbal IQ is above some minimum level (a cutoff of 80 is often used). However, with this definition, one may end up including many children whose verbal and nonverbal abilities are not very discrepant, and so it becomes questionable whether one should continue to talk of "specific" language impairment.

An even more radical view is that nonverbal IQ is irrelevant to the diagnosis of SLI, and so one should use neither a discrepancy nor a cutoff approach. After all, why should the presence of a language impairment protect one against a low IQ? Surely we should expect to see this kind of developmental problem in children of all IQ levels. In support of this position, it can be argued that some of the language functions that are most markedly impaired in children with SLI, such as ability to use adult grammar (see Chapter 5), bear little relationship to nonverbal IQ in any case (see *Good language despite low general ability*, p.33). Furthermore, language-impaired children of low IQ benefit just as much from speech-language therapy as those of average IQ (Fey, Long, & Cleave, 1994).

There are two reasons for approaching with caution the idea of abandoning nonverbal IQ criteria. The first is a methodological issue. If one is doing research on the underlying nature of SLI, then it is advisable to study children with as pure a disorder as possible. This way, if one finds evidence for a particular cognitive deficit, then it is clear that it is a correlate of the language impairment, rather than a correlate of low IQ. The second point is motivated by concern that if the

diagnostic criteria for SLI become too lax, then we might end up with an over-inclusive category that contains a mixture of children with different etiologies and underlying causes, and so reduce our chances of finding orderly patterns of results. Note, though, that both of these arguments reflect the concerns of researchers rather than clinicians. In our current state of knowledge there seems to be no justification for using stringent research-based criteria to decide who should receive remedial help. Those decisions should be based on whether or not therapy is effective, and all the research to date suggests that IQ has surprisingly little impact on response to therapy (although most studies do exclude children with IQs below 70, where this generalisation may no longer apply). A second point to note is that if our interest is in investigating etiology, an under-inclusive definition of disorder may be as misleading as an over-inclusive one. For instance, in Bishop's (1994b) genetic study, a less stringent definition of SLI gave a much more clearcut pattern of results than a highly restrictive one.

One possibility given serious consideration in this book is that the core deficits in SLI affect language abilities that are largely independent of the skills measured by IQ tests. If this is correct, then the rationale for using IQ as a baseline against which to assess language function crumbles. However, this view does not entail that we simply broaden our definition to incorporate anyone with a low score on a language test, irrespective of nonverbal ability. Rather, it necessitates that we rely solely on those language indices that tap the putative underlying cognitive deficit. This remains a speculative hypothesis in need of validation, but it seems likely that, far from opening the floodgates to a heterogeneous array of children with different etiologies and problems, it could lead to a tighter and more homogeneous definition of language impairment.

4. Exclusionary criteria

A typical list of co-existing conditions that preclude a diagnosis of SLI include low IQ, hearing loss, neurological disease, severe environmental deprivation, "emotional disorder", which is usually taken to mean autistic disorder, and physical

Good language despite low general ability

Look at the following description of what it was like to have a brain scan and see if you can find any evidence for language impairment:

> There is a huge magnetic machine. It took a picture inside the brain. You could talk but not move your head because that would ruin the whole thing and they would have to start all over again. After it's all done they show you your brain on a computer and they see how large it is. And the machine on the other side of the room takes pictures from the computer. They can take pictures instantly. Oh, and it was very exciting.

The interesting fact about this sample of speech is that it was produced by a 17-year-old woman with an IQ of 50 (Bellugi, Marks, Bihrle, & Sabo, 1988). Relatively good language skills coupled with low IQ are not uncommon in individuals who, like this woman, suffer from Williams syndrome, a rare genetic disorder in which there is an abnormality of calcium metabolism. Affected individuals often use unusual vocabulary items and seem to have no difficulty in generating sentences with complex syntactic structures. Despite a low IQ, they can have far greater facility with language in everyday contexts than the typical person with SLI.

Williams syndrome is not the only context where complex language is seen in association with low IQ. Cromer (1994) described a case of a young woman with hydrocephalus who had a full scale IQ of only 44, and yet whose conversational language was full of complex grammatical constructions and relatively adult vocabulary. A particularly intriguing example of dissociation between verbal and nonverbal abilities was reported by Smith and Tsimpli (1995), who described a man who had a normal verbal IQ and an amazing ability to learn foreign languages, despite having a nonverbal IQ below 70 and some autistic features. He had suffered brain damage after a difficult birth and was unable to live independently, and yet he was fluent in several languages and had a wide vocabulary.

The ability to repeat nonwords, regarded as an index of phonological short-term memory, is a skill that is often particularly impaired in SLI (see Chapter 4), and yet may be intact in some people with Down's syndrome or Williams syndrome, despite a low IQ (Barisnikov, Van der Linden, & Poncelet, 1996; Vallar & Papagno, 1993).

Such developmental dissociations in ability are rare, but they undermine any notion that an early plateau in language attainment is a necessary consequence of a low nonverbal IQ. Some have taken the argument further, and used such cases as evidence that language can develop in a modular fashion, independent of other cognitive functions. That position, however, is more debatable. Typically, the mismatch between verbal and nonverbal abilities looks much less striking when both domains are assessed using formal tests. Thus, with the exception of the Smith and Tsimpli case, the individuals described here have verbal IQs in the mentally handicapped range, despite the impression of linguistic competence on the basis of informal analysis of spontaneous language. Thus, the skill discrepancy may be less between language and nonverbal abilities, as between nonreflective, automatic behaviour and reflective, test-taking behaviour. In addition, most of the studies demonstrating good verbal skills in people of low IQ are carried out with adults, and little is known about their early language acquisition. It would be misleading to conclude that development of language comprehension and expression are entirely normal in such cases. Notwithstanding these qualifications, one cannot fail to be impressed by the complexity of syntax, vocabulary, and phonology in spontaneous language that can be attained by people with a low nonverbal IQ, particularly when one compares this with the kind of expressive language seen in children of normal intelligence who have SLI.

malformation of the articulators. The logical difficulties raised by the first of these was discussed in the previous section. What of the others?

Rapin (1982) and Rapin and Allen (1987) questioned the appropriateness of at least two of these exclusions, autism and neurological disease, on the grounds that this confounds different levels of description. They proposed that a language disorder should be identified on the basis of the child's language symptoms; the presence of associated disorders and presumptive etiology are separate issues. On this view, developmental language disorder and autistic disorder are not mutually exclusive diagnoses: they describe patterns of impairment in different domains which may occur alone or in combination. Furthermore, where the disorders do co-occur, the pattern of language disorder may be very variable: thus, some autistic children are mute and have limited verbal comprehension, others are talkative and have unusual discourse. In a similar vein, Rapin (1982) noted that a range of language profiles may be seen in children with neurological disease.

This approach emphasises how our contemporary diagnostic criteria may obscure relationships between different conditions. For instance, the traditional insistence on making a differential diagnosis between autistic disorder and SLI has caused much confusion in implying that there is a sharp diagnostic boundary. In fact, as will be discussed further in Chapter 8, autistic-like symptoms can co-occur with varying degrees of language impairment, and many children do not fit neatly within a single diagnostic category.

There is also a danger that in using exclusionary criteria we beg important questions about cause and effect. Suppose we have one child who had several febrile convulsions in the first year of life, and another with a history of recurrent otitis media, which was successfully treated, and a third who has been sexually abused. If we exclude a diagnosis of SLI on the basis of such histories we imply that the convulsions, otitis media, or sexual abuse in some sense explain the language impairment. Yet many other children with such histories have no language impairment.

Does this mean that we should forget exclusionary criteria altogether? That would be too strong a conclusion. It seems reasonable to exclude children with any kind of permanent, pre-lingual, bilateral hearing loss sufficient to merit use of hearing aids, because there is clear evidence of a reliable association between this kind of history and impairment of oral language development (Bamford & Saunders, 1985). It would seem advisable to maintain a distinction between SLI and aphasia that is acquired in childhood after a period of normal language development, either as a result of brain damage or in association with epileptic phenomena, where there is ample evidence that both symptoms and prognosis are very different from those seen in developmental disorders (Bishop, 1988b).

As far as the other exclusionary criteria are concerned, the decision whether to apply them will depend on the purposes of making a diagnosis. In many research contexts, it is desirable to study as pure a group as possible, and so it would be sensible to exclude from study children with co-existing conditions that might complicate interpretation of results. (Although, as noted, there are situations when too stringent exclusionary criteria may distort findings, with the researcher ending up studying a highly atypical subgroup of children with SLI.) However, in clinical settings, it is inappropriate to exclude children with co-existing conditions whose relationship to the language impairment is only speculative. Indeed, by attributing all the child's problems to a co-existing condition such as prematurity, otitis media, or sexual abuse, one may be doing the child a disservice by reducing the probability that the language difficulties will be properly assessed and treated.

5. Changes with age

SLI is not a static condition. There are many children who are slow to pass through early milestones but then catch up (see reviews by Paul, 1996; Whitehurst & Fischel, 1994), and in children with more persisting difficulties, the pattern of impairment can change with age (Bishop, 1994b; Bishop & Edmundson, 1987a). In many people, the overt language handicap resolves with age but persisting underlying impairments can be demonstrated on formal tests (Bishop, North, & Donlan, 1996; Lewis & Freebairn, 1992; Tomblin, Freese, & Records, 1992). What we do not know, however, is whether this is the case for all individuals with early indications of SLI, or whether there is a distinct subset of children who have a genuine delay, from which they can catch up with no long-term consequences. There is some evidence for a subgroup of "late bloomers" who have a good outcome with no residual problems after a slow start in language (Fischel, Whitehurst, Caulfield, & Debaryshe, 1989; Paul, 1996). In such cases, it seems more accurate to talk of "language delay" rather than "language disorder"; presumably the underlying neurobiological basis is a maturational lag rather than any abnormality of brain organisation or functioning.

SUBTYPES

So far, we have talked about SLI as if it were a single, uniform condition. However, most people who have had any experience of language-impaired children will agree that there is considerable variability from child to child. At one extreme, we might have the child who has very poor understanding of what others say, and who produces nothing but single words which are frequently unintelligible. Another child might appear to understand well, but speaks only in very simple three- or four-word phrases, omitting many grammatical endings from words. Yet another child speaks clearly and fluently and yet we have difficulty in understanding what is said. Awareness of this variation has led several investigators to propose that the broad category of SLI includes a variety of distinct disorders, and to attempt to devise a rational way of subclassifying this population.

One distinction that was common in early writing on SLI, and persists in some contemporary accounts (e.g. World Health Organization, 1992), is that between expressive and receptive forms of language impairment. In the former, only language expression is impaired, whereas in the latter,

comprehension is also affected. This distinction, which was copied from early classifications of acquired aphasia, is of limited usefulness for a number of reasons:

1. Most children with SLI prove to have some impairment of comprehension if tested using sensitive age-appropriate tests (Bishop, 1979).
2. The distinction between expressive and receptive subtypes is more a matter of degree than a sharp divide.
3. The classification of an individual as a case of receptive or expressive disorder may change with age.
4. As will be discussed in later chapters, among those with receptive difficulties, very different types of language problem may be observed.

It is noteworthy that the expressive vs. receptive distinction has largely been abandoned in the study of acquired aphasia, and has been superseded by linguistically based schemes that attempt to specify the stage of processing that is impaired. The same approach seems appropriate for SLI. However, in adult aphasiology, as in the study of SLI, while there is widespread dissatisfaction with a simple classification, it has proved difficult to develop a workable diagnostic system based on more sophisticated psycholinguistic criteria.

There have been attempts at classification using statistical methods, such as cluster analysis, to look for patterns of association and dissociation between different language deficits in children with SLI (Aram & Nation, 1975; Wolfus, Moskovitch, & Kinsbourne, 1980). These have not been conspicuously successful, and it is probably true to say that very few clinicians use the categories that resulted. These studies were limited by several factors. First, the statistical techniques they employed require that the sample size be substantially larger than the number of variables in the analysis if they are to give reliable results (see Tabachnick & Fidell, 1989, for a discussion), but SLI is rare enough to make recruitment of large numbers a problem. Second, as Wilson and Risucci (1986) pointed out, output of a cluster analysis is critically dependent on the data that are input to the analysis; or, to put it more trenchantly, "garbage in, garbage out". Even if our analysis is based on well-standardised and reliable language assessments, they will typically fail to capture many important aspects of language. For instance, as we shall see in later chapters, experimental studies find that some children with SLI are poor at discriminating between speech sounds, some have especial problems with understanding contrasts in meaning that are signalled by grammatical devices, whereas others can usually understand individual sentences, but have difficulty in keeping track of meaning and relating one utterance to another in continuous discourse. Contemporary standardised tests are not adequate to measure or discriminate between these different kinds of comprehension problem. Thus, it seems best to proceed by first defining which aspects of language behaviour seem, on clinical grounds, to distinguish between different subtypes of language disorder, and then devise measures of these to input into a classificatory analysis.

Descriptive, clinically based accounts of subtypes of language disorder have been proposed in the UK by Bishop and Rosenbloom (1987), and in the US by Rapin and Allen (1983) (see Table 2.4, below). However, a great deal of work needs to be done to validate and refine these systems, and, in particular, to specify clear and objective diagnostic criteria and to find out whether there really are sharp borders between the different subgroups.

TABLE 2.4

Brief Outline of Rapin and Allen's (1987) Clinical Language Subtypes*

Verbal auditory agnosia/word deafness
Inability to comprehend spoken language, with intact understanding of gestures. Speech is absent or very limited with poor articulation

Verbal dyspraxia
Comprehension is adequate, but speech is extremely limited, with impaired production of speech sounds and short utterances. There may be signs of oromotor dyspraxia (i.e. difficulties in producing nonspeech oral movements), but the child's difficulty with speech sounds cannot be accounted for in terms of dysarthria (i.e. muscle weakness or inco-ordination of articulators of neurological origin)

Phonologic programming deficit syndrome
The child speaks fluently in fairly long utterances, but speech is hard to understand. Comprehension is adequate

Phonologic-syntactic deficit syndrome
The child mispronounces words and speech is dysfluent. Utterances are short and grammatically defective, with omission of function words and grammatical inflections. Although the deficit may appear superficially to affect only expressive language, comprehension problems can be seen for complex utterances and abstract language

Lexical-syntactic deficit syndrome
Production of speech sounds is normal, but the child has word-finding problems and difficulty in formulating connected language, e.g. in conversation, or when narrating a story. Expressive syntax is immature rather than faulty. Comprehension of abstract language is worse than understanding of the "here and now"

Semantic-pragmatic deficit syndrome
The child speaks in fluent and well-formed utterances with adequate articulation. However, the content of language is bizarre and the child may be echolalic or use overlearned scripts. Comprehension may be over-literal, or the child may respond to just one or two words in a sentence. Language use is odd, and the child may chatter incessantly or produce language without apparently understanding it. The child is poor at turn-taking in conversation and at maintaining a topic

---

*Rapin and Allen regard this framework as appropriate for children with autistic disorder as well as those with SLI.

Anyone familiar with a range of children with SLI will be able to think of individuals who fit these categories, but there are always many cases who are less clearcut.

One important factor that is all too often overlooked is age. The pattern of language deficits that children show can vary quite markedly as they grow older. This was brought home to me when I did an informal survey of school records of eight- to twelve-year old children who had the characteristics of semantic-pragmatic disorder, i.e. they were often verbose, and spoke in fluent and complex utterances, but appeared to give tangential responses to questions and to have problems in conversing. Most of these children had been very late in starting to speak, often beginning to talk at the age of three or four years. When they did start to speak, many of them produced unintelligible jargon and/or very primitive one- or two-word utterances, and comprehension and auditory attention were very poor. Clearly, the language profile in the preschool years was very different from that observed when they were in primary school. Changing patterns of language impairment were also documented by Bishop and Edmundson (1987a) in a longitudinal study of four-year-old children. Age variation in language profiles poses a particular problem for researchers interested in classification, because it means that we might mistakenly conclude that there are different subgroups, when in fact what we are seeing is the same disorder manifesting at different points in development.

The question of whether there are distinct subgroups of SLI is a fundamental one for researchers. If we treat SLI as a homogeneous condition, when in fact there are several distinct disorders, our studies could give very misleading results. On the other hand, if we try to focus on a distinct subgroup of children, e.g. those with semantic-pragmatic difficulties, we find that there are no agreed objective diagnostic criteria, making it difficult for other investigators to replicate findings. Furthermore, the difficulties of finding enough children to study, already a problem for many researchers in this field, are greatly magnified. At present, most research on underlying

processes in SLI has treated this as a single, unitary disorder and researchers have reached very different conclusions about what is the fundamental problem. There are several possible reasons for such disagreement, but one that should be given serious consideration is that there may really be a whole range of different language impairments, so that investigators are studying different subgroups of children. It is my belief that research on classification and research on underlying cognitive processes must go hand in hand. Issues of classification are never solved in a single step; rather, there has to be an iterative process, whereby a tentative classification is formulated, measures devised to assess crucial discriminating characteristics, and the classification framework is then tested to see if distinct groups emerge. Basic research on psycholinguistic processes should be used not only to try to discover the basis of SLI, but also to explore the range of variation in cognitive deficits, and how this relates to language profile. Once we understand what it is about language that can give children particular difficulty, we can devise better ways of indexing underlying problems, and it is these indices, rather than current assessment tools, that have the best chance of providing us with a meaningful classificatory framework.

In later chapters, I have attempted to describe the characteristics of children participating in studies of SLI, but this is often a frustrating exercise, because the criteria for selection are often specified in broad or general terms that makes it difficult to get an impression of the children's language characteristics.

ASSOCIATED CHARACTERISTICS

It is useful to ask whether there are any characteristics, other than the language difficulties, that distinguish children with SLI from other children, because factors that go together with language impairment can provide clues as to underlying causes and mechanisms. The answer is yes, there are indeed some reliable correlates of SLI.

Gender

The most noticeable and regularly observed correlate is gender: two to three times as many boys as girls are affected (Robinson, 1991). It may be that SLI is on a continuum with normality, and is simply an exaggeration of the usual tendency for boys to be somewhat slower than girls in language development (Neligan & Prudham, 1969). However, this does not get us very far unless we can specify the factors responsible for the sex difference in normally developing children.

An epidemiological study on *reading* disability by Shaywitz, Shaywitz, Fletcher, and Escobar (1990) suggested that sex differences in developmental disorders may be more apparent than real. When they screened a whole population of schoolchildren in the US, they found equal numbers of affected boys and girls, and concluded that the sex difference had more to do with who was referred for assessment or intervention than with a true difference in rates of literacy problems. Reading impaired boys were seen as more conspicuous because they often had additional behavioural or attentional problems. However, other studies using similar epidemiological methods have found a clear excess of boys with both reading problems (Lewis, Hitch, & Walker, 1994; Rutter, Tizard, & Whitmore, 1970), and speech-language disorders (Fundudis, Kolvin, & Garside, 1979; Morley, 1972), suggesting referral bias is not the whole story.

It may be that the sex difference has a biological explanation. Geschwind and Galaburda (1987) argued that testosterone retards development of the left cerebral hemisphere in the developing foetus. However, individuals with hormonal abnormalities tend not to show the neuropsychological profiles that this theory would predict (see Bishop, 1990, for a brief description and critique of the theory, and commentaries on Bryden, McManus, and Bulman-Fleming, 1994, for a wider spectrum of views).

Birth order

One well-established finding is that first-born children tend to develop language faster than later-born children (Pine, 1995; Siegel, 1982). There are at least two factors that could be important here: the amount of one-to-one attention that the child receives from an adult, which will decline with family size, and the extent to which the infant hears talk from other children rather than from adults. However, although several studies have demonstrated a link between late birth order and poor communication status (Bishop, 1997; Fundudis et al., 1979; Tomblin, Hardy, & Hein, 1991) the effect is small and most children with older brothers and sisters do not have SLI.

Social background

Social background, as assessed by indices such as parental occupation or parental educational level, is another factor known to relate to rate of language development in the population at large, and which is sometimes found to be associated with SLI (e.g. Fundudis et al., 1979). However, as with birth order, the link with language impairment is not strong, and many children with SLI have parents who are affluent and well-educated.

Nevertheless, it is worth a brief digression to consider what is known about the language correlates of social background in the general population, because this may shed light on potential etiological agents for SLI. The first point to note, stressed by Puckering and Rutter (1987), is that social class effects on children's development tend not to be specific to language. Thus, where language differences are seen between social classes, they are typically mirrored by similar size effects on nonverbal abilities.

Furthermore, British researchers have tended to conclude that language differences between social classes are small and not of clinical importance. For instance, in a survey of language development in preschool children, Wells (1979) noted that although the mean language ability differed for those in the highest and lowest social classes, there was substantial overlap between the groups. Puckering and Rutter (1987, p.107) reviewed the evidence and concluded that "the main social class effect seen in children's language is a matter of patterns of usage, rather than basic language skills". However, studies from the US have reported more substantial effects (Whitehurst, 1997). The different emphasis put on social factors in the two countries might reflect the range of social conditions that are studied. Some US studies, such as that of Whitehurst (1997) were concerned with children growing up in poverty, often with single parents. On formal testing, the language skills of these children were substantially below age level, corresponding to a mean score 1 SD below the population average on some tests. Nevertheless, the profile of language impairment was quite different from that typically seen in SLI; measures of vocabulary and narrative skills were poor, but syntax scores were well within normal limits.

It is usually assumed that links between social class and language learning reflect a direct influence of the ways in which parents talk to their children. And, indeed, there are well-documented differences in communicative style between parents from different social classes (Hart & Risley, 1992). However, there are a host of other correlates of social class that could underpin the correlation (e.g. health and nutritional status of mother and child, family size, and overcrowding). In a later section, we will also consider possible heritable influences on SLI. Similarities between parent and child in terms of verbal skills and educational attainments may reflect the influence of shared genes. Because high verbal skills are required for most high status jobs, this kind of association could account for observed links between low social status in the parent and low language skills in the child (see Hardy-Brown & Plomin, 1985).

Other developmental difficulties

Although SLI is regarded as a "specific" disorder, and diagnostic definitions usually specify there must be a normal nonverbal IQ, we have seen that there are reasons to question this aspect of the definition. Interestingly, even if we do restrict consideration to those language-impaired children who achieve a normal nonverbal IQ, we typically find an increased rate of nonlanguage developmental difficulties, indicating that the problem may be less specific than is often assumed. Several studies have found that motor co-ordination is poor in children with SLI (Bishop & Edmundson, 1987b; Johnston, Stark, Mellits, & Tallal, 1981; Robinson, 1987; Stark & Tallal,

1981a; Vargha-Khadem et al., 1995), and they do poorly on visual perceptual tasks requiring discrimination of similar shapes (Powell & Bishop, 1992) or memory for spatial arrays (Wyke & Asso, 1979). We know very little about the causes of such associations. Powell and Bishop suggested that poor performance on certain psychophysical and motor tests, which require persistence and are not intrinsically motivating, might reflect short attention span. It is usually assumed that by controlling for nonverbal IQ one controls for this kind of general influence on test-taking, but, as Powell and Bishop noted, IQ tests seldom require prolonged concentration on the same tedious task, and perhaps provide more reward and variety for children than more experimental tests. Certainly, a high proportion of children with SLI also meet diagnostic criteria for attention deficit disorder (Beitchman, Nair, Clegg, Ferguson, & Patel, 1986), and various behaviour problems are unusually common, especially in those with poor comprehension (Baker & Cantwell, 1982; Stevenson, Richman, & Graham, 1985).

NEUROBIOLOGY

Brain damage

Early investigators noted the parallels between SLI and acquired aphasia in adults: in both conditions there was a relatively specific impairment of language, with preservation of other mental faculties. The obvious next step was to postulate that SLI was caused by damage to the same areas that led to acquired aphasia in adults, i.e. specific regions of the left frontal and temporo-parietal lobes (see Fig. 2.7, overleaf). There are two ways of investigating this hypothesis. One can look for evidence of brain damage in children with SLI, or one can look for evidence of SLI in children with brain damage. However, as research evidence accumulates it is increasingly clear that neither approach provides good evidence for an association.

Until recently, investigation of brain damage in children with SLI was necessarily indirect. Even now, when brain imaging techniques are increasingly available, there are few research

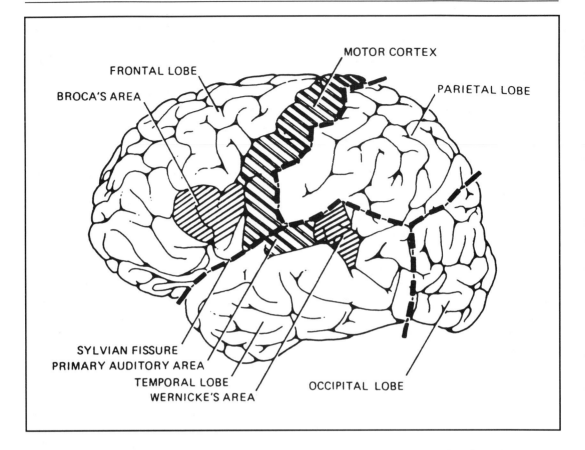

FIG. 2.7   Side view of left cerebral hemisphere (reprinted from Bishop, 1988b). In adults, damage to Broca's area is associated with nonfluent aphasia, with impairments of phonology and syntax which are particularly evident in expressive language. Damage to Wernicke's area is associated with fluent aphasia with severe comprehension impairment. The precise location and boundaries of these areas is a matter of debate and may well vary from person to person. Gender differences in location of language areas have been described by Hier, Yoon, Mohr, Price, and Wolf (1994).

studies of SLI. This is because some of the methods, such as CT scanning, involve small amounts of radiation and their use with children purely for research purposes is ethically questionable; other methods, such as magnetic resonance imaging, have only recently been developed to the point where data can be quickly gathered from young children who will not lie still for a long period of time. Most of these methods are expensive enough to make assessment of large series of individuals impossible without generous research funding.

In reviewing the small number of studies that had been published prior to 1986, Bishop (1987a) noted that positive findings of brain damage were

typically reported only in cases where severe language problems were accompanied by other significant symptoms such as behaviour problems or seizures. Two studies which used CT scan with SLI children without additional neurological handicaps were carried out by Rosenberger and Hier (1980) and Harcherik et al. (1985). Neither study found any structural lesions associated with SLI. A controlled study of a carefully selected sample of children with SLI using blind analysis of MRI came to similar conclusions (Jernigan, Hesselink, Sowell, & Tallal, 1991). As we shall see, these studies did find some peculiarities in the proportionate size of different brain areas, but they did not find any evidence of damaged brain tissue.

Negative findings on brain imaging are not conclusive, however, because some kinds of early brain damage may be invisible using such methods. In particular, we know that premature infants are at high risk of bleeding into the ventricles of the brain (intraventricular haemorrhage), a condition that is clearly visible on ultrasound scanning of the newborn, but which may leave no long-term evidence a few years later. However, several studies have investigated perinatal risk factors, and there is no indication that those who develop SLI are at any greater risk than other children for the types of perinatal hazard that can lead to brain injury (see review by Bishop, 1997).

Perhaps the most convincing evidence, however, comes from studies that turn the question on its head to ask whether a focal left hemisphere lesion early in life leads to a specific interference with language development. The surprising answer is that it does not seem to have any serious long-term consequences specifically for language. A lesion that, in an adult, would lead to a total and persistent aphasia may be compatible with development of good comprehension and fluent, complex speech, provided that the injury is unilateral and acquired very early in life. Most studies in this area have explicitly compared children with focal left and right hemisphere lesions acquired before the first year of life. Right hemisphere lesions in children lead to a typical pattern of deficit similar to that seen in injury in adulthood, with normal language and depressed visuospatial skills (for example, assessed with tasks like Block Design and Object Assembly, see *Assessment of nonverbal ability*, pp.24–25). However, visuospatial skills are also depressed after left hemisphere damage in childhood, with language often being relatively spared. There is some debate as to whether those with early left lesions may follow a slower or different course in early language development than those with right-sided damage, and whether they are at greater risk of having subtle deficiencies in processing complex syntax (see review by Bishop, 1988a). Also, in the early stages of development, unilateral brain damage is associated with considerable variation in language profile from child to child, but this is not accounted for purely in terms of

lesion side (Dall'Oglio, Bates, Volterra, Di Capua, & Pezzini, 1994). Because the numbers of children with focal brain damage are so small, it is difficult to do a definitive study that identifies which variables determine language outcome. However, one thing that all researchers are agreed upon is that an early focal left hemisphere lesion does not lead to a clinical picture in childhood resembling adult acquired aphasia or SLI.

In sum, although early focal brain damage would seem to be the most obvious and plausible explanation for SLI, the evidence simply does not support this hypothesis. We need to look elsewhere for the cause of SLI.

Early influences on brain development

When thinking of a neurological basis for language impairment, the natural tendency is to consider factors that might damage brain tissue. However, if adverse influences are encountered very early in development, while the brain is still being formed, the consequence may be a brain that is superficially normal, with no obvious areas of damage, but which is structurally abnormal.

Brain cells (neurons) are formed and organised into a coherent structure during the first 20 weeks of foetal life. Neurons are formed in particular areas of the brain, known as the ventricular and subventricular proliferative zones, and must migrate to their final positions. An abnormal brain will result if insufficient neurons are formed, in which case the brain will be unusually small (microcephaly), or if neurons fail to arrive at the correct destination, so that different types of brain cell, which normally occur in distinct cortical layers, may occur in the wrong region (heterotopias and cortical dysplasias). Gross brain malformations are typically associated with global cognitive impairment. However, in recent years there has been mounting interest in the notion that relatively mild brain abnormalities affecting circumscribed regions of the brain may be at the basis of developmental disorders affecting higher cognitive functions.

One of the first case studies to provide direct evidence for this kind of basis to SLI, was conducted by Cohen, Campbell, and Yaghmai (1989), who conducted a post mortem analysis of a girl with "developmental dysphasia", who died from an infectious disease. They reported that her brain looked normal on gross examination, but more microscopic inspection revealed clusters of misplaced brain cells in the left frontal region. Similar findings were reported by Galaburda, Sherman, Rosen, Aboitiz, and Geschwind (1985) in the brains of dyslexic individuals. Such reports have generated great excitement in suggesting that early abnormalities of neuronal migration might be responsible for causing developmental disorders. However, as Lyon and Gadisseux (1991) have remarked, minor changes in the usual cortical pattern can be seen in many normal individuals, so if one looks for microscopic abnormalities in a brain at post mortem it is usually possible to find something. As they noted: " 'microneuropathology' may lead to 'macro-errors' " (p.12). Where misplaced tissue is found in areas such as the perisylvian region, it seems very likely that the areas of abnormal development are causally linked to developmental disorders of language. However, to be confident of these findings, we need much more information on the range of variation in brain structure that is found in normally developing individuals.

The basic organisation of the brain of the foetus is laid down during the first half of pregnancy, but neurological development continues after this stage. Neurons form immense numbers of interconnections with one another, but only those connections that are functional survive, and a major feature of normal early development is massive destruction of neurons and their connections. The formation of a functional brain has been likened to a process of sculpting a structure from a block of stone. Recognition of this fact raises the intriguing possibility that developmental disorders might arise if there were insufficient cell death, leaving a brain cluttered with suboptimal connections. Considered in this light, reports that language-impaired children have abnormal patterns of morphological brain asymmetry (Jernigan et al., 1991; Plante, Swisher, Vance, & Rapcsak, 1991; Rosenberger & Hier, 1980) are of interest given that asymmetry normally arises through more rapid cell death on one side (Galaburda et al., 1987). However, although

unusually large brain size has been reported in a subgroup of children with "semantic-pragmatic disorder" (Woodhouse et al., 1996), in most children with SLI, certain brain regions are significantly smaller, on both sides, than in the brains of control children (Jernigan et al., 1991). Insufficient cell death, therefore, does not seem to be a likely candidate for causing the more typical forms of SLI.

There are plenty of other possible mechanisms that could result in abnormal brain development, but these remain more speculative still. Lyon and Gadisseux (1991) note that in the second half of pregnancy, continuing into early postnatal life, there is development of the blood vessels that are responsible for nourishing the brain, as well as the glial fibres that provide support for the neurons and facilitate rapid transmission of nerve impulses. Delayed maturation of these structures could lead to immature brain function. The function of the brain is also heavily dependent on chemical substances, neurotransmitters, which control the state of excitation and inhibition of different neuronal circuits. Where a brain appears structurally normal but fails to function as it should, the question arises as to whether abnormal levels of neurotransmitters might be implicated.

After birth, the development of neuronal interconnections can be influenced by the stimulation that the individual experiences. It has been known for over 30 years that rats reared in a stimulating environment with plenty of playthings and opportunities for exploration develop larger brains than those kept in bare cages (see Rosenzweig, 1966). As well as general effects on overall brain development, there are also highly specific ways in which sensory stimulation can affect neuronal connections. This has been most extensively studied in the visual system, where the responsiveness of individual neurons in the visual cortex to particular patterns of stimulation has been studied by inserting an electrode into a cell, recording its rates of firing when different visual inputs are encountered. In the cat, there are usually many neurons that require simultaneous input from both eyes in order to be activated. However, if kittens are raised with monocular vision (by allowing only one eye to see the world at a time), these "binocular" cells do not develop. A temporary interference with normal binocular vision early in development can lead to permanent and irreversible effects on how the nervous system is wired up (see Daw, 1995, for a review). Some analogous work has been done on the auditory system, where it has been shown that temporary interference with hearing, by inserting earplugs, or exposure to particular types of auditory stimuli, can alter the sensitivity of cells in the auditory cortex (King & Moore, 1991; Moore, 1990). Although this work is based on studies of experimental animals, there is great interest in its possible relevance to humans. Of particular importance is the notion that there may be a "critical period" during which patterns of neuronal interconnection are being established, when even a temporary disturbance in sensory input can have long-term impact on how the brain functions (Ruben & Rapin, 1980).

Clearly, there are plenty of ways in which brain function may be affected in the developing child, other than as a consequence of damage to brain cells.

ETIOLOGY

It is evident that the biological basis of disorders such as SLI is still poorly understood, although the most plausible line of explanation is in terms of some kind of early developmental disorder of neurological development, perhaps in the form of disrupted neuronal migration, leading to a brain that is not optimally interconnected. We can push questions about causation back a stage further, i.e. what has caused the brain to develop this way. If we accept, as seems likely, that destruction of brain tissue through infection, lack of oxygen, or trauma is not a plausible cause, then we need to consider three other broad classes of explanation. Three types of influence will be considered in this section: the postnatal environment, the prenatal environment, and the genetic make-up of the child.

The language environment
It is sometimes assumed that SLI results simply from an impoverished linguistic environment.

After all, a child cannot learn language without being exposed to it. Perhaps those children who fail to acquire language at the normal age simply have had inadequate language experience.

In its simple form, this hypothesis is hard to sustain, because quite wide variations in language input to the child have only small effects on rate of development. There are rather few studies that have directly measured language progress in relation to quantitative aspects of maternal speech to the infant, but those that do exist suggest that, rather than there being some kind of linear relationship between language input and rate of learning, the average child requires a surprisingly small amount of verbal stimulation in order to trigger language development. In a review of studies relating maternal language to children's language development, Harris (1992, pp.44–45) concluded:

It seems to me that there are quite tight constraints upon the maximum amount of influence that input can have upon development. So what I am proposing is a kind of threshold model in which what matters is that there be a sufficiency of the right kind of experience. If the child receives linguistic input that does not provide such a sufficiency, then early language development will be affected. But if this sufficiency is greatly exceeded, there will be little or no additional facilitatory effect.

Harris also noted that where maternal input had a measurable effect, this tended to be on semantic rather than syntactic development, a view that is supported by Huttenlocher, Haight, Bryk, Seltzer, and Lyons (1991), who showed that the number of words spoken by mothers to their 16-month-old children was predictive of subsequent rate of growth of vocabulary.

The best evidence for relationships between language input and children's language learning come from studies that look at the interaction between caregiver and child, e.g. by using measures that assess how far a mother relates what she is saying to the child's current focus of interest (e.g. Ellis & Wells, 1980; Harris, Jones, Brookes, & Grant, 1986). Research with depressed mothers, who are often relatively unresponsive to their infants' communicative attempts, provides some evidence for effects on language development (Murray, Kempton, Woolgar, & Hooper, 1993). However, the effect was relatively small and diminished with age (Murray, Hipwell, Hooper, Stein, & Cooper, 1996).

The most striking findings come from children whose parents have limited oral language skills because they are deaf. Although small scale studies have stressed the difficulties such children can experience (Sachs, Bard, & Johnson, 1981), more systematic study of larger groups of children has found that the majority had no problems in language learning, provided they heard normal speech patterns from other adults for 5 to 10 hours per week (see review by Schiff-Myers, 1988).

In sum, any review of the effects of language stimulation on language development comes to the rather surprising conclusion that grammatical development is relatively insensitive to the quality and quantity of language input from parents and other caregivers, although effects on semantic development are easier to document. If we exclude cases of extreme neglect (see Skuse, 1988), there is no dimension of the child's communicative environment that seems a plausible candidate for causing language problems severe and specific enough to count as a case of SLI. Indeed, as has been found in cases of brain damage, when circumstances are weighing against the child, language seems to be one of the more resilient functions. Can we, then, take seriously the quote from Pinker (1984) at the start of this chapter? Is language development immune to all but the most extreme environmental influences? Like all sweeping generalisations, this claim for the resilience of language needs some qualification, but, insofar as we are talking about causes of *persistent* and *specific* language impairments in children, it does seem fair to conclude that the language environment is not the culprit.

However, two points need to be stressed. First, we have to be clear about what effects we are talking about. Those interested in the etiology of SLI are concerned with children who have impairments in language development that are both large enough to interfere with everyday life, and which typically persist well beyond the initial stages of language learning. For most of these children, the acquisition of phonology and syntax poses particular problems, and an adult level of grammatical competence may never be acquired. Much of the research on relationships between maternal language input to the child and language development is concerned with accounting for individual differences in the rate of language acquisition in children who are functioning within the normal range. To argue against a major role for maternal language in the etiology of SLI is not to deny any effect of language input on the course of development. Rather, the case is that the research that does demonstrate links between maternal language finds effects that are relatively slight, and there is no indication that less optimal language stimulation on its own is a sufficient explanation for clinically significant problems in language learning.

A second qualification is discussed by Mogford and Bishop (1988), namely the need to be aware of possible interactions between causal factors. One commonly encounters the following kind of argument. We are testing the hypothesis that factor X causes SLI. We find cases of children who have experienced factor X and who do not have SLI. Hence we conclude X is not implicated in the etiology of SLI. This is a reasonable conclusion if our concern is only to test whether X is a necessary and sufficient cause of SLI. However, suppose X does assume importance in the etiology, but only when it occurs in combination with another factor, Y. Such synergistic causal mechanisms are much harder to demonstrate, and have barely been considered in the context of children's language learning. However, they are well recognised in the field of developmental psychopathology, where simple cause–effect relationships are the exception rather than the rule, and where the typical finding is that a factor, X, is associated with increased risk of disorder, but is neither a necessary or sufficient cause (for examples, see Rolf, Masten, Cicchetti, Nuechterlein, & Weintraub, 1990). This approach to risk factors seems appropriate when considering variables such as the impact of a deaf parent on a hearing child's language development. Schiff-Myers (1988) noted that, while the most frequent outcome was that the child had no language impairment, the rates of language difficulty were higher than in the general population, suggesting that the limited language environment could lead to problems in a child exposed to other risk factors. We may give a similar interpretation to the findings by Sharp, Hay, Pawlby, Schmücker, Allen, and Kumar (1995) and Murray et al. (1993, 1996), which, taken together, suggest that the effects of maternal depression on the cognitive and linguistic development of the infant depend both on the child's gender (with boys more at risk than girls) and on social background (with much more striking effects in boys from disadvantaged backgrounds).

Perceptual limitations

As noted previously, early in life, the way in which the brain develops will depend on the perceptual stimulation the individual is exposed to. In the 1960s, research was published which created great excitement in suggesting that language development could be compromised by transient hearing problems caused by a common disorder of the middle ear, otitis media with effusion (OME). In this disease, the middle ear fills with fluid, muffling the reception of sound and typically causing a conductive hearing loss of some 20 to 40 dB. To get an idea of what effect this has on language perception, try inserting a couple of foam earplugs loosely in the ear canal: you should have no difficulty in understanding what someone is saying at normal volume, but it may become difficult when there is background noise or a group of people in conversation, and over time the extra effort required to listen will become oppressive. In the past, OME was not thought to have any adverse long-term consequences, except in cases where the condition became chronic, when the fluid in the middle ear can become thick and glue-like and persist for months at a time. In most children, the condition resolves fairly rapidly, either spontaneously or in response to antibiotics.

In 1969, however, Holm and Kunze published a study that raised the possibility that OME might be a more serious condition than had previously been thought. They compared language test scores of an OME group, recruited through an otolaryngology department, with a control group of similar social background. The children with OME were consistently poorer on a range of language measures. Over the next few years, other studies were conducted, with variable results, but often confirming the original findings of language deficits in the children with OME. The disturbing suggestion was raised that, in children, the temporary sensory deprivation induced by OME might have long-term effects on the brain, by affecting neural interconnectivity in developing language areas. An analogy was drawn with the work demonstrating a "sensitive period" for neuronal development in the visual system; perhaps the auditory and language areas of the brain could be permanently impaired if critical auditory stimulation was muffled or distorted early in life just when the child was mastering language (Ruben, 1986). Thus, OME became a strong candidate for explaining cases of SLI.

However, later studies began to raise questions about the early research. In reviewing the literature, Bishop and Edmundson (1986) noted that poor language scores in children with OME were much less commonly found if testing was deferred until hearing had returned to normal. Thus, the notion of permanent deficits caused by a transient hearing disorder seemed less plausible. Studies which identified cases of OME through whole population screening rather than from clinics found much less dramatic evidence of language impairment, in some cases reporting no difference between those with and without histories of OME (e.g. Lous & Fiellau-Nikolajsen, 1984; Roberts et al., 1986) and in others reporting differences that were so small as to be of little clinical importance (Peters, Grievink, van Bon, & Schilder, 1994). Other surveys made it clear that OME was a widespread problem in young children; a study in south London found that 41% of five- to six-year-olds had evidence of abnormal middle ear function on initial screening, although in about half of these the problem was no longer present on retesting (Portoian-Shuhaiber & Cullinan, 1984). In many cases the middle ear disease had gone unrecognised until the child was screened for study purposes. This drew attention to a possible source of unwitting bias in the early research. Suppose that a high proportion of children have OME at a given time, but that this is often unrecognised. A subset of the population will have language difficulties such that the parent seeks advice from a family doctor or paediatrician. Because hearing problems can cause language difficulties, the doctor is likely to investigate the child's hearing and so OME will be detected if present. In such a case, the doctor may feel that the language difficulties are of sufficient concern that the OME should be treated by an expert, and so the child is referred on for treatment to a hospital specialist. The point is that OME of similar severity might have gone undetected, or, if detected, have been left untreated, in a child who did not have a language problem. The very fact that a child has language difficulties makes it more likely that OME will be looked for, and treated seriously if found. In short, children attending hospital clinics for treatment of OME cannot be regarded as a typical cross-section of those with OME; they are likely to include an over-representation of children with language difficulties. For this reason, when looking for consequences of OME, we can trust only those studies which have used whole population screening. As noted earlier, these typically do not find large language differences between children with a history of OME and those who are unaffected, especially if language testing is deferred until after the OME has resolved.

It would be premature to rule out any role of OME in causing language impairments. In those rare cases where the condition is chronic, sometimes leading to perforation of the eardrum, and associated with conductive hearing loss lasting months or even years, there is evidence of more serious and persistent language deficits (e.g. Kaplan, Fleshman, Bender, Baum, & Clark, 1973). Furthermore, there is a suggestion that OME may act as a risk factor which assumes significance if it occurs in combination with other factors, such as perinatal hazard (Bishop & Edmundson, 1986), especially if there are multiple episodes in the first year of life (Friel-Patti, Finitzo-Hieber, Conti, & Clinton Brown, 1982). However, most children with SLI do not have unusually frequent or severe OME, and middle ear disease is not an adequate general explanation for the cause of SLI.

The prenatal environment

If experiences in early life do not seem adequate to explain SLI, perhaps we need to move to an even earlier stage of development, to ask whether prenatal factors might be implicated. In the second half of gestation, after neurons have been formed and moved to their final positions, a variety of environmental influences can affect growth and maturation of the brain. If a pregnant woman is exposed to infection, poisonous substances, or irradiation, is intoxicated with alcohol or other drugs, or eats a deficient diet, this may influence how the foetus develops (see Jacobson, 1991; Sparks, 1984 for introductory reviews). It has been speculated also that levels of circulating testosterone, which is known to affect sexual differentiation of the brain in rats, may influence brain lateralisation (Geschwind & Galaburda, 1987). Animal experiments have shown that stressful events experienced by a pregnant rat can influence the offspring's brain development, learning and behaviour, presumably through the operation of hormones that are secreted in response to stress (Fleming, Anderson, Rhees, Kinghorn, & Bakaitis, 1986; Weller et al., 1988).

To date, there is no firm evidence that any of these mechanisms is implicated in the etiology of SLI, but the lack of evidence mostly reflects a lack of research, rather than studies with negative findings. One hypothesis that has been scrutinised in several studies is Geschwind and Galaburda's proposal that levels of testosterone in pregnancy influence brain lateralisation, and that failure to establish normal patterns of lateralisation is associated with developmental disorders of language and literacy. However, there is little support for this view; evidence for atypical cerebral lateralisation in SLI is weak, and individuals who are either exposed to abnormal levels of testosterone, or who are insensitive to its effects, do not show the expected language deficits (see Bishop, 1990). The testosterone explanation for developmental disorders does not seem likely to provide an adequate account of the etiology of SLI.

Genes

Over the past decade, a number of studies reported that language disorders run in families; if a child has SLI, then the risk of other relatives having similar problems is much higher than it is for the general population. It is important to stress that this "familiality" does not in itself prove that a disorder is inherited. First, we have to take into account the possibility of "cultural transmission", i.e. the passing on of a disorder from parent to child by learning and imitation. A parent who has a language disorder could provide a poor language model for the child; if the child imitated the parent, the same pattern of difficulties might be seen. Cultural transmission may play some role in SLI, but it is usually discounted as a general explanation because, within the same family, it is often the case that some children are affected and others not. If SLI arose simply from imitating disordered language from parents, then all children growing up with that parent should show the same problem. Another possible explanation for familiality of SLI is shared environment. Family members typically live in the same home, eat the same food, are exposed to the same diseases, and so on. Thus, if there were an environmental factor that increased the risk for SLI, related individuals would be likely to share it, and this alone could account for the increased rate of disorder.

One way of disentangling effects of genes and environment is the twin study method. Twins share many environmental experiences, and would be expected to be similar insofar as these are important for language development. However, twins differ in their genetic similarity. Non-identical or dizygotic (DZ) twins are just like any other brothers and sisters: they share, on average, half their genes. Identical or monozygotic (MZ) twins, however, are formed by the splitting of a single embryo and have exactly the same genes. The crucial comparison for a twin study is between MZ and DZ twins. If genes are important in causing disorder, MZ twins should resemble each other more closely than DZ twins. The simplest way of testing this is simply to classify each twin as affected or unaffected and then to see how many pairs of twins are concordant, i.e. both affected by the disorder. If the MZ concordance is significantly higher than DZ concordance, we conclude that genes are involved in causing disorder. At the time of writing, there have been three twin studies of SLI

and related conditions, and all report significantly higher concordance for MZ than DZ twins (Bishop, North, & Donlan, 1995; Lewis & Thompson, 1992; Tomblin & Buckwalter, 1994). When the definition of SLI was extended to include children with a low language test score and/or a history of speech therapy, Bishop et al. found that concordance for MZ twins was close to 100%, whereas for DZ twins it was around 50% (see Fig. 2.8, overleaf). This implies that genes have a strong influence in determining which children develop language difficulties.

The genetic mechanism is not understood, but it is plausible that it involves disruption of the timing of early neurodevelopmental events, such as neuronal migration. Lyon and Gadisseux (1991) noted that most neurodevelopmental anomalies in the first 20 weeks of foetal life are the result of an inherited anomaly, and it is plausible that genes associated with SLI affect brain development well before the child is born.

Many people are uncomfortable with genetic explanations for disorder, because they fear that if something is inherited, nothing can be done about it. As Dawkins (1982, p.13) complains, there is widespread belief in "genetic determinism":

> People seem to have little difficulty in accepting the modifiability of "environmental" effects on human development. If a child has had bad teaching in mathematics, it is accepted that the resulting deficiency can be remedied by extra good teaching the following year. But any suggestion that the child's mathematical deficiency might have a genetic origin is likely to be greeted with something approaching despair: if it is in the genes "it is written", it is "determined" and nothing can be done about it: you might as well give up attempting to teach the child mathematics. This is pernicious rubbish on an almost astrological scale ... What did genes do to deserve their sinister juggernaut-like reputation? Why do we not make a similar bogey out of, say, nursery education or confirmation classes? Why are genes thought to be so much more fixed and inescapable in their effects than television, nuns, or books?

The error of the genetic determinist is to assume that the gene causes behaviour, in a direct and unmodifiable fashion, and to thus interpret a high heritability as indicating no role for environmental factors in affecting that behaviour. This is a serious misconception. Behaviour genetics is concerned with understanding the causes of individual differences in a particular population. Suppose we consider something relatively uncontroversial like height. We could use a twin study to establish how far differences in the heights of eight-year-olds in the UK were related to differences in their genes, or were determined by non-genetic factors (which might include such things as diet, level of exercise, and so on). If we found very high heritability, this

would not justify us in concluding that diet was unimportant for growth; only that the variations in diet existing in the population under study did not play a major role in causing height differences between children. Rutter (1991) noted that the height of London boys has, in fact, risen sharply over the period 1909 to 1959, though heritability of height in the UK has always been high. The genes have not changed during this century, but the average diet has improved, and the height in the whole population reflects this effect. Suppose now, that we repeated the study in an area of the world where there was a much wider range of diet, and where some children were severely malnourished while others were adequately fed, we would expect

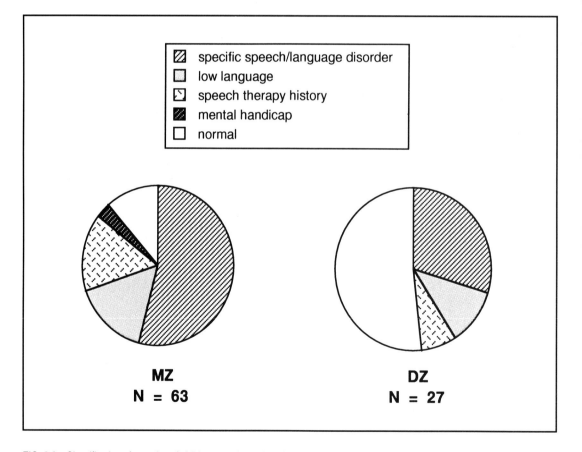

FIG. 2.8   Classification of co-twins of children meeting strict criteria for specific speech/language disorder. The hatched area on the right side of each figure shows the pairwise concordance for strictly defined SLI. The total area with any shading shows pairwise concordance for broadly defined speech/language disorder, including those without a large verbal–nonverbal discrepancy (the "low language group") and those with a history of speech-language problems who now score in the normal range on language tests ("speech therapy history" group). (Data from Bishop, North, and Donlan, 1995.)

the heritability estimates to decrease, because we would now be including children whose poor diets were having a significant impact on their growth, regardless of their genotype. Or suppose we were sufficiently unethical to give growth hormone to a random 50% of London boys and recompute the genetic analysis one year later. Heritability estimates would once again fall dramatically, because a large proportion of the variation in height would now be accounted for by this environmental manipulation. For further discussion of these issues, see Geschwind (1983) and Rutter (1991).

Genes do not act in isolation to cause behaviour: they are simply biochemical messengers, determining which substances are manufactured in the growing organism at different points in time. All human behaviour is the product of complex interactions between biological make-up and environmental experiences; the aim of behaviour genetics is to identify how far differences in genotype, as opposed to differences in environment, are associated with individual differences in a behavioural trait, but, as we have seen, heritability estimates are specific to a given population and not cast in stone. The message is that we should not be misled into thinking that high heritability means a characteristic cannot be influenced by non-genetic factors. It simply means that for children undergoing the usual range of experiences, genetic make-up is more important than their environment in determining who has a language impairment. However, it tells us nothing about what might be possible if we were to expose children to different environments, outside the usual range of experience (i.e. interventions designed to counteract the impairment). In the long run, if we understand how a gene works, we may be able to intervene biochemically and counteract its effect. But we do not need to wait for science to progress to this point to develop effective therapies. If we can understand a child's language deficit in terms of the psycholinguistic processes that are involved, we should be able to devise remedial approaches to facilitate language learning.

FOOTNOTE

1. Pinker's quotation should not be taken as implying any ignorance of specific language impairment. His point was to stress the robustness of language learning in the face of diverse environmental experiences. Pinker (1994) discusses specific language impairment as an exception to this general rule.

3

Speech perception

The articulate voice is more distracting than mere noise.
Seneca the Younger, Letters to Lucilius (1st c.) 56 (trans. E.P. Barker)

OVERVIEW

1. Speech perception involves two complementary skills; the ability to distinguish different sounds (discrimination), and the ability to treat sounds that are acoustically different as equivalent (phoneme constancy).
2. In many children with SLI, there is a relationship between deficits in speech perception and poor speech production. However, this relationship is dependent both on the age of the child and the nature of the language difficulties.
3. Some children with expressive phonological problems perform normally on tests that require them to discriminate those sounds they cannot produce distinctively. However, they usually have difficulty with tests that require them to perceive phonological constancy, e.g. to judge that "sat" and "seem" both begin with the same sound. In such cases, the child persists in using immature perceptual strategies, encoding words in terms of entire syllables, without awareness that speech can be analysed in terms of smaller subsyllabic units.

4. A large body of work supports the view that many children with SLI have unusual difficulty in discriminating brief or rapidly changing sounds. Since many speech sounds have such characteristics, this provides a plausible account of difficulties in learning and comprehending language.
5. Some children have receptive difficulties so severe that they resemble adult cases of auditory agnosia, where sounds are heard but not interpreted. For these children, there often appears to be disruption of auditory processing at an early stage, leading to very limited ability to discriminate and interpret auditory input, whether verbal or nonverbal. However, such children are rare and often have a distinctive etiology. Most children with SLI do not have such marked auditory impairments.

INTRODUCTION

In this chapter we shall be concerned with the first stages of language comprehension, those shown in Fig. 3.1. In Chapter 1, we saw that speech

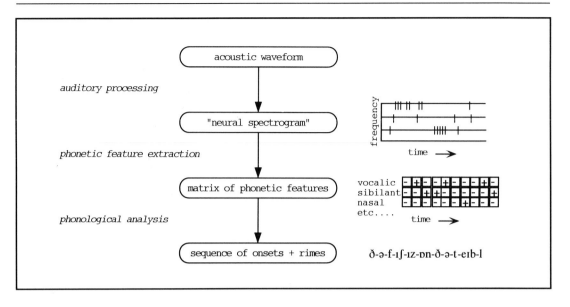

FIG. 3.1   Model of the stages of processing in the earliest stage of speech perception. Note that this model has been modified to take into account developmental research that will be reviewed in this chapter, which shows that normally developing young children have little ability to analyse speech at the level of individual phonemes, although they do develop awareness of the subsyllabic units of onset and rime (see Table 1.1, p.10, for definitions).

perception is far more complex than is often realised. Liberman, Mattingly, and Turvey (1972) have estimated that speech perception involves converting an auditory signal that contains 70,000 bits of information per second into one that contains less than 40 bits per second. Thus, an enormous amount of information is compressed into a form appropriate for storage in short-term memory.

In considering the development of auditory perception, it is helpful to draw a three-fold distinction between:

- *detection* of sounds: the ability to tell that a sound has occurred;
- *discrimination* between sounds: the ability to tell different sounds apart; and
- *classification* of sounds: interpreting sounds by relating them to categories based on prior experience.

Detection of sounds: Methods of assessment

The definition of SLI excludes children whose language problems are secondary to hearing loss;

thus, the ability to detect sound must be adequate for language learning.

In practice, this is typically interpreted to mean that there are normal thresholds for detecting sounds across the range of frequencies from 250 to 4000 Hz (see Fig. 3.2, opposite).

This is not always so easy to demonstrate. The fact that a child responds to soft sounds in everyday settings is not sufficient evidence of normal hearing; different regions of the cochlea are sensitive to different frequencies, so it is possible for a child to have a selective problem in hearing sounds of a given frequency. We can still learn from a study by Ewing (1967), who found that six out of ten children who had a diagnosis of "developmental aphasia" turned out to have high frequency hearing losses when properly assessed.

Nowadays, a wide range of methods is available to assess the integrity of the peripheral auditory system, so that even if a child is too young or unco-operative to be tested using behavioural audiometry (where the child is trained to perform some action, such as dropping a brick in a box, on hearing a tone) one can use physical methods to

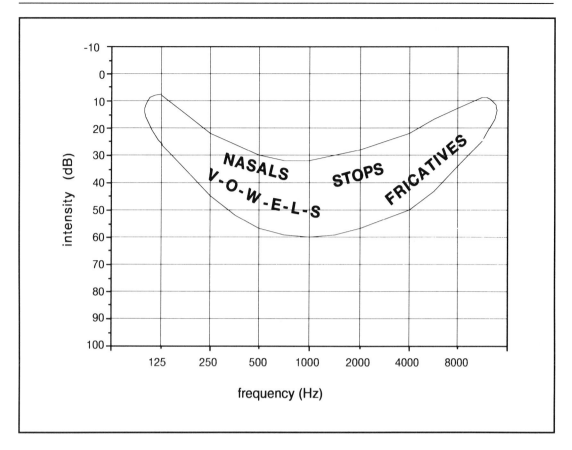

FIG. 3.2   Frequency/intensity plot, with bounded area showing region occupied by English speech sounds.

record the responses to sound of the middle ear (tympanography), or the cochlea (electrocochleography). However, an intact middle ear and inner ear do not necessarily mean that later stages of processing are normal; there may be disruption of the pathway from ear to brain. There are a handful of studies in the literature that compare brainstem auditory evoked responses (see *Auditory evoked responses*, overleaf) for children with SLI and normally developing children. Results have been rather uneven, but no study has found any unambiguous abnormalities (Akshoomoff, Courchesne, Yeung-Courchesne, & Costello, 1989; Grillon, Akshoomoff, & Courchesne, 1989; Mason & Mellor, 1984), and one reported reduced latency of brainstem response in children with SLI, which is the opposite to what would be seen with hearing loss (Roncagliolo, Benitez, & Perez, 1994).

Discrimination of speech sounds: Normal development

Because the child can detect sound, it does not follow that later stages of processing are intact. One may draw an analogy with colour-blindness, where visual discrimination is impaired (in the commonest form, red and green are indistinguishable) but there is no problem in stimulus detection (the child can see the stimulus, despite confusion about its colour). To learn language, the child must not just be able to tell that a sound has occurred, but also to distinguish or classify sounds in terms of critical dimensions.

The remarkable discovery made over the past 25 years is that most children show excellent speech discrimination from a very early age. We know this thanks to the ingenuity of investigators who have developed reliable techniques for assessing auditory discrimination even in very

Auditory evoked responses

Neural responses to sound within the auditory pathway can be recorded from electrodes placed on the scalp; an auditory click evokes a classic sequence of responses reflecting activity at different locations in the brainstem and related structures, and the latency and amplitude of these gives an indication of the integrity of the pathway. The activity produced by a single auditory stimulus is negligible and impossible to separate from background activity, but by presenting a repeated train of auditory stimuli and averaging the response over all presentations, a characteristic waveform can be observed, as in Fig. 3.3, below.

Studies of animals and of human patients with localised pathology have enabled us to trace the areas of the brain where the different waves originate, making the auditory evoked response a useful tool in diagnosing the locus of impairment in individuals with lesions of the auditory pathway. The auditory brain-stem response (ABR) occurs in the first 10 msec following an auditory click stimulus. The response may be absent or delayed in cases of peripheral hearing loss. This method is not, however, sensitive to hearing loss affecting only the low frequencies.

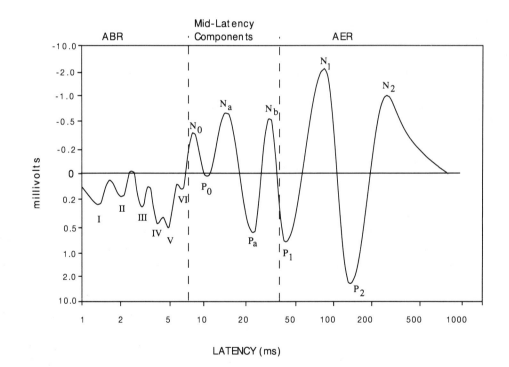

FIG. 3.3 The gross electrical response recorded from scalp electrodes in response to auditory stimulation. Latency shows the interval after the auditory signal (delivered at time 0). Waves are labelled as N (negative) or P (positive). Based on Aslin, Pisoni, and Jusczyk (1983).

young babies (see *What can a baby hear?*, overleaf). In 1971 two laboratories reported that categorical perception (see *Categorical perception*, p.57) could be demonstrated in infants (Eimas, Siqueland, Jusczyk, & Vigorito, 1971; Moffitt, 1971). Later work has gone on to show that at one month of age they can discriminate consonantal contrasts from foreign languages, even those that are not present in their own language (see Jusczyk, 1995, for a review). Language acquisition seems to involve a process of selection: i.e. infants have the potential to make contrasts between phonemes of any of the world's languages, but, with exposure to the native tongue, meaningless contrasts become assimilated into a single category, while the distinction between sounds that convey differences in meaning is retained. Jusczyk (1994) has described this process as reflecting a change in attentional bias; the child learns to attend to acoustic dimensions that are important for signalling meaning differences, and to ignore those that do not convey meaningful information.

Does this mean that there is no improvement in discrimination ability from infancy to adulthood? The question is a difficult one to answer because the methods used to test discrimination in infants are so very different from those used with older children and adults, where discrimination is usually assessed using psychophysical methods that allow one to establish how small a difference between two stimuli can reliably be detected. This involves using long series of stimuli, which would tax the attention and concentration of many younger children. Psychophysical methods typically do show developmental trends towards improvement of auditory discrimination thresholds with age on a range of dimensions, but it can be hard to establish how far this reflects a genuine improvement in the sensitivity of the brain in processing auditory information.

Wightman and colleagues (Wightman & Allen, 1992; Wightman, Allen, Dolan, Kistler, & Jamieson, 1989) stressed the importance of attentional factors in psychophysical tasks with young children, noting that although normal preschool children gave fairly stable patterns of responding within a test session, they showed substantial variation from day to day in threshold on an auditory gap detection task. This was not a simple learning effect, because there was no stable trend of improvement. Wightman and colleagues carried out computer simulations of the effect on threshold estimation of the child periodically switching off attention and guessing randomly. They found that this produced very realistic performance functions, mimicking those of the youngest children. Thus, fluctuating attention is a plausible explanation for the difference between adult and child auditory thresholds in psychophysical tasks. In general, provided children are attending to the task, they appear to have adequate sensitivity to detect very fine differences between speech sounds from a very early age.

Classification of and identification of speech sounds: Moving from syllables to smaller units

Studies of normally developing children emphasise that the ability to identify speech sounds is quite different from the ability to discriminate sounds. We are so accustomed to relating spoken to written language, that we have no difficulty in treating a word like "cat" as composed of the three sounds /k/, /a/, and /t/, and we assume that in "kit" we have the same initial and final sounds, with a different vowel in the middle. However, as we saw in Chapter 1, in acoustic terms, both /k/ and /t/ will differ depending on the adjacent vowel. Although there is fairly good constancy in terms of the articulatory correlates of consonant phonemes,[1] in acoustic terms there is striking variation, resulting from the effects of phonetic context on the sound envelope that is produced by the articulators. As Nygaard and Pisoni (1995, p.66) put it: "The process of coarticulation results in the smearing together of information in the acoustic signal about individual phonemes." The net result is that it is not an easy task for a child to recognise that speech can be decomposed into a small set of building blocks, phonemes.

The young child does not need to be aware of phonemes in order to learn a language. In principle, a child could learn to speak by mimicry: speech would involve imitating the whole acoustic

What can a baby hear?

Babies cannot tell us what they perceive, and, even if they could, they would probably have little motivation to take part in tedious psychophysical experiments. Experimenters have, however, devised a range of behavioural methods for throwing light on the perceptual world of the infant.

One technique that has been used to assess auditory perception is the elicited head-turn method, illustrated in Fig. 3.4. The child is trained to make a head turn when a repetitive background sound changes, and is reinforced for doing so by being shown an exciting toy. In the set-up illustrated here (based on Kuhl, 1980), the three adults in the experiment are all listening to music over headphones. The only participant who hears the sounds coming through the speaker is the infant, who is held by the parent, and is entertained with silent toys by the assistant. If the infant makes a head turn when the sound from the speaker changes, then the visual reinforcer (a mechanical toy) is activated. Both the experimenter and the assistant "vote" as to whether the infant's head has turned. Using this method, one can see, for instance, if the infant notices a change when the stimulus changes from /pa/ to /ba/.

Other techniques rely on the fact that a novel stimulus typically evokes a behavioural response in an infant, but as the stimulus is repeated, this response dies down (i.e. habituation occurs). However, a change in stimulus will cause the original behaviour to return, i.e. dishabituation. If habituation persists though the stimulus has changed, we can conclude that the infant treats the stimuli as equivalent. Various versions of this method are possible. For instance, sucking rate can be measured using a specially modified dummy (Eimas et al., 1971). The infant is then presented with repeated instances of the sound /ba/. Sucking initially increases and then dies down. The sound is then changed. If the new sound is another example of /ba/ with different voice onset time, the sucking rate remains low.

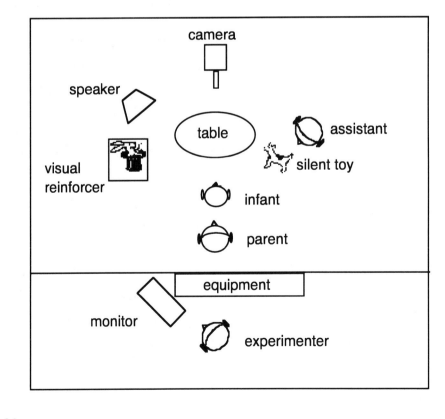

FIG. 3.4

Categorical perception

If we modify acoustic features of a synthesised consonant along a continuum, we typically do not see a gradual change in how the stimulus is perceived. For instance, if we vary voice-onset time (VOT) for a stimulus corresponding to a bilabial stop, we find that the stimulus is clearly perceived as /p/ up to a certain point, after which it is perceived as an unambiguous /b/. Furthermore, ability to discriminate between two stimuli on the continuum is entirely predictable from how they are labelled. Thus acoustically different stimuli that are both labelled as /b/ are very difficult to discriminate in a same–different judgement, even though in acoustic terms they may be as far apart as exemplars of /b/ and /p/ that are easy to discriminate. Figure 3.5 contrasts the pattern of results that corresponds to this kind of "categorical perception" with the pattern of "continuous perception" that one would expect if ability to identify and discriminate pairs of stimuli were simply a function of the amount of acoustic difference between them.

When categorical perception was first described, it was thought to be evidence for a specific perceptual mechanism dedicated to speech processing. However, subsequent research has shown that categorical perception is seen for other types of stimulus and, perhaps most damningly for the "speech specialisation" interpretation, it can also be demonstrated in animals (see Kuhl, 1982). It seems rather, that the sensitivity of the auditory system is not linear along all dimensions, and that speech categories have evolved to capitalise on this fact, with phonemes contrasting acoustically at maximally sensitive points. (See Kluender (1994) for a review.)

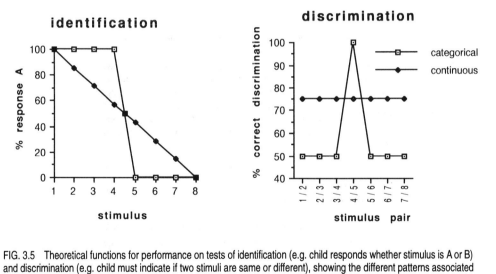

FIG. 3.5 Theoretical functions for performance on tests of identification (e.g. child responds whether stimulus is A or B) and discrimination (e.g. child must indicate if two stimuli are same or different), showing the different patterns associated with categorical vs. continuous perception.

envelope of a heard word, and word recognition would proceed by a kind of template matching. However, this is likely to be inefficient in terms of word retrieval. During the child's second year of life, vocabulary typically shows a rapid increase. Jusczyk (1986) has argued that, as vocabulary grows, there is a need to impose a clear organisation on lexical storage if words are to be recognised and retrieved rapidly. If, as Waterson (1971) has suggested, the young child merely extracts a stress pattern and salient acoustic features from words, then there will be little differentiation between representations of closely related words such as "mad", "nap", "pan", "tan", "mat", "bang", "tang", "mac", all of which are monosyllabic with the same vowel, a plosive and a nasal. Word recognition will thus get slower and more inefficient as vocabulary increases. In contrast, a system that categorises words not just in terms of the syllabic structure and the content of those syllables, but also in terms of the serial order of the segments that constitute syllables, should allow for a much more rapid lexical retrieval (e.g. on hearing /ma-/, only three of the eight words listed here would be activated).

Another problem with learning by mimicry is that it allows for little generalisation of learning to new stimuli. Suppose I say a nonsense word such as "keev". If I fail to appreciate that this syllable is composed of familiar units, I will have to go through a process of trial and error in learning exactly how to articulate it. However, if I recognise it as composed of familiar elements (the onset /k/ as in "cat", "cake", or "come", and the rime /iv/ as in "leave", "sleeve", "weave"), I can use this knowledge to assemble an accurate articulatory programme. It thus becomes much easier to learn new vocabulary, because once the component sounds in a word have been identified, the child can work out how to produce the whole word in terms of familiar speech motor patterns.

Locke (1988, p.18) suggested that the child's own speech production may make the task of analysing and organising speech sounds more explicit:

> Since speech movements are tightly linked to phonemic categories it seems that if the child feels himself producing discrete articulations while targeting for and hearing auditory-vocal shapes, the conversion of templates to syllabic and segmental sequences might occur just that much quicker.

On this view, phonological perception and production interact in early language acquisition; repetition entails recoding auditory input in articulatory form and this facilitates a phonological analysis of the input. Initially, when the child has only a crude perceptual analysis of incoming speech, attempts to repeat will contain many errors;

we will expect basic stress patterns and vowels to be accurately reproduced, but there will be only an imprecise rendering of specific consonants. However, by repeated imitation of speech, the child becomes more accurate and common patterns of articulatory production will be extracted. It then becomes easier for the child to identify abstract underlying segments, and form long-term representations of words on the basis of these, rather than in terms of more superficial acoustic features. Locke's account has potential importance for SLI, because it predicts that immature auditory perception could be a consequence of poor speech production: the child who cannot speak clearly will take longer to learn about the subsyllabic levels of representation.

There has been a great deal of research on the development of awareness of the internal structure of spoken words. Experimental studies have shown that children gradually move from an analysis of speech input in terms of words and syllables to awareness of the subsyllabic units of onset and rime. It is often assumed that accurate speech perception and production requires the ability to analyse speech in terms of even smaller units, i.e. at the level of phoneme segments, but this is questionable. Many children below the age of five years show little explicit awareness of phonemes, despite being competent at speaking and recognising words, and identifying onsets and rimes (see *Methods of testing children's awareness of phonological segments*, opposite). Awareness of phonemes is a late developing skill, and may be in part dependent on exposure to written language, which makes this level of analysis much more transparent (see, e.g. Wimmer, Landerl, Linortner, & Hummer, 1991).

SPEECH PERCEPTION IN SLI

For anyone attempting to review the literature on auditory-phonological processing, the heterogeneity of SLI immediately becomes a source of concern. Some studies have focused on children with severe comprehension problems, asking how far their difficulties are auditory or linguistic.

Methods for testing children's awareness of phonological segments

This is just a selection of some of the methods that have been used to assess children's awareness of phonological segments. They vary in their task demands, especially in terms of memory load, and the extent to which the child is required to manipulate phonological representations. In addition, methods vary in terms of how far they require the child to segment material into phonemes, or whether success can be attained by operating with the subsyllabic units of onset and rime (see *Units of phonological analysis*, p.10). Much of the research interest has focused on the relationship between phonological awareness, as assessed by these kinds of measure, and reading ability.

Tapping number of phonemes/syllables (Liberman, Shankweiler, Fischer, & Carter, 1974). After plenty of practice examples, the child is given a word and asked to tap out the number of syllables or phonemes. Most children aged four to five years can tap out the number of syllables in a word, but have great difficulty in learning to tap the number of phonemes.

Odd man out (Bryant & Bradley, 1985). After pre-training with nursery rhymes to give the child the idea of which words belong together and "sound right", the child is given lists of three or four words and has to say which was "odd one out":

e.g.				
"alliteration"	rot	rock	rod	box
"middle sound"	mop	hop	tap	lop
"rhyme"	doll	hop	top	pop

Note that these tasks could be successfully done by a child who recognised onset and rimes only.

Word decomposition (Barton, Miller, & Macken, 1980). After training with simple words, children are asked to say the first sound of a word such as "swing". Many four- to five-year-olds would say /sw/ rather than /s/, i.e. they would segment into onset/rime rather than in terms of phonemes.

Phoneme substitution (Treiman, 1985). Children are taught by example to play a "word game" where the first two or last two segments of a syllable are replaced with a new set of sounds. Target words varied in consonant (C) and vowel (V) structure; included CCV and CVC. For instance, for a CVC syllable, the child would learn to alter the first two sounds to /lʌ/, or, in another condition, the last two sounds to /ʌl/ so that /fɛg/ became /lʌg/, or /fʌl/. Eight-year-olds found it easier to learn games that treated onsets and rimes as units, as opposed to games that involved identifying phonemes.

Others have concentrated on looking for a link between defective speech production and abnormal speech perception. Because there are no consistent criteria, it can be difficult to generalise from one study to another. In reviewing this field, I have attempted to make a broad distinction between:

(a) children with no physical or motor abnormality of the speech apparatus who nevertheless make errors in speech sound production;

(b) more typical SLI, where language comprehension is usually impaired to some extent, but the most obvious problems are with expressive syntax and phonology;

(c) severe comprehension problems, where the child is regarded as having "auditory imperception" or "verbal-auditory agnosia".

As was noted in Chapter 2, it is unclear how far these correspond to points on a continuum of severity, or distinct disorders with different underlying bases. As we shall see, identification of speech sounds appears to be a problem for all three groups. For the last two groups, discrimination of auditory stimuli is often also compromised, raising the question of how far the language problems might be secondary to more fundamental disturbances in processing stimuli in the auditory modality.

CHILDREN WITH EXPRESSIVE PHONOLOGICAL IMPAIRMENTS

In the past, children who had difficulties in producing speech sounds with no apparent physical cause were regarded as having a "functional articulation disorder". Nowadays, the term "articulation disorder" is usually reserved for impairments with some physical (i.e. motor or structural) basis, and researchers make rather different subdivisions within the "functional" (i.e. not motor or structural) group. One distinction is between children who fail to mark phonemic distinctions reliably in their native language, i.e. those with phonological impairments, and those who mark all the phonemic distinctions, but produce some sounds in an idiosyncratic fashion, i.e. those with phonetic distortions. Another important factor on which children differ is the extent to which broader language difficulties (e.g. weak vocabulary, immature use or understanding of grammar) are associated with the problems in speech sound production. Although language may appear reasonably normal on the surface, many children with phonological impairments do have some language deficits when appropriate tests are used.

Relationships between discrimination and production of phoneme contrasts

Review of the literature on links between speech perception and impaired expressive phonology is hampered by the fact that many early studies do not specify sufficient detail about the children who were studied.

For children with "functional articulation disorders", a very mixed picture emerges, with some studies finding evidence of discrimination difficulties, and others obtaining normal findings. Differences in the nature and severity of children's speech difficulties are almost certainly responsible for the diversity of findings, though methodological factors may also be implicated.

Locke (1980) and Seymour, Baran, and Peaper (1981) pointed out that many researchers used unsatisfactory procedures to test speech discrimination. Most tests used in research settings adopt one of two paradigms. The first involves presenting the child with words that constitute "minimal pairs", i.e. they differ by one phoneme, e.g. "goat"–"coat". The child is shown a set of pictures and has to select the one whose name is spoken. A major disadvantage of this approach is

that it is difficult to find a vocabulary of minimal pairs of words that are pictureable and familiar to young children. This limits the phoneme contrasts that can be assessed, and many tests adopting this format include contrasts that are seldom confused in children's speech. Failure to find impairments on such a test may simply reflect the poor sensitivity of the test.

An alternative approach is to use nonwords, in a same–different paradigm. The child hears a minimal pair, such as "gub"–"guv" and must say if they are the same or different. However, this type of task is often impracticable with young children, who may quickly tire attending to pairs of meaningless verbal stimuli. Given that there is a 50% chance of giving a correct answer by guessing, it is necessary to use a long sequence of items to get a sensitive index of performance, raising all the problems of confounding poor discrimination with poor attention, as noted above.

Locke (1980) proposed a novel approach in which the child is shown a picture with a familiar name (e.g. dog) and has merely to judge whether or not the tester says the name correctly (e.g. "is this gog?"). This procedure overcomes the major problems of other test methods, and also has the advantage that one can design a test individually for a child so as to assess whether contrasts that are not distinguished in the child's speech are also misperceived. Bird and Bishop (1992) included a test based on Locke's procedure in a study of 14 children with phonological disorders but normal receptive vocabulary. They found that this group performed significantly less well than control children, individually matched on age and nonverbal ability. However, there was wide individual variation, and several children had no difficulty in discriminating phonological contrasts that they did not produce distinctively in their speech. There are two possible ways of viewing this result. One is to conclude that children with phonological impairments are heterogeneous, with some having perceptual deficits and others not. If this is so, one would expect to find other characteristics correlated with presence of perceptual deficit, e.g. the type of phonological problem or its prognosis. An alternative interpretation is that a perceptual impairment early in life is sufficient to cause a phonological disorder, which persists even after the perceptual impairment has resolved. Thus, to demonstrate a link between expressive phonological problems and perceptual impairment it may be necessary to study children at a very early age.

Identification of phoneme constancy in children with expressive phonological impairments

Studies by Bird and colleagues (Bird & Bishop, 1992; Bird, Bishop, & Freeman, 1995) indicate that while impaired speech discrimination is seen in only a subset of children with expressive phonological impairments, problems in perceiving phoneme constancy across different word contexts is widespread. The children studied by Bird et al. (1995) were selected on the basis that they all had persisting problems with expressive phonology. For some of them, this was the only measureable language problem, but others had additional impairments in receptive and expressive vocabulary and/or grammar. In one task, children were shown a puppet who liked things that began with the first sound of his name, "Sam". They were then required to judge, e.g. whether the puppet liked the "sock" or the "ball". The contrasting sounds (in this case, /b/ and /s/) were deliberately selected to be perceptually distinctive, avoiding sounds that children had difficulty in producing contrastively. In another task, children were given training in rhyme generation and then asked to produce rhyming words (e.g. "tell me something that rhymes with cat"). These tasks revealed substantial deficits in children with phonological problems. They could not judge that the initial sound of "Sam" was the same as the initial sound in "sock", and hence match "Sam" with "sock" rather than "ball", despite the substantial differences between the sounds /s/ and /b/. In many cases, the performance of phonologically impaired children on these tasks was no better than if they were guessing. Also, they were very poor at rhyme generation. Whether or not the child had additional language difficulties or a "pure" phonological problem made little difference to the pattern of results.

Such findings cannot be accounted for in terms of poor discrimination. If the child had difficulty in distinguishing two phonemes, then certain classes of sounds would be collapsed together. For instance, if the child treated /t/ and /k/ as instances of the same sound, we might then expect that when asked for a rhyme for cat, the response "back" would be given. However, this was not the type of error that was observed. When asked to generate rhymes, the commonest type of response seen in phonologically impaired children was for the child to give a semantic associate (e.g. replying "dog" or "hamster" to "cat"). These children seemed to have no idea of what was required of them, despite repeated demonstration. Their difficulty seemed to be in identifying and classifying speech sounds. This suggests that impaired ability to judge that two different acoustic patterns correspond to the same phoneme could for some children be a far greater problem than the discrimination of differences.

Bird and colleagues explained these findings by arguing that children with phonological problems failed to segment words into subsyllabic units. As we have seen, the syllable appears to be the preferred unit of analysis for all young children at the earliest stages of language acquisition, but by four years of age, most children develop awareness first of intermediate subsyllabic units, such as onset (initial consonant(s)) and rime (vowel and any subsequent consonants). Children with phonological problems appear to persist in using an immature perceptual strategy, and to continue to operate at the level of the word or syllable well past the normal age at which segmentation skills are acquired. This means that each new word must be learned as an entire unsegmented pattern. Consequently, they do not appreciate that words are composed of a small number of building blocks, and their language learning is inefficient and protracted.

Most children with SLI have expressive phonological problems at some point in their development, and in the sample studied by Bird et al. (1995) half of the children had low scores on tests of expressive or receptive language. Interestingly, language status had no effect on ability to do the phonological classification tasks. Other studies have shown that samples of children selected for having SLI also do poorly on various tasks involving phonological segmentation (Kamhi & Catts, 1986; Kamhi, Catts, Mauer, Apel, & Gentry,

1988). Tallal, Stark, Kallman, and Mellits (1980) showed that most (though not all) children with SLI had great difficulty with a task which required them to give one response to consonant-vowel syllables beginning with /d/ and a different response to those beginning with /b/ (i.e. /da/, /dɛ/, /di/ vs. /bɑ/, /bɛ/, and /bi/). (Phonetic symbols are shown in the Table inside the front cover.) However, this is perhaps not surprising; as we shall see in the next section, the same children had great difficulty even mastering a simple discrimination between /ba/ and /da/. What would be interesting would be to repeat this study using stimuli that children found easy to distinguish (e.g. /s/ vs. /d/) to see if their difficulties in perceptual classification extended to situations when there was no discrimination problem.

Bird et al. (1995) went on to show that children who had persistent problems in perceiving phoneme constancy were at high risk for literacy problems, especially in spelling. In many cases, the children had learned the letter–sound correspondences of the alphabet, but nevertheless failed in reading or spelling nonsense words such as "feg". For instance, the child given FEG to read might say /f/—/ɛ/—/g/, but then go on to pronounce the whole word as "John". This pattern of performance starts to make sense if we realise that the child has no understanding of the relationship between phonemic segments and whole syllables, because the latter remain processed as unanalysed global Gestalts. The problems go beyond simply collapsing phonological contrasts into a single category: rather, there is a failure to identify the basic units necessary for efficient perception and storage of the sounds of words.

An important question for future researchers is to discover whether this immature style of phonological processing is a secondary consequence of deficient auditory discrimination, or whether it is a quite different kind of problem, reflecting impairment of a language-specific modular system. It is often argued that problems in auditory discrimination cannot explain difficulties with phonological segmentation, because poor segmentation can be seen in children who have no evident difficulties in discriminating between

speech sounds. This was the case, for instance, in the study by Bird and Bishop (1992), and in a study of phonemic constancy by Tallal et al. (1980), where many of the young normally developing control children had difficulty with the task. The point to remember, however, is that we are dealing with a developmental disorder. It is possible that the deficits that one sees are age-dependent, and that discrimination difficulties might have been evident earlier on in those who currently have problems in segmentation. A very young child who was slow and inefficient in processing auditory signals might have difficulty in establishing an optimal phonological system, and this could lead to lasting problems, even if auditory discrimination subsequently matures to reach normal levels. This line of explanation is speculative and can only be assessed by longitudinal studies, but it is important to be aware of such possibilities, if we are not to dismiss causal links prematurely.

CHILDREN WITH TYPICAL SLI

We turn now to research on children with more typical SLI. Many of these children have similar impairments of expressive phonology to those described in the previous section, but in addition, their mastery of syntax and/or semantics is impaired. As we have seen, these children resemble children with more selective phonological impairments in having difficulties with tasks that involve phoneme identification. However, in children with typical SLI it has been proposed that the difficulties in identifying speech sounds are just the tip of the iceberg, and that their poor phoneme perception reflects much more fundamental problems in discriminating a wide range of auditory stimuli, nonverbal as well as verbal.

An early advocate of auditory perception deficits in SLI was Eisenson (1968, 1972), who maintained (1972, p.69):

The use of the term developmental aphasia, or one of its synonyms, implies that the child's perceptual abilities for auditory (speech) events underlies his impairment for the acquisition of auditory symbols. His expressive disturbances are a manifestation of his intake or decoding impairment.

Eisenson (1968) proposed that children with SLI had the kind of difficulty in identification of speech sounds that was discussed in the previous section, failing to form phonemic categories, but rather treating the /t/ in "ten" as different from the /t/ in "city", and storing each sound as a discrete entity. However, this was seen as linked to basic problems in discriminating between sounds. Eisenson's views were based predominantly on clinical observation rather than experimentation, and, in this chapter, the experimental evidence that has accumulated over the past 25 years will be reviewed. As we shall see, there is considerable support for his notion that at the heart of SLI there is an impairment of auditory perception.

By far the most comprehensive investigations of auditory processing in SLI have been carried out by Tallal and her colleagues in a series of studies conducted over the past two decades. Tallal concluded that the temporal characteristics of auditory stimuli are critical for children with SLI. When stimuli are either brief or rapid, children have difficulty in discriminating them, although they have no difficulty in differentiating the same stimuli when they are lengthened or presented at a slower rate. According to the current version of the theory, the impairment is not seen as specific to the auditory modality: similar difficulties in coping with brief or rapid events can be seen in other sensory modalities. However, this multimodal rapid processing deficit has an especially severe impact on language development, which is crucially dependent on the ability to recognise very brief auditory stimuli. Tallal's work has made a major impact in the field, and we shall spend some time looking at the evidence for this theory, as well as criticisms that have been levelled against it.

Tallal's hypothesis of a "temporal processing" impairment

Interest in temporal constraints on auditory processing goes back to an early report by Lowe and Campbell (1965) who studied temporal sequencing of children with SLI (referred to by these authors as "aphasoid" children). They found that children with SLI required a substantially longer gap between tones, or inter-stimulus interval (ISI), than other children to judge the sequential order of a high and low tone, although they performed normally on a similar task in which they simply had to say whether one or two tones had been presented.

In their first study, using a group of 12 children with SLI recruited from a British residential school, Tallal and Piercy (1973a, 1973b) replicated and extended this work, building into the study a number of important controls. First, they removed the need for children to make any verbal response, arguing that if a child had a language impairment, it may be a difficulty with the encoding of verbal concepts such as "high" or "low" that was impairing performance (see Fig. 3.6, overleaf, for details of the procedure). Tallal and Piercy (1973a) reported that control children performed significantly better than chance at the shortest ISI of 8 msec, whereas children with SLI attained this level of performance only at an ISI of 305 msec. A second control was to test tone discrimination using two different methods, the Repetition method, where the child had to identify and repeat the order of the stimuli, and the Same–Different method, where it was necessary only to discriminate the two tones. The same pattern of results was obtained on both tasks. Tallal and Piercy (1973b) went on to show that similar results were obtained if the tone duration, rather than ISI, was manipulated. When tone duration was 250 msec rather than 75 msec, children with SLI had no difficulty in doing the task at the shortest ISIs.

A third control was to include a parallel visual task, where the stimuli were two coloured patches (shades of green that did not readily lend themselves to verbal labelling), to see how specific the problem was to auditory stimuli. With these visual stimuli, children with SLI were indistinguishable from a control group (Tallal & Piercy, 1973b). Another factor associated with poor performance by children with SLI in auditory conditions was amount of information. When the Repetition Test was used to test memory, by requiring the child to repeat sequences of three to five tones, performance of the SLI started to fall

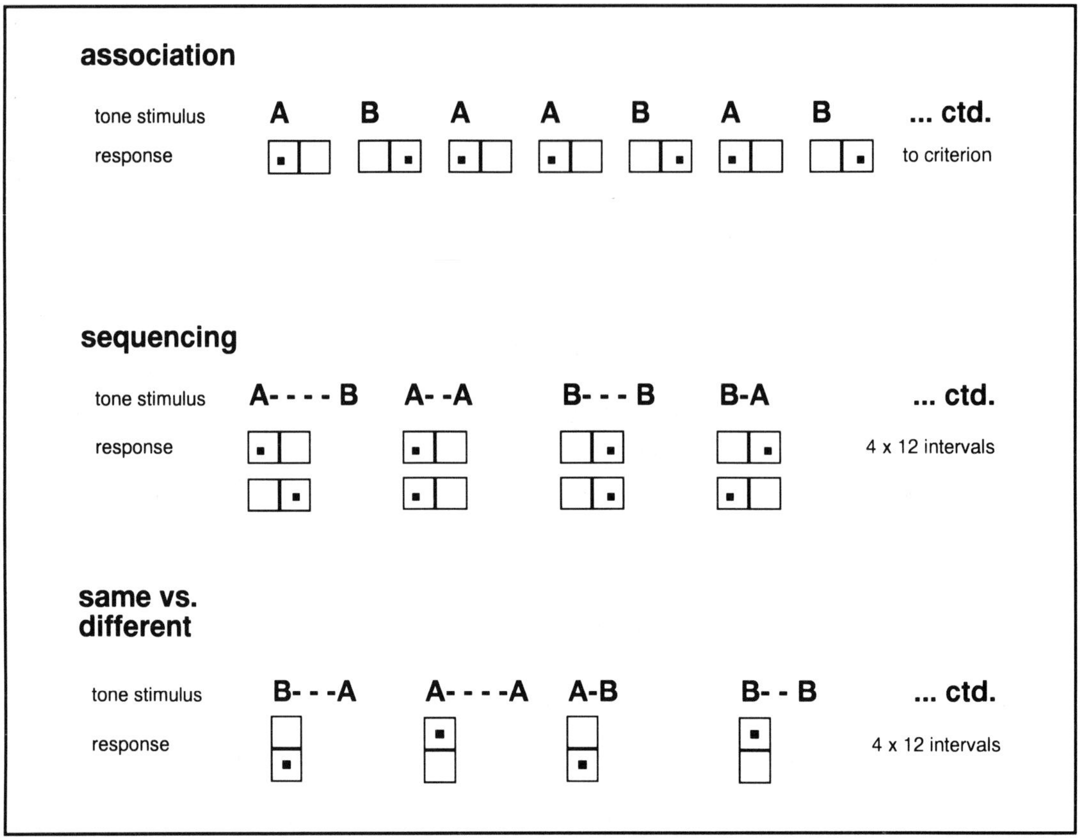

FIG. 3.6 Three phases of Tallal and Piercy's (1973a) procedure. The tones A and B (fundamental frequency of 100 vs. 305 Hz, duration 75 msec) were easy to discriminate and presented at intensities well above threshold. In the Association phase, the child was trained to associate each tone with a specific response panel (left or right) on a response box. Training with reinforcement continued until a criterion of 20 out of 24 consecutive responses correct was achieved. In the Sequencing phase, children were presented with pairs of tones, varying in the interval between tones (interstimulus interval, or ISI). The task was to press the sequence of panels corresponding to the tones. Longer sequences of three or four tones were then given (not shown). In the Same–different phase of the test, the response box was rotated through 90 degrees, and the child trained at a long ISI to select the top panel if two tones were identical, and the bottom panel if they were different. Once this association had been learned, the series of tone pairs randomly varying in ISI was presented. The Association and Sequencing phases together are referred to in later literature as the Repetition Test.

behind that of the control group on the longer sequences, even when there was a long ISI.

Tallal (1976) showed that the pattern of performance seen in children with SLI did not resemble that of normal children at any age. For two-tone sequences, when the interval between stimuli was long, children with SLI performed better than younger control children, but they did substantially worse than this group when the interval was less than 300 msec (see Fig. 3.7,

opposite). These experiments provided support for Eisenson's (1972, p.66, my emphasis) claim that "the aphasic child's basic perceptual impairment [is] one for auditory perception for speech *at the rate at which speech is normally presented*".

On the basis of findings with nonverbal tone stimuli, Tallal and colleagues made predictions about the types of speech sounds that children with SLI should find difficult to discriminate and produce. Stop consonants, which are differentiated

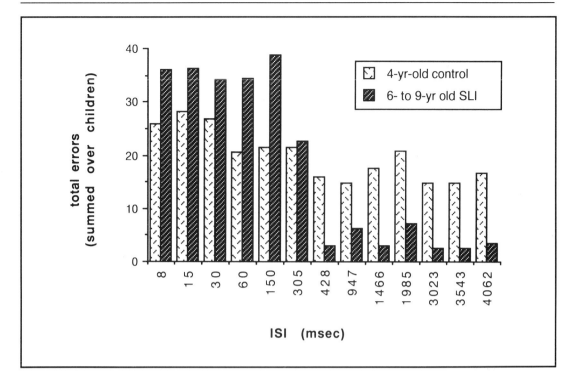

FIG. 3.7   Error rates on two element tone sequences tested using the Repetition method; redrawn from Tallal's (1976) data.

on the basis of information occurring in the first 40–50 msec, should be hard to tell apart, whereas vowels, which have critical information spread over a longer duration, should be easier. These predictions were broadly confirmed (Tallal & Piercy, 1974; Tallal, Stark, & Curtiss, 1976), with poor discrimination found for stop consonants, such as /ba/ vs. /ga/ and relatively good performance with vowels.

The initial experiments with tones provided a rationale for expecting a difference in difficulty for consonants and vowels, because consonants are differentiated principally by a very brief initial segment of sound, whereas the distinguishing information for vowels is more prolonged. However, there is another difference between these two types of speech sound: vowels are "steady state", i.e. there is little change in the levels of energy in a given frequency band over the course of the vowel, whereas stop consonants are characterised by a changing pattern of intensity at different frequencies (i.e. formant transitions) (see *Acoustic cues in speech perception,* p.8). Tallal and

Piercy (1975) went on to demonstrate that the advantage for vowels over consonants was due to their longer duration rather than to the transitional nature of consonants, by showing that the advantage for vowels could be reversed by altering temporal characteristics of synthetic speech stimuli, i.e. stretching formant transitions of consonants or truncating vowels (see Fig 3.8, overleaf). However, Tallal and Stark (1981), while broadly replicating earlier findings, reported that the perceptual deficit of children with SLI was not limited to those sounds differing only on formant transitions. These children also did poorly when asked to discriminate /sa/ and /ʃa/, which differ primarily on spectral cues. Furthermore, they had little difficulty in discriminating between /ɛ/ vs. /a/, even though the duration of each vowel was only 40 msec. They concluded that brief steady-state stimuli were difficult to discriminate only if rapidly followed by another acoustic stimulus.

Leonard, McGregor, and Allen (1992) replicated and extended the study of Tallal and

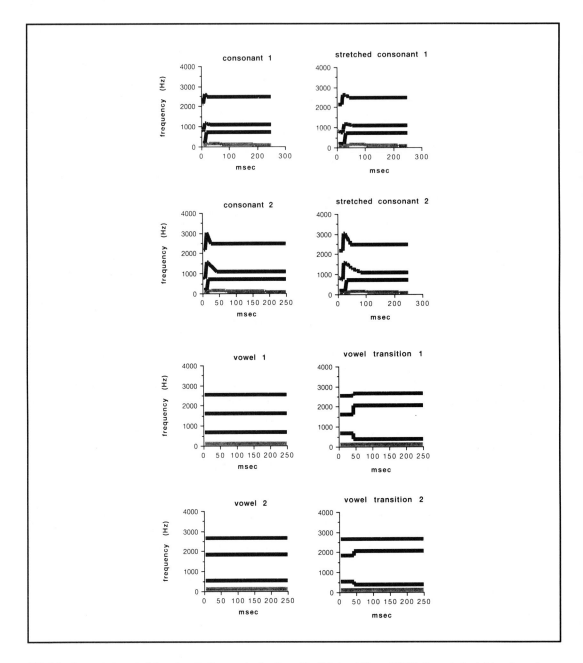

FIG. 3.8   Formant characteristics of synthetic speech stimuli used by Tallal and Piercy (1975). Those in the left-hand panel are the original consonant and vowel stimuli used by Tallal and Piercy (1974). The consonants are perceived as /bɑ/ and /dɑ/ and the vowels are perceived as /ɛ/ and /a/. Children with SLI had great difficulty in discriminating between consonants 1 and 2, but performed normally on the contrast between vowels 1 and 2. The right-hand panel shows the modified stimuli used in the 1975 study. The duration of the initial transient portion of the consonant stimuli has been more than doubled, making the discrimination between stimulus 1 and 2 much easier for children with SLI. The distinctive portion of the vowel stimuli has been truncated to 43 msec, leading to very high error rates by children with SLI. N.B. for stimuli where the distinctive portion was brief, a high proportion of children with SLI were unable to distinguish the stimuli on the association phase, and did not proceed to the sequencing phase.

Stark (1981). Like the latter authors, they used a "go-no go" task rather than the Repetition method. The child was first trained to press a button when a "target" stimulus (e.g. /bɑ/) was presented, and then given a series of trials where the task was to press the button on hearing the target and withhold the response when a contrasting stimulus (e.g. /dɑ/) was presented. They compared eight four- to five-year-old children with SLI and eight control children and, following Tallal and Stark, presented data in terms of the numbers of children reaching a criterion of 12 correct responses in a sequence of 16. Results are shown in Table 3.1.

The results were compatible with those of Tallal and colleagues, in that discriminations of the stop consonants /b/ vs. /d/ and the fricatives /s/ vs. /ʃ/ was difficult, whereas the vowel contrasts were much easier, except where the vowel was followed by another syllable within a very short space of time (i.e. in the polysyllabic stimuli, where the interval between syllables was 35 msec). It is worth noting that this demonstration of worsening discrimination when a speech sound is embedded in a nonsense word is compatible with findings from an early study by McReynolds (1966), who showed that language-impaired children could learn a discrimination between /m/ and /ʒ/ much more easily than a discrimination between /həmɒk/ and /həʒɒk/.

Up to this point, all the studies in this series tell a coherent story: children with SLI had a selective impairment in discriminating between auditory stimuli if the critical distinguishing information was brief, or if stimuli occurred in rapid succession. However, the next study led to a qualification of this conclusion. Tallal, Stark, Kallman, and Mellits (1981) conducted a larger investigation of 35 children with SLI aged from five to nine years, selected by stringent test criteria. In this study, discrimination of auditory and visual stimuli was explicitly compared. The auditory stimuli included complex tones, as used by Tallal and Piercy (1973a,b) as well as synthesised speech sounds (/bɑ/ and /dɑ/). The visual stimuli were letter-like forms. As in the earlier studies, there were striking differences between SLI and control children in their ability to discriminate tone pairs when a variable ISI was used. There were, however, some interesting differences from the previous sample. First, some children with SLI performed poorly with auditory stimuli that were neither brief nor rapid. Two children failed to reach criterion on a task which simply required them to learn to associate a different response with each tone. A further seven children performed at chance with auditory sequences of two tones even when there was a long interval between stimuli. The SLI group

TABLE 3.1

Numbers of Children Achieving Discrimination (Out of 8) in a Study by Leonard et al. (1992)

	Control	SLI
Vowels		
/i/ vs. /u/	8	7
/dɑb/ vs. /dɑb/	8	6
Consonants		
/bɑ/ vs. /dɑ/	6	2
/dɑs/ vs. /dɑʃ/	5	1
Vowels embedded in polysyllabic form		
/dɑb-i-bɑ/ vs. /dɑb-u-bɑ/	6	0

in general was significantly impaired in ability to process sequences of more than two stimuli, even when the interval between stimuli was relatively long. Another striking difference from earlier work was that the SLI group was deficient relative to controls with visual as well as auditory stimuli on tests of sequencing, rate processing, and serial memory. Post hoc analysis indicated that this finding was a function of the age of the subjects: the younger children with SLI were impaired in visual and auditory modalities, whereas the older ones were impaired with the auditory stimuli only.

This age effect could reflect sampling factors, but it could also indicate that the profile of impairment changes as the child grows older. To investigate this possibility, Bernstein and Stark (1985) traced 29 children from the original study and retested them on perception of synthetic /ba/–/da/ contrasts four years after the initial testing. Overall, there was a substantial improvement in children's performance. When first tested, 19 of the 29 children with SLI had failed to discriminate reliably between these synthetic speech sounds, whereas on retest 24 of them reached criterion, and there was no overall difference between the SLI group and controls. When presented with sequences of stimuli at a fixed inter-stimulus interval, performance of children with SLI was variable. Most of them did very well, but a few made many errors. All those who did pass this subtest were able to reach criterion on a rate processing subtest which included trials with brief inter-stimulus intervals. Furthermore, most of the SLI and control children could repeat sequences of four or five items on a serial memory subtest. This good performance with auditory stimuli was obtained even though, on retest, 23 of the children still met psychometric criteria for SLI.

Bernstein and Stark (1985, p.28) noted: "Considering time 2 results alone, we could not conclude that specific language impairment in older children is caused by perceptual deficits in rapid rate processing of phonemes." However, there are two points to note when interpreting these results. First, it would be erroneous to conclude that the language disorder was not caused by perceptual impairments just because no perceptual impairment was evident at time 2. As Bernstein and Stark concluded (p.28): "Language disabilities may

result when inadequate processing of sensory information occurs during early childhood although the original processing deficit may no longer exist." In other words, a delay in the maturation of normal perceptual systems early in development might impair learning during a critical period, leaving lasting residual language problems even after auditory perception had matured to normal levels. A second point was that performance was near ceiling levels on retest, so it could be the case that children with SLI still had an auditory perceptual deficit, but the tests were too insensitive to detect this.

Further evidence for amelioration of a rapid processing deficit with age comes from Lincoln, Dickstein, Courchesne, Elmasian, and Tallal (1992), who compared three groups of adolescents and young adults: one group had autistic disorder, one had receptive developmental language disorders, and the third was a normal control group. The groups were matched on age, and the two clinical samples were similar in terms of verbal IQ. The test methods were closely similar to those used by Tallal and colleagues, but they included sequences of up to seven tones at both rapid and slower presentation rates. Results are shown in Fig. 3.9. When the task involved only two stimuli at rapid rates of presentation all groups performed near ceiling levels (similar to the Bernstein and Stark study). The deficits of language-impaired children were apparent with trains of six or seven tones. However, in contrast to predictions made on the basis of Tallal's earlier work, rapid presentation rate did not pose particular problems for children with SLI: they were impaired relative to the other groups on long sequences whether fast or slow.

Temporal processing deficit or poor discrimination of brief/rapid stimuli?

While there is widespread agreement that the work of Tallal and her collaborators provides evidence of abnormalities in auditory processing in children with SLI, there has been some debate as to what exactly this deficit is. Studdert-Kennedy and Mody (1995) have objected to Tallal's usage of the term "temporal processing" to describe the perceptual deficit in SLI, arguing that it confuses rate of perception with perception of rate. They point out

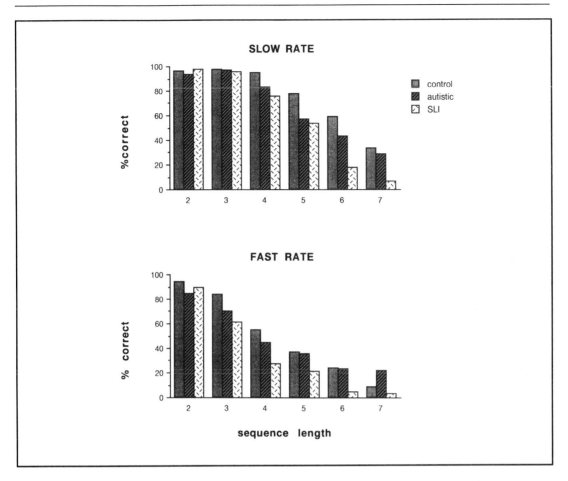

FIG. 3.9   Mean percentage correct (adjusted for performance IQ and age) of adolescents and young adults on a computerised version of the repetition test. Scores on list lengths five and above were extrapolated by assigning maximum errors to those who did not meet criterion at a previous level. (Figure based on data from Table 2, p. 618 of Lincoln et al., 1992.)

that Tallal's own studies, as well as others, show no evidence of a primary problem in sorting out temporal order of incoming stimuli, but rather a difficulty in identifying stimuli that are brief or rapidly followed by another stimulus. For instance, in Tallal and Piercy's original same–different task (see Fig. 3.6, p.64), performance was just as bad when children had simply to indicate whether the two stimuli were identical, as when they had to report the order of occurrence. The point made by Studdert-Kennedy and Mody is well taken and it seems prudent to use a term such as "rapid perception" rather than "temporal processing", to avoid ambiguity and confusion.

Sensory trace, or stimulus recoding impairment?

An information-processing model by Cutting and Pisoni (1978) provides a useful starting point for analysing the nature of the auditory processing deficit. They reviewed experimental evidence that points to the existence of a sensory information store, or echoic memory, that holds auditory information in relatively unprocessed form for a period of 50 to 250 msec. Information from this store is transmitted to a recognition device, where it undergoes further analysis in terms of both auditory and phonetic features. Cutting and Pisoni suggested that Tallal's data implicated a deficit in the sensory information store and perhaps also at the level of auditory analysis.

Evidence for a defective sensory trace.   This conclusion by Cutting and Pisoni was influenced by the early work of Tallal and Piercy (1973a,b), which showed that processing of brief tones was impaired regardless of whether the task was to give a sequence of responses that matched the tones, or to simply identify a tone pair as same or different. In the latter task, it does not matter if the child cannot identify the stimuli; all that is needed is the ability to recognise that a change has occurred. A similar methodology was used by Elliott and her collaborators (Elliott & Hammer, 1988, 1993; Elliott, Hammer, & Scholl, 1989) in a psycho-physical study of "fine-grained auditory discrimi-nation" in a large sample of children covering a wide range of age and ability. Elliott et al. used synthesised speech stimuli to test the ability to discriminate stimuli on the /ba/–/da/–/ga/ dimension, and also those varying in voice onset time, i.e. /ba/ vs. /pa/. A computer-controlled procedure was used, with children having to make a same–different judgement about pairs of stimuli. They found clear deficits in children with language problems, but unfortunately the interpretation of this result is not entirely straightforward. Psychophysical methods are problematic when the children are inattentive or poorly motivated. The task of making fine judgements about series of closely similar stimuli is repetitive and boring for adults, let alone children. There is ample evidence that children with SLI have a high rate of attentional problems, and a hallmark of attentional problems is that children do not persist well on boring tasks. Indeed, Powell and Bishop (1992) found poor results on tests of *visual* discrimination in children with SLI and argued these could very well be artefactual and arise because inattentive children found these tests rather less interesting than nonverbal IQ subtests, on which they typically obtained normal scores. In a different kind of experimental context, Stark and Montgomery (1995, p.150) gave a revealing description of typical behaviour of some of their language-impaired participants: "In spite of the reminder, before each sentence pair was presented,

to listen for the (pictured) target word, the LI children would sometimes gaze around the test room, play with the headphones, or slump, glassy-eyed, while the sentences were being presented. Afterward, they might or might not be able to say that they had heard the target word." Such observations mean that we need to take very seriously the possibility that performance deficits on a discrimination task such as that used by Elliott and colleagues might reflect generalised attentional problems rather than a selective impairment in early stages of auditory discrimi-nation.

So how are we to distinguish these possibilities? It is difficult (if not impossible!) to prevent children being inattentive, but we can build into the task some kind of control that allows us to identify when this is a problem. One way of doing this is to design the task so we can contrast competence in one condition, with defective performance in another. In effect, this is what we see in Tallal's Repetition Test, where a general explanation in terms of inattention cannot explain how within a session the same child makes errors when the ISI is short but does well when it is long. Unfortunately, no such control was used in the studies by Elliott and colleagues. It is usually assumed that random attentional failures can be excluded by a study of individual performance curves, which, in adaptive procedures, should show gradual convergence on a threshold, without any indication of a drift from good to poorer performance. However, the simulations by Wightman et al. (1989), described earlier, indicate that one would need very high rates of inattentiveness, persisting over long periods, before their impact could be detectable. One aspect of individual performance that can be informative is the nature of errors. If poor discrimination is the critical factor, then most errors should involve "same" responses to "different" stimuli. In this regard, there is reason to question the logic of Elliott, Hammer et al. (1989), who interpreted errors on "catch trials" (where both stimuli were identical and so a "same" response was correct) as poor auditory discrimination. The task used by Elliott et al. reveals clear problems in children with SLI, but the specificity of the deficit remains unclear, and this study cannot be taken as providing unambiguous support for an early sensory impairment.

An intact auditory sensory trace? One reason for looking especially carefully and critically at studies that suggest a disturbance of early sensory processing is that it is hard to reconcile this idea with Tallal's later theoretical position which implicates a multimodal impairment of rate processing. Given that early sensory processing of auditory and visual stimuli are mediated by different brain areas which develop at different rates, it is difficult to imagine a single neurobiological impairment that would impair the early stages of both auditory and visual processing.

There are also a number of studies that appear to demonstrate that children with SLI have an intact sensory trace, with problems only at a later stage of processing. One such piece of evidence comes from a method devised by Stefanatos, Green, and Ratcliff (1989), which will be described more fully in a later section, where cortical evoked potentials are recorded as the child listens to a repeatedly modulated tone that warbles between high and low frequencies at a steady rate, to establish whether there is a brain response that mimics the frequency modulation. Two studies have adopted this approach (Stefanatos et al., 1989; Tomblin, Abbas, Records, & Brenneman, 1995), and neither has shown any deficits in children with typical SLI, (although, as will be discussed in a later section, Stefanatos et al. did find abnormalities in children who had severe receptive impairments). These studies do rule out a deficit in detection of frequency modulation at a very early stage of cortical processing. However, as Tomblin et al. pointed out, children in their study had not been given a discrimination task such as the Repetition Test, so it is not possible to establish whether the electrophysiological results are discrepant with a behavioural index of discrimination.

Direct comparison of electrophysiological and behavioural approaches was achieved in a study by Neville, Coffey, Holcomb, and Tallal (1993), who also obtained predominantly normal results on a measure of neuronal refractoriness in children with SLI. Children were presented with sequences of 2000 Hz tones (each of 50 msec duration), within which they had to listen for occasional occurrences (on 10% of trials) of a 1000 Hz "target" tone. The interval between tones was varied from 200 to 2000 msec; at more rapid presentation rates, the evoked response decreases, because neurons have a "refractory period", i.e. a period of low responsivity, immediately after firing. The prediction was that performance of control children and those with SLI might diverge when the ISI was less then 300 msec. However, in a global comparison between 22 nine-year-olds with SLI and 12 control children, Neville et al. found no difference in either amplitude or latency of cortical auditory evoked responses, even at short ISIs. These same children had participated in other studies by Tallal and individual children with SLI did vary in the extent to which they had behavioural evidence of rapid auditory processing deficits. Therefore, they subdivided the SLI sample into two equal-sized groups on the basis of their performance on Tallal's repetition test, and compared their evoked potentials. Although they reported significant three-way interactions between group, electrode site, and ISI, the main interaction between group and ISI was not statistically significant.[2] Thus, overall, electrophysiological studies appear to reveal that the brain of a child with SLI does differentiate between auditory stimuli that are not discriminated on behavioural testing.

Further evidence for an intact auditory trace comes from a behavioural study by Sussman (1993). He compared a group of children with SLI with younger normally developing control children on their ability to discriminate between synthetic speech stimuli that fell on a continuum between /ba/ and /da/. Thus, this task involved making judgements about stimuli that differed only for a short portion of their duration. Sussman found that the results depended crucially on how children's discrimination was tested. In one condition, the child would hear a sequence of four syllables, and was asked to touch a red X if a change was detected. In another condition, the child was presented with a single stimulus and asked to label it as an instance of /ba/ or /da/. In the first task, performance of children with SLI was as good or better than that of control children. However, in the second task the

SLI group showed evidence of problems. They were more variable than control children in how they labelled the stimuli and did not have such a clear categorical boundary between /bɑ/ and /dɑ/. In this regard, the results resembled those obtained in a previous study of categorical perception by Thibodeau and Sussman (1979). Sussman concluded that the sensory trace of a speech stimulus was probably normal in children with SLI, enabling them to detect even subtle changes in an auditory signal. However, sensory trace information decays rapidly unless encoded in some other form, and Sussman suggested that it may be this encoding process which is defective in SLI. In the model of Cutting and Pisoni (1978) this would correspond to an impairment in the recognition system, rather than in the sensory trace itself.

Sussman's findings seem completely at odds with Tallal and Piercy's (1973a,b, 1974, 1975) demonstration of impaired same–different judgements with brief tone sequences or synthetic speech stimuli. It is tempting to explain away this discrepancy in terms of differences in the samples of children studied by the two groups, but before dismissing incompatible results as due to sampling factors, it would be worth doing more systematic comparisons of the methods used by the different investigators, because, though they seem similar in terms of the discriminations they require of children, they do differ in their response requirements. In the same–different task used by Tallal and Piercy, the child had to remember which of two panels to press to indicate "same" or "different"; it seems likely that this would be more difficult to learn than the response used by Sussman, i.e. making a response if any change was detected in a sequence of four syllables. Although Tallal and Piercy did everything possible to minimise verbal mediation in their studies, children with SLI may have found it harder to remember the response coding, and this might have disproportionately affected their performance in the more difficult conditions, when ISI was very short.

If we do want to argue that the sensory trace is unimpaired, we need to ask why discrimination of tone pairs is so dependent on duration in young children with SLI. The argument would be that the encoding of an auditory trace into a more durable representation is much slower than in normally developing children. This will not matter if there is an adequate interval between stimuli, or if stimulus duration is long, but, for brief stimuli, most of the information from the trace will have decayed before it has been encoded. If two stimuli occur in rapid succession, the second will occur before encoding of the first is complete. Thus, an account that argues that some kind of additional processing must be done on a sensory trace to encode it in a less fragile form could account for the dual problem seen in SLI with both rapid and brief stimuli being affected, while at the same time being consistent with those electrophysiological or behavioural studies that suggest integrity of the sensory trace.

One approach that holds out future promise for addressing these methodological and interpretative concerns is the study of auditory evoked potentials. Kraus, McGee, Carrell, and Sharma (1995) reviewed work using an index called mismatch negativity or MMN. The idea is very simple. One records an evoked response to a series of identical standard auditory stimuli (e.g. a synthetic /dɑ/). Occasionally, a slightly different stimulus is inserted into the series (e.g. another synthetic /dɑ/ with slightly different auditory characteristics, termed the "deviant" stimulus). In general, work with both adults and children shows that if the deviant stimulus is discriminable using a behavioural test, then it will be associated with a different waveform in the evoked response. One can index the brain's discrimination of the stimuli by subtracting the evoked response to the standard stimulus from that obtained with the new stimulus. The difference between waves is the MMN, as shown in Fig. 3.10.

There are two features of the MMN that make it particularly attractive as a tool for studying impaired auditory perception in children. First, the MMN is very similar for adults and school-aged children, even though the waves from which it is derived do differ in their early components. Second, MMN does not require the child to attend and respond to the stimuli; indeed, Kraus et al. made recordings while the child was watching videos. Thus, this method overcomes many of the

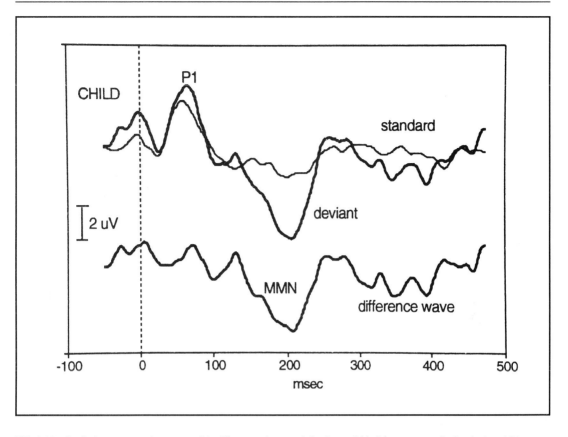

FIG. 3.10   Cortical response to just perceptible differences in speech (variants of /da/) from a normally developing child. Averaged responses to standard and deviant stimuli are shown in the top half of the graph; the "difference wave" in the lower half of the figure is obtained by subtracting the deviant wave from the standard wave. (Reprinted from Kraus, McGee, Carrell, & Sharma, 1995.)

problems associated with psychophysical procedures, where thresholds may be affected by wandering attention, and it does not require the child explicitly to encode the stimulus. MMN is a relatively new technique in the study of children's auditory processing. Kraus et al. presented an illustrative case study of a boy with SLI in whom MMN was absent, not only to a fine distinction between different variants of /da/, but also when /ga/ was presented as the mismatch stimulus in the context of /da/. In a later study, Kraus et al. (1996) went on to argue that MMN to synthetic speech stimuli revealed poor discrimination skills at an early stage of auditory processing in a group of children who were described as "learning disabled". It is too early to know whether children

who fail Tallal's repetition test will reliably show similar abnormalities on MMN.

Memory for auditory sequences.   Regardless of whether the impairment is in sensory storage or later identification, we need also to explain why individuals with SLI have problems in retaining long sequences of items even when there is a long inter-stimulus interval (Lincoln et al., 1992). Encoding an initial sensory trace allows incoming information to be stored in a more durable form, but the memory representations are nevertheless subject to decay unless actively attended to and rehearsed. The child who encodes incoming stimuli rapidly and efficiently will have time to refresh the traces of stimuli earlier in the series;

however, the child who takes much longer at the encoding process will have little spare capacity for rehearsal. If this account is correct, we might expect to see different serial position recall functions in short-term memory for children with SLI vs. control children. A study by Gillam, Cowan, and Day (1995) addressed just this question. They compared children with SLI with both age-matched controls and also with younger children matched on memory span. These groups were then compared in terms of their ability to recall digits at different serial positions, and in terms of their susceptibility to the "suffix effect", i.e. the detrimental effect of adding an irrelevant spoken syllable to the end of the list of digits. Task difficulty was equated by giving all children lists that were one item longer than digit span, with data then compared for the first and last three serial positions (see Fig. 3.11, below). Children with SLI

showed a smaller primacy effect than age-matched controls, but were similar in this respect to memory-span matched controls. However, they showed a significantly larger suffix effect, i.e. their performance was more impaired by the irrelevant spoken item at the end of the list. The conclusions drawn by Gillam et al. were closely in line with the argument advanced here: they proposed that, in children with SLI, interpretation of incoming auditory information was slowed, leading to over-reliance on an auditory-phonetic trace that was vulnerable to overwriting by new speech input.

Auditory perception or speech perception deficit?

A major criticism raised by Studdert-Kennedy and Mody (1995) has to do with the characterisation of the perceptual deficit as an auditory processing problem. These authors were specifically

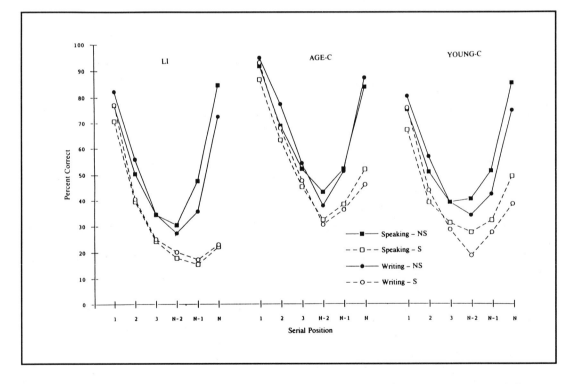

FIG. 3.11   Mean percent recall as a function of list position, response modality (speaking vs. writing), and item time (NS = no suffix, S = suffix), for three groups of subjects in study by Gillam et al. (1995). LI = language impaired, AGE-C = age matched controls; YOUNG-C = younger controls matched on digit span. Because different children were tested at different list lengths, the recency portion of the curve is shown in relation to the list length (N), rather than absolute serial position. Reprinted with permission.

interested in the application of Tallal's theory to children with reading problems, but the issues they raised are relevant also to SLI. They argued that perceptual deficits similar to those reported by Tallal and colleagues can be seen in poor readers when one uses speech stimuli (synthetic /ba/ vs. /da/), but not when one uses nonverbal auditory stimuli that are carefully selected to be matched with the speech stimuli in terms of acoustic properties (Mody, Studdert-Kennedy, & Brady, 1997). The nonverbal stimuli were sine waves with durations and frequency trajectories identical to the second and third formants of the /ba/–/da/ stimuli. Mody et al. reported that poor readers who were selected for doing poorly in the /ba/–/da/ discrimination did not differ from a control group in discrimination of the nonverbal stimuli, regardless of inter-stimulus interval, and they concluded that the deficit of these children was specifically phonological, and not auditory.

As we have seen, Tallal's own studies, starting with the original Tallal and Piercy (1973a,b) reports, provided ample evidence for deficits on nonverbal auditory discrimination tasks in children with SLI. The question then is, why should Mody et al. obtain different results? The two obvious explanations are in terms of (1) differences between subject populations and (2) differences between auditory stimuli.

Mody et al. freely admit that the poor readers in their sample had reading problems that were much milder than those of Tallal's subjects.[3] Furthermore, their receptive vocabulary was average, and there was no indication of associated language difficulties. Unfortunately, Mody et al. did not include tone stimuli similar to those used by Tallal and colleagues with these children, so we cannot tell whether this sample would have shown the same kind of deficit as reported by Tallal et al. Nevertheless, Mody et al. did not see this as particularly relevant. They accepted that other studies of children with serious reading difficulties have found problems in processing tones, but they argued that this was a co-occurring deficit in stimulus classification speed which was much more variable in occurrence than phonological deficits, and not causally related to them. Specifically, they stated (p.206): "We have no

reason to suppose that the two weaknesses reflect the same underlying discriminative deficit, because tones and syllables contrast on entirely different acoustic dimensions." In brief, Mody et al. argue that, while a more general explanation of both speech and nonspeech impairments in terms of an auditory perceptual deficit may be parsimonious, it is simply implausible, given the very different acoustic characteristics of tone and speech stimuli. However, it is hard to see how slow classification of incoming auditory stimuli (which Mody et al. accept as a correlate of reading problems) could fail to have an impact on how a phonological system develops. The fact that deficits with nonspeech auditory stimuli are less reliable and less severe than deficits with speech stimuli is not strong evidence that the two are unrelated; it could simply mean that slow auditory processing early in development has a particularly pronounced effect on how the phonological system develops. We need further studies charting the relationship between auditory and phonological discrimination deficits over time, starting at an early age (say, four years old) to establish whether there is a causal link between the two, or whether, as Mody et al. would argue, the deficits in processing nonverbal auditory stimuli are just a red herring for those seeking the primary underlying cause of SLI.

A question of particular interest is whether MMN will reveal deficits in discriminating nonspeech auditory stimuli of the kind used by Mody et al. (1997). The MMN method has promise, both for clarifying the nature and locus of auditory deficits, and for identifying which children with SLI do have poor discrimination arising at an early stage in auditory processing.

CHILDREN WITH SEVERE COMPREHENSION DIFFICULTIES

Occasionally one encounters children who have such severe impairments of auditory comprehension that they appear to make little sense of sound and behave as if deaf. Case descriptions of such children have been provided by Worster-Drought and Allen (1929) (under the label of congenital auditory imperception) and Rapin, Mattis, and Rowan (1977) (under the label of verbal auditory agnosia).

One reason for keeping such cases separate from other language impairments is that a distinctive etiology is commonly associated with this clinical picture. Bishop and Rosenbloom (1987) noted that severe auditory comprehension problems in the absence of autism were usually seen in children whose language skills regressed after a period of normal development, and who showed disturbances of the electrical activity of the brain, leading to the diagnosis of acquired epileptic aphasia or Landau–Kleffner syndrome (Landau & Kleffner, 1957). It seems more appropriate to classify this disorder with acquired childhood aphasias rather than with SLI, because the course suggests an acquired etiology, although the precise pathological process remains to be identified.

Acquired epileptic aphasia is a rare disorder that often goes undiagnosed and some studies may have unwittingly included unrecognised cases within groups of children classified as having a receptive SLI. Epileptic seizures are seldom observed in these children, and they do not usually have any hard neurological signs, so unless a clinician is alerted by the history to conduct EEG investigations, the child might be regarded as neurologically normal. Indeed, EEG abnormalities may be intermittent and/or only apparent when a sleep EEG is recorded, and they may disappear altogether over time (Deonna, 1993). In my early studies of children with SLI, I encountered several with the diagnosis of "receptive aphasia", where the history of regression was suggestive of acquired epileptic aphasia, but where the child had never had seizures and no EEG recording had been taken around the time of onset, so the diagnosis could not be confirmed. It would be misleading to give the impression that all children with severe receptive impairments have an epileptic etiology (whether recognised or undiagnosed). However, in my experience, those rare children who seem able to make little sense of sound, despite having adequate hearing and normal development in other respects, do not seem to be on a continuum with other types of developmental language disorder, at

least as far as etiology is concerned, and it seems prudent to study them as a separate group until we have stronger justification for treating them as simply a severe variant of SLI.

Clinically, these children look as if they have major problems in processing auditory stimuli, but relatively little research has been done to pinpoint the locus of the impairment. In particular, there is uncertainty as to whether there is difficulty in discriminating all auditory stimuli or whether this is restricted to verbal materials. Rapin et al. used the diagnostic label of verbal auditory agnosia; this amounts to a theoretical statement that the problem is restricted to impaired processing of speech sounds, leaving processing of other auditory stimuli intact.

Frumkin and Rapin (1980) studied four children with the diagnosis of verbal auditory agnosia and found that they did indeed have extreme difficulty in discriminating between synthetic speech sounds. They based their task on Tallal's Repetition test. They found that two children performed at chance level and the other two showed adequate discrimination of vowels but very poor performance with consonants, the same pattern of impairment as described by Tallal and Piercy (1974, 1975).

If, as the label "verbal auditory agnosia" implies, the impairment in these children is restricted to the processing of speech sounds, one should find normal perception of nonverbal auditory stimuli. Frequently, the only evidence for this is unimpaired discrimination of environmental sounds. This, however, is not very satisfactory. Often the choices are between environmental sounds that differ substantially in acoustic characteristics and performance is near ceiling.

In one of the few studies to examine the characteristics of auditory stimuli that children with receptive language disorders responded to, Stefanatos et al. (1989) recorded cortical evoked potentials as the child listened to a repeatedly modulated tone that warbled between high and low frequencies at a steady rate. One can record cortical activity that modulates at the same rate as the stimulus. If a child had an impairment of auditory registration at a very early stage of processing, we might expect to see an abnormal evoked response, reflecting a lack of cortical neurons sensitive to changing frequency. This is exactly what Stefanatos et al. found in a subgroup of children with severe "receptive aphasia" (see Fig. 3.12, overleaf). This indicates that the underlying impairment operates at a stage prior to perceptual recognition and is not restricted to verbal materials. Thus the limited evidence available suggests that it may be more accurate to speak of a general "auditory agnosia" in these children, rather than a specifically verbal impairment. However, subsequent accounts of this work have suggested that the children studied by Stefanatos et al. included cases of Landau–Kleffner syndrome (Tomblin et al., 1995), and so these results may not generalise to children who are free from any epileptic activity.

What if one by-passes the postulated auditory perceptual deficit and presents children with visual forms of language? If an auditory processing problem were responsible for comprehension failure, then it seems reasonable to predict that one should observe much better understanding for written or signed language, provided the child had had adequate opportunity to learn these. The answer to this question is more complicated than we might imagine. Cases have been described of children who can understand written language much better than spoken language (e.g. Denes, Balliello, Volterra, & Pellegrini, 1986), and most authorities recommend using written or signed language as a route into language learning for cases of acquired epileptic aphasia. However, visual language is no panacea, and grammatical difficulties are evident in written language (Bishop, 1982). We will defer discussion of the implications of such findings until Chapter 5.

DEFECTIVE AUDITORY PROCESSING IN CHILDREN WITH SLI: CAUSE, CONSEQUENCE, OR CORRELATE?

The review of research in this area emphasises the methodological problems that researchers encounter when they try to answer the question "is defective auditory perception a causal factor in specific language impairment?" One can get very

different results to that question depending on the precise methods adopted; studies of brain evoked responses may reveal capacities that do not seem to be present on behavioural testing. The child who is asked to detect when a stimulus changes may show superior discrimination ability to one who is asked to identify each stimulus. Top-down influences mean that speech discrimination may also vary depending on whether stimuli are familiar words or nonsense words, or whether stimuli are easily nameable. There are major difficulties in distinguishing genuine perceptual problems from poor concentration and attention. Furthermore, there may be variation from one child to another, depending on the type of speech-language problem they manifest, and even in the same child over a long period of time.

Interpretation of deficits on auditory perceptual tasks is hence fraught with difficulties. If we find poor auditory processing correlated with SLI, this may be an indicator of a fundamental underlying deficit that has caused the language difficulties, but it could reflect a causal relationship in the other direction, with language level dictating perceptual test performance, or we may simply be seeing deficits that are correlated but not causally related in any interesting way. To make matters worse, the fact that we are dealing with a developmental disorder means that we cannot even rely with confidence on negative evidence to rule out certain hypotheses. If we find a child with SLI can do a speech discrimination task, we cannot be certain that an earlier impairment of speech perception might have resolved but left a lasting legacy of language difficulties.

Given these tremendous difficulties of methodology and interpretation, it is perhaps all the more impressive that we do seem able to draw some conclusions from the growing literature on this topic. The view that language impairments are linked to auditory processing problems has stood the test of time remarkably well. The work of Tallal and colleagues has demonstrated that children with SLI do have problems in discriminating nonverbal auditory stimuli when these are brief or rapid, or when there is a large amount of information to be processed. Tallal (1990) stressed that the underlying deficit in these children is not specific

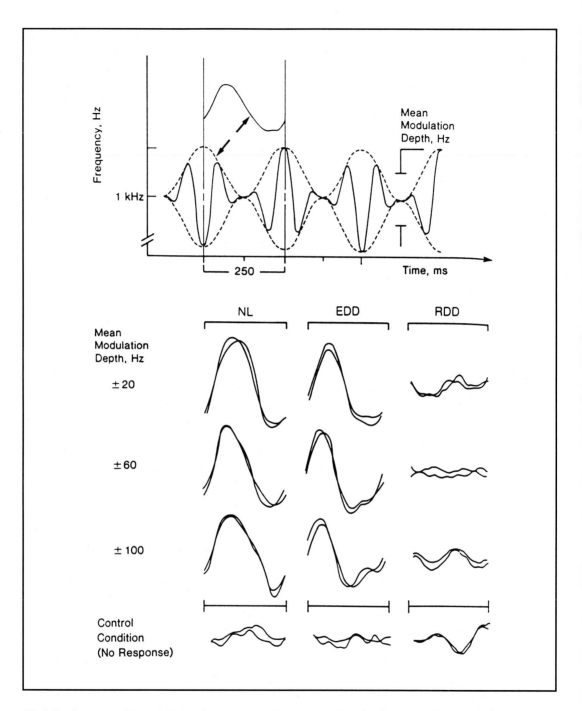

FIG. 3.12 Bottom panel shows typical cortical responses to frequency modulated auditory stimuli for children in three groups: those with normal language (NL), with expressive language disorders (EDD), and receptive language disorders (RDD). The stimulus that elicits these responses (top panel) is of constant amplitude, but varies in frequency in a sinusoidal fashion 10 times per second. "Modulation depth" refers to the size of the frequency deviations, which vary sinusoidally four times per second. The cortical responses are locked to this depth-modulation waveform, as shown by the arrows. Figure reprinted from Stefanatos et al. (1989).

to the auditory modality, but is a more general impairment in processing rapid transient information. However, because language learning depends critically on the ability to detect rapidly changing auditory signals, the impact of this multimodal impairment will be particularly pronounced in the verbal domain.

Although the findings of auditory processing impairments in SLI appear to be robust and have now been replicated by several research teams, controversy continues as to how these findings should be interpreted, and not everyone accepts Tallal's causal account. Most of the evidence for causal theories in the field of SLI is correlational, and thus open to more than one interpretation. For instance, rather than language impairment being a secondary consequence of an auditory processing problem, the relation might work the other way around (see Bishop, 1992). Perhaps a defective language-learning module leads to poor performance on auditory tasks. This could be the case if, for example, covert labelling of stimuli in the repetition task facilitated performance, and if skill in rapidly generating such labels was directly related to language level. Although the stimuli in Tallal's studies were explicitly designed to be difficult to verbalise, when only two stimuli are used, it is not too difficult to learn to give them names (e.g. tones may be labelled as "high" and "low", or as "beep" and "boop"). If children with SLI were slow and inefficient at generating names, we might expect their deficit to be most marked in contexts where there was little time available for generating a name code, i.e. when stimuli were rapid or brief. In effect, we would argue that there is a problem in encoding the auditory sensory trace, but this would be a top-down problem, caused by lack of facility with verbal labels, rather than a bottom-up problem in processing sensory information. Insofar as perceptual deficits are found for speech stimuli, a top-down account is even easier to formulate, because it could be argued that stimulus encoding is facilitated by good phonemic awareness.

The main method used to rule out an explanation of a deficit as a consequence of language impairment is to contrast children with SLI with a younger control group matched on language level. This is not a straightforward matter, because language level may vary markedly depending on the index one chooses to use. However, if we can show that children with SLI perform even more poorly than younger children who seem to have comparable verbal skills, then this is strong evidence that their auditory impairment cannot be explained away in this fashion. Although she did not use language-matched controls, Tallal (1976) produced data showing that the distinctive pattern of impairment in children with SLI was not seen in much younger normally developing children. These young control children found the task difficult and made many errors, but they did not show the sudden drop in performance at short inter-stimulus intervals that characterised children with SLI (see Fig. 3.7, p.65).

Another possibility is that auditory impairment might be a correlate of SLI, rather than a causal factor. There are many areas of deficit seen in children with SLI that would appear to fit this picture. For instance, the neuromotor impairments demonstrated by Tallal's own group (Johnston et al., 1981) provide a good example. Could the auditory processing deficits simply be one (of many) indicators of general brain immaturity? One argument advanced in favour of this view is that an auditory impairment could not account for the detailed linguistic phenomena seen in SLI. Leonard (1979, p.227) concluded a review of the area by stating that "The very nature of the restricted speech used by language impaired children seems to suggest that auditory processing deficits may be a corollary to, rather than a cause of language difficulties." However, more recent work by Leonard and colleagues has dramatically revised that opinion (see Leonard, McGregor, & Allen, 1992, and work reviewed in Chapter 5), and it is clearly unwise to assume that one can specify precisely how auditory impairment will affect grammatical development. What of the phonological impairments seen in many children with SLI? Tallal et al. (1976) noted that in general the phoneme contrasts that children failed to make in their expressive speech were between sounds characterised by rapid transitional information; it is unusual for children with SLI to make errors on vowels, which are relatively long in duration, and common for there to be confusions between stop consonants such as /t/ and /k/, where the critical distinguishing information is very brief. However, not all of the common speech errors seen in SLI are readily accounted for in this way, e.g. confusions between /w/ vs. /r/ are frequently seen, and "stopping", i.e. substitution of stop consonants (e.g. /t/, /d/) for fricatives at the same place of articulation (/f/, /v/) is not uncommon.

Furthermore, children with SLI do not characteristically confuse /b/ and /d/ in their speech, although there is ample experimental evidence that they find these sounds difficult to discriminate. However, this latter finding is not necessarily a serious problem for Tallal's position, because children use cues from lip-reading as well as acoustic information when learning about phonemic contrasts, and /b/ is easy to discriminate from other stop consonants on this basis. Frumkin and Rapin (1980) considered whether individual differences in phonological status are related to auditory perceptual processing. They subdivided a group of children with SLI according to whether they had any phonological impairment at the time of testing. Children with phonological disorders showed the characteristic deficit described by Tallal and Piercy. They had difficulty in discriminating between synthetic /ba/ and /da/, but their performance improved when the duration of the formant transition was increased from 40 to 80 msec. In contrast, children with SLI with normal phonology were unimpaired on this task, but they were poor at discriminating between brief vowel sounds, and had difficulty in reporting the order of pairs of consonants presented in quick succession. Overall, the relationship between expressive phonology and auditory perceptual problems is broadly in line with predictions from the rate processing deficit hypothesis, but there are discrepancies that remain to be explained.

The strongest evidence in support of a causal account would be if one could improve the language impairment by improving auditory functioning. This is exactly what Tallal and colleagues (Merzenich et al., 1996; Tallal et al., 1996) claim to have done in a recent intervention study. They took as their starting point animal experiments that showed that the capacity for

segmentation of successive events in sensory input streams can be sharpened by intensive practice, even in adult animals. Encouraged by this evidence of learning-induced changes in sensory cortex, they devised an intervention package designed to train children to discriminate stimuli on the basis of brief acoustic cues. First, they used a computer game based on Tallal's Repetition Test, in which the child had to reproduce the order of two sound sequences, starting with a long ISI and progressively reducing this as the child's performance improved. In another game, synthetic speech sounds were used, and the child's task was to identify the sequence position of a target syllable. In two separate studies, using the computer games for between 19 to 28 sessions of 20 minutes each, children with SLI showed clear improvement on these tasks over time, which were paralleled by gains on the original Repetition Test. In addition, Tallal et al. (1996) exposed children to acoustically modified speech in which the duration of the speech signal was prolonged and the transitional elements were amplified. Control children received a similar package of interventions, but using unmodified speech and computer games based on discriminations that did not involve rapid processing. The outcomes reported by Tallal et al. were dramatic, with children who received the "temporal processing" intervention showing significantly greater improvement than control children on language measures. This work, which has excited considerable controversy, is still at an early phase, and further evaluation studies are under way. It remains unclear which components of the intervention package are critical. If the early promise of the method is fulfilled, with auditory training producing improved language abilities in everyday contexts, this would be the strongest support yet for the view that linguistic difficulties in these children are secondary to more fundamental auditory limitations.

FOOTNOTES

1. This should not be taken as implying that a phoneme can be identified with a particular

articulatory configuration. Remember, the phoneme is a mental abstraction. Co-articulation refers to the fact that the way in which a consonant is articulated will be affected by preceding and following phonemes, so that, for instance the /s/ in "soup" is produced with lips rounded, whereas /s/ in "seat" is produced with lips spread. Nevertheless, if one read a record showing the pattern of articulatory activity over time, it would be possible to identify the sequence of consonants more easily than if the only source of evidence were a spectrogram. For vowels, the situation is reversed: their acoustic correlates are rather more reliable than their articulatory correlates.

2. The authors do interpret the three-way interaction as compatible with the notion of an impairment in early auditory processing, but this is hard to evaluate, because the control group were excluded from the analysis.

3. It is not possible to establish whether they had clinically significant problems because their reading data are presented only as age equivalent scores. Studdert-Kennedy and Mody (1995) noted that they would not be regarded as dyslexic.

4

Understanding word meaning

Children pick up words as pigeons peas, And utter them again as God shall please
John Ray, *English Proverbs* (1670)

OVERVIEW

1. Vocabulary learning involves identifying recurring phonological strings in the speech input, identifying the concepts that words express, and mapping the first domain (phonology) on to the second (conceptual).

2. Most children with SLI are poor at learning new vocabulary: this can be seen both in terms of their performance on tests of receptive vocabulary, and more directly in studies that assess learning of new words under naturalistic or experimental conditions.

3. There is little evidence of a deficit in the conceptual bases for language, or in abstract symbolic thought in the majority of children with SLI.

4. In many children with SLI, word learning appears to be affected by problems in phonological perception and/or memory.

5. In addition, syntactic limitations in children with SLI limit their ability to use syntactic knowledge to infer word meanings ("syntactic bootstrapping").

6. Limited literacy skills can restrict further vocabulary learning as children grow older.

7. There is some evidence suggesting that even after a word has been learned, retrieval of the lexical representation is less efficient and accurate than in a normally developing child, perhaps because the phonological representation is underspecified.

INTRODUCTION

Vocabulary is one aspect of language that continues to develop throughout and beyond childhood. Using Templin's (1957) estimate of vocabulary size for a six-year-old as some 14,000 words, Carey (1978) noted that the young child must learn an average of nine new words a day between the ages of 18 months and six years (see *Estimating vocabulary size*, overleaf).

Most studies that have looked at the question find that children with SLI know fewer words than other children of the same age. The first question to ask is how far this is just an output problem. You

Estimating vocabulary size

In the earliest stages of language development, size of a child's expressive vocabulary can be directly measured by counting each new word that the child uses. However, this soon becomes impractical as vocabulary increases. In older children, the usual method for estimating vocabulary size is to take a random sample of words from an unabridged dictionary and test children's knowledge of these. The proportion of words in the random sample that is known to the child is then multiplied by the total number of words in the dictionary to obtain an estimate of total vocabulary size. As Anglin (1993) has pointed out, the method is fraught with methodological difficulties, and has in the past led to wildly different estimates. Problems include deciding which dictionary to use, and settling on criteria for accepting that a word is "known". Estimates of vocabulary growth in the early school years from Anglin's study are shown in Fig. 4.1.

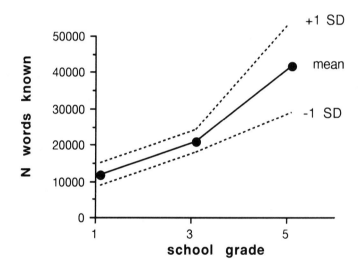

FIG. 4.1   Increase in vocabulary size is accompanied by increase in individual differences in children's vocabulary with age. These data come from Anglin (1993). The average ages of children would be 6–7 years for first graders, 8–9 years for third graders, and 10–11 years for fifth graders.

are no doubt familiar with the "tip of the tongue" phenomenon, where you find yourself unable to generate a word despite knowing it (see *The "tip of the tongue" phenomenon*, opposite). This demonstrates how knowledge of a word does not guarantee correct production. Although explicit "tip of the tongue" states are not commonly reported by children (Wellman, 1977), one does find instances of mismatch between knowledge of a word and ability to produce it on demand, i.e. so-called "word finding" problems, which can be elicited by asking the child to name pictures (Fried-Oken, 1987; German, 1982). However, although there are some children for whom word-finding is the principal symptom of language difficulties, in most cases of SLI, the problem is not restricted to retrieving words from memory; understanding of vocabulary is also limited (see *Testing children's understanding of words*, p.86). Figure 4.4 (p.88) shows illustrative data from children with SLI.

Furthermore, studies of incidental learning of word meanings have confirmed that children with SLI understand fewer new words than

The "tip of the tongue" phenomenon

Accounts of the "tip of the tongue" (TOT) experience go back at least as far as William James (1893, p.251), who wrote:

Suppose we try to recall a forgotten name. The state of our consciousness is peculiar. There is a gap therein; but no mere gap. It is a gap that is intensely active. A sort of wraith of the name is in it, beckoning us in a given direction, making us at moments tingle with the sense of our closeness and then letting us sink back without the longed-for term.

Interest in TOT experiences was rekindled by Brown and McNeill (1966) who found it was possible to induce such states in people by reading them dictionary definitions of rare words and asking them to supply the word. Try Brown and McNeill's procedure with the following words, noting down any wrong words that pop into your head. If you are aware of knowing the correct word but being unable to produce it, see if you can specify which letter it starts with and how many syllables it has.

1. The lowest order of mammals, having a single opening for the genital and digestive organs.
2. An instrument for measuring angular distances, used especially in navigation to observe altitudes of celestial bodies.
3. The middle of the three chief divisions of the body of an insect.

4. A disordered, giddy state in which the individual or his surroundings seem to whirl dizzily.
5. The picture script of ancient Egypt.
6. A whirling motion of a fluid forming a cavity in the centre; a whirlpool, an eddy.
7. Adjective applied to someone after whom a book or an institution or anything else is named.
8. Transmission of a disease by direct contact.
9. A lamb-skin with a curled wool from the middle East.
10. The bones in the fingers.
11. A large flightless bird, found in New Guinea, etc., brightly coloured, with a large bony projection on top of its head.
12. Acting to prevent something, especially to prevent spread of disease.
13. The art of juggling or conjuring, sleight of hand, manual skill or dexterity in executing tricks.

Often, one can recall fragmentary information about the target word, including the number of syllables, rhythmic contours, and initial sound, but the complete phonological form is elusive. Words that are similar in sound to the target often pop into mind. Brown and McNeill (p.326) described a subject in the TOT state as being in "mild torment, something like the brink of a sneeze, and if he found the word his relief was considerable". Readers who are in such torment will find relief in the footnote on page 89.

---

age-matched controls after a few brief exposures in the naturalistic context of a TV programme (Oetting, Rice, & Swank, 1995; Rice, Buhr, & Oetting, 1992). Such findings indicate that we need to consider what might be limiting the child's ability to learn new words.

Gleitman (1994) summarised the problems facing children acquiring new vocabulary: (1) they have to achieve knowledge of the concepts that words express; (2) they have to extract recurrent phonological patterns from incoming speech; and (3) they have to solve what has been termed "the mapping problem"; lining up each concept with one of these phonological patterns. Weak vocabulary could reflect difficulty with any one of these processes.

In this chapter, we consider whether poor word learning in children with SLI can be clearly linked with a deficit at one of these specific stages. We will start by examining conceptual development in SLI, and then go on to consider children's ability to extract phoneme sequences corresponding to words. Then we will move on to look at how they put phonological and conceptual information together, i.e. how they solve the mapping problem. We then proceed to ask whether poor vocabulary learning in children with SLI might be a consequence of reduced opportunity to learn arising from poor literacy skills. Finally, we consider how far comprehension of everyday speech may be hampered by problems in rapidly accessing words that are in the child's vocabulary.

Testing children's understanding of words (receptive vocabulary)

The typical method used for assessing receptive vocabulary in children aged around three years and over is the multiple choice picture-pointing format. This requires no expressive language from the child, who simply has to select a picture to match a word spoken by the tester. Figure 4.2 shows a sample item from the British Picture Vocabulary Scale (Dunn et al., 1982), the UK equivalent of the widely used Peabody Picture Vocabulary Test (PPVT) (Dunn, 1965). Item difficulty increases progressively, with vocabulary becoming more abstract and more specialised.

Children with poor concentration may be difficult to test in this way because they do not scan all the alternatives, and may be distracted by visually salient foils. For normally developing children below the age of about 30 months, multiple choice comprehension tests do not give reliable results (Bates et al., 1988).

Bates (1993) gives a useful summary of the advantages and disadvantages of alternative methods that can be used with very young or inattentive children. These are:

• *parental report*   Bates et al. (1988) found that parental report of the words their child understood at 13 months correlated significantly with PPVT scores at 28 months, indicating that this method of assessing comprehension does have some validity.

• *evoked response methods*   Molfese (1990) developed a method, subsequently used by Mills, Coffey-Corina, and Neville (1993) in which brain evoked responses in young children are compared for familiar and unfamiliar words. The latency and amplitude of components of the evoked response differ in relation to word familiarity. This is a promising method for assessing receptive language in very young children, but not all children will co-operate with the procedure. Furthermore, the evoked response cannot tell us whether the child understands the meaning of a word.

1

2

3

4

FIG. 4.2   Training plate from the British Picture Vocabulary Scale. The child's task is to point to the picture named by the examiner, e.g. "dog".

Testing children's understanding of words (receptive vocabulary) (continued)

• *preferential looking*   Golinkoff, Hirsh-Pasek, Cauley, and Gordon (1987) and Reznick (1990) showed that children as young as 14–16 months will look longer at a picture that matches a spoken utterance than one that does not (see Fig. 4.3, below).

This method has provided evidence that young infants have some comprehension of language that they cannot yet produce. However, it is not suitable for individual assessment: to obtain robust results, one needs to pool data from several children.

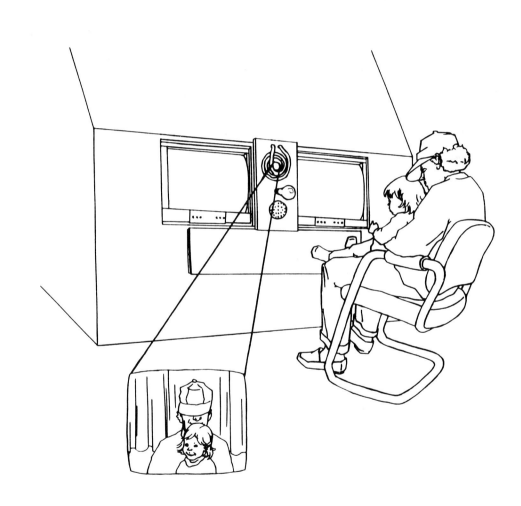

FIG. 4.3 Experimental set-up for preferential looking paradigm. The child is seated on mother's lap and presented with two simultaneous video cartoons. A voice relayed through the speaker speaks a word or sentence that matches one of the videos. The mother is instructed not to watch the videos and is given a visor to wear over her eyes, so she does not unwittingly cue the infant to make the correct response. The child's face is filmed by a camcorder hidden behind the arrangement of lights. If the infant looks significantly longer at the screen that matches the spoken message, this is evidence of comprehension. (Reproduced from Naigles and Kako, 1993, Fig. 1.)

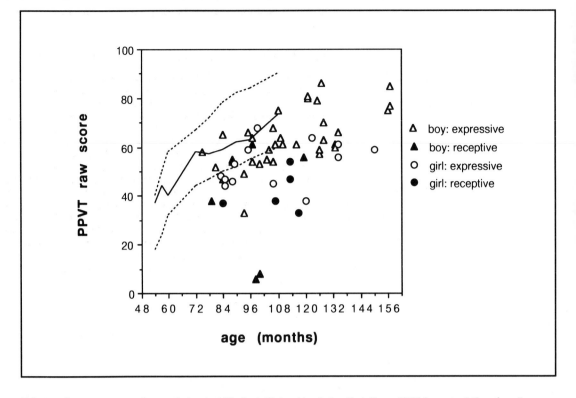

FIG. 4.4   Scores on a receptive vocabulary test (Peabody Picture Vocabulary Test; Dunn, 1965) by a population of pupils attending three British residential schools specialising in the education of children with SLI. Median raw scores of control children aged four to nine years are plotted as bold line; dotted lines denote smoothed 10th and 90th centiles. Data from children with SLI are plotted as points. Although pupils are subdivided for educational purposes into "receptive" and "expressive" subtypes, it is apparent that receptive vocabulary is poor relative to age for many of those in the "expressive" group. Data are same as those reported by Bishop (1979), except that more stringent criteria have been applied to exclude any child with evidence of middle ear disease.

VOCABULARY LEARNING

Meaning and conceptual development

The preverbal infant categorises the world along dimensions such as mass substance vs. object, animate vs. inanimate, and recognises properties such as numerosity before learning the words to refer to these (Spelke, Breinlinger, & Macomber, 1992). To some extent, then, the task of learning vocabulary is that of learning to map words on to pre-existing nonverbal concepts.[1] But how does the child know which word to relate to which concept? The philosopher Quine (1960) drew attention to the difficulty of this task, with the following example. Suppose we are in a foreign land and we hear a native say "Gavagai" as a rabbit

scurries past. How do we infer what "Gavagai" means? The speaker could be referring to the animal, its colour, its tail, the act of scurrying, the place where the animal is, and so on, or he could be issuing a command such as "Look!".

In fact, although these are all logical possibilities, it is unlikely that we would entertain many of them were we placed in Quine's hypothetical situation. The reason is that we are biased to treat some interpretations as more likely than others. Thus, it is much more likely that, all else being equal, the referent of "Gavagai" will be the rabbit than some part of the rabbit or some action that it is carrying out.[2] This has been termed the "whole object" bias. There has been considerable interest among developmental psychologists in establishing just what biases children bring to the word-learning task, and how early these can be manifest (see Markman, 1990, for a review). In general, children show biases such as a predisposition to treat words as referring to whole objects from the earliest stages of language learning.

If a child failed to develop preverbal concepts normally, or lacked the normal interpretative biases, this would affect vocabulary development, but one would expect to see evidence of this in nonverbal as well as verbal behaviour. By definition, children with SLI have normal nonverbal abilities and behaviour, and it is generally assumed that prelinguistic concepts must therefore be adequately acquired. There is little published research on conceptual development in SLI, and this is a thorny topic to investigate because, by the time we are aware that a child has a language problem, conceptual development and language development are inextricably inter-twined. In general, though, any conceptual problems that are seen in children with SLI seem to be a consequence of their weak language skills, rather than indications of more basic difficulties in concept formation. This was the conclusion reached in a study by Siegel, Lees, Allan, and Bolton (1981) who devised nonverbal tests to assess concept development in children with SLI. Children with SLI had no difficulty with simple concepts such as "more" (demonstrated by pointing to the member of a pair of cards which depicted more elements), but they did make a disproportionate number of errors on more complex concepts such as understanding of spatial order and conservation of number. However, Siegel et al. noted that the more complex items involved remembering information or marking a place in a sequence, and they suggested that the deficit in those with SLI might reflect their failure to use inner language to reason and remember.

Donlan, Bishop, and Hitch (in press) demon-strated normal conceptual understanding in a task that does not seem to involve any verbalising. Children with SLI had entirely normal ability to interpret the numerical significance of digits, showing the standard symbolic distance effect (see *Children's encoding of number: The symbolic distance effect*, overleaf) when asked to judge which of two digits was the larger.

This result provides convincing evidence against a view popularised by Morehead and Ingram (1976) who proposed that children with SLI might have a general cognitive deficit in forming representations. This notion has its origins in Piagetian theory (see Piaget, 1970) which argues for a developmental shift from concrete operations to symbolic thought. In the first two years of life, children's experience of acting upon the world enables them to represent external reality by sensori-motor schemata. For instance, the child who has experience of shaking a rattle might be observed to make a shaking motion when the rattle is absent, as a means of representing the absent object. These early representations of the world are concrete, in that there is a close tie between the sensori-motor behaviours that are elicited by the object, and those that are used to represent it when it is absent. Language development requires that the child move from this concrete mode of representation to a much more abstract level of thought, where there is no iconic relationship between the sign and the signified. Thus the phonological string that corresponds to the word "dog" has only an arbitrary relationship to the class of entities that it refers to. A child who was unable to operate with abstract symbols would have immense difficulty learning language. However, this is implausible as an account of SLI, because it would predict far more profound and pervasive language difficulties than are typically seen. Children with SLI do use words and sentences to talk about the world; the problem is that they learn more slowly than other children. However, if they had not developed a capacity for symbolic thought, they should be unable to attain even this basic level of language competence.

Overall, then, the general ability to use abstract symbols to represent concepts appears to be intact in most children with SLI.

Answers: *The "tip of the tongue" phenomenon* (1) monotremes; (2) sextant; (3) thorax; (4) vertigo; (5) hieroglyphic; (6) vortex; (7) eponymous; (8) contagion; (9) astrakhan; (10) phalanges; (11) cassowary; (12) prophylactic; (13) prestidigitation.

Children's encoding of number:
The symbolic distance effect

If a child is shown two written digits and asked to judge which one is larger, the speed of response is inversely proportional to the distance between numbers. Thus, for instance, it takes longer to judge that 5 is bigger than 4 than to judge that 5 is bigger than 2. Note that this result is the opposite of what you would expect if the child counted up from one digit to the next. This symbolic distance effect was first described by Moyer and Landauer (1967) and has since been demonstrated for a wide range of tasks, such as judging the order of letters of the alphabet, or judging the relative real-life size of animals which are depicted scaled to the same size.

Donlan et al. (in press) investigated the symbolic distance effect in normally developing and SLI children who were matched in terms of language comprehension level. They found a normal symbolic distance effect in children with SLI when judging relative size for a range of materials (illustrated in Fig. 4.5, below). This suggests that the encoding of conceptual meaning of numerical stimuli (digits) is just as efficient as encoding of physical characteristics (in dot arrays or pictures).

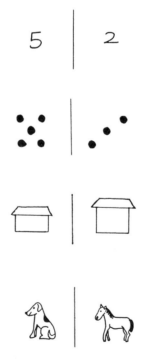

FIG. 4.5   Sample stimuli by Donlan et al. (in press) for measuring symbolic distance effect in children with SLI and younger controls matched on comprehension level. The dot arrays and house stimuli are examples of numerical and nonnumerical stimuli that can be compared purely on physical characteristics. The animals must be judged in terms of real-life size from pictures that are scaled to the same size, and so this judgement requires accessing a mental representation. The digits are purely abstract symbols of numerosity.

Phonological skills and formation of long-term representations

When we learn a new word, we form a permanent, long-term representation that links a sound pattern (phonological representation) with a meaning (semantic representation) in a "mental lexicon". If we find that a child has an impoverished vocabulary, one possible reason is that there might be a specific difficulty in establishing long-term phonological representations.

In Chapter 3, we reviewed evidence for deficits in phonological analysis in children with SLI. A developmental deficit in phonological analysis will have knock-on effects at later stages of understanding, because the input to the process that extracts word patterns will be degraded. The crucial question is whether weak vocabulary in children with SLI reflects problems in forming new phonological representations and if so, whether this is a consequence of deficient perceptual analysis at an earlier stage, or a more specific impairment of a memory system that is specialised for vocabulary learning.

Segmenting the speech stream into words. In Chapter 1 it was noted that the problem of segmenting the incoming speech stream into words was a far from trivial problem. In English, stress and rhythm are salient cues to word boundaries (Gleitman & Wanner, 1982), and there is good evidence that young children rely heavily on these when learning language (Cutler, 1994).

Rice et al. (1992) considered whether a problem in segmenting unfamiliar verbal material might play a part in delaying word learning in children with SLI. Using a naturalistic task where new words were presented in the context of a TV programme, Rice et al. used a multiple choice comprehension test to assess learning of vocabulary in three groups of children: five-year-olds with SLI, normal three-year-olds who were matched on mean length of utterance (MLU) (see *Matching for "language level": Mean length of utterance (MLU)*, overleaf), and normal five-year-olds, matched on chronological age. Their interest was in whether vocabulary learning would be easier if a pause was inserted before a novel word. As can be seen in Fig. 4.7 (p.93), there was no evidence that a pause helped children with SLI; on the cont-

rary, they showed no evidence of any learning in this condition. Overall, their performance was significantly worse than that of age-matched control children, and comparable to that of the language-matched children who were some two years younger. Ellis Weismer and Hesketh (1993) studied the effect of prosodic cues on word learning, using a more artificial word-learning task in which children were taught monosyllabic nonwords in "outer space language". Those with SLI did more poorly overall than age-matched controls on this task, but there was no selective benefit to this group from use of a slower presentation rate, or from stressing the novel words. However, the authors noted that the sample sizes were small and there was substantial individual variation within each group. Taking these two studies together, however, it appears that difficulty in extracting unfamiliar words from a continuous speech stream is not the major factor constraining vocabulary learning in children with SLI.

Underspecification of phonological representations in the lexicon. Another possibility is that, even if they segment an unfamiliar string correctly, children form an inadequate phonological representation. In 1982, Schwartz and Leonard published a study investigating the influence of phonological characteristics on word learning in normal young children. The paper was entitled "Do children pick and choose?", and the conclusion was "Yes, they do". When presented with a range of novel words, children's learning was not arbitrary; rather, they tended to learn those words that were phonologically similar to the words already in their expressive vocabulary. This finding, which was also supported by work by Leonard, Schwartz, Morris, and Chapman (1981), has important implications for children with SLI, many of whom have limitations of expressive phonology. It suggests that if children have persistent difficulties in producing phonemic contrasts, this will limit their ability to learn new words.

Leonard et al. (1982) devised an experimental word-learning procedure that made it possible to compare children's learning of novel words according to their phonological composition. They

Matching for "language level":
Mean length of utterance (MLU)

MLU is the most popular index to use in studies that match children with SLI with younger normally developing children on "language level". It is an index of grammatical development, a topic that will be dealt with more fully in Chapter 5. MLU was first proposed by Brown (1973), in his classic study of the early grammatical development of three children, Adam, Eve, and Sarah. Brown recommended computing MLU in morphemes rather than words, which means a child is credited with two units for words with grammatical inflections such as "sing-ing", "brok-en", "bigg-est". Researchers typically use samples of 50 to 100 utterances as a basis for the computation. One reason why MLU is a popular index of grammatical complexity is that it is relatively easy to compute. Another is that in normally developing children there is a fairly linear relationship between MLU and age (see Fig. 4.6, below). However, because expressive language usually lags behind receptive language in SLI, children who are matched on MLU are unlikely to be matched in their level of understanding. Usually, this will be higher in children with SLI than in MLU-matched controls. Also, one cannot assume that children who are matched on MLU necessarily have similar vocabulary levels.

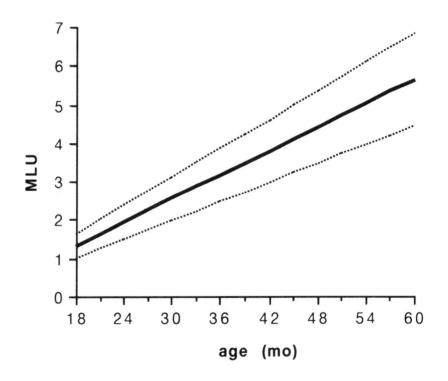

FIG. 4.6 Average level and range of MLU in relation to age in normally developing children. The dotted lines show ± 1 *SD* from the mean. These data come from Chapman (1981), who also gives guidelines for computing MLU.

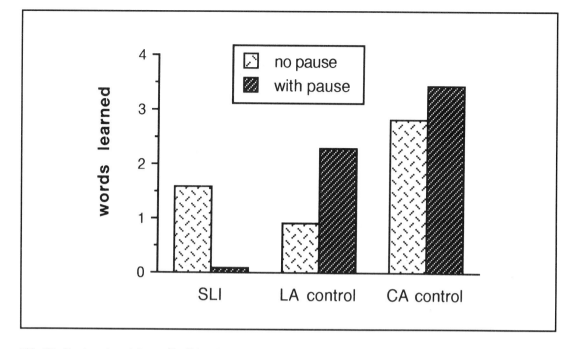

FIG. 4.7   Number of words learned by SLI and control groups in study by Rice et al., 1992. The SLI children were five-year-olds, the language age (LA) controls were normally developing three-year-olds who were matched on mean length of utterance (MLU), and the chronological age (CA) controls were normally developing five-year-olds. The y-axis shows the difference between the number of words recognised before and after exposure to several occurrences of each word in the context of a TV programme.

studied two groups of children who were producing only single words; a group of normally developing children ranging in age from 1;5 to 2;0, and a group of children with SLI aged from 2;8 to 3;4. Estimates of expressive vocabulary size (based on examination of their speech supplemented by parental report) were similar for both groups, at around 40 words. When tested using the methods shown in Table 4.1, Leonard et al. again confirmed that children tended to produce those novel words which were phonologically similar to items already in their expressive vocabularies. However, on the comprehension test, phonological composition did not affect performance of either group.

One critical difference between production and comprehension is that comprehension can proceed on the basis of a less than complete phonological representation. If you were asked to select from an array of toy animals the [dʒəʔ'ɑ] you could correctly find the giraffe, because it is the only one that starts with /dʒ/ and has two syllables with the stress on the second

(see table on inside front cover for pronunciation of phonetic symbols). A partial phonological representation is compatible with perfect performance on a simple multiple choice test. It is not, however, sufficient for accurate production. The interesting possibility is thus raised that children with SLI may be slow at vocabulary learning because their phonological representations of words tend to be underspecified. It should be possible to demonstrate this by testing comprehension using a different method, similar to that described by Locke (1980) (see p.60). Rather than presenting a word and asking the child to select an object to match it, one could present an object with a name and see how far the child would be willing to accept a slightly modified version. For instance, having taught the child the new word "gourd", one could see whether the child would accept the label "dourd", or "gourt", and so on. Such a procedure might reveal differences between groups that were not apparent on the more conventional form of comprehension test.

TABLE 4.1

Experimental Procedure Used by Leonard et al. (1982)

	Nouns	*Verbs*
Materials	eight objects with unfamiliar names, e.g. gourd, whisk, snail, hoop, etc.	eight actions with unfamiliar names, e.g. nudge, kneel, dive, crouch, etc.
Pre-test		
production	present novel item: ask "what's this?"	demonstrate novel action on doll: ask "what's the baby doing?"
comprehension	present all 8 items in an array: ask e.g. "where's the *gourd*?" repeat for all 8 items	present the doll: say "Make the baby *kneel*" repeat for all 8 actions
Experimental procedure	10 × 45 minute sessions, each resembling informal play, in course of which training is interspersed	
training	adult shows novel item and says, e.g. "here's the *gourd*"	adult demonstrates novel action on doll and says, e.g. "watch the baby *kneel*"
Post-test		
production and comprehension probes	as in pre-test	as in pre-test

This view of defective word learning is compatible with the ideas reviewed in Chapter 3, suggesting that for children with SLI, awareness of constancy of phoneme segments might be an area of difficulty, so that words would be represented in the lexicon as "Gestalt" phonological representations of whole syllables or polysyllabic forms. On this view, the fact that children with SLI tend to have both persisting problems with expressive phonology, and acquire vocabulary slowly could be related consequences of a single underlying problem in developing a differentiated system for representing subsyllabic units. It is worth noting that this would not correspond to a developmental deviance. There is evidence from the speech errors of normally developing young children that incomplete phonological specifications are often set up, particularly for polysyllabic words (e.g. Aitchison, 1972). The claim, rather, is that children with SLI may persist in using underspecified, global, representations well after the age when

most children have moved to a more efficient style of phonological processing.

This conceptualisation leads to another intriguing prediction concerning the impact of phonological complexity on comprehension vs. production of newly learned vocabulary. If the child is required to produce a novel word, there is a straightforward prediction that the more phonological material, i.e. the longer the word, the more difficult the task will be. This does not, however, necessarily apply in comprehension in a multiple choice task, where the most important determinant of performance will be how distinctive the novel word is in relation to other words in the child's vocabulary. Length could be a positive advantage here, because polysyllabic words have more possible features (including stress pattern) on which they may be distinguished from other words, so that if the child retains partial information about the sound of a word, it could still be sufficient for recognition. It would be interesting explicitly to contrast comprehension and production: if underspecification of lexical representations is implicated in SLI, then we would predict that different patterns should be seen for production and comprehension when children learned novel words: shorter words would be easier to produce but harder to comprehend.

Phonological short-term memory.   Gathercole and Baddeley (1990a) have proposed that SLI involves a core deficit in phonological short-term memory. This theory has an interesting history. Its roots lie in early research by Baddeley and Hitch (1974), who were concerned with the structure of short-term memory. One of the oldest methods for assessing short-term memory is digit span—the experimenter dictates a series of digits and the subject is required to repeat them back. Most adults can repeat a sequence of around seven digits without error, leading to the postulation of some kind of short-term verbal store. By manipulating the features of the to-be-remembered material, it was possible to identify some properties of this store. Even if word lists were presented in written form, it was found that people were poorer at remembering polysyllabic as compared with monosyllabic words, and they were worse with phonologically similar words (e.g. rat, cat, bat) than with distinctive ones (e.g. mouse, dog, bat). However, the semantic relationships between words did not influence recall. It was concluded that what was stored were phonological representations. But what purpose did this store serve? Baddeley and Hitch showed that if you occupied the store (by requiring the subject to maintain a string of digits in memory), this had remarkably little impact on cognitive processes such as reasoning or comprehension in normal adults. Furthermore, PV, a woman who had severe and selective limitations of digit span as a consequence of acquired brain damage, could nevertheless comprehend complex utterances and had no obvious speech difficulties (Vallar & Baddeley, 1984a,b). The researchers were faced with the perplexing situation that humans possessed an efficient short-term memory store for phono-

logical information whose only function seemed to be to retain series of digits spoken by psychologists! A breakthrough came in a further study of PV. Her ability to process language was excellent; however, what she could not do was to learn new vocabulary (Baddeley, Papagno, & Vallar, 1988) (see Fig. 4.8, overleaf). This result suggested that investigators had been looking in the wrong direction for a function of the phonological store —it had been assumed that it played a role in on-line processing of language; instead, it seemed to be important for the learning of language. The existence of a specialised memory system dedicated to setting up long-term representations of phonological forms would help explain why young children are so good at vocabulary learning. Research by Carey (1978) and colleagues demonstrated that even a single encounter with a new word is often sufficient for a long-term memory representation to be set up (although the fleshing out of complete semantic and phonological information takes much longer). Could phonological short-term memory (STM) be critical for such efficient learning?

This question motivated studies by Gathercole and Baddeley (1989), who looked at the relationship between phonological short-term memory and vocabulary learning in normally developing children. They showed that children's performance on tests of phonological short-term memory accounted for a significant amount of variation in receptive vocabulary growth over a two-year period, after allowing for the effects of nonverbal IQ. They found that, rather than the traditional digit span, the most powerful predictor was a test of nonword repetition. Sample test items are shown in Table 4.2, overleaf.

In another study, Gathercole and Baddeley (1990a) studied new vocabulary learning in an experimental setting; children were presented with novel toys which were given specific names which were either familiar boys' names (e.g. Thomas, Michael) or invented two-syllable words (e.g. Meton, Pimas). The task was simply to learn the name to go with each toy, and performance was contrasted for children from the Gathercole and Baddeley (1989) study who had been selected as particularly good or poor at nonword repetition.

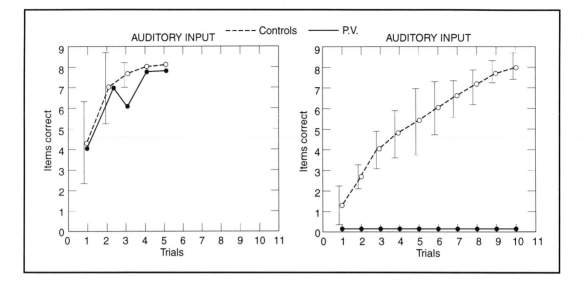

FIG. 4.8   Impairment of new vocabulary learning in the adult patient PV, who had a severe impairment of phonological short-term memory after brain damage. The left-hand panel shows learning of word–word paired associates (e.g. apple–robin), the right-hand panel depicts learning of word–nonword pairings (e.g. apple–svieti). (The actual word stimuli were in PV's native language, Italian.) Word–word learning is entirely normal. On word–nonword learning, it is easy to be misled into thinking PV's data have been omitted from the plot: in fact, her performance remained on the test floor for 10 trials. Figures reproduced from Baddeley et al., 1988.

TABLE 4.2

Sample Items from the Children's Nonword Repetition Test (Gathercole, Willis, Baddeley, & Emslie, 1994)

Nonword	Phonemic form	N syllables	Simple/complex*
pennel	ˈpɛnəl	2	s
hampent	ˈhampənt	2	c
dopelate	ˈdɒpəleɪt	3	s
glistering	ˈglɪstərɪŋ	3	c
woog**alam**ic	wugəˈlamɪk	4	s
contr**amp**onist	kɒnˈtrampənɪst	4	c
defer**mi**cation	difɜmɪˈkeɪʃn	5	s
detrata**pill**ic	ditratəˈpɪlɪk	5	c

*Complex nonwords contain consonant clusters; simple nonwords do not.

Even though children in both groups were capable of repeating the names, those with good nonword repetition skills learned them faster (see Fig. 4.9, opposite). Similar results were obtained using a different method for teaching word meanings in a study by Michas and Henry (1994).

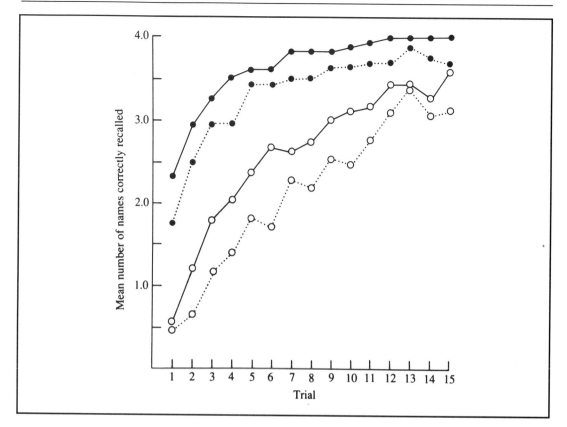

FIG. 4.9 Mean number of real (filled circles) and nonsense (open circles) names correctly recalled on each learning trial for children with low (dotted line) and high (bold line) scores on nonword repetition. Reproduced from Gathercole and Baddeley (1990a).

Gathercole and Baddeley (1990b) also studied a small group of children with SLI. On traditional short-term memory tasks involving word lists, they found that these children were impaired in relation to others of the same age, but the pattern of performance was similar, i.e. they showed the usual effects of word length and phonological similarity. They did, however, show striking deficits on the test of nonword repetition, especially for nonwords with three or more syllables. This has been replicated by Montgomery (1995) and Bishop et al. (1996) (see Fig. 4.10, overleaf).

There is thus mounting evidence that the skills implicated in the nonword repetition task play a role in learning new words, and that performance on this task is defective in children with SLI. But what does the nonword repetition test measure? Gathercole and Baddeley favour the notion that the test detects a primary memory deficit—either the capacity of the phonological store is unusually small, limited to one or two syllables, or its contents decay unusually rapidly. However, it could be argued that the problem is not so much one of retaining phonological information, as of encoding that information appropriately.

We noted in Chapter 3 that there is good evidence for abnormal encoding of speech in children with SLI, and it was suggested earlier that underspecification of phonological information in lexical representations might constrain vocabulary learning in SLI. Thus, it seems plausible that poor nonword repetition in SLI might simply reflect the fact that initial perception and encoding of phonological information was inadequate. There are several reasons why Gathercole and Baddeley rejected this view. First, in their 1990b study, they

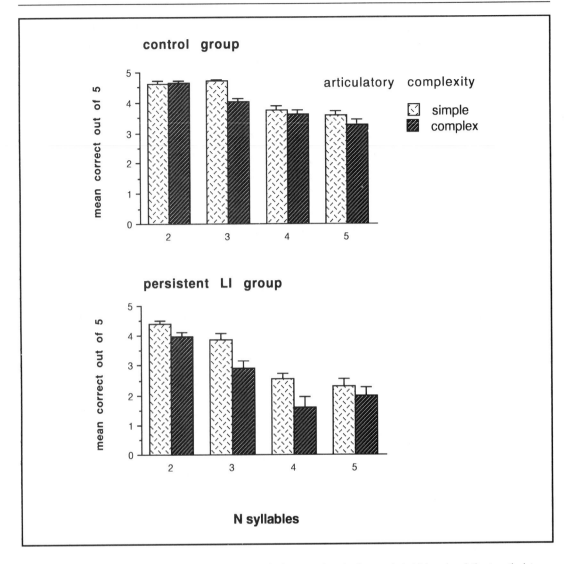

FIG. 4.10   Data on the Children's Nonword Repetition test for language-impaired vs. control children, in relation to articulatory complexity (i.e. whether the nonword contains consonant clusters or not) and length in syllables. Error bars show standard errors. The language-impaired children obtain lower scores at all lengths except the two-syllable items, where both groups are at ceiling. Data from Bishop et al. (1996).

showed that children with SLI performed normally on a speech discrimination test that involved judging whether pairs of nonwords were the same or different. However, the discrimination task used by Gathercole and Baddeley was a very easy one, and ceiling effects could have obscured group differences. Contrasts which children with SLI often find difficult, such as /ba/ vs. /ga/, or /da/ vs. /ga/ were not tested. Furthermore, as we saw in

Chapter 3, normal speech discrimination does not rule out abnormalities of phoneme identification. Children who persist in an immature perceptual categorisation of speech input and who operate at the level of the syllable, rather than identifying subsyllabic elements might be expected to have particular difficulty in remembering novel phonological strings because, unlike other children, they fail to recognise that they are composed of a common set of elements, and so encode them inefficiently (see *Memory depends on initial encoding*, below). On this view, the poor repetition of children with SLI would reflect a lack of expertise in phonological analysis, rather than a primary memory disorder.

Memory depends on initial encoding

Study the sequence of words in Fig. 4.11 written in Chinese script for a few seconds, cover it up, and then try to reproduce it. How did you get on? The answer should depend on whether or not you are familiar with Chinese. If you don't know any Chinese, you will have seen three visually complex figures and you will probably feel totally overwhelmed by the amount of visual detail. If you know Chinese you should find the task much easier, even if you have not previously encountered these specific words*. A person fluent at reading and writing Chinese is aware that there are eight basic strokes which are used to create Chinese characters, and will therefore recognise an unfamiliar word as being composed of those familiar elements. This will provide a framework for analysing and storing a new character, reducing the memory load. Thus, knowledge of the elements of which a new item is composed makes new learning much easier. Let us go on to suppose that an English reader who knows no Chinese is nevertheless determined to learn these characters and so practises the first two repeatedly until they can be reproduced without error. Now we present the third character, which has not been studied, and compare recall of the figure for our fictitious reader and a native Chinese speaker. The expectation is that the native speaker will still be superior in recalling this word. This is because the Chinese speaker has knowledge that can be used to analyse and reproduce novel forms, whereas the knowledge of characters that the English speaker has slowly and painfully acquired is largely specific to the two characters that have been learned, and does not generalise usefully to a new character†.

Exactly analogous arguments can be applied to the nonword repetition task: if the child does not analyse novel phonological strings in terms of familiar elements (in this case onsets and rimes, rather than brush strokes), but attempts to retain detailed information about the whole syllable, there is much more to remember and so vocabulary learning is that much harder. Furthermore, although new vocabulary may be learned, each lexical entry is represented as a unique auditory-phonetic pattern and so there will be little generalisation to new words. This is a speculative explanation that needs further investigation. One strong prediction from this hypothesis is that children with nonword repetition deficits should be poor at identifying phoneme constancy across different phonetic contexts. Methods for demonstrating this were reviewed in *Methods for testing children's awareness of phonological segments* (p.59); e.g. the child might be asked to select from an array of four items the two whose names begin with the same sound, or to identify rhyming pairs.

*The examples of characters were deliberately selected to be obscure, with the aim that most Chinese readers would not have encountered them before, though they would recognise component elements, and may be able to deduce the meaning from these. Of course, if the characters are already in the vocabulary of a reader, we would expect excellent recall after even a brief presentation, because the task then becomes one of retrieving an orthographic representation of a familiar word from the lexicon.

†In order to make a visual analogy that is as close as possible to the case of phonological memory for nonwords, I am using an example for which, as far as I know, there is no empirical support. I would be interested to hear from any reader who has the opportunity to run this experiment whether my predictions about different memory and generalisation by native and non-native Chinese speakers is borne out! My confidence in the predictions is based on a large literature demonstrating differences in how experts and novices remember material in a wide range of domains, including chess, mathematics, and map reading (Gilhooly & Green, 1988).

FIG. 4.11

Gathercole and Baddeley raised a second objection to an explanation in terms of initial encoding of phonological stimuli: they noted that performance on the nonword repetition task was strongly related to the length of nonwords. Indeed, on two-syllable nonwords, children with SLI did not differ significantly from age-matched controls: both groups performed near ceiling level (see Fig. 4.10, p.98). If encoding is a problem, they reasoned, this should be apparent regardless of the amount of material to be recalled. However, here again, the argument hinges on just what we mean by an encoding deficit. If encoding is slow and inefficient, then processing of later-arriving material may be disrupted because of the time it takes to encode the early-arriving material. The reasoning here has much in common with that used when discussing Tallal's findings on perception and

memory for tone sequences (see pp.63–66). Slow encoding of incoming information will have increasingly severe consequences the more material needs to be processed, and hence a basic perceptual problem can lead to poor memory.

Indirect evidence for a decay rather than an encoding account of the phonological memory data comes from a study by Rice, Oetting, Marquis, Bode, and Pae (1994). These authors used the same Quick Incidental Learning (QUIL) paradigm as in previous studies, where children are exposed to novel words in the context of television cartoons with voice-over commentary. Rice et al. varied the number of presentations of the novel words, using three or ten exposures of each of eight words, and they also compared children's understanding of these words in a multiple choice format both immediately after presentation and after a delay. Findings are summarised in Fig. 4.12. It is clear that

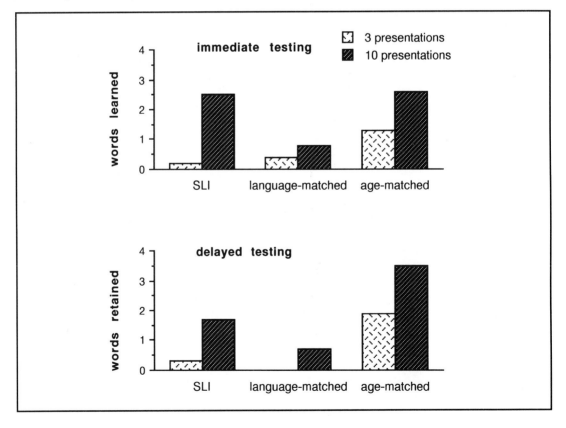

FIG. 4.12   Word learning by SLI and control children in relation to number of presentations of the novel words, and interval before testing. Data from Rice et al., 1994.

children with SLI do as well as age-matched controls on immediate testing only if they have ten rather than three exposures to the novel word. However, when retested a few days later, their performance had declined below the control level. Thus material that had been learned appeared subject to unusually rapid decay. However, intriguingly, the difference between SLI and LA control groups after a delay reflected not just decline in the scores of the SLI group, but also improvement in the control children. Perhaps the problem for the SLI group was not the rate of decay in memory, but a failure to organise material in the lexicon so as to achieve efficient retrieval. This example illustrates just how difficult it is to differentiate explanations in terms of rate of decay with explanations in terms of encoding strategy.

Rice et al. pointed out some difficulties for an explanation of their findings solely in terms of phonological factors. First, they noted that number of syllables in the novel words was unrelated to word learning. Indeed, in another study by this group (Oetting et al., 1995), a set of verbs with a mean length of only 1.6 syllables was substantially harder to learn than other parts of speech which were on average a whole syllable longer. This is not, however, a serious difficulty for a phonological account, given the way in which word knowledge was tested, i.e. by a multiple choice comprehension test. As noted above, a degraded phonological representation will yield different patterns of performance on production vs. comprehension. In comprehension, where it is not necessary to recall the whole phonological form, the critical factor is distinctiveness of the phonological representation. The second point noted by Rice et al. (1994) was that verbs in this study were significantly harder to retain over a delay than nouns for the children with SLI, leading them to argue that grammatical factors were an important constraint on vocabulary learning. However, the evidence is not compelling. Only four verbs and four nouns were tested and there was substantial variation between items in the effects observed. To be confident that it was indeed part of speech that was determining performance, rather than some other word-specific characteristics, we would need to have a statistical analysis that demonstrated that effects generalised across items as well as subjects (see H. Clark, 1973).

The role of imitation in vocabulary learning.
The account advanced so far maintains that learning of phonological strings is poor in SLI and that this is likely to reflect how the information is encoded and organised. An early impairment of rapid auditory processing could influence how the phonological system develops and hence how speech material is encoded. However, another factor that could affect phonological memory is speech production. Might learning of phonological forms depend not just on hearing new spoken words, but on the experience of speaking them? Could imitation of a word help establish a phonological representation in the lexicon by supplementing perceptual information with articulatory information? This line of argument is motivated by naturalistic observations, which show that verbal imitation is a naturally occurring phenomenon seen in infants at the earliest stages of language acquisition (Veneziano, 1988). Young children tend not to imitate words that are already established in their vocabulary (Ramer, 1976), but, on the other hand, they do not imitate structures that are completely absent from their own spontaneous speech (Bloom, Hood, & Lightbown, 1974). Bloom et al. proposed that children imitated utterances when they recognised that "some aspect of the utterance was in that grey area of what [they] knew about language" (p.417). Imitation thus enabled them to use the adult utterance to help them to encode a state of affairs. Bloom et al. also found substantial variation from child to child in the amount of imitation that was engaged in. Others have shown that below two years of age, children whose speech contains a high proportion of imitative utterances have higher expressive vocabularies than other children (Rodgon & Kurdek, 1977; Snow, 1989). Such observations raise questions about the function of imitation, and suggest that it might be to facilitate vocabulary learning. A handful of experimental studies have investigated this more systematically. Leonard, Schwartz, Folger, Newhoff, and Wilcox (1979) presented 16- to 24-month-old children with 12 nonsense names for unfamiliar objects in a series

of five play sessions over a period of three weeks. They confirmed that young children have a strong tendency to imitate; over 70% of the novel words were imitated, most in the first session. However, children's subsequent spontaneous use of the object names was no greater for items that had been imitated than for those that had not. In another study, children were given either familiar or unfamiliar items with a statement such as "Here's a cup" or "Here's a zib", and then asked "What's this?" In line with observational studies, the researchers found that spontaneous imitation of the item name was more common for the unfamiliar than for the familiar objects, but, once again, correct responding on the naming task was not related to whether the child had spontaneously imitated the word. Leonard et al. (p.26) concluded that imitation might be less important for vocabulary acquisition than hitherto thought: "Rather than constituting a means of acquiring the spontaneous use of particular lexical items, imitation seems best characterised as a strategy enabling children to participate in the communicative act under conditions of limited lexical knowledge." However, a replication and extension of this study by Leonard and Schwartz (1985) led to some tempering of this conclusion. One way of assessing the effect of imitation was to see how many exposures of object–name pairs were needed in the training phase before the child produced the word. On this measure of spontaneous production, there was no effect of prior imitation. However, when success in producing the name on a post-test was the dependent measure (i.e. the examiner attempted to elicit the name, rather than waiting for the child to produce it spontaneously), it was found that scores were higher for words that had previously been imitated. Leonard and Schwartz suggested that imitation in conjunction with spontaneous production may serve as some type of overt rehearsal facilitating subsequent productions.

If imitation does facilitate vocabulary learning, then we would expect to see weak vocabulary in children who had difficulty imitating. Tentative support for this view was obtained by Bishop, Byers-Brown, and Robson (1990), who studied receptive language skills in cerebral palsied children whose difficulties in speaking had a purely physical cause. In relation to cerebral palsied control children with normal speech, the speech-impaired participants had no problems on a test of comprehension of complex sentences. However, their receptive vocabularies were poor in relation to their other language skills and they had difficulty with a test that involved judging whether two nonwords were the same or different. The latter difficulty seemed to reflect memory rather than perceptual problems, because the same children could readily discriminate whether a word was spoken correctly or with one phonetic feature changed. Bishop et al. concluded that ability to repeat heard speech does facilitate memory for novel phonological sequences and acquisition of new vocabulary.

Clearly, cerebral palsied children, whose speech difficulties are due to neurological damage affecting motor control, have different kinds of problems from children with SLI, where difficulties with speech production have no physical basis. However, the two groups may have some similarities insofar as both find it difficult to imitate speech. Supplementing information about a word's perception with information about production appears to have a facilitatory effect on word learning, and children who do not have this additional source of information available might be expected to have poor vocabularies. Nevertheless, even totally speechless children can learn to recognise an impressive amount of vocabulary, so the role of imitation must be seen as supplementary to other mechanisms for word learning, rather than essential.

Top-down influences: Influence of vocabulary knowledge on perception and memory for novel phonological strings.   Our review of vocabulary learning so far has adopted a "bottom-up" approach. We hear a novel phonological string, segment it into subsyllabic units, retain it in memory, and ultimately form a long-term representation in the lexicon, as depicted in the sequence of stages linked by bold arrows in Fig. 4.13. Our emphasis has been on the extent to which problems in encoding or remembering phonological strings might affect vocabulary acquisition

But could influences operate the other way around, with vocabulary level affecting memory for phonological material? This would be a top-down influence, as illustrated by the dotted line in Fig. 4.13, whereby pre-existing lexical knowledge influenced how new incoming phonological information was processed.

Gathercole and Baddeley had attempted to avoid such influences by using novel phonological strings rather than familiar words in their tests of short-term memory. However, over the years, there has been a steady accretion of studies demonstrating that "wordlikeness" of nonwords, and the extent to which they have real words embedded in them, influence accuracy of repetition (Dollaghan, Biber, & Campbell, 1993, 1995; Gathercole, 1995; Gathercole, Willis, Emslie, & Baddeley, 1991); the more a nonword resembles an item already in a person's vocabulary, the easier it is to remember. Now, it follows that the more words a child knows, the greater is the opportunity for such influences to operate, and thus existing vocabulary knowledge could facilitate repetition of nonwords. Snowling, Chiat, and Hulme (1991)

developed this line of argument, suggesting that the nonword repetition deficit seen in children with SLI might be an index of the consequences rather than the cause of language impairment. This might be especially true for longer nonwords, where it is possible to draw upon prior knowledge of stress patterns of polysyllabic words to aid retrieval. This view was bolstered by Van der Lely and Howard (1995), who showed that memory for nonwords was no worse in children with SLI than in language-matched controls when the task involved sequential recall of a series of monosyllabic nonwords.

Taking this argument to its logical conclusion, one could argue that the only reason that there is a positive correlation between measures of phonological STM and vocabulary development is because of top-down effects (i.e. the path traced by the dotted line), and that intrinsic variability in children's memory capacity plays no part in causing individual differences in size of the lexicon. However, this is probably too extreme. In young children, early measures of phonological STM predict vocabulary growth, even after

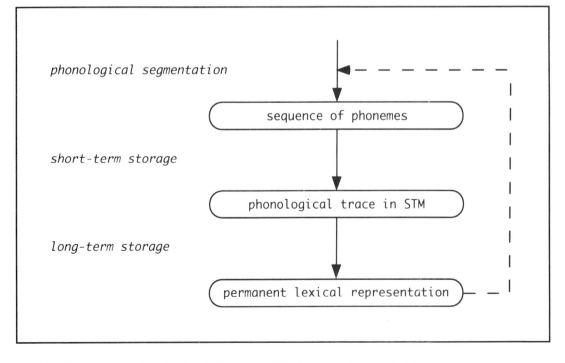

FIG. 4.13   Stages of processing in forming a lexical representation from a novel phonological string.

allowing for initial level of vocabulary, whereas the converse is not the case (Gathercole, Willis, Emslie, & Baddeley, 1992). As children grow older, the prediction from phonological STM to vocabulary growth becomes weaker, and Gathercole et al. suggested that other factors, such as richness of the child's linguistic background, and the child's ability to derive meaning from context assume more importance in vocabulary learning. If weak phonological STM affects early vocabulary acquisition, but then becomes less important, we would expect to find evidence of weak phonological STM in children with a history of language delay, even if their problems subsequently resolved. This is exactly what was reported in the study by Bishop et al. (1996), where school-aged children with a past history of SLI did just as poorly on nonword repetition as those who still had signs of SLI. Poor nonword repetition in "resolved" cases could not be explained in terms of weak "top-down" influence from the lexicon, because vocabulary level in this group was age-appropriate. Rather, Bishop et al. argued that a low score on nonword repetition in this group was a residual marker of abnormal phonological processing.

Defective phonological short-term memory: Evaluation. It is clear that ability to remember phonological information is poor in children with SLI. However, the underlying nature of this impairment is still a matter for debate. My own analysis, in our current state of knowledge, is that the available evidence could be parsimoniously explained in terms of a primary auditory deficit in speed of encoding information that affects the development of phonological classification, so that children persist in using immature strategies for encoding speech, and hence have inefficient organisation of phonological representations in the lexicon. The memory difficulties would be seen then as secondary to atypical encoding of phonological information. However, we cannot rule out other factors; encoding may be impoverished if the child relies solely on perceptual information, rather than supplementing this with information about a word's articulation. And, as argued by Gathercole and Baddeley, there may be a primary memory

impairment, with limited capacity in, or more rapid decay from, a short-term store, so there will be poor retention even if phonological information is encoded normally.

Whichever explanation for weak phonological memory is embraced, we have to ask whether it can account not just for weak vocabulary, but also for the broader range of language problems seen in children with SLI, especially problems with grammatical morphology. Adams and Gathercole (1995) suggested that phonological short-term memory was important for retaining word sequences for grammatical analysis, and they demonstrated that for normally developing three-year-old children, nonword repetition was a good predictor of syntactic proficiency. Grammatical limitations in SLI will be considered in detail in Chapter 5. For the present we simply note that if, as Adams and Gathercole maintain, phonological memory is important for learning syntax as well as vocabulary, then a core deficit in this system could have wide-ranging effects on language learning.

Mapping from phonology to meaning: Syntactic and semantic bootstrapping

It would be possible to have adequate phonological analysis, normal conceptual representations, appreciation of the symbolic function of language, and yet still have weak vocabulary, because the mappings between phonology and meaning had not been learned. Just how do children solve the mapping problem and work out what a phonological string refers to?

It is often assumed that children succeed by observing the contexts in which words are uttered. For instance, the word "elephant" is uttered when a large grey animal with a trunk is present, and so the child deduces that this is the referent. The process of selecting the correct referent is facilitated in normally developing children by their strong tendency to monitor the direction of gaze of other people, and hence to locate the focus of attention (Baron-Cohen, Baldwin, & Crowson, 1997). This is a very effective strategy for learning concrete nouns, but it is hard to see how other words, such as verbs, could be mastered in this way (Fisher, Hall, Rakowitz, & Gleitman, 1994).

One clue to meaning is the syntactic context in which a word is used. An early demonstration of this was by Roger Brown (1957, see Fig. 4.14, below). Children were presented with a novel word in the context of a picture depicting a nonsense activity with an unfamiliar substance in an unfamiliar container. For instance, a pair of hands were depicted kneading a red confetti-like substance in an oddly shaped container, and the child was told "In this picture you can see sibbing/a sib/some sib". Then they were given a choice of three pictures: one repeating the action with different materials, one showing a different action on the same material, and one showing a different action and material with the original container. They reliably selected the previously pictured object if, for instance, asked "show me a sib", the previous substance if asked "show me some sib", and the previous action if asked "show me sibbing". Children are able to identify recurring phonological elements that indicate part of speech, i.e. function words and inflections such as "the", "a", "-ing", or "-ed", and use this information to deduce the part of speech of an unfamiliar word that occurs in association with these; in this way they considerably refine the range of possible meanings.

FIG. 4.14   Picture stimuli based on those described by Brown (1957) in his experiment assessing children's use of grammatical inflections and function words in attributing word meaning. (The original stimuli were described but not depicted by Brown: his stimuli were brightly coloured and designed to be attractive to children.) The child would be asked: "Do you know what it means to sib? In this picture" (first picture in the set) "you can see sibbing. Now show me another picture of sibbing" (presenting the other three pictures of the set). If the stem was to function as a particular noun, the instruction would be "Do you know what a sib is?" and proceed in consistent fashion. If the word was to function as a mass noun, the initial statement was "Have you ever seen any sib?"

Syntactic relationships between an unknown word and other sentence elements can also give critical cues to meaning. Landau and Gleitman (1985) noted that if the visual context was the major cue to meaning and structure, then congenitally blind children should have major difficulties in language acquisition. They reported a case study demonstrating this need not be so. To explain how a blind child can learn to use verbs like "look" and "see" they proposed that, once some grammatical knowledge is available, a child may perform a syntactic analysis on an input sentence containing an unfamiliar word, and deduce the meaning of the unfamiliar word from its syntactic characteristics. For instance, if an adult describing a cartoon to a blind child says: "Tom really walloped Jerry", the child can deduce that the word wallop refers to an action in which Tom was agent and Jerry was patient. The grammatical elements associated with a verb provide information as to whether it refers to self-caused actions (typically expressed by an intransitive verb, i.e. with a subject and no object, such as "stand" or "swim"), an act that affects another's state (typically a transitive verb with subject and direct object, such as "kick" or "tickle"), or a propositional attitude (where the verb typically takes a sentence as a complement, such as "think" or "know"). So if the child has to deduce what "gorp" means, a different conclusion will be reached if the adult says "John is gorping", "John is gorping Max", or "John gorps that Max is nice". This ability to use syntactic context to infer meaning is referred to as syntactic bootstrapping (a term that originates in the notion of pulling oneself up by one's bootstraps).

Another source of information about verb meanings comes from awareness of the semantic roles played by participants in an action. Suppose the child observes a bear hitting a tiger in a distinctive way while the speaker says "the bear is kaboozling"; as noted previously, the syntactic context would suggest an intransitive verb; however the salient activity would be an action whereby the bear influenced the tiger, and so could lead the child to infer that "kaboozle" was a transitive verb. Had the same sentence been uttered in the context of a bear simply jumping around in an odd fashion, this would have supported the notion that "kaboozle" was an intransitive verb, and it would probably be interpreted as referring to that action. Semantic bootstrapping refers to the use of nonlinguistic contextual information about the semantic roles of entities that affect or are influenced by events to infer word meaning.

The question arises as to whether children with SLI use semantic and syntactic bootstrapping appropriately to infer word meanings. Early research relevant to this issue was the study described earlier on verb and noun learning by Leonard et al. (1982) (see Table 4.1, p.94). Fourteen children with SLI and fourteen language-matched control children were exposed to real but unfamiliar words depicting objects or actions in a play session. Leonard et al. were surprised to find that, overall, there were close similarities between SLI children and control children in the comprehension and production of the experimental words, as this result is quite discrepant with most of the other research reviewed in this chapter finding weak vocabulary in children with SLI. Leonard (1989), however, pointed out that an analysis in terms of bootstrapping processes could help understand these findings. He argued that the apparent ease of learning new words shown by children with SLI could be a consequence of the fact that the new words were presented in an inflectionally bare context, e.g. "Here's the gourd"; "Watch the baby kneel", and thus the main factor determining learning was the child's ability to perform a conceptual analysis of the object or action from which a semantic representation could be formed, i.e. semantic bootstrapping. However, he suggested that in more naturalistic situations where novel words are presented in a range of grammatical contexts, syntactic bootstrapping assumes importance.[3] In Chapter 5, we will review evidence that shows that children with SLI have major difficulties in processing syntactic structures. Leonard's analysis suggests that weak vocabulary could be a secondary effect of syntactic limitations in this population.

Van der Lely (1994) carried out a study explicitly designed to compare semantic and syntactic bootstrapping processes. Six children with SLI were compared with seventeen younger children who were matched on "language age" as measured by tests of single word vocabulary and expressive morphology. In the semantic bootstrapping task, the child was shown toys performing novel actions, accompanied by novel words. For instance, toy A jumps up and down on the back of toy B and the experimenter says "this is voozing". Children's ability to infer grammatical relations was then tested by asking them to (1) describe the behaviour of new toys carrying out the same actions; and (2) act out sentences such as "the horse voozes the lion" or "the lion is voozed by the horse". In contrast, in the syntactic bootstrapping task, no semantic information or contextual cues were provided. Children were simply asked to make up a meaning for a new word, and to show this to the experimenter by acting out sentences such as "the lorry yols the car". Responses were scored in terms of the semantic relations between the toys. In the example given, the expected response would be one where the lorry performs some action on the car, i.e. lorry is agent and car is patient, because the agent is usually the subject of an active sentence. In the semantic bootstrapping task, Van der Lely found that children with SLI used novel verbs to describe the behaviour of toys at least as much as language-age matched controls. Furthermore, the groups did not differ in terms of the number of elicited sentences that used word

order in a standard, or "canonical", fashion to express thematic roles. Thus, shown toy A "voozing" toy B, and then presented with other toys carrying out analogous actions, children with SLI were just as capable as the control children of saying "the dog is voozing the cow", reflecting the same thematic relations as in the demonstration item. Furthermore, on the acting out component of the semantic bootstrapping task, both sets of children succeeded fairly well in acting out sentences such as "the horse voozes the lion" or "the horse is voozed by the lion", with a much higher error rate on locative sentences such as "the lorry zeks the car to the train" or "the lorry is zeked by the car to the train". Although there was a trend for the children with SLI to do more poorly on this comprehension test, it was not statistically significant.

In contrast to their similar profiles on the semantic bootstrapping task, children with SLI were significantly impaired on the syntactic bootstrapping task (see Fig. 4.15, below). Typically, children who did poorly on this test were able to invent an appropriate event corresponding to the verb, involving the toys mentioned in the sentence. However, the assignment of thematic roles did not correspond to the canonical mapping. So when asked to demonstrate "the lorry yols the car", the

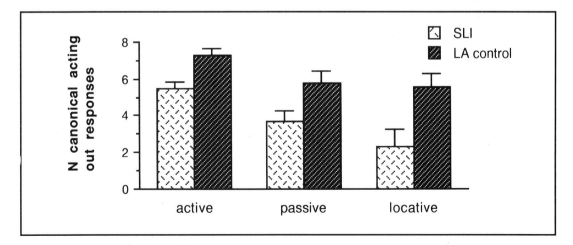

FIG. 4.15 Data from Van der Lely (1994). The graph shows the number of canonical responses (i.e. those where the agent, patient, and location agreed with the usual interpretation of grammatical roles for three sentence types) for sentences including a nonsense verb. The sentence types were: active, e.g. "the man yols the lady"; passive, e.g. "the man is yolled by the lady"; and locative, e.g. "the man jids the girl to the lady".

child might make the car do something to the lorry rather than the other way around.

Taken together, these results indicate that children with SLI can form a representation of verb argument structure (i.e. the relationships between entities that the verb refers to) on the basis of contextual information. However, they do appear to be impaired in deducing meaning relations from grammatical structure. Van der Lely argued that lack of grammatical competence limits the child's ability to use syntactic bootstrapping to infer word meanings. Hence, a primary grammatical deficit could lead to poor word learning.

Van der Lely's study was replicated by O'Hara and Johnston (1997), who obtained closely similar results. However, these authors favoured a different line of explanation for the findings, noting that although children with SLI were poor at the syntactic bootstrapping task, they nevertheless inferred important components of verb meaning and performed at well above chance levels. They suggested that attentional or memory limitations might be implicated in poor performance, and noted that errors of omission or selection were most common for the last-named noun. Also, sentences involving three toys were more difficult than those with two. Both Van der Lely and O'Hara and Johnston agree that children with SLI are poor at inferring verb meaning from the syntactic frame in which the verb occurs, but whether this reflects some specifically syntactic difficulty with mapping between syntactic and semantic domains, or a more general limitation in dealing with large amounts of sequential information remains unclear at this point. We shall return to this issue in Chapter 6. For the present, the point that again emerges from this work is the extent to which different linguistic levels interact in development. If we find that a child has a weak vocabulary, it is tempting to assume that the underlying deficit must be in either phonological analysis or semantic analysis. However, the work on syntactic bootstrapping demonstrates that a child who had a weak grasp of grammatical principles would have difficulty in learning vocabulary because an important source of information about word meaning would be deficient.

Anglin (1993) drew attention to a related mechanism in vocabulary learning, namely deducing word meaning from word structure. When children are asked to define words, or to select an appropriate meaning from a set of alternatives, one strategy they may adopt is to work out the meaning by using knowledge of how derivational morphemes and word compounding rules operate (see *Morphemes*, opposite). For instance, the child who knows the meaning of "nice" but has never heard the word "niceness", may nevertheless be able to deduce the correct meaning from a knowledge of how derivational inflections such as "-ness" alter the part of speech of a word root. Anglin showed that the most substantial vocabulary growth in the early school years (US grades one to five) was in knowledge of morphologically complex words, and he suggested that what he termed "morphological problem solving skills" are responsible for much of this development. I am not aware of comparable research on children with SLI, but it would seem worth investigating whether they are deficient in this kind of analysis; if so, they would be expected to fall increasingly further behind their peer group in vocabulary comprehension.

Vocabulary learning through the written word

As well as providing data on the types of words that children learned, Anglin's (1993) research emphasised that the dramatic growth in vocabulary with age during the early school years is accompanied by an equal increase in variability from child to child (see *Estimating vocabulary size*, p.84). One reason proposed for the widening individual differences as children grow older is the impact of literacy skills on vocabulary learning. Books provide access to a much wider range of words than are encountered in everyday talk. Furthermore, the written word emphasises the morphological similarities between words that may not be recognised as sharing a common root when spoken, because of changes to the stress and vowel forms, e.g. major/majority, excite/excitation. If a child has difficulty in learning to read, then an important opportunity for learning new vocabulary will be lost.

It seems unlikely that lack of literacy skills is the whole explanation for poor vocabulary in SLI:

many of the studies demonstrating poor vocabulary learning (e.g. those by Rice and her colleagues) were conducted with preschool children, where this could not be a factor. However, the role of literacy in vocabulary learning becomes increasingly important as the child grows older and it seems likely that this is a factor compounding the problems of children with SLI (see e.g. Bishop & Adams, 1990). One prediction from this hypothesis is that the deficit in vocabulary relative to a peer group should become increasingly marked in the early school years. Furthermore, rate of progress in vocabulary learning should be related to level of literacy.

LEXICAL ACCESS

We have focused so far on comprehension problems that reflect lack of vocabulary knowledge. In real-life situations, however, it is important not just to know the meaning of a phonological string; but also to be able to extract that string from a continuous stream of speech and match it to a representation in the lexicon. A receptive vocabulary test, where words are presented in isolation with no time pressure, might overestimate how well a child will understand word meanings in everyday speech.

Morphemes

The term "morpheme" is used to refer to the most basic element of meaning. A useful definition provided by Fromkin and Rodman (1978, p.142) is of the morpheme as "a minimal linguistic sign, i.e. a grammatical unit in which there is an arbitrary union of a sound and a meaning and which cannot be further analysed".

A single word may contain a single morpheme as in:

boy, house, knit, beauty, wise

two morphemes, as in:

boy+s, boy+ish, house+hold, knitt+ing, beauti+ful, wis+est, Piaget+ian

three morphemes, as in:

boy+ish+ness, house+hold+s, beauti+ful+ness, un+wise+ly

or four or more:

anti+neo+Piaget+ian, un+thought+ful+ly

Grammatical morphemes are morphemes that serve grammatical functions, and include inflections (such as -ing, -ed, or -en endings on verbs) and function words, such as "a", "some", "not", or "because". These words signal such characteristics as tense, aspect, or plurality, or express relationships between content words in a sentence. The inflectional endings are known as bound morphemes, because they cannot occur on their own and must be attached to a word. They contrast with free morphemes, which can stand alone.

Another type of bound morpheme is the derivational morpheme, which alters the meaning of a word, sometimes changing its grammatical class, as when "beauty" (noun) becomes "beautiful" (adjective), or "private" (adjective) becomes "privatise" (verb). In English, bound grammatical morphemes are added to the ends of words they modify, but derivational morphemes may occur as prefixes (e.g. un-, pre-, neo-, anti-) or suffixes (e.g. -ful, -ness, -ity, -ism). In other languages, grammatical morphemes may occur as prefixes, suffixes, or infixes (i.e. modifying the word internally rather than being appended at front or end).

A compound word is a word made from two free morphemes, such as "blackbird" or "greenhouse". In many cases, the meaning of the compound is not readily deducible from the component morphemes, e.g. "gooseberry".

Addition of a derivational morpheme or formation of a compound frequently alters the pronunciation of the component morphemes. For instance, we say "sincere" with a long vowel on the second syllable, but "sincerity" with a short vowel. For "blackboard" the stress is on the first morpheme, whereas if we were to use the two morphemes in a phrase, "black board", the stress would be on the second morpheme.

Even though segmentation of the speech stream does not appear to be a specific problem for children with SLI (Rice et al., 1992), we still have the formidable problem of matching a spoken input with a representation in the mental lexicon, which, in an average child, contains thousands of words by the age of six years. One way of conceptualising this is to pursue the analogy with a "mental dictionary". Suppose we were given a written word to look up, and we proceeded by simply starting at the beginning and working through to the end of the dictionary: the task would be impossible. In practice, looking up a word is much easier than that because the dictionary imposes an organisation in terms of alphabetic principles so we can home in on the right section immediately. Contemporary models of lexical access adopt the notion that phonological characteristics of words are used in retrieval, but the process is seen as far more active and dynamic than a dictionary search. Morton (1969) popularised the Logogen Model in which each word has a lexical entry that has a particular level of activation. When the level of activation exceeds a certain threshold level, then the word is recognised. Perceptual input that matches the phonological specification of a lexical entry boosts its activation. The Cohort Model of Marslen-Wilson and Tyler (1980) develops this kind of idea further. According to this model, phonological information is processed as soon as it is encountered, with identification of a word proceeding in a left-to-right fashion. This enables the model to explain why many words can be recognised on the basis of partial information, before the utterance of the word has terminated. Suppose the word "trellis" is presented. Initially, all the lexical entries beginning with /t/ are activated, i.e. some several thousand lexical entries. However, as the next segment of the word is encountered, only those beginning /tr/ remain activated. By the time we reach /trɛ/, only 19 words remain as candidates, and when the next phoneme is processed and we have /trɛl/, we have sufficient information to identify the word "trellis" unambiguously, even though it has not been completed, i.e. we have reached a "uniqueness point". This process is illustrated in Table 4.3.

Another feature of contemporary models that was part of the original Logogen Model is the fact that activation levels of lexical units can be influenced by factors other than perceptual input. Thus, in the Logogen model, words that have a high frequency of occurrence have higher levels of resting activation than low frequency words, and hence are recognised more rapidly. However, there is also a dynamic aspect to top-down influences on activation, i.e. it can vary from moment to moment depending on the context. For instance, words corresponding to animal names will be recognised more readily in the context of a conversation about the zoo than in the context of a conversation about theoretical physics. This kind of contextual effect can be demonstrated both in terms of faster recognition time, and in ease of recognition when the word is degraded by omitting some portions or playing it through noise.

The Cohort Model has performed well in experimental tests of predictions about speed of word recognition for different vocabulary items, but it has in recent years been both modified by the authors and challenged by other models of speech recognition (see Lively, Pisoni, & Goldinger, 1994; Massaro, 1994, for reviews). This is not the place to go into a detailed account of the similarities and differences between these models; the important point to note is that experimental data strongly support a model of lexical access that involves simultaneous activation of representations of words that have perceptual similarities to the incoming stimulus, with identification occurring at the point when one lexical representation becomes activated above a threshold level.

Given that word recognition involves activating lexical representations with common phonological properties, it follows that efficient processing depends on organisation of the lexicon in terms of phonological principles. As was noted in Chapter 3, very young children do not seem to analyse words into subsyllabic units, and there is a suspicion that, in children with SLI, this immature style of phonological processing persists. Normal young infants may recognise familiar words purely on the basis of a few salient auditory characteristics, including stress pattern and specific features such as nasality or sibilance. The

TABLE 4.3

Cohort Model of Word Recognition (Cohorts Activated at Different Time Points on Hearing the Phoneme String /ˈtrɛlɪs/)

/t/	/tr/	/trɛ/	/trɛl/	/trɛlɪ/	/trɛlɪs/
tap	train	treacherous	trellis	trellis	trellis
tax	trace	treachery			
toe	tremulous	tread			
train	:	treadle			
:	:	treadmill			
:	trigger	treasure			
treat	:	treasury			
:	:	treble			
:	trust	trek			
tripod	:	trellis			
:	:	tremble			
:	trial	tremolo			
truce	true	tremulous			
:	:	trench			
:	:	trenchant			
:	:	trend			
:	:	trepidation			
:	treacle	trespass			
tungsten	treat	trestle			
cohort of approx. 3500 words	*cohort of approx. 900 words*	*cohort of 19 words*	*cohort of 1 word* **UNIQUENESS POINT**		

time ⟶

problem with this kind of representation is not only that it does not specify sufficient information for accurate production of the word, but also that word recognition gets increasingly difficult as vocabulary size increases (see also Charles-Luce & Luce, 1990). Jusczyk (1986) proposed that one reason for children to develop a phonologically based representation of words was that it enabled the lexicon to be organised more efficiently, so that an incoming word could be rapidly compared with all lexical items with a common onset. If, as argued in Chapter 3, some children with SLI persist in a more global syllabic analysis of word structure, this would have the consequence that not only would new word learning be retarded, but also that, once words were learned, lexical access would be slow and inefficient. In contrast, if the only reason for slow vocabulary learning were difficulty at the mapping stage, and limited ability to use syntactic bootstrapping, then we would expect that, once acquired, lexical entries should be normally organised. Indeed, since there would be a smaller pool of words to search through in the mental dictionary, we might even anticipate rather better lexical retrieval in children with SLI than in their normally developing peers.

The few studies that have been conducted on lexical retrieval support the notion that children with SLI don't just have fewer lexical representations than their normally developing peers, but that the storage of those lexical representations they do have is non-optimally organised, making rapid retrieval problematic. On a Rapid Automated Naming task, where the child must say the names of pictured items (from a small set of familiar objects) as rapidly as possible, children with SLI perform more slowly than normally developing controls (Katz, Curtiss, & Tallal, 1992; Leonard et al., 1983; Wiig, Semel, & Nystrom, 1982). Also, anecdotal evidence suggests that underspecification of lexical representations may be common in SLI, with children making phonological errors where the overall syllabic and prosodic shape of the word is preserved, but the detail is in error (e.g. "trelliscope" for "telescope"). The limitation of this kind of production data is that its interpretation remains ambiguous. The fact that word production is slow and error-prone could simply reflect a problem in translating an accurate phonological representation in the lexicon into an articulatory program. A great deal of computation is involved in deriving a set of rapidly sequenced articulatory movements from an abstract under-lying phonological representation, and there is plentiful evidence to support the notion that this kind of motor programming is defective in at least some children with SLI. Ideally, therefore, to be certain that word-finding problems are more a function of lexical impairments rather than a motor output difficulty, we need converging evidence from tasks which require no speech production on the part of the child.

Montgomery, Scudder, and Moore (1990) used a word detection paradigm based on the work of Marslen-Wilson and Tyler (1980), in which the child heard a spoken sentence and was required to press a key as soon as a predetermined target word occurred. Compared with younger normally developing control children, language-impaired children were significantly more likely to miss target words.[4] The authors also noted that the children with language impairments did show normal sensitivity to syntactic and semantic constraints, responding faster when a word occurred in a context that was semantically and/or syntactically plausible than when it was presented in a random word list. Stark and Montgomery (1995) did a similar study, this time comparing language-impaired children with an age-matched control group. Words were presented both in word lists and in sentence contexts. Overall, children with language impairments were both slower and less accurate in responding to target words. They showed normal effects of sentence context, however, being faster to respond to words in sentences, especially those occurring at the ends of sentences where there was more opportunity for contextual effects to develop. Interestingly, in view of the debates about speed of phonological processing in SLI (see Chapter 3), neither time compression of the stimuli nor auditory filtering exerted significant effects on either group of children.

These two studies are consistent with the notion that word retrieval is slow and inaccurate in children with SLI, but we need to treat the data cautiously. Stark and Montgomery commented on the problems that many children with SLI had in attending to the task, and it seems possible that their poor performance may be more a function of a tendency to lose concentration intermittently, rather than any consistent slowing of retrieval processes.

One study that must be mentioned at this point is by Kail, Hale, Leonard, and Nippold (1984), who explicitly set out to test between storage and retrieval accounts of lexical deficits in SLI. This study is, however, rather difficult to integrate with the other work reviewed here, because the paradigm that was used was a free-recall task, where the stimuli were all familiar words falling into natural categories such as colours or fruits. Thus, what Kail et al. refer to as "storage" is temporary activation of a set of words in memory for later recall, not the setting up of a new lexical representation. Likewise, "retrieval" in this task is the ability to recall which words in the mental lexicon have recently been activated, which is rather a different task from rapidly recognising a familiar spoken word. Kail et al. argued that if children with SLI had a retrieval deficit, then they should show more improvement than other children when given retrieval cues consisting of category names. It was found that children with SLI were equally poor at free and cued recall, with performance resembling that of language-age-matched controls. It was also argued that a retrieval problem should be associated with more trial by trial variability in recall, when children were asked for repeated recall of the same list on several occasions. Although children with SLI did give evidence of more retrieval problems than their age-matched controls, their retrieval profiles were similar to language-age-matched control children. Overall, this study suggests that semantic organisation of material in memory is not a major source of difficulty for children with SLI, but it does not address the issue of how phonological representations are initially set up in the lexicon.

CONCLUSIONS

Vocabulary learning is deficient in children with SLI, but the explanations for this deficiency are quite varied. We can rule out any strong form of a hypothesis that attributes poor learning to abnormal conceptual development or lack of symbolic representations. We are left with two plausible accounts that focus on different stages of the word learning process. On the one hand we have what we might term the "bottom-up" theorists, who stress that vocabulary acquisition depends on the setting up of long-term phonological representations in the lexicon, and argue that this process will be hampered by poor phonological perception and memory. Whether normal phonological representations decay rapidly, or whether the initial encoding of phonological information is inadequate remains unclear, but there is ample evidence that children with SLI do have major difficulties in retaining novel strings of phonological material. An alternative view of SLI stresses the "top-down" processes involved in vocabulary learning. Both semantic and syntactic sources of information are

used in new word learning. The more vocabulary a child already knows, the easier it is to learn new words, by generalising from existing knowledge about phonological, prosodic and morphological structure. Syntactic information can be used to deduce word meaning and hence solve the mapping task. The child who is a fluent reader will have numerous opportunities for incidental learning of words from contextual information, and will also have more direct clues, from a word's spelling, as to its morphological composition.

There is no doubt that top-down influences operate in word learning. The critical question is whether they are sufficient to explain vocabulary limitations in children with SLI. There is relatively little work bearing directly on this question, but there is suggestive evidence that phonological representations in the lexicon may be underspecified. This kind of evidence is hard to explain away in terms of a "top-down" model, because inadequate use of top-down processing should simply retard vocabulary acquisition without affecting how phonological information is encoded. Experimental studies of the word learning process have been particularly fruitful in documenting the factors that influence vocabulary acquisition in some children. However, it is important to be aware that the results obtained may be crucially dependent on how we test vocabulary knowledge: whether we look at production or comprehension, and, if the latter, whether the interest is in awareness of phonological composition of the word or its meaning. A final way forward is to conduct longitudinal studies of individuals with SLI. The severity and pattern of impairments can change quite markedly over time, and a longitudinal approach may allow us to see which deficits constitute an unchanging core disorder, and which are secondary consequences that may be overcome by alternative compensatory strategies.

FOOTNOTES

1. Only "to some extent" because there is evidence that word learning can influence conceptual boundaries (e.g. Choi & Bowerman, 1991).

2. It is important, however, to qualify this statement with "all else being equal", because the salience of an object or event also determines whether it is likely to be talked about. Suppose 10 white rabbits had already scurried past and suddenly a pink one appeared, whereupon the native said "Gavagai". In that case, it is very unlikely that "Gavagai" would mean "rabbit": it would be more likely to mean "pink" or "look!"

3. Another potential reason for different findings between studies was that Leonard et al. used monosyllabic words, whereas in other research, such as the QUIL studies by Rice and colleagues, polysyllabic words were included.

4. Interpretation of reaction time (RT) data was complicated by the fact that the language impaired children were compared to a younger control group. On the word detection task these two groups did not differ in RT, but on a nonverbal tone-detection task overall RTs were faster for the language-impaired children. Montgomery et al. argued that the tone detection RT could be used as a measure of baseline speed, which was then subtracted from the word detection RT: on this difference measure there was a nonsignificant trend for the language-impaired children to have larger scores (i.e. word detection was slow relative to tone detection).

5

Grammatical knowledge in sentence comprehension

The author is testing a normally developing control child on a sentence comprehension test which involves saying "yes" or "no", depending on whether a test sentence matches a picture:
DB: "Mowgli says every monkey is tickling himself"
Child: You mean they are tickling themselves?
DB: Listen again: "Mowgli says every monkey is tickling himself"
Child: Right, so they are tickling themselves. Is that what you mean?
DB: You try and work it out.
Child: (frustrated) Well, I could do it if you would say it properly.

OVERVIEW

1. In this chapter, we shall consider how the child uses knowledge of word order, grammatical inflections, and function words to derive meaning from a sentence.

2. An influential theory proposed by Chomsky maintains that language acquisition can be explained only by assuming that the child has innate knowledge of a Universal Grammar, which specifies principles common to all human languages. Fundamental tenets of this theory are that (1) linguistic knowledge takes the form of abstract symbolic rules and (2) language processing is carried out by a specialised brain module that is relatively independent of the operation of other cognitive systems.

3. The bulk of research on grammar in SLI is concerned with deficits in expressive language. Evidence from receptive language tests is important for establishing how far these difficulties reflect lack of grammatical knowledge. The few studies that have been done specifically to look at comprehension of grammatical contrasts show that many children with SLI have unusual difficulty in understanding meaning distinctions that are signalled by syntactic relationships or grammatical inflections.

4. Chomskyan theory has been challenged by those who reject the notion that children's

knowledge takes the form of abstract symbolic rules. Connectionist approaches regard language acquisition as involving probabilistic learning, with modularity as a gradually emergent property rather than an innately specified characteristic.

5. Several linguistic accounts of SLI have been formulated on the basis of Chomskyan theory. These maintain that components of the innate grammar are defective or absent. However, these theories typically predict more extreme grammatical deficits than are seen in SLI.

6. A non-modular approach to language acquisition sits well with an alternative account of SLI that treat grammatical deficits as secondary to more general perceptual deficits.

INTRODUCTION

When words are put together, the whole is far greater than the sum of the parts. By combining words one can generate an enormously complex range of meanings. Verbs provide a means for expressing relationships between entities; who did what to whom, who experienced what, how an object was acted upon, and so on. Adverbs and adjectives enable one to describe qualities of actions, events or objects. But this is not all. Our powers of expression are enormously increased by the use of linguistic terms that function solely to modify meanings of content words. Some of these are "function words", such as "but", "not", "in", or "from", which express logical, spatial, and temporal relationships. Others are grammatical inflections, which cannot stand alone, and are always appended to a content word, such as plural "-s", past tense "-ed", or comparative "-er". Both uninflected words and inflections are morphemes, i.e. minimal units of meaning. Morphemes that cannot stand alone are known as bound morphemes, and those that can do so are free morphemes.

Meaning is expressed not just by the morphemes that are present in a sentence, but by the order in which they occur. Languages vary both in the ways in which they use word order to convey

meaning, and in the flexibility of word order that is permitted.

For instance, in English, the typical, or canonical, word order is subject–verb–object (SVO) as in:

John hit Fred

whereas in Japanese, the canonical order is SOV:

John-ga Fred-o but-ta

Grammatical difficulties are one of the most striking features in the expressive language of many children with SLI (see examples in Table 5.1, opposite). Typically one sees omission of grammatical inflections and persistence of immature sentence structures long after the age when most children would have mastered the basics of grammar of their language. How these language deficits are interpreted is one of the most controversial topics in the study of SLI. This chapter will consider a crucial, but often neglected, source of evidence for this debate: how children *understand* grammatical contrasts. Before we review such evidence, it is first necessary to discuss what we know about normal acquisition of grammatical knowledge.

WHAT DO CHILDREN LEARN ABOUT GRAMMAR?

Morphological paradigms

Imagine you visit the delightful country of Slaka (Bradbury, 1986), where you speak not a word of Slakan. The natives are, however, friendly, and you gradually pick up fragments of the language. You master a simple vocabulary, and know how to buy a book (*toma*), newspaper (*blatta*), bag (*bagga*), shoes (*suli*), and hat (*krapa*). When you next enter the local shop, you hear someone buying books refer to *tomi*, and later on your hear someone talk about *blatti*. Gradually you become aware that *tomi* is the plural of *toma*, and *blatti* the plural of *blatta*. Armed with this knowledge, you confidently generate plurals for *bagga* (*baggi*) and *krapa* (*krapi*). You also deduce that a single shoe is

TABLE 5.1

Some Examples of Grammatical Errors Observed in 8- to 12-year-old Children with SLI*

Child's version	Correct version
Noun plural omission	
and not **spot** on	and it didn't have spots on
cakes erm **sandwich**	cakes and sandwiches
Verb tense	
he **say**, I'm a monster	he said, I'm a monster
and they had like a round circle and they **hide** in it	and they had like a round circle and they hid in it
the car has **broked** down	the car has broken down
Genitive inflection	
my sister use my **Dad** car but she keep smashing it	my sister used my Dad's car but she kept smashing it
he went up the stairs with **Bernard** teddy bear	he went up the stairs with Bernard's teddy bear
Pronoun case	
and **him** jumped on the television	and he jumped on the television
them can rush to try to help him	they can rush to try to help him
Omission of "to be" as main verb (copula)	
cos they her favourites	cos they're her favourites
he a Jack Russell	he's a Jack Russell
Determiner error	
maybe have **a** chickenpox or maybe have something	maybe he has chickenpox or something
Omission of subject in obligatory context	
eat up Bernard except training shoes	he ate up Bernard except for his training shoes
bit Daddy leg no notice	he bit Daddy's leg but he took no notice

*All examples taken from the sample of transcripts studied by Bishop (1994a).

referred to as *sula*. What you have just done, in fact, is to establish a general morphological paradigm, i.e. learned a productive rule for marking plurality that can be applied to new forms, even those where you have never encountered the spoken plural.

When children first use inflected forms, they appear unaware of the significance of the inflectional endings; thus, a child might use the words "walked" and "walk" to refer to past and current actions, without recognising that there is a general rule for deriving one form from the other. At this stage, as each new form is encountered, it is entered in a word-specific paradigm, with entries for both present and past forms (see *Formation of morphological paradigms*, overleaf). However, as more and more forms are encountered, a general

rule is abstracted for forming the past tense. Studies of young children support the view that rule-based morphology is acquired by a gradual process of first learning specific instances of inflected words, and then identifying a general pattern that enables one to generalise knowledge to inflect a word that has never been heard in the inflected form.

One source of evidence for general paradigms comes from observations of children's errors. Normally developing young children are heard to produce such forms as "comed" instead of "came", and "goed" instead of "went". In overgeneralising a regular inflection to an irregular verb, children indicate that they have formulated a general principle for forming the past tense of a verb. A more systematic analysis of this tendency was

Formation of morphological paradigms

Pinker (1984) proposed that adult knowledge about grammatical inflections is represented in the form of general paradigms, with particular affixes listed in a matrix according to the grammatical features that they correspond to. However, it is necessary also to postulate the existence of word-specific paradigms, to account for the ability to use irregularly inflected forms. Pinker proposed that, early in development, children treat all words as if they were irregular forms, setting up morphological paradigms for each specific lexical item.

However, as vocabulary expands, they begin to segment inflected forms and recognise common inflectional patterns. At this point, a general paradigm is formed. This leads to more economical storage, because there is no need to store all the inflected forms with each stem; inflections can be generated by rule if no inflected form is found in the word-specific paradigm. This means that lexical representations change during development, as illustrated for English verb tense in Table 5.2 opposite.

carried out by Berko (1958), who tested children's ability to apply inflections in completely unfamiliar circumstances, i.e. when given non-sense words, as in the task illustrated in Fig. 5.1 (p.120). Children as young as four years demonstrated some ability to inflect nonsense forms with endings such as plural, past "-ed", and progressive "-ing", demonstrating that they had general knowledge of principles of grammatical morphology and were not simply rote learning inflected forms. However, while general morphological paradigms are important in enabling a child to generate novel inflected forms, in English, as in many other languages, there are numerous words that are irregular and must be rote-learned, e.g. child–children; go–went.

Different languages mark morphosyntactic features in different ways. Many languages mark gender and case as well as features such as number and tense, and the morphological paradigms may be highly complex. In fusional languages a single inflection can simultaneously denote more than one feature. For instance, in German, the inflection appended to an adjective simultaneously denotes case, gender, and number. In contrast, agglutinating languages (e.g. Turkish) have a different inflection for each grammatical feature, and these are strung together in a sequence. Some languages, such as Hebrew, mark grammatical features by altering vowels within words, rather than appending inflections (just as English does with

irregular verbs, e.g. sing, sang, sung). Other languages, such as Chinese, make little or no use of inflectional morphology. Although there are exceptions, it is usually the case that, the richer the inflectional morphology of a language, the less use is made of word order for expressing grammatical functions. In English, which has a relatively sparse inflectional morphology, word order is far more important than in Italian, which has a rich inflectional system. These major variations in the richness, complexity and regularity of inflectional morphology make cross-linguistic comparisons of language learning of particular interest.

Syntactic structures

Not all sequences of morphemes are acceptable. This is evident when we ask people to make grammaticality judgements, i.e. judging whether a sequence of words is a legal sentence, given examples such as:

John asked Mary to help him

or

*John asked Mary to help himself

(An asterisk preceding a sentence denotes that it is ungrammatical.)

Speakers of a language are able to make intuitive judgements about the grammaticality of a

TABLE 5.2

Change in Morphological Representations from Initial to Final State

Initial state	Final state

GENERAL PARADIGM

	person		
tense	1st	2nd	3rd
present	–	–	-s
past	-ed	-ed	-ed

WORD-SPECIFIC PARADIGMS	WORD-SPECIFIC PARADIGMS

Initial state — WORD-SPECIFIC PARADIGMS

	person		
tense	1st	2nd	3rd
present	look	look	looks
past	looked	looked	looked

	person		
tense	1st	2nd	3rd
present	jump	jump	jumps
past	jumped	jumped	jumped

	person		
tense	1st	2nd	3rd
present	walk	walk	walks
past	walked	walked	walked

	person		
tense	1st	2nd	3rd
present	have	have	has
past	had	had	had

	person		
tense	1st	2nd	3rd
present	come	come	comes
past	came	came	came

Final state — WORD-SPECIFIC PARADIGMS

	person		
tense	1st	2nd	3rd
present	look	•	•
past	•	•	•

	person		
tense	1st	2nd	3rd
present	jump	•	•
past	•	•	•

	person		
tense	1st	2nd	3rd
present	walk	•	•
past	•	•	•

	person		
tense	1st	2nd	3rd
present	have	•	has
past	had	had	had

	person		
tense	1st	2nd	3rd
present	come	•	•
past	came	came	came

In the initial state, each cell of the paradigm is filled for each word. In the final state, a general paradigm is set up which specifies the inflectional ending that is applied in any case where the cell is unfilled (denoted by •).

FIG. 5.1   Sample item from Berko's (1958) study. Berko noted that (p.150): "if a child knows that the plural of *witch* is *witches*, he may simply have memorized the plural form. If, however, he tells us that the plural of *gutch* is *gutches*, we have evidence that he actually knows, albeit unconsciously, one of those rules which the descriptive linguist, too, would set forth in his grammar."

whole range of sentences in the language, usually without any explicit understanding of the underlying rules that are guiding their judgements. Linguists aim to specify what these underlying rules are, i.e. to make explicit the implicit knowledge that people use. This is a far from simple task (see *Rules of grammar*, opposite). It is important to appreciate that this enterprise is quite different from that of dictating how people ought to talk. We are not concerned here with prescriptive grammars that judge double negatives or split infinitives as improper. Rather, the aim is to

understand what are the principles that determine how people do talk, and which would be agreed upon by all competent speakers, regardless of class or dialect.

One sometimes has the impression that formal grammarians are interested only in people's ability to judge sentences as grammatical or un-grammatical, but there is, of course, far more to grammatical competence than this. Most importantly, we need to be able to decode the meaning conveyed by grammatical variations, and to recognise, for instance, that:

the boy gave the man the hat

and

the boy gave the hat to the man

describe the same event, whereas:

the dog chased the cat

and

the dog was chased by the cat

do not.

Specifying how a sentence expresses who did what to whom involves assigning thematic roles to noun phrases, a process that is dependent on the verb's lexical properties and the noun's syntactic relationship to the verb (see *Thematic roles and argument structure*, p.123). For instance, "the boy" corresponds to the entity being pushed (i.e. the theme, or patient) in sentences such as "the boy is pushed by the girl", "the boy was pushed", or "the girl who was on the bus pushed the boy", but is the person doing the pushing (the agent) in "the boy

pushed the girl", "it was the girl that the boy pushed", or "the boy who was running past John pushed the girl". These latter examples illustrate that recognition of who did what to whom requires knowledge of syntactic relationships that go beyond simple temporal order.

HOW DO CHILDREN LEARN GRAMMAR? THE PRINCIPLES AND PARAMETERS FRAMEWORK

Some 25 years ago, the attention of linguists was drawn to a major problem in the study of language acquisition—on a logical analysis, it should be impossible for children ever to learn the rules of grammar! (see *Learnability*, p.124). It was concluded that since children clearly do learn grammatical rules, they must come to the language-learning task with some pre-existing innate knowledge of what grammar is like.

The notion of an innate grammar, which is a fundamental tenet of Chomsky's (1976) theoretical

---

Rules of grammar

As a competent speaker of English, you frequently ask questions, and make negative statements. One can see some regular patterns in how these types of sentence are constructed, as illustrated in the examples in Table 5.3, below. We have no difficulty in recognising these as legal English sentences, but do you know what rules you are using?

Try to formulate a general rule that specifies the type of utterance that makes a legitimate statement, and the rules for turning this into a question or negative statement. Then turn to *Rules of grammar (continued)* on the next page.

TABLE 5.3

Statement	Question	Negative
Mary likes fish	Does Mary like fish?	Mary doesn't like fish
The boy went to the park yesterday	Did the boy go to the park yesterday?	The boy didn't go to the park yesterday

Rules of grammar (continued)

When you attempt the exercise in *Rules of grammar*, on the previous page, you will find the problem impossible unless you think in terms of sentences as a collection of abstract elements of particular types, such as nouns, verbs, and so on. If you simply tried to derive a rule based on serial order (e.g. insert "not" after the third word to form a negative), this would not work. You will notice that the phrase "the boy" seems to serve the same function in the sentence as the proper name "Mary", and its position in the sentence changes in the same way when a question is formed. You might formulate a simple rule such as:

statement: NP + V + tense marking + (preposition) + NP + (adverb)

where NP is a noun phrase such as "Mary" or "the boy", and the brackets enclose an optional element. Reordering and adding elements as below will then give the corresponding questions and negatives:

question: do + tense marking + NP + V + (preposition) + NP + (adverb)
negative: NP + do + tense marking + "not" + (preposition) + NP + (adverb)

However, these rules are not adequate, because they cannot handle the more complex examples shown in Table 5.4, below. Although you generate questions and negatives all the time and clearly have implicit knowledge of how to do this, this exercise is useful in demonstrating how little insight most of us have into the grammatical processes used in generating sentences.

Can you generate rules for questions and negatives that work on these more complicated examples?

The task for linguists is to derive rules which capture generalities about grammatical structure simply and elegantly. In attempting to make rules for the examples in Table 5.4, you will find that you need to specify these in terms of hierarchical structure, listing acceptable orders for abstract elements that are themselves composed of smaller elements. For instance "Brian and Jeff", "The boy with ginger hair", "The girl whose mother is over there", and "Sharon" all have something in common, in that they correspond to the entity that carries out the action specified by the verb. Our intuition is that these all behave in a similar fashion, even though the form of words varies from a single proper noun to a whole phrase which contains another verb.

TABLE 5.4

Statement	*Question*	*Negative*
Brian and Jeff might want to come.	Might Brian and Jeff want to come?	Brian and Jeff might not want to come.
The boy with ginger hair was finishing his paper.	Was the boy with ginger hair finishing his paper?	The boy with ginger hair wasn't finishing his paper.
The boy with ginger hair has been finishing his paper.	Has the boy with ginger hair been finishing his paper?	The boy with ginger hair hasn't been finishing his paper.
The girl whose mother is over there wants some tea.	Does the girl whose mother is over there want some tea?	The girl whose mother is over there doesn't want any tea.
Sharon could have asked Pete to help her.	Could Sharon have asked Pete to help her?	Sharon couldn't have asked Pete to help her.

---

approach, strikes many people as decidedly odd. However, all that one is really claiming is that when confronted with language input, the brain is pre-wired to derive a special class of mental representations from the input. We know that in other cognitive domains such specialisation exists; for instance, newborn infants show an orienting response to faces, preferring them to other similar

Thematic roles and argument structure

Certain words, most notably verbs and prepositions, express relations between other sentence elements, and furthermore they require that appropriate elements are present in a sentence in order for it to be grammatical.

For instance, the verb "put" requires a subject, an object, and a prepositional phrase, and omission of any of these will render a sentence containing this verb ungrammatical (denoted *):

*John puts
*puts the book
*John puts the book
*John puts on the table
*puts the book on the table
John puts the book on the table

Other verbs, such as "eat", may have optional requirements; a subject is essential, but an object is not:

Jason eats
Jason eats the avocado
*eats the avocado

Elements such as subject, object, etc. are referred to as arguments and the grammatical requirements of a word for a subject, object, or other element are its argument structure. The item that the argument structure is associated with (in these examples the verb), is the predicate. According to current linguistic theory, argument structure is specified as part of a word's lexical entry. This is a different view from earlier notions that treated syntax and lexicon separately; the grammaticality of a sentence depends not just on whether particular elements occur in a

certain order, but also on whether the verb's obligatory arguments are present.

Here is one way of formally representing argument structure, where the placement of the lexical item in relation to other elements is shown by a line:

eat: NP_1 __ (NP_2)

NP_1 denotes the subject (e.g. "Jason" in the previous example), and NP_2 denotes the object (e.g. "the avocado"). The fact that the verb takes an optional subject is shown by the placement of NP_2 in brackets.

The verb "put" requires both an object (NP_2) and a prepositional phrase (PP) denoting the location. The argument structure is therefore:

put: NP_1 __ NP_2 PP

Associated with each argument is a thematic role (or theta role). This specifies the type of meaning relation that obtains between the argument and the predicate. Here are some examples of thematic roles (for a fuller account, see Parsons, 1995):

agent: instigator of an action
theme: object asserted to have a particular
            location or change in location
location: where the theme is
source: where theme is moving from
goal: where theme is moving to

As well as specifying the types of arguments a predicate takes, the lexical entry also specifies the mapping between arguments and thematic roles. Thus for the verb "put", NP_1 corresponds to an agent, NP_2 to the theme, and PP to the goal.

stimuli, thereby demonstrating some innate knowledge of the structure of faces (Morton & Johnson, 1991). What makes an innate grammar a particularly peculiar idea is the fact that innate knowledge must be general enough to account for acquisition of Italian, Japanese, Turkish, Malay, as well as sign language acquisition by congenitally deaf children (see e.g. Poizner, Klima, & Bellugi, 1987). Thus, the Chomskyan position is that humans have an innate brain system that contains knowledge that is extremely abstract, not a function of simple perceptual properties, not tied to any one modality, and highly specialised just for language learning. It is

this combination of characteristics that make the innateness claims quite remarkable, with no obvious parallel in any other domain of cognition.

Until the 1970s, the study of how children learn grammar was almost exclusively concerned with the English language, but the arguments for an innate grammar forced developmental psycholinguists to adopt a wider frame of reference, and to do cross-linguistic studies to identify the general structural features that are shared by all human languages, i.e. Universal Grammar. In contemporary grammatical theory, the quest is to define principles that are sufficiently abstract to apply to

Learnability

In formal linguistics, the task of language learning is seen as somewhat akin to the problem confronting a rat, pigeon, or child participating in the kind of concept learning experiment that was much beloved of experimental psychologists around the 1960s. Just as language learning involves abstracting underlying rules that distinguish grammatical from ungrammatical sentences, so concept learning involves identifying the rule that distinguishes "positive" (rewarded) instances from "negative" ones. Suppose the exemplars consist of patterns such as those shown in Fig 5.2.

The experimenter presents you with the task of deducing the rule that has been used to generate these five stimuli. If you try to do this, you will find that the task is made difficult by the fact that you have been shown only positive instances. There are many possible rules that could have generated this set, and no way of choosing between them, e.g.:

rule A: take two or three shapes, each inside the other, with any shading

rule B: take any number of shapes, each inside the other, with the constraint that exactly one of the shapes must be unshaded.

rule C: select two or three shapes with these constraints: if the outermost shape is a circle, the innermost one must be a lozenge; if the outermost is a lozenge, the innermost must be a triangle; if the outermost is a triangle, the innermost must be a circle.

Now, suppose that the task is altered, and the experimenter shows you a random sequence of patterns, including both the positive exemplars shown in Fig. 5.2, and others, as in the array in Fig. 5.3, all of which are labelled as negative cases.

Although the rule is still not easy to work out, the existence of the negative exemplars makes an enormous difference to the task, because it allows one rapidly to rule out certain hypotheses. Rule A and rule C would generate the first negative exemplar. Rule B seems more promising, as it would correctly reject the first three negative examples. However, it is rejected when we come to the fourth negative exemplar, which fits rule B but is nevertheless wrong.

The actual rule which was used to generate the positive set was: rule D: take two or three shapes, each within the other, with the constraint that adjacent shapes must differ in terms of both shading and shape.

Once we have formulated a rule, we are in a position to generate new instances of the category that we have not seen before. After exposure to a small set of positive and negative exemplars, we may hit on a rule which is only partially correct, e.g. rule E: take two or three shapes, each within the other, with the constraint that adjacent shapes must differ in terms of shading.

If we generate new instances using such a rule, then we will make some mistakes, but we will do much better than if we were simply guessing, and a high proportion of the patterns that we generate will be correct positive instances.

Of course, there is an alternative way of approaching this task, and that is to learn by rote each instance of a correct figure. However, this would impose an immense load on memory, and it would not allow us to generate new instances of patterns that obeyed the rule but which we had not been trained on.

What, you might be asking, has this to do with language learning? The answer is that, according to those working in the area of linguistics known as Learnability Theory, the concept formation task can be seen as providing several parallels with the process of acquiring a grammar. First, the process of learning a

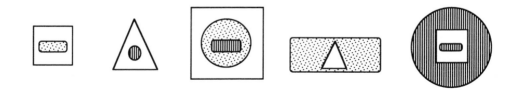

FIG. 5.2   Positive instances: Patterns that agree with the rule.

Learnability (continued)

language is seen as analogous to the concept learning task in that what one is trying to do is to work out an underlying rule system that generates exemplars—in this case sentences rather than patterns. Learning is seen as involving generation and testing of hypotheses in relation to incoming evidence. However, instead of being presented with the more tractable task of discovering the rules from both positive and negative examples, the child who is learning language is typically given only positive evidence. That is to say, parents seldom correct their child's ungrammatical utterances, and they certainly do not deliberately teach grammar by overt contrasts between grammatical and ungrammatical forms (Grimshaw & Pinker, 1989). So the child has the logical problem of trying to learn grammar from a set of positive instances that could have been generated by many different rules. A very general rule (e.g. rule A) will fit positive exemplars that were in fact generated by a more specific rule (e.g. rule D), but the child has no way of telling which is correct. And, just as in the concept formation task, rote learning is not a solution, because it cannot explain the child's ability to produce novel grammatical utterances.

It must be stressed that the analogy between concept formation and issues of language learnability is far from perfect. Learnability theory is a highly technical area where formal logic is used to analyse the conditions under which different types of rules could be learned on the basis of a particular type of input. However, the analogy is useful in illustrating the point that when trying to uncover underlying structure on the basis of a set of examples, one can never be 100%

certain that the correct rule has been deduced if one is exposed only to positive instances.

To continue the analogy a little further, suppose that the person doing the concept formation task is told at the outset to focus on the differences between adjacent shapes within a pattern. This single piece of information will make the learning task very much easier. Similarly, advocates of Chomskyan theory argue that the task of learning the structure of a grammar on the basis of positive information will be made tractable if, and only if, the learner approaches the task with some knowledge of what types of information will be relevant in defining grammatical rules. When linguists talk of innate grammatical knowledge, this is what they mean: the child comes to the learning task with some prior information that constrains the types of rules that will be hypothesised. For a more detailed account of Learnability Theory, see Atkinson (1992).

Although this theoretical analysis of language learning has been highly influential, it is under increasing attack from theories that make different assumptions about the nature of the language-learning task. In particular, if one regards learning as involving probabilistic convergence on a solution rather than inductive hypothesis-testing, then the traditional Learnability analysis is not appropriate, and learning from positive instances does become feasible under certain conditions. In a later section, we will consider connectionist approaches to language learning, which adopt a probabilistic approach (see *Connectionism*, p.132).

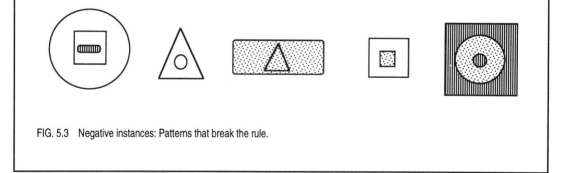

FIG. 5.3   Negative instances: Patterns that break the rule.

all the world's grammars. One approach that was originated by Chomsky (1981) is referred to as Government and Binding theory, or Principles and Parameters theory. In this theory, grammar is decomposed into several subsystems, each of

which contains a set of principles. This area evolves so rapidly that any account is soon out of date. However, one component is introduced in *X-bar syntax*, overleaf, to give the reader the flavour of this approach.

X-bar syntax

For many years, attempts to write grammars consisted of rules for a given language, that specified how elements such as noun phrases (NP), verb phrases (VP), adjective phrases (AP), or prepositional phrases (PP) could be formed, manipulated, and combined. As pressures grew to develop more general rules that would be applicable to all languages, much more abstract formalisms were developed, of which X-bar syntax is one of the best-known.

X-bar syntax proposes that all phrases can be regarded as having the same basic hierarchical structure, as shown in Fig. 5.4:

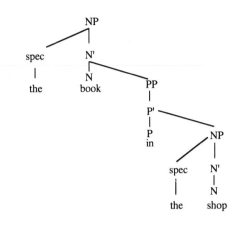

FIG. 5.5

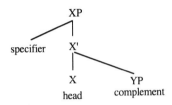

FIG. 5.4

What this means is that any phrase can be decomposed into three basic elements: a specifier (spec), a head (X), and a complement (YP). Only the head is obligatory. The complement, if present, has the same X-bar structure. For the basic phrase types of NP, VP, AP, and PP, the head corresponds to a lexical item, whose grammatical class determines the phrase type. Thus a NP has a noun as its head, a VP has a verb as its head, and so on.

Let us illustrate the framework with an example. The tree in Fig. 5.5 shows the structure of the NP "the book in the shop". In this phrase, the X-bar structure is repeated three times, because there are three embedded phrases. The lowest level is the NP "the shop", which has just a specifier and head. This is combined with "in" to form a PP, "in the shop", with "the shop" as its complement and the preposition "in" as its head. This PP does not have a specifier. Combining the PP with the "the book" we get the entire NP "the book in the shop".

You may wonder why each phrase contains two points where branching can occur: a topmost level, from which the specifier branches, and the X' level, from which the complement branches. It would seem simpler to have a single topmost node, with specifier, head and complement all branching from this, e.g. as in Fig. 5.6.

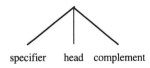

FIG. 5.6

The reason for adopting the more complex X' structure with two binary branches is that it allows us to depict hierarchical relationships between sentence elements in a way that is critical when we come to specify grammatical rules such as those concerned with agreement or permissible movement of sentence elements. The relationships between a specifier and a head, between a head and a complement, and between a specifier and a complement are not equivalent, and this needs to be recognised in a syntactic representation.

An important insight was that by postulating some more abstract elements whose overt expression in the sentence was less transparent, it is possible to use the

X-bar syntax (continued)

same X-bar framework to depict the relationships between higher level sentence elements. The phrase structures considered so far have all had lexical heads; i.e. the head corresponds to a lexical item such as noun, verb, etc. By postulating the existence of functional heads, which are more abstract elements, we can treat a whole sentence as an X-bar structure, with the subject corresponding to the specifier, the verb phrase to the complement, and an abstract element INFL as the head. INFL (short for inflection) determines information about tense, person, number, aspect, and modality. In English, it will be realised as a lexical item only if the sentence contains an auxiliary or modal verb. Otherwise, it will generate an inflection that is attached to the main verb. The tree structure in Fig. 5.7 shows the underlying X-bar structure that would generate the sentence "the man might bribe the guard" or "the man bribed the guard".

This characterisation of the hierarchical structure of sentences and phrases provides a formal way of depicting relations between sentence elements which allows one to specify precisely the circumstances under which:

1. a single pronoun may be substituted for a string of words; e.g. "he will do it" for "the man might bribe the guard".
2. two expressions in a sentence can refer to the same entity; e.g. "the man" and "the guard" cannot be one and the same person.
3. features such as gender and number of one sentence element will influence expression of

other elements in the sentence. In the tree in Fig. 5.7, any inflection generated by the head INFL will agree in number with the specifier "the man". Hence we may have: "the man bribes the guard" vs. "the men bribe the guard".

4. rearrangements of the words in the sentence are possible, e.g. the following rearrangements are possible, and serve to bring the italicised elements of the sentence into focus:

    it is *the man* who will bribe the guard
    it is *the guard* that the man will bribe

X-bar syntax is regarded by its proponents as a core component of Universal Grammar, and hence this kind of underlying structure is assumed to be part of a child's innate knowledge of language. This implies, among other things, that the child's brain is set up to extract hierarchical structures from strings of words, with each node in the hierarchy having only two branches.

In more recent treatments, X-bar syntax has been developed further, with other types of functional head being proposed. Furthermore, X-bar syntax is but one element of a complex set of interlocking theories that interact with one another to constitute Universal Grammar. It is impossible to do justice to the elegance and complexity of contemporary syntactic theory in this brief treatment. For an accessible introduction to this kind of theorising, see Cook (1988); for a fuller treatment see Haegeman (1994) and Radford (1988).

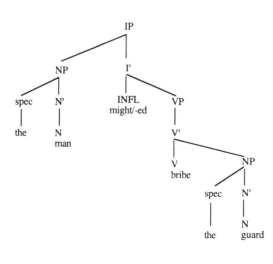

FIG. 5.7

Linguists face the challenge of not only specifying the characteristics of Universal Grammar, but also explaining how the child learns to relate this abstract innate knowledge to the specific language being learned. It has been proposed that children's innate knowledge specifies parameters on which languages might vary, and that language acquisition involves working out from the ambient language which settings of parameters apply. For example, word order varies from one language to another: SVO is the canonical word order for English, and SOV for Japanese. This difference is also seen in the structure of phrases, where complements follow heads in English, but precede them in Japanese. We can economically summarise differences between the two languages by postulating a Head-Direction parameter, which is set to head-first for English and head-last for Japanese. It is further proposed that each parameter has a default setting which is assumed to apply unless evidence to the contrary is obtained.

There are so many differences between languages that the amount of information contained in Universal Grammar would be enormous if every dimension of variation corresponded to one parameter. When

parameter setting theory was first formulated, it was thought that it would be possible to specify parameters that could determine several different properties of the language simultaneously. *Parameter setting: An example*, below, gives an illustrative example, the "Pro-drop" parameter. However, the original parameters that were proposed as part of Universal Grammar have been challenged by counterexamples. For instance, some languages, such as Chinese, do not behave in accordance with the Pro-drop parameter. Those wishing to retain parameter setting theory have been forced to specify new parameters which are much more ad hoc and inelegant (see Atkinson, 1992, ch. 4).

NONMODULAR ACCOUNTS OF GRAMMATICAL DEVELOPMENT

In recent years, a number of questions have been raised about the hypothesis of an innate Universal Grammar, and the account of language learning as a process of parameter setting has been questioned.

Parameter setting: An example

Compare:

English	Italian
it is raining	piove
	(rains)
it is very beautiful	e bellissimo
	(is very beautiful)
I go to London	vado a Londra
	(go to London)

In English, the subject of a verb must always be expressed, so much so that an "empty" pronoun will be placed in subject position if there is nothing else to fill it.* In Italian, however, the subject is typically omitted unless it is needed for emphasis or contrast. When we look across languages, we find that those like Italian that have optional subjects usually also have richly elaborated verb inflectional systems, with the inflection indicating features such as person, number, and gender as well as tense. There is therefore little

ambiguity even if the subject is not present. In a language such as English, where the verb inflectional system is not well elaborated, omission of the subject could lead to ambiguity (e.g. "go to London" could have as its subject "I", "you", "we", or "they"). Hyams (1986) applied Parameter Setting theory to such phenomena, proposing that optionality of subject and richness of verb inflectional system are treated together as aspects of a single parameter, known as "Pro-drop". She suggested that young children learning English start with the parameter setting appropriate for Italian, and hence they freely omit subjects. Once the correct setting of the parameter is triggered by exposure to appropriate input, the child ceases to omit obligatory subjects, and at the same time related phenomena are observed, such as the use of modal auxiliary verbs.

*The subject can be omitted in cases of ellipsis, where it is recoverable from a prior utterance, e.g. no subject is present in B's utterance because it can be deduced from A's prior question. A: What is the boy doing? B: Reading a paper.

Challenge 1: The Chomskyan account ignores nonsyntactic sources of information in acquisition of grammatical competence

In *Learnability* (p.124), an analogy was drawn between concept learning and discovery of grammatical rules; this reflects the view of language learning as a process of discovering the principles that determine what is a legal sequence of morphemes. Bates and MacWhinney (1989) are among those who have vociferously challenged this view, arguing that learning of grammar is better conceptualised as a process of mapping between two domains, form and function. For instance, in learning how word order is used in a language, the child can apply knowledge of basic concepts such as actor and acted-upon. A given language will tend to express these semantic notions in a regular way, by word order and/or grammatical morphology, and the child can therefore use knowledge of semantic relationships to learn how to express grammatical notions such as subject and object.

Those defending the Chomskyan position reply to this argument with evidence that even young children show awareness of grammatical principles that are entirely arbitrary and have no significance with regard to meaning. We have discussed grammatical morphemes such as plural "-s" or past tense "-ed" which do affect meaning, but there are many cases of morphemes which have no specific interpretation. For instance, the difference between "he go there" and "he goes there" is not a difference in meaning; rather it is simply a difference in well-formedness, with the morphological variants between go/goes serving to signal the structural relationships between sentence elements. This line of reasoning has its roots in Chomsky's famous example "colourless green ideas sleep furiously" which we can identify as a well-formed, though nonsensical sentence, in contrast to "ideas green furiously colourless sleep", which is ill-formed. Because we can recognise abstract structural patterns as grammatically well-formed, regardless of whether they make sense, it is argued that the processing of meaning is independent from the processing of abstract syntactic representations.

To Bates and MacWhinney (1989) this is a misguided conclusion that arises from treating the role of meaning in learning grammar as an either/or question; either children do make use of meaning, or they don't. Bates and MacWhinney reject this analysis, arguing that there are many different cues that are used in learning form-function mappings, of which meaning is a particularly useful and salient one. Certainly language learning also involves "distributional learning", i.e. recognition of sequential patterns among categories in language input. But meaning provides additional information that facilitates such learning. In short, they argue that because children learn some syntactic facts that are unrelated to meaning, this does not entail that meaning is processed quite independently from syntax.

Another body of work has emphasised the important cues to syntax learning that are provided by stress, timing, and intonation, i.e. prosody. Morgan, Meier, and Newport (1987) have made a strong case that prosodic cues facilitate the learning of grammatical rules. Thus, the child's task is not simply to learn grammar from exposure to the sequential information present in correct sentences: they can use additional information provided by the grouping and stress of morphemes to identify those that form higher level units, i.e. phrases and clauses, and to distinguish the content words from grammatical "function" words and inflections.

Challenge 2: Incomplete understanding of grammar in young children

The Chomskyan account maintains that children possess a great deal of grammatical knowledge right from the outset. However, attempts to demonstrate this innate knowledge have not always been successful. For instance, Matthei (1981) studied children's ability to act out sentences such as:

the horses said that the cows jumped over each other

The interpretation of "each other" is determined by a component of Universal Grammar known as "Binding Principle A". Children aware of this principle should perform correctly on such sentences. Matthei found that children aged from four to six years often made errors in which they made both groups of animals actors, e.g. in the above example, the horses jumped over the cows and vice versa. Does such a result contradict the tenets of Universal Grammar in demonstrating that young children do not have knowledge of the Binding Principles? Atkinson (1992) argued this conclusion was premature, offering the following alternative interpretations of the result:

1. Knowledge of Binding Principles may be innate but not available; just as genetically determined biological processes such as dentition, puberty, and so on, may occur at particular points in maturation, so might the principles of Universal Grammar come onstream at specific stages of development.

2. Children may misclassify the part of speech of "each other" and so may not recognise that the Binding Principles apply to it.

3. The sentence might approach the limit of the child's parsing abilities, leading to a misrepresentation such as: "The horses and the cows jumped over each other"

4. The child might feel it is expected that the horses should do something, and "saying" is not something they can demonstrate, and so they involve the horses in the action. This would in effect be a pragmatic influence on behaviour.

Atkinson pointed out this is not an exhaustive list of possibilities. He concluded his analysis thus (p.161):

a child producing or comprehending language tokens in naturalistic or experimental environments is just one source of evidence bearing on the nature of the internalised grammar. There is no reason in principle why it should be more compelling than [the] abstract speculations [described in the previous chapter].

Cook (1988, p.56) echoed this view, pointing out that for those working in the Principles and Parameters framework, language acquisition is viewed as a logical problem that can be solved

without necessarily looking at the development of children. Although Chomsky (1980, p.80) claimed that "An innatist hypothesis is a refutable hypothesis", children's use or understanding of language is clearly not the place to look for refutation. This is because one can always invoke performance errors as a factor in children's poor comprehension; i.e. the problem is not that the child does not have the knowledge represented, but rather that limitations of memory and attention, biases to prefer particular options, or motivational factors interfere with their ability to demonstrate this knowledge. Of course, the same performance factors that lead to comprehension errors in normally developing children must also be considered when accounting for comprehension problems in children with language impairments.

Challenge 3: Learning is probabilistic, not all-or-none

The parameter-setting model of language learning implies that learning takes place in an all-or-none fashion: as Atkinson (1992, p.103) remarked: "the process of learning is (much more) deterministic, with large chunks of grammar falling into place on the basis of a single parametric decision". A parameter is either set or not, but once set there seems little opportunity for backtracking and changing a setting on the basis of new evidence. Furthermore, we have to assume that a child either knows a rule or does not; it does not seem plausible that a rule should be partly acquired, although it may seem reasonable to assume that when it is first learned the child's knowledge may be a little unsteady and uncertain. On this view, we would expect that when they first start to learn language, and the parameter is at the "default" setting, all children should look very similar in how they use and interpret syntax. Then, with exposure to the native language, ability to use particular rules should pass fairly rapidly from a state of no knowledge to a state of complete knowledge. Furthermore, when a parameter such as pro-drop is acquired, a set of related grammatical characteristics should be observed together. Yet this is not what is seen. Children show much more variability in how they use grammar than would be expected on a parameter-setting account. For instance, the same child might, in a relatively short space of time, say "break", "breaked", and "broke" in past tense contexts (Chapman et al., 1992). Many children show partial mastery of the rules of grammar, and one does not see the co-ordinated acquisition of the constellation of features corresponding to a parameter.

Challenge 4: Connectionist nets can learn rule-like behaviour with no explicit representations of rules

A fundamental tenet of Chomskyan theory has been that the regularities of language can be described in terms of a set of principles that can be formalised in terms of operations on abstract symbols. The whole of the learnability question revolves around the idea that there is no way in which grammatical regularities can be extracted from the input without some prior knowledge of the form they will take. But what if children don't learn rules? For many years this idea was not even countenanced because the alternatives seemed unworkable. However, when computer science developed to the point where it became possible to simulate human learning using connectionist networks it became clear that a network trained with an input that showed certain regularities could demonstrate apparently rule-governed behaviour without having any explicit representation of symbolic rules in its architecture (see *Connectionism*, overleaf). The specific example used in the early work, that of learning past tense verb endings (Rumelhart & McClelland, 1986), is a controversial one, with much debate centring on the question of whether a realistic simulation of children's learning can be achieved without building certain "fudges" into the simulation (see Pinker & Prince, 1988). But for many psycholinguists, the ability of this early model to simulate the detailed course of language acquisition was not the central issue; the important advance made by the connectionist modellers was that they suggested that the intractable problems faced by those trying to account for language acquisition might have arisen because they were asking the wrong question, in assuming that in the absence of innate principles, the child would be faced with an impossible task of acquiring from positive evidence a set of abstract

symbolic rules, learned by a process resembling hypothesis-testing. A connectionist network set up to learn the concept formation task shown in *Learnability* (p.124) could learn to recognise correlations between shapes, shading and position in the pattern, eventually acquiring the ability to complete a partial pattern and to sort novel patterns into positive and negative instances. The connectionist view would be that what is acquired in language learning is implicit knowledge of probabilistic relationships between sequences of grammatical elements and meanings, learned by a process that involves strengthening connections between related elements and weakening those that are unrelated. Simple networks, such as the one used by McClelland and Rumelhart for the past tense simulation, cannot learn hierarchical dependencies between linearly organised sentence elements far removed from one another, but with a relatively minor modification to network structure, grammatical regularities can be extracted (Elman, 1992). Admittedly, connectionist modellers are still a long way from developing a plausible simulation of language learning, but what is clear is that the objections that have been put forward to early learning accounts such as that proposed by Skinner (1957) do not necessarily apply to learning by a connectionist network. The Competition Model of Bates and MacWhinney (1989) provides a theoretical approach to language acquisition that rejects most of the central tenets of the Principles and Parameters approach and sits much more comfortably with a connectionist account: grammatical knowledge is not processed separately from other types of information, learning is probabilistic, and relies on general processes of pattern perception and associative learning, rather than involving a specialised module. Some linguists feel that connectionism is a storm in a teacup, and that over time we will find that it cannot resolve the difficult questions of language acquisition (Pinker & Mehler, 1988). However, the debate about symbolic vs. connectionist approaches to language-learning, if it has achieved nothing else, has highlighted the questionable nature of some of the assumptions that have been made about the nature of the learning process. The debate also has important implications for the way in which comprehension deficits in SLI are conceptualised.

Connectionism

In the 1980s there was a surge of interest in modelling processes of perception, memory, and cognition using simulated neural networks.

These networks have a number of properties that differentiate them from earlier box-and-arrow information-processing models. A simple demonstration model is shown in Fig. 5.8. This shows relationships between a layer of units that represents the input (I1 to I5) and a layer representing the output (O1 to O4). The kinds of language mapping that have been simulated this way includes mapping from written words to pronunciation (i.e. reading aloud) (Seidenberg, 1992), mapping from verb stems to past tense inflected forms (Rumelhart & McClelland, 1986), or mapping from phonetic features to words (McClelland & Elman, 1986).

The first point to note is that the representation of inputs and outputs is distributed in parallel units (hence the alternative name for connectionism: parallel distributed processing). Instead of having one unit representing each stimulus or response, each input and output is represented by a given pattern of activation across a whole array of units. If each unit has two possible states, on or off, this means that 16 different outputs can be represented by four units, and 32 inputs by five units.

A crucial feature is the pattern of interconnection between units, shown by the connecting lines. The strength of connections is not fixed, but changes as learning of input–output relationships proceeds. A positive connection strength corresponds to an excitatory connection; a negative strength to an inhibitory connection. When a set of input units is activated, activation propagates through the network, with each unit influencing those to which it is connected. One method for computing the effect on the activation of an output unit is to multiply the activation of each input unit with the strength of the connection from that unit to the output unit, and then to sum these values across all input units. The principle is the same for all networks, although more complex mathematical functions may be used.

Learning is achieved by training the system by presenting examples of input, together with a training pattern on the output layer. The actual activation produced in the output layer is compared with the training pattern, and the strengths of connections between units adjusted according to the degree of match or mismatch. With repeated presentation of such pairings, the network converges towards a stable state of interconnections that enables it to reproduce the appropriate output pattern when presented with a given input.

Provided there is some degree of structure in the input–output mappings, such a network will exhibit evidence of having learned something of the underlying structure. In particular, it will show ability to generalise to new inputs that it has not been trained on. So, for instance, a network trained on a set of stem-past tense verb mappings may output a plausible past tense form for a verb it had not been trained on (Rumelhart & McClelland, 1986). For a detailed review of connectionist modelling of developmental processes, see Elman et al. (1996).

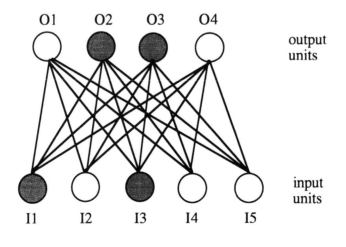

FIG. 5.8   Illustrative connectionist model for learning an input–output mapping.

MODULAR THEORIES OF GRAMMATICAL DEFICITS IN SLI

Whichever approach we adopt to explain language acquisition, we need to explain why some children fail to learn language normally. One influential view, based in the Chomskyan tradition, maintains that language acquisition depends on innate grammatical modules that are defective (or even absent) in SLI. As a consequence, it is argued, one sees very selective problems with particular components of the grammar. This is an extreme type of theory that maintains that a biological system that is crucially important for language learning is defective in children with SLI, so that their grammatical knowledge is qualitatively different from that seen in normal children. This approach has appealed to theoretical linguists, who see the study of SLI as having the potential to throw light on fundamental issues of what it is about language that is innate.

Later in this chapter, we shall contrast this theoretical perspective with a nonmodular approach which attributes grammatical problems to perceptual deficits.

The "feature-blindness" hypothesis

In 1990, Gopnik published an account of a fascinating three-generation family, of which about half the members were affected by a severe form of SLI. One reason why this family was of particular interest to linguists was because their impairment appeared to be genetic, with a family pedigree compatible with a dominant pattern of inheritance (Hurst, Baraitser, Auger, Graham, & Norell, 1990) (see Fig. 5.9, below). Given that innate Principles and Parameters are postulated, it was tempting to propose that these individuals lacked part of this genetic endowment.

In early accounts of the family, Gopnik proposed just such a theory, affecting one component of the grammar. She reported striking deficits in the ability of affected individuals to mark features such as number, gender, animacy, mass/count, proper nouns vs. common names, tense, and aspect. These features are usually marked by inflectional endings and they also constrain the form of other items in the sentence. Thus, in English a plural noun is marked by a plural morpheme (/s/, /z/, or /ɪz/, depending on the phonological form of the word), and this also constrains the form of the verb of which it is subject, and the form of preceding determiners

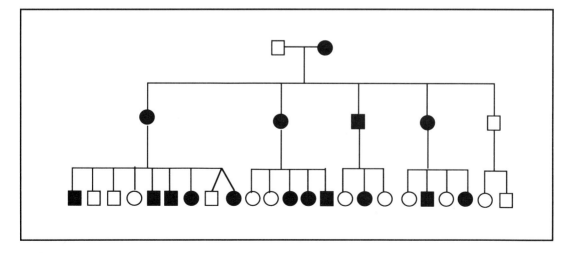

FIG. 5.9 Pedigree of family studied by Hurst et al. (1990), Gopnik (1990), and Vargha-Khadem et al. (1995). Females denoted by circles, and males by squares. Filled symbols are affected individuals. Around 50% of offspring of affected individuals are affected, consistent with a dominant pattern of inheritance.

(*the*, *some*, or *two* would be permissible, whereas *a*, *one*, or *this* would not). Extracts from notebooks kept by some of the family members illustrate their problems with features such as number ("All the children got present"), aspect ("Carol is cry in the church"), and proper names ("A Patrick is naughty"). To investigate mastery of the plural feature, Gopnik administered an experimental task in which the tester presented a nonsense creature and said, for example, "this is a zoop". The testee was then shown several such creatures and asked: "These are ——?" She found that people with SLI were poor at this task and did not appear to have an internalised, unconscious set of rules for forming plurals. Another test was used to assess ability to use tense features. The format was that a sentence was presented in one tense, and the testee then prompted to produce an analogous sentence in a different tense. For example, the tester would say "Every day the man walks eight miles. Yesterday he ——(walked eight miles)". The individuals with SLI gave semantically relevant answers but seldom made appropriate changes to verb tense. They also had difficulty with a related test in which sentences were given to elicit similar forms with different morphological endings, e.g. "There is a lot of sun. It is very —— (sunny)".

Of course, if a person lacks grammatical features in underlying representations, there should be problems not just in producing grammatical inflections, but in understanding their significance. In another test, Gopnik (1994a) used a grammaticality judgement task (see *Grammaticality judgement tasks*, opposite). Family members with SLI could judge as correct those sentences that were correct. However, they tended also to accept as correct sentences that had errors in feature-marking, and if they did detect the error they had difficulty in correcting it.

However, a different type of comprehension test yielded findings that were problematic for the theory: affected individuals showed good understanding for some items on a task testing understanding of inflectional endings, and were able, for instance, reliably to select the picture of several books (rather than a single book) when asked "point to the books". Gopnik accounted for this by suggesting that a word like "books" might

be rote-learned to refer to a group of objects. Just as the young child might learn "cornflakes" without realising this is the plural of "cornflake", so the child with SLI might learn a wide range of plural or other inflected forms, without appreciating their morphological composition. Unfortunately, a critical test of this hypothesis, i.e. checking whether the affected individuals could understand the plural "-s" in a nonsense word context (e.g. "show me the zoops") was not conducted. Subsequent studies, however, have led to the abandonment of the "feature blindness" hypothesis as too extreme an account of the impairment in SLI. Rather than supposing that such children have no representation of grammatical features in the grammar, Gopnik and her colleagues proposed a new hypothesis, that their problem is with the rule-based nature of learning that is involved in building morphological paradigms.

Rule learning in morphological paradigms

Gopnik and Crago (1991) proposed that the problem for children with SLI is that, in effect, they approach the language-learning task as if all words were irregular. The child with SLI is aware of the grammatical features that need to be marked, but does not realise that the appropriate marking for a specific word can usually be derived by rule, rather than rote-learned. In the earlier section on paradigm building we considered Pinker's (1984) proposal that, in normal development, children initially place each inflected form in a word-specific paradigm, but then come to recognise the regularities in inflectional morphology, creating a differentiation in the lexicon between the storage of regular and irregular forms. In contrast to connectionist modellers (e.g. Plunkett & Marchman, 1993), who maintain that a single system can account for knowledge of regular and irregular forms, Pinker (1991) argued that different processes are implicated in producing a regularly inflected word, which involves assembling the word from stem and inflection, and in producing an irregularly inflected form, which is retrieved directly from long-term memory. If, as proposed by Gopnik and Crago, the child with SLI lacks the specialised system for learning morphological rules, then this differentiation between regular and

Grammaticality judgement tasks

Most receptive language tasks require a person to interpret spoken language, e.g. by obeying a command, acting out an instruction, or selecting a picture from an array of possibilities. The grammaticality judgement task measures a different aspect of receptive language knowledge, the ability to detect well-formedness. The testee is presented with a set of sentences, some of which contain grammatical errors, and the task is to say whether or not the sentence is acceptable. If the sentence is judged unacceptable, then the testee is asked to correct it.

Sample items from a test used by Gopnik (1994a) are shown here:

2a) Bill was expecting his phone to ring at any moment.
Still, when it ringed he was surprised.
Still, when it ring he was surprised.
Still, when it rang he was surprised.

2b) When your eyeglasses get dirty you have to wipe them.
Yesterday when my eyeglasses got dirty, I wipe them.
Yesterday when my eyeglasses got dirty, I wope them.
Yesterday when my eyeglasses got dirty, I wiped them.

For each option, the testee is asked to rate, on a seven-point scale, whether the completion is unnatural or natural-sounding.

Grammaticality judgement tasks are useful for assessing a person's knowledge of grammatical contrasts that do not affect meaning, and so are not amenable to conventional comprehension testing, e.g. the difference between "him saw that" and "he saw that". They can help specify the locus of a grammatical

deficit: for instance, if a child who has problems producing specific grammatical morphemes also has difficulty in distinguishing the accuracy of sentences which do and do not contain correctly inflected forms, this is good evidence that the problem is not simply that the child has a phonological problem that makes it hard to say the morpheme. The contrast between grammaticality judgement and comprehension test performance can also be useful: many adults with acquired agrammatic aphasia are surprisingly good at grammaticality judgements, despite very poor comprehension of grammatically complex sentences (Linebarger, Schwartz, & Saffran, 1983): this has been taken as evidence that they are able to perform an adequate on-line parse of incoming sentences, but have problems mapping the grammatical representation on to a semantic form. (However, alternative interpretations are possible: see e.g. Mauner, Fromkin, & Cornell, 1993).

Because the overwhelming proportion of errors on this kind of task involve accepting an ill-formed sentence (rather than rejecting a well-formed one), one needs to be careful in interpreting data from children, who may have a response bias to say "yes", perhaps because they are reluctant to judge something that an adult has said as "wrong". One way of reducing this kind of bias is to present the test sentences via a puppet "who sometimes says things wrong", and needs correcting (e.g. Kamhi & Catts, 1986). In addition, it is useful to include control sentences with semantic anomalies (e.g. "the dog writes the food"); if the child is willing to reject these, then this provides evidence against a global response bias (Liles, Shulman, & Bartlett, 1977). Signal detection analysis (McNicol, 1972) provides a method for combining data from "yes" and "no" responses to establish if the child can discriminate well-formed from ill-formed utterances at above chance level.

---

irregular inflected forms will not be made; both will be learned by associative processes. This will have two consequences. First, it means that inflected forms will take up far more space in long-term memory, because a great deal of redundant information will be stored. This is likely to make word retrieval more difficult. Second, it follows that these children will not be able to use inflections spontaneously and creatively, although they will be able to produce and understand those

that have been rote-learned and which have a lexical representation.

However, as with the original "feature blindness" account, any theory that maintains that children with SLI are completely deficient in building morphological paradigms is hard to sustain. Leonard, Bortolini et al. (1992) noted that children with SLI, like normally developing children, sometimes made over-regularisation errors, producing forms such as "comed" or "goed", which provide evidence of rule application. Furthermore, there have been several experimental demonstrations that children with language impairments show some ability to generalise a novel bound morpheme to new vocabulary (Bellaire, Plante, & Swisher, 1994; Connell & Stone, 1992). In addition, studies have demonstrated that children with SLI are impaired at producing irregular as well as regular inflections (Bishop, 1994a; Ullman & Gopnik, 1994). Furthermore, some regular morphemes, such as plural "-s", are much easier for children with SLI than others, such as past tense "-ed". Vargha-Khadem et al. (1995) assessed the same family as had been studied by Gopnik and colleagues, and reported that they made over-regularisation errors and had difficulties with irregular inflections.

In response to such findings, research on SLI has moved in several directions. As will be discussed in a later section, some researchers have rejected altogether the notion of an impaired language module. However, others have continued to pursue this line of explanation. On the one hand, Gopnik's team at McGill University have pushed the rule-abstraction hypothesis to the limit, noting the importance of looking at the data in detail, and arguing that use of compensatory strategies, especially by older individuals, may cloud the picture. For instance, Goad and Rebellati (1994) noted that the apparently correct use of noun plural inflections seemed to be achieved in some cases by the explicit application of the taught rule: "add -s to form a plural". Not only did this lead to slow and effortful production, but detailed phonetic analysis showed that the apparently correct plural "-s" forms produced by language-impaired individuals lacked voicing assimilation; for instance, when asked for the plural of "wug", the response was /wʌgs/ rather than /wʌgz/ (see *Phonological influences on inflectional endings*, opposite). Gopnik (1994a) further argued that individuals with SLI appeared to treat past tense marking on a verb as a semantic means of referring to an earlier point in time, rather than as a syntactic feature. On this view, an "-ed" marker on a verb expresses a similar meaning as terms such as "yesterday" or "then". Most critically, if a sentence does include

such temporal adverbs, then there is no semantic motivation for using the past tense; for the person with SLI, a sentence such as "then the branch fall off" is acceptable, because the past time is expressed by the adverbial "then"; there would be more reason to use the past tense "fell" if the adverbial were omitted. The point stressed by these researchers is that correct performance on a language test need not necessarily reflect true competence in underlying ability. Grammatical morphemes might be used without appreciation of their syntactic significance, either as semantic markers, or applied consciously after explicit instruction in their use.

Others working in the tradition of formal linguistics have argued for different kinds of specific modular language deficits in SLI. Although distinct aspects of syntax are emphasised by different researchers, and their hypotheses have different levels of generality, the work reviewed in the next three sections, focusing on marking of grammatical agreement, appreciation of hierarchical structure, and representation of dependent relationships, all have in common the idea that what is defective in SLI is the ability to compute or represent grammatical relationships between elements.

Marking of agreement in SLI

Clahsen (1989) studied grammatical errors produced by German children with SLI and found that they were not impaired on all aspects of grammatical morphology and showed some evidence of forming morphological paradigms. However, they did have undue difficulty using inflectional endings that marked grammatical agreement. Thus gender and number agreement in the noun phrase were often in error, and subject–verb agreement and use of case markers for accusative, genitive, and dative caused great difficulty. Verbs were restricted largely to uninflected stem forms, infinitive forms, and those suffixed with "-t". However, some kinds of verb morphology (e.g. rules for participles) were unimpaired. Clahsen, Rothweiler, Woest, and Marcus (1992) went on to show that German children with SLI had good control of noun plural morphology, and made errors of

Phonological influences on inflectional endings

Most people would agree that the general rule for forming plurals in English is to add -s, and the rule for forming a past tense from a verb stem is to add -ed. However, although the inflections are typically written this way, they will be produced differently, depending on the phonological context. After a vowel or voiced consonant, the plural will involve adding /z/ rather than /s/, and after a sibilant (/s/, /z/, /ʃ/, /ʒ/, /tʃ/, /dʒ/), the plural is /ɪz/. Thus, we have:

+s+	z	+ɪz
cats	dogs	horses
minutes	hours	ages

Similarly, the past tense inflection is pronounced as /t/ after an unvoiced consonant, as /d/ after a voiced consonant or vowel, and as /ɪd/ after /t/ or /d/.

+t	+d	+ɪd
ripped	begged	loaded
kissed	buzzed	tilted

Instead of having three different rules for plural or past tense formation, each corresponding to one of these forms, these patterns can be captured by specifying a single rule that states that a voiced inflection is attached to a word ending in a voiced sound, and unvoiced inflection is added to a word ending in an unvoiced sound, except that an unstressed vowel is inserted if the inflection would otherwise merge with a preceding consonant. This is a good illustration of a rule that speakers of English automatically observe without being aware that they are doing so.

The fact that the form of an inflection is determined by the phonological environment suggests that the grammatical system specifies an abstract representation of the inflection, which is then automatically converted to a phonological form at the speech output stage, using phonological rules to take the context into account.

over-regularisation, indicating that they had formed productive morphological paradigms. Further striking evidence of intactness of at least some aspects of morphosyntax came from studies by Leonard and his colleagues (Leonard, Sabbadini, Leonard, & Volterra, 1987), showing that Italian children with SLI who are learning a language with a particularly complex morphology, seem to have rather less difficulty with morphosyntax than those learning English.

This has led to the proposal that the principal problem for these children is not in learning morphological paradigms, but rather in computing agreement between sentence constituents and so recognising when it is appropriate to use those morphemes that mark agreement (see also Ullman & Gopnik, 1994, for a related proposal). For instance, whether one says "the girl drinks" or "the girl and boy drink" depends on the relationship between the noun phrase and the verb, which must agree in number. On the other hand, whether one says "girl" or "girls" is simply a function of the number of people being referred to, and no agreement between sentence elements is encoded in this inflection. This kind of theory can thus explain why, in English, plural marking on nouns is relatively intact in SLI, whereas number marking on the verb is not (e.g. Bishop, 1994a). However, the data by Leonard et al. (1987), demonstrating adequate marking of agreement in Italian-speaking children with SLI, is less easy to accommodate.

Failure to extract hierarchical structure

If children with SLI have problems marking agreement, could this be part of a more pervasive problem in representing relationships between sequentially presented items? As was demonstrated in *X-bar syntax*, (pp.126–127), a core feature of language is its underlying hierarchical structure. If we want to understand relationships between sentence elements, we cannot depict them in a linear string; we have to have a method for depicting nested relationships. Failure to extract hierarchical structure from a linear input would lead to numerous problems in language learning. If one tried simply to associate each word with the next, then there would be difficulties in appreciating relationships between sentence elements, and the kinds of errors of grammatical morphology and marking of agreement described previously would follow as consequences.

This kind of explanation was considered by Cromer (1978), and it implies that there is a far more pervasive problem than the difficulty in marking agreement that Clahsen and colleagues had proposed.

Cromer's position is sometimes described as a general nonlinguistic account of SLI, but this was not really the case. His view was that extraction of hierarchical structure was what the innate language-learning system might be specialised for, but he argued that defects in this system might be evident in other domains (Cromer, 1983). In fact, the notion of nonverbal deficits in processing hierarchically organised material has not been substantiated (Kamhi, Ward, & Mills, 1995). Nevertheless, there is plentiful evidence that hierarchical aspects of language processing give children with SLI particular difficulty.

An early piece of evidence was provided by Cromer (1978), who gathered samples of written story descriptions from children with receptive language disorders and concluded that they were restricted to simple sentence patterns that could be interpreted in terms of sequential dependencies (see Table 5.5, below). Note that, in contrast with the individuals described by Gopnik and Crago (1991), the problems of these children extended beyond grammatical morphology; for instance, they appear to have problems with verb argument structure.

A clear prediction from Cromer's account is that children with SLI should have selective impairments in understanding sentences whose interpretation depends on appreciation of hierarchical structure. Early evidence for such problems was obtained by Bishop (1979), who used a multiple choice picture-pointing task to compare children's ability to understand different kinds of constructions. Children with SLI, like normally developing children, scored near ceiling levels on items which simply involved remembering and integrating the meanings of up to four content words, such as that shown in Fig. 5.10.

However, they showed much poorer performance on items where grammar was used to signal contrasts in meaning, by function words, inflections or word order. Their greatest difficulty was with potentially reversible sentences, such as that shown in Fig. 5.11. On these items, children with SLI did more poorly even than younger normally developing children who were matched on level of receptive vocabulary.

Bishop (1982), went on to show that children with severe receptive SLI often misinterpreted passives such as "the boy is chased by the dog" as having subject–verb–object structure (boy chase dog), even if the sentence was presented in written form, so the child did not have to remember the words. Even more striking were the errors that these children made on sentences with postmodified subjects, such as that shown in Fig. 5.12 (p.140).

All items had the structure "The X in/on/under/behind the Y is Z", where X and Y were nouns and Z a colour term. Understanding of all nouns and colours was first established in a pre-test. Unlike normal young children, children with receptive language disorders tended to attach the adjective, Z, to the nearest noun, Y. Thus for the item in Fig. 5.12, they would select the top right-hand picture rather than the correct picture, that in the bottom right-hand corner. Bishop argued that if the problem was in remembering sentence elements, one might find a mixture of correct and incorrect responses, rather than what was observed

---

TABLE 5.5

Example of Story Description by a Child with a Receptive Language Disorder from a Study by Cromer (1978)

The child is describing a story which was acted out with puppets. The names of the principal characters (a wolf, a monkey, a duck) were written on the blackboard as the characters were introduced.

The wolf is taking his table tennis ball. He is putting in the tube. The monkey is bitting the wolf's ear.

The wolf is running the monkey. The duck is taking round the tube. The ball is in the basket. The wolf is saying oh gone the ball. Again the wolf is taking his table tennis ball in the tube. The monkey is bitting the wolf's ear. The wolf is chasing him. The duck is saying oh again ball in the tube. The duck is bitting the duck's ear.

FIG. 5.10   Item from the Word Combinations section of Bishop's (1979) comprehension test: "the spotty cat sits under the tree". Note that to select the correct answer, all that is required is that the child finds the picture showing the combination of content words: spotty, sit, and tree. Success does not depend on the ability to process word order or inflectional morphology.

which was a systematic tendency to misinterpret these sentences, suggesting the wrong underlying structure was assigned, e.g. "the chicken is on the ball: the ball is black". Furthermore, it was found that this tendency was not restricted to auditory presentation but was even more marked when the

test was given using written presentation, where the child did not have to remember the words, and where correct perception of the sentence could be verified by having the child read it aloud.

This study, then, seemed to provide strong support for the notion that children with SLI had

FIG. 5.11   Item from the Word Order section of Bishop's (1979) comprehension test: "the bcy is pushed by the cow".

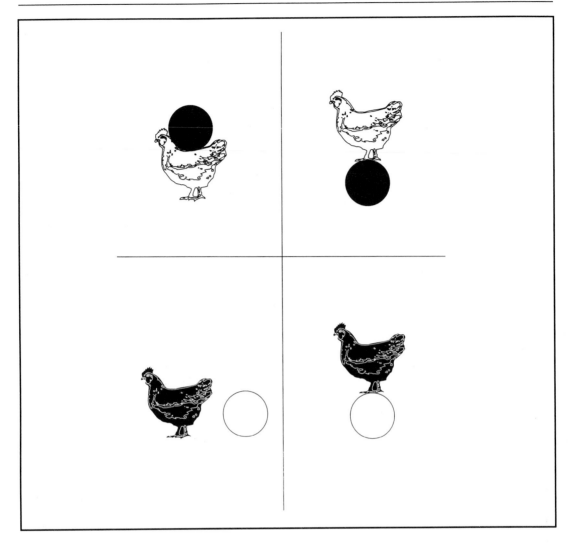

FIG. 5.12   Item from the study by Bishop (1982): "the chicken on the ball is black".

difficulty in forming a representation of hierarchical syntactic structure. However, a note of caution should be sounded. The most striking difficulties in understanding complex sentences seen in the Bishop (1982) study were found in only a minority of children with unusually severe receptive disorders, some of whom had a regressive language disorder that suggested an underlying epileptic etiology, and all of whom conformed to Rapin and Allen's (1987) description of "verbal auditory agnosia". Other children in the study had less severe language difficulties, and although they made errors with the postmodified sentences of the kind shown in Fig. 5.12, their performance was better than chance level. Second, although these results supported Cromer's account as a description of the comprehension problems of children with SLI, one may take issue with the interpretation of these results as evidence for impairment of an innate language-processing module. An alternative, nonlinguistic account of the origin of these difficulties will be considered more fully in a later section (pp.149–153).

Representational deficit for dependent relationships

Particularly detailed studies of grammatical aspects of sentence comprehension have been carried out by Van der Lely and her colleagues, who proposed that there is a subset of children with SLI who have a representational deficit for dependent relationships. This notion is closely allied to Cromer's position, though more fully specified.

The claim is that children have difficulty in using and understanding sentence elements that mark syntactic dependencies. Like Clahsen's (1989) account, this hypothesis predicts deficits in marking subject–verb agreement, but it also predicts more widespread syntactic problems. For instance, marking of pronoun case (e.g. in English, the contrast between he vs. him) should be impaired, because this depends on the syntactic relationship between a noun phrase and the verb phrase.

One might wonder how such a theory explains errors of verb tense, which might seem simply to refer to time of occurrence of an event. In fact, correct use of tense is much more complicated than this. Consider, for instance, three contrasting sentences referring to the future, one with the main verb ("submit") inflected with "-s", one inflected with "-ing", and the last uninflected:

John submits his thesis tomorrow
John is submitting his thesis tomorrow
John will submit his thesis tomorrow

The treatment of tense in contemporary linguistic theory is complex and controversial, but it is clear that expression of tense depends on syntactic relationships and not just on the time period referred to. (In Government and Binding theory, the expression of tense depends on syntactic relations with a functional head, INFL, see *X-bar syntax*, pp.126–127.) Thus, problems with verb tense would be predicted for a child who had problems with dependent relationships.

As far as sentence comprehension is concerned, Van der Lely argued that a child with a representational deficit for dependent relations will generate a syntactic representation that does not fully specify the relationship between sentence constituents. The result is that the representation may be ambiguous and open to more than one interpretation. If that were the whole explanation, then one might expect children with SLI simply to perform at chance when given complex sentences where word order was critical. However, in practice they may succeed in decoding sentences by using pragmatic and semantic strategies, e.g. in treating the first-mentioned noun phrase as the entity that carries out an action.

The studies by Van der Lely and her colleagues are noteworthy because of the care taken to select relatively homogeneous groups of children in order to see clear patterns of deficit in SLI. The children studied by these authors are described as having "grammatical SLI", and they were selected on the basis that they do more poorly on expressive and receptive tests of grammatical-morphological abilities than on those testing semantic-lexical skills. Furthermore, Van der Lely and colleagues used language-matched as well as age-matched control groups. The rationale is that it is relatively uninteresting to show that children with SLI are impaired on a language task; the crucial point is whether one can demonstrate a selective pattern of deficit that is not just equivalent to what is seen in a younger normally developing child with immature language.

In an early study, Van der Lely and Harris (1990) showed that children with SLI have major problems in working out the thematic roles encoded by word order. They found that children with SLI did poorly with reversible sentences, particularly if nonstandard (noncanonical) word order was used. They compared a group of children with SLI, aged around six years, with a "language age" control group of younger children (mean chronological age three and a half years), who obtained equivalent raw scores on a receptive vocabulary test and an expressive morphology test. Despite this matching, children with SLI obtained significantly poorer scores than controls on comprehension tests that involved either acting out sentences or selecting a picture to match a sentence (see Fig. 5.13, overleaf; this also shows data from a control group matched on chronological age, who scored near ceiling on most items). Like Bishop

(1979, 1982), Van der Lely and Harris found major deficits in comprehension of reversible passive structures (e.g. "the boy is pushed by the girl"), but problems were also seen on active sentences and locative and dative constructions. They concluded that the processes of performing a syntactic analysis and relating this to thematic roles posed particular problems for children with SLI. Note

that this type of problem is not predicted by theories that focus solely on deficits in inflectional morphology.

A subset of the same group of children went on to participate in the bootstrapping experiments by Van der Lely (1994), which were described in Chapter 4 (see pp.106–108). These confirmed their difficulties with mapping thematic roles onto

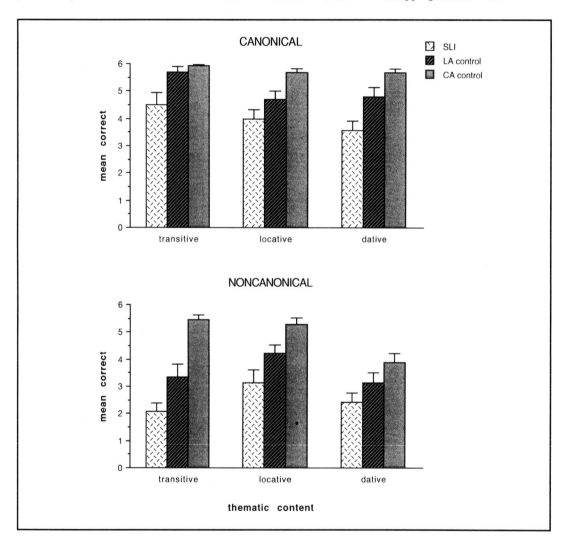

FIG. 5.13   Results from Van der Lely and Harris (1990). Mean items correct for children with SLI vs. language-age (LA) and chronological-age (CA) matched control groups for acting out sentences. Error bars show standard errors. Canonical transitive sentences are simple actives such as "the boy pushes the girl", and noncanonical transitives are passives (e.g. "the girl is pushed by the boy"). Canonical locatives are sentences such as "the book is on the paper", whereas noncanonical locatives are sentences such as "on the paper is the book". Canonical datives are "give the girl to the boy" and noncanonical datives are "give the boy the girl".

syntactic functions; children had problems in identifying thematic roles when nonsense verbs were inserted into sentence frames such as "the lorry yols the car", and the task was to invent a plausible meaning.[1]

Van der Lely (1990) noted that children with SLI performed better with short passives, (e.g. "the boy is chased") than with full passives (e.g. "the boy is chased by the girl"). At first glance, this seems incompatible with an underlying deficit in representing dependent relations, because the short passives are regarded as having a complex underlying structure with a noncanonical relation between thematic roles and grammatical functions. She proposed, however, that children with SLI could succeed with these structures if they treated the verb like an adjective (Van der Lely, 1996a). For instance, on hearing "the toy is broken", one can regard "broken" as a simple adjective, so that the sentence has the same type of structure as "the toy is red" or "the toy is big". And indeed, a word like "broken" can play an explicitly adjectival role in sentences such as "the broken toy is in the cupboard". This adjectival interpretation is syntactically much simpler. In a study using picture arrays like the one shown in Fig. 5.14, overleaf, Van der Lely (1996a) obtained evidence that children with SLI do tend to adopt an adjectival interpretation of short passives.

With active sentences, Van der Lely found that all children, both SLI and control, performed near ceiling. (Note that this indicates that none of the children had any major problems interpreting the pictures.) On full and short progressive passives, which do not permit an adjectival interpretation of the verb, the children with SLI performed well above chance but their scores were significantly worse than the control children, with fewer correct responses even than those of the youngest control group. The most striking difference between groups, however, was on the short ambiguous passives (e.g. "the fish is eaten"). On these, children with SLI were biased in favour of the adjectival interpretation, whereas other children were equally likely to select passive and adjectival readings. Furthermore, on around 30% of trials, children with SLI selected the (wrong) adjectival reading for the short progressive passives, so they

would, for instance, point to the picture of the eaten fish (choice 3) when given the sentence "the fish is being eaten". Although control children sometimes made this error, this occurred on significantly fewer trials. A graphical summary of the most stringent comparison, between children with SLI, who had a mean age of 11 years, and the youngest control group, who were aged 5 years, is shown in Fig. 5.15 (p.145).

In a further study, Van der Lely and Stollwerck (1997) went on to test predictions from the "representational deficit for dependent relations" hypothesis using a different syntactic relationship, that between reflexive and personal pronouns and the entities they refer to. Consider the following sentences:

Mowgli is pointing to him.
Baloo Bear says Mowgli is pointing to him.
Mowgli is pointing to himself.
Baloo Bear says Mowgli is pointing to himself.

In the first two sentences, "him" cannot refer to Mowgli, whereas in the last two it must. Formal syntactic theory captures the generalisations of how pronouns are interpreted with two principles:

Principle A. A reflexive must be bound in its governing category.
Principle B. A pronoun must be free in its governing category.

The words "bound", "free", and "governing" here all have technical meanings, referring to the syntactic relationships between different sentence elements, but, in essence, these principles specify that a reflexive must have an antecedent to which it refers, this antecedent must be local (in most, but not all cases, this means it will refer to a noun phrase within the same clause), and the antecedent must have a particular syntactic relationship to the reflexive. In contrast, a personal pronoun cannot refer to a noun phrase meeting these criteria. The principles specify what the referent for a reflexive must be, and what a referent for a personal pronoun must not be. For those working in the Chomskyan tradition, these principles are not just linguistic abstractions; they apply in all languages and are

FIG. 5.14   Sample test page from the study by Van der Lely (1996a) testing understanding of full and short passives. A total of 12 such picture arrays were used. On each trial, the child heard a spoken sentence and had to point to the picture that matched it. Each picture array was used on four trials to test understanding of the following sentence types: Simple active: e.g. the fish eats the man (correct response 4); Full passive: e.g. the man is eaten by the fish (correct response 4); Short progressive passive: e.g. the fish is being eaten (correct response 2); Short ambiguous (potentially adjectival) passive: e.g. the fish is eaten: correct response 2 (passive) or 3 (adjectival). (Thanks to Heather Van der Lely and Peter Hudspith for making copies of original artwork available.)

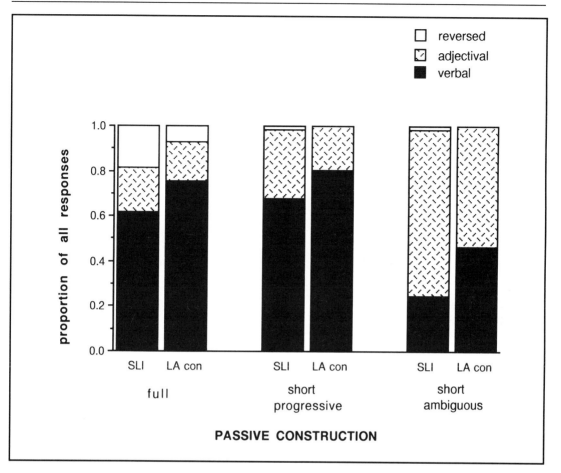

FIG. 5.15   Results from the Test of Active and Passive Sentences from Van der Lely (1996a). The mean proportion of responses of each type is shown for children with SLI (mean age 11 years) and language-age matched controls (mean age 5 years). In Fig. 5.14, for the "short ambiguous" passive "the fish is eaten", picture 4 depicts the reversed choice, picture 3 depicts the adjectival interpretation, and picture 2 depicts the verbal interpretation.

part of the innate knowledge that constitutes Universal Grammar.

Suppose a child had difficulty in analysing syntactic relationships. Van der Lely and Stollwerck argued that this will cause problems in working out what pronouns refer to, because in order to apply the Binding Principles, one must be able to compute syntactic relationships between sentence elements, in order to identify the "governing category". However, in most everyday contexts one may succeed without this knowledge because there are many nonsyntactic cues to meaning. The child may be able to use contextual cues and pronoun gender to help decode what is meant, but will run into trouble in more complex situations where these cues are not adequate. Van der Lely and Stollwerck argued that it should be possible to demonstrate this difficulty using specially designed materials.

They carried out two experiments, whose results will be shown here combined. For each item, the child was shown a picture while a single sentence was spoken, and was asked to say YES or NO. One set of items used pictures such as those in Fig. 5.16. The first point to note was that all children scored at ceiling in a control condition where both figures were named (e.g. "is Baloo Bear tickling Mowgli?"), and performance was close to

FIG. 5.16   Sample items from the study by Van der Lely and Stollwerck (1997). The child is shown a single picture and provided with a test sentence. The task is to say YES or NO depending on whether the sentence matches the picture. For sample test sentences and results see Fig. 5.17, opposite. (Thanks to Heather Van der Lely and Peter Hudspith for making copies of original artwork available.)

ceiling when knowledge of pronoun gender could be used; e.g. when the picture showed Mother Wolf tickling Mowgli, and the child was asked questions such as "Is Mother Wolf tickling him?" or "Is Mother Wolf tickling herself?". Thus there was evidence that children could cope with the basic task demands, and were aware of the different gender of the characters and the corresponding pronouns.

Figure 5.17 shows the pattern of results obtained by Van der Lely and Stollwerck for children with SLI and for the youngest control group (mean age around six years, matched on

grammatical-morphology test scores).[2]   The children with SLI did do more poorly overall than all three control groups on those items that could not be interpreted by using gender or contextual cues, but their errors were not random.

The children with grammatical SLI appeared to be aware that a reflexive pronoun expresses a self-oriented action. With this knowledge, a child could perform correctly on sentences such as "Is Mowgli tickling himself?" without doing any grammatical analysis, simply by selecting the picture where the character was acting on himself

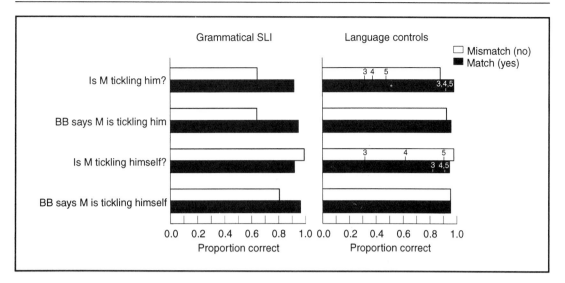

FIG. 5.17   Results from study on Binding Principles by Van der Lely and Stollwerck (1997). To simplify presentation, this summary figure shows only the youngest control group from Van der Lely and Stollwerck's study, and excludes data from control conditions and from other items that included quantifiers. The points marked 3, 4, and 5 on the control plot indicate mean levels of performance by normal three-, four-, and five-year-olds using different items to test comparable constructions in a study by Chien and Wexler (1990).

rather than on the other. However, this strategy would not work for sentences such as "Mowgli says Baloo Bear is tickling himself" paired with picture B (which depicts a self-directed action carried out by the wrong character). On items of this type, children with SLI made more errors.

On personal pronouns, 11-year-old children with SLI had a level of performance that is usually found in normally developing children only below 6 years of age (Chien &Wexler, 1990). It seems that children with grammatical SLI treat a personal pronoun as if it can refer to either a self-oriented or an other-oriented action. The difficulty was not simply due to the child assuming that the pronoun must refer to a character who has already been mentioned, because performance on "mismatch" personal pronouns was equally poor when picture B was paired with the sentence "Baloo Bear says Mowgli is tickling him" (where the referent of "him" was mentioned) as when the sentence was "Is Mowgli tickling him?" In both cases, children with SLI tended to respond YES.

Such results provide strong evidence that children with SLI are poor at working out pronoun

reference on the basis of syntactic information. They tended to rely on other cues: gender, number, or pragmatic and semantic constraints. The results are particularly impressive in view of the fact that the impairment is seen relative to much younger control children who are matched on overall performance on a standardised comprehension test. However, can we conclude that the results support the view that children with grammatical SLI lack the syntactic knowledge that is needed to apply the Binding Principles to rule out inappropriate co-reference? This is an extreme view that would mean that, in the absence of other cues to pronoun reference, children with SLI should perform at chance, either showing a systematic response bias (e.g. YES to everything) or guessing and saying YES or NO at random. In fact, there is no type of construction where this was the case. Van der Lely and Stollwerck analysed match (correct answer = YES) and mismatch (correct answer = NO) items separately, noting chance levels of performance on some of the mismatch conditions. However, the proper test for random responding is how responses pattern across both match and mismatch items for a given structure (cf. Grimshaw & Rosen, 1990). On the items shown in Fig. 5.10 (p.139), children with SLI showed a systematically different pattern of responding to match and mismatch items, both with personal and reflexive items. On the personal pronoun items it is unclear what cue other than syntax could be used.

Van der Lely and her colleagues have produced an impressive range of evidence using a wide range of syntactic constructions to show that children with SLI do poorly on comprehension tasks which involve extracting grammatical structure in sentences with noncanonical word order or complex structural dependencies. In every case, their performance is worse even than younger children matched on various indices of language level. Clearly these tasks do pinpoint areas of disproportionate and unusual difficulty for children with SLI, and the control stimuli incorporated in the experimental design allow us to rule out any simple explanation in terms of a general difficulty in understanding component words or processing long sentences. But do the results support the notion of a representational deficit for dependent relationships? I would argue that the deficits that are seen in SLI, although undoubtedly severe, are not fully compatible with any hypothesis arguing that these children are *unable* to use certain kinds of syntactic information. Performance on critical constructions is typically above chance level, even when it is not possible to identify any plausible nonsyntactic strategy that a child could use to perform correctly.

A further complication is that normally developing children do not perform perfectly on items designed to test knowledge of supposedly innate grammatical principles. Indeed, the five-year-olds studied by Chien and Wexler show a pattern of performance similar to that of Van der Lely and Stollwerck's SLI group. Adherents of Principles and Parameters theory have proposed a range of processing limitations and pragmatic constraints that could explain the errors made by normally developing children (Atkinson, 1992, ch. 6; Chien & Wexler, 1990; Grimshaw & Rosen, 1990), and they deny that high error rates contravene the innateness hypothesis. However, if

errors by normally developing children are attributable to performance factors, then couldn't the errors of children with SLI be explained in a similar fashion? Van der Lely and Stollwerck argued no, because Chien and Wexler's four- to five-year-olds scored only 83% correct on mismatch items in the control condition (e.g. "This is Mama Bear; this is Goldilocks. Is Mama Bear touching Goldilocks?—correct response "no"). This indicated that they had some general difficulty with task demands even when no pronouns were involved. They concluded that "whilst the evidence from the comprehension and production of pronouns and reflexives in young children indicate that their failures to obey Binding Principles are due to performance factors, we see no convincing evidence to indicate that this is so for the Grammatical SLI children".

In discussing their findings, Van der Lely and Stollwerck (1997) define a more specific version of the "representational deficit for dependent relations" hypothesis which sits more comfortably with the data from normal children, and which does not propose any absolute inability to compute syntactic relations in SLI. Rather, they argue, children with SLI resemble younger normal children in that they build a concatenation of simple phrase structure trees, rather than integrating these into a complex tree which represents higher level hierarchical syntactic dependencies. Local syntactic relations are likely to be handled correctly, because these can be represented in simple phrase structures. However, more distant relationships will not be adequately specified, and so we will see a breakdown of performance on more complex structures involving operations such as movement, agreement, and case assignment. Van der Lely and Stollwerck stay within the framework of Principles and Parameter theory, arguing that the factor that prevents the child from generating more complex syntactic structures is a failure of maturation of innate syntactic abilities. However, their account opens up the possibility that the factor that impairs syntactic development may be some extra-linguistic, and possibly nonmodular limitation of information processing.

A NONMODULAR EXPLANATION OF POOR GRAMMATICAL COMPETENCE: PERCEPTUAL DEFICIT

In Chapter 3, evidence was reviewed for an auditory perceptual deficit in children with SLI. How far could such a perceptual deficit account for grammatical impairment? In 1989, Leonard proposed what he termed the "surface hypothesis", which maintained that it is the perceptual and articulatory characteristics of grammatical morphemes that make the task of morphological paradigm building unduly difficult for children learning English. The precise details of the hypothesis have changed somewhat over the years, but in the earliest accounts, Leonard emphasised the evidence for auditory processing deficits in children with SLI, implying that there might be a straightforward link between ease of perceiving phonological material and its incorporation into a morphological paradigm. Many grammatical morphemes are brief, unstressed, and tend not to occur in a salient word-final position (e.g. past tense "-ed", plural "-s"), and the kind of auditory perceptual impairment proposed by Tallal could conceivably make such morphemes hard to detect. Thus, formation of morphological paradigms could be unduly difficult and protracted, not because of any impairment of the innate language-learning module itself, but because of inadequate perception of language input.

An important prediction of the surface hypothesis is that there will be cross-linguistic differences in the presentation of SLI, depending on the perceptual salience of grammatical morphemes. This contrasts with theories that attribute problems to lack of innate grammatical principles, where the main determinant of the child's difficulties with language learning should be grammatical function. To date, most attempts to test this notion have focused on expressive language. Leonard et al. (1987, 1988) compared expressive difficulties of SLI children in two different languages, English and Italian. In English, many grammatical contrasts are marked by morphemes that are unstressed, brief, and of low perceptual salience (e.g. -s or -ed). In contrast, in

Italian, grammatical morphemes are often syllabic and much more salient. In the study by Leonard et al., eight English-speaking children were contrasted with eight Italian-speaking children, all diagnosed as cases of SLI. The English children all used word final /s/, /z/, /t/, and /d/ in singular nouns such as *bus*, and *bed*, so any failure to produce plural or past tense morphemes could not be attributed to difficulty in articulating these phonemes. The two groups of children were matched in terms of mean length of utterance in words. Samples of their language were collected, using pictures to elicit examples of grammatical forms of interest. Italian children did not show striking differences between regular noun plurals and third person singular verb inflections: both were produced in obligatory contexts at a much higher rate than was observed in English children. While there was no overall difference between Italian and English children in the production of articles, the Italian children used the feminine forms of the definite and indefinite articles, *la* and *una*, significantly more often than the corresponding masculine forms, *il* and *un*. Given that the number of obligatory contexts for *il* and *un* was as high as for *la* and *una*, it is difficult to explain this difference except in terms of phonological structure. Most errors with articles involved omission of the article rather than substitution of an alternative. Finally, Leonard et al. (1987) also noted that Italian children with SLI correctly marked gender agreement of possessive pronouns and adjectives in nearly all instances where this was required.

Leonard (1989) argued that many of the errors made by children with SLI could be accounted for by assuming that they have difficulty in learning features represented by nonsyllabic consonant segments (e.g. in English, plural, possessive, or third person singular -s, past -ed, and contracted forms of *to be*) and those represented by unstressed syllables (e.g. *a*, *the*, infinitive particle *to*, complementiser *that*). On this interpretation, Italian children find it easier to learn verb inflections because most of these consist of stressed syllabic affixes. Their ability to handle gender agreement is attributed to the fact that the relevant affixes have a very clear relationship to one another; in most cases the final vowels of adjectives match those of the nouns they modify. Leonard and his collaborators have gone on to investigate production of grammatical morphemes in a wide range of languages. They conclude that many, but not all, of their findings fit the hypothesis that children with SLI have particular difficulty in learning morphemes of weak perceptual salience.

There are three lines of evidence that have been advanced against perceptual deficit explanations for morphosyntactic deficits in SLĪ.

1. First, it has been noted that grammatical problems can be seen with written as well as spoken language. For instance, in the study of comprehension of sentences with postmodified subjects, Bishop (1982) found that children with SLI actually performed more poorly with written input than with spoken input, even though they could read all the individual words. If an auditory processing problem is at the root of a comprehension difficulty, then shouldn't we be able to by-pass the problem by using the visual modality, i.e. written presentation?

The logic clearly works in the case of an acquired language disorder, where one can see people with aphasia who are unable to make sense of spoken language but demonstrate excellent understanding of written language (e.g. Caramazza, Berndt, and Basili, 1983). But in the course of acquisition, written language is parasitic on oral language; the child must have some understanding of the language that is represented by the written word in order to make sense of it. This is why children with severe congenital hearing loss have so much difficulty in learning to read: their mastery of the phonology, syntax, and semantics of oral language is severely compromised by the auditory deficit, and this hampers learning of written language.[3] This is apparent from Cromer's (1978) examples of written language samples of language-impaired and hearing-impaired children (see Table 5.5, p.138). Although Cromer was keen to stress the differences between groups, the written stories of hearing-impaired children were far from normal and not easy to distinguish from those of language-impaired children on casual inspection.

Other researchers have emphasised the abnormalities of syntactic structure that are apparent in the written language expression and comprehension of children with hearing impairments (Bishop, 1982, 1983a; Quigley, Power, & Steinkamp, 1977).

In short, any language learning device needs adequate auditory input if oral language is to be learned successfully. If it is not, then written language problems will ensue. Thus, in a developmental disorder, the fact that a grammatical impairment is seen for both written and spoken language does not constitute evidence that the primary cause is impairment of an innate language acquisition module.

2. A second objection to an auditory processing account is that children with SLI can discriminate very accurately between inflected and uninflected forms (Gopnik, 1994b). This demonstration, however, is not very convincing. The critical issue is not whether the child is capable of discriminating between different phonological forms, but whether auditory discrimination is impaired relative to other individuals when listening under non-optimal conditions, i.e. when words are spoken rapidly, in the context of a sentence, and against competing noise. The evidence reviewed in Chapter 3 strongly suggests that, for many children with SLI, discrimination between certain speech sounds is not at chance, but is below normal levels. A relatively slight degradation in quality of speech input, affecting perception of a minority of utterances, could have a disruptive effect on language learning.

Furthermore, one conclusion from Chapter 3 was that there is more to auditory perception than the ability to discriminate. Classification of speech input is also important, so that the child learns to recognise acoustically different stimuli as exemplars of the same phoneme. In Chapter 3, it was suggested that this ability to perceive phoneme constancy might pose a more severe problem for children with SLI than the ability to tell two speech sounds apart. Evidence was reviewed showing that children with SLI, especially those with expressive phonological impairments, might be poor at phonological segmentation, treating words as Gestalts rather than breaking them into strings of phonemes. One can see that a fundamental deficit in segmentation could be responsible for exactly the kind of paradigm-building problem that Gopnik and Crago (1991) describe, because, in order to detect similarities between inflected forms, the child must be able to segment the inflectional ending and appreciate that this is equivalent for different words such as "book+s", "cat+s", and "ship+s". This kind of account could not explain the whole gamut of grammatical difficulties seen in SLI. However, given that the family members studied by Gopnik and Crago did have unusually severe problems with expressive phonology (Hurst et al., 1990; Vargha-Khadem et al., 1995), it would be interesting to test further the notion that their phonological and morphological difficulties might to some extent reflect a common problem of identifying the segments of which speech is composed.

3. The final objection to perceptual deficit accounts is that there is no direct correlation between the perceptual salience of a morphological marker and its risk of being impaired (e.g. Gopnik, 1994b), as the difficulty of a particular phonological form varies with its grammatical function. Watkins and Rice (1991), for instance, found that children with SLI had much more difficulty in producing prepositions such as "over" or "on" when these were in the role of verb particle (e.g. "put on the hat", "kick over the fence") than when they functioned as prepositions (e.g. "sit on the chair", "jump over the fence"). To take another example, children with SLI were far less accurate in their use of the morpheme "-s" in possessive contexts or to mark third person singular than when it served to mark a noun plural (see, e.g. Bishop, 1994a; Rice & Oetting, 1993). Evidence such as this has been used to conclude that difficulties with auditory perception of speech input are not adequate to explain syntactic problems in SLI.

Furthermore, children with SLI have difficulty with some morphemes that can by no stretch of the imagination be regarded as phonetically weak, e.g. in English, irregular past tense forms, and the distinction between nominative and accusative pronouns (he/him; she/her). These types of error, it is argued, cannot be attributed to auditory perceptual difficulties.

The question one has to ask of this line of explanation is whether it is safe to assume that a problem in perception at an early stage of input will simply interfere with acquisition of those parts of syntax signalled by hard-to-perceive elements, leaving the rest of the system to develop normally. This ignores interdependence of components of the grammar. For a start, there is ample evidence that function words such as "the" and "a" and inflected endings such as "-s" or "-ed" are important cues to children about the grammatical category of words with which they are associated. Thus, for instance, if I tell you that "the zod prungled a verd" you will be able to deduce that "zod" and "verd" are nouns and "prungle" is a verb, just on the basis of the related function words and inflections they occur with. Problems in perceiving grammatical morphemes should, therefore, not just affect morphological skills, but will also have a more pervasive impact on grammatical knowledge, making it harder to establish grammatical category information when learning new lexical items (Leonard & Eyer, 1996). Poor perception of phonologically weak morphemes could also delay acquisition of a wide range of syntactic structures by increasing the ambiguity not just of structures where inflections are important, but also those which they usually contrast with. Consider the following example: suppose a child has perceptual problems such that the sentence "the boy is hit by the girl" will sometimes be heard as "boy hit girl". Clearly, such a child will find it difficult to learn passive constructions, which are characterised by unstressed morphemes "-ed" and "by". Now suppose the same child hears "the boy hits the girl". Once again, this is sometimes perceived as "boy hit girl". Now, although low salience morphemes are not at all critical to decode this sentence, we might expect problems, because to this child "boy hit girl" can refer to the boy as agent or the girl as agent. Clearly, school-aged children with SLI can distinguish between active and passive sentences (see Van der Lely, 1996b) and it would be far too extreme to argue that they have no ability to detect inflectional morphemes or function words. However, the point is that if perceptual processing is impaired, then there will be occasions when words of weak salience will be missed, and so form-function mappings will be less reliable and harder to learn. To take another example at a more formal level, we may note that if the child has problems perceiving morphemes signalling verb tense and agreement, then this will lead to difficulties in forming functional categories such as INFL (see *X-bar syntax*, pp.126–127). Without INFL, it is not possible to assign case to noun phrases, and hence we would predict problems with distinctions such as "he" vs. "him". Thus, a simple perceptual problem could have a widespread impact on learning how the grammar represents thematic roles, and this will lead to problems affecting salient as well as nonsalient morphemes.

How, then, are we to distinguish the pattern of impairment predicted by a perceptual deficit account and a modular linguistic deficit? The complex interdependencies between components of the grammar would seem to make it impossible to specify in advance precisely how an auditory processing deficit might affect language acquisition. This leaves us with two ways forward. One method is to compare grammatical impairments in SLI with those seen in children who are known to have peripheral auditory impairments, i.e. those with prelingual hearing losses, to establish just how far a limitation of auditory perception can disrupt ability to learn the grammar of an oral language. Most research on oral language development of hearing impaired children has focused on cases of severe or profound congenital hearing loss, which can be problematic for several reasons: (1) speech of severely deaf children is often hard to understand, making it difficult to judge whether grammatical morphemes are present; (2) where there is little functional hearing, the child will tend to learn language through the eye rather than the ear, and so learning of spoken language will involve all the problems of second language acquisition, compounded by difficulties introduced by the very different properties of visual and auditory devices for expressing syntax (see Bishop, 1983a). For comparisons with children with SLI, it would be of considerable interest to look at children with milder or partial hearing losses, where oral rather than signed language is the main medium of communication, but where

perception of critical grammatical morphemes may be compromised. It is noteworthy that an early study with a "hard of hearing" sample found no correlation between the child's ability to discriminate phonemes, and accuracy of repetition of grammatical structures that incorporated those phonemes (Wilcox & Tobin, 1974), lending support to the argument that one cannot predict a priori how a perceptual problem will influence the course of acquisition of grammar.

In the future, a second approach, that of using connectionist modelling to predict the effects of auditory perceptual deficits on language learning, may be feasible.

"Perceptual deficit" explanations of impaired grammatical comprehension have relatively few contemporary adherents among those interested in formal linguistics, but it may be that the rejection of this line of explanation has been premature and is based on a limited view of the nature of perceptual impairment, together with inaccurate assumptions about what the consequences of a perceptual deficit should look like.

In this chapter, we have concentrated on lack of grammatical knowledge as a factor affecting children's sentence comprehension. In the next chapter, we turn to consider a related question, namely, how far sentence comprehension problems might arise because of limitations of attention, perception or memory, which tax a limited capacity system and hence lead to errors with grammatically complex material.

FOOTNOTES

1. Surprisingly, in the 1994 study, the same children did not differ from language-matched controls in acting out sentences containing a nonsense verb whose meaning they had previously seen demonstrated, even when passives were used. This contrasts with their poor performance in the Van der Lely and Harris (1990) study. However, the small number of language-impaired children in the later study (N = 6) meant that there was low statistical power to detect a difference. Also, the

children were a year or so older than when first assessed by Van der Lely and Harris.

2. Van der Lely and Stollwerck also included test items including quantified subjects, e.g. "is every monkey tickling himself?" I have excluded these items from discussion because results using this more complex structure can be problematic to interpret: these items are included in linguistic studies because they rule out the possibility of "accidental" co-indexing with a definite referent. However, correct performance also requires that the child appreciates that a term such as "himself", which usually has a singular referent, is now referring to each member of a group of individuals. The quote at the beginning of this chapter reinforces this point. Errors could reflect a tendency to avoid selecting a plural referent for "himself", rather than any deeper syntactic difficulty.

3. I have found that when I use data from hearing-impaired children to illustrate the kinds of syntactic difficulties that can arise as a secondary consequence of lack of auditory input, people often respond by saying: "That can't be right! Deaf children have normal language competence, provided they are exposed to a sign language." And indeeed, painstaking research by linguists since the 1960s has confirmed that the natural sign languages that deaf children usually learn so readily do have a complex syntactic structure, and cannot merely be dismissed as iconic gestures (see e.g. Bellugi, van Hoek, Lillo-Martin, & O'Grady, 1988). The fact remains, however, that syntax of a sign language is very different from syntax of spoken languages. The visual modality is well-designed for processing simultaneous, spatial patterns. It is much less competent at detecting sequential information. In the auditory modality we see the converse: excellent ability to detect temporal patterning, but less ability to process large amounts of simultaneous information. Syntactic information in sign language is conveyed more by spatial configuration than by temporal order, and there appears to be little or no transfer of syntactic competence from signed to spoken language. Consequently, when tested on their knowledge of the syntax of oral language, whether in spoken or written form, most congenitally deaf people show marked impairments (Bishop, 1983a).

6

Understanding sentences in real time

The tests that people give him just don't capture the difficulties he has in the real world, when people are talking rapidly, and one sentence follows another, without any pause. He is overwhelmed by all that information. I just wish they'd realise he needs time to understand.

Parent of a child with SLI

OVERVIEW

1. Sentence understanding places heavy processing demands on an interpretative system that must decode language input on-line, and which will run into trouble if the rate of new input exceeds the system's processing speed.
2. We may distinguish between accounts of SLI that assume there are defective grammatical representations from accounts that attribute poor sentence comprehension to processing limitations, e.g. weak capacity of a working memory system that is involved in computing the interpretation of sentences on line. Representational accounts (reviewed in Chapter 5) assume that there is defective language competence, whereas explanations in terms of processing limitations treat SLI as a performance deficit.

3. Language production data offers some support to the notion that children with SLI have impairments of language performance, because they show partial mastery of grammatical rules.
4. Furthermore, children with SLI have significant problems with comprehension tasks that require them to process large amounts of information, even when the syntactic structure is simple.
5. There are five types of evidence that can be used to distinguish between representational and processing accounts of comprehension deficits in SLI: (a) examination of the pattern of errors on a given structure; (b) profile of performance across different structures; (c) interaction between syntactic complexity and other language demands; (d) manipulation of task demands to affect processing load; (e) simulation of the effects of capacity limitations on sentence interpretation.

INTRODUCTION

In Chapter 5, we reviewed work on sentence comprehension that was concerned with investigating grammatical competence in SLI. Various hypotheses were considered, but they all had in common the notion that SLI was characterised by some deficiency in the child's underlying grammatical representations. This approach follows naturally from the Chomskyan tradition, where grammatical knowledge is described in static terms. However, it completely ignores the way in which grammatical knowledge is deployed in real time when generating meaning from incoming speech. This is an important limitation, because there is ample evidence that decoding of grammatical structure does not wait until a whole sentence has been encountered. Rather, the identification of the grammatical structure of a sentence (parsing) takes place incrementally as each word is heard. Even if we are perfectly competent in the grammar of our native language, comprehension can break down if we overload the listener with sentences that are rapid and/or syntactically complex. Comprehension problems can result from performance limitations in a listener who cannot simultaneously cope with the task of remembering incoming material while computing the meaning of what has already been heard.

To illustrate the distinction between competence and performance limitations, try the following experiment on a friend. Read the list of digits below at a constant rate of one per second:

3, 7, 8, 2, 4, 9, 1, 3, 6, 4, 2, 7, 9, 3, 8, 5, 3, 7, 4

and ask your friend to reply with the sum of the current number and the last number but one.

The correct response to the sequence above would be:

11, 9, 12, 11, 5, 12, 7, 7, 8, 11, 11, 10, 17, 8, 11, 12, 7

Your friend is likely to complain that this is a taxing task. You can make it even more taxing by speeding up the rate of presentation, by using two-digit numbers, or by asking that the current number be added to the last number but two. If you do all three things, even the most intelligent and attentive testee is likely to make mistakes. Yet on the surface, this seems a trivially easy task. The arithmetical knowledge that is required is simple and highly overlearned, so we cannot blame failure on lack of competence. And, indeed, if you were to present the numbers at a very slow rate, or, better still, in written form, the task becomes much easier. What makes it difficult is the need to hold one thing in memory while performing an operation on another. Each operation is easy enough on its own, but keeping track in memory of both results of computations and new incoming material is what taxes most people. The task makes heavy performance demands, and these are what lead to errors.

We may draw a loose analogy between this task and comprehension of spoken sentences, where new material continues to arrive as computations are performed on what has just been heard. For the average intelligent adult, problems with these operations are seldom observed in real-life comprehension, because the encoding of meaning in language is so redundant, and contextual cues as well as syntactic form can be used. However, in more experimental settings, it is not too difficult to induce comprehension failure in normal adults (see *Comprehension failure despite adequate grammatical competence*, opposite).

How do we build up a representation of sentence structure moment-by-moment as each word is encountered? Most of the research on this problem has been done by computational linguists, who have developed computer simulations of real life comprehension. On-line extraction of syntactic structure, or parsing, is a complex and controversial topic (for reviews see Garnham, 1985; Mitchell, 1994), but to illustrate this approach, we will take one example, Briscoe's (1987) Lexicat. This parser uses a form of categorial grammar (see *Categorial grammar*, p.159), which enables it to generate an incremental representation of syntactic relationships as words are encountered. In Lexicat, incoming information is stored on a memory stack, with analysis proceeding on the basis of a three-cell

Comprehension failure despite adequate grammatical competence

Read the following sentences, and put a tick if the sentence is true, and a cross if it is false:

A follows B   B A   ☐
C does not precede D C D   ☐
E is not followed by F F E   ☐

Although the language involved in this task is within the competence of most adults, it is surprisingly difficult to work out the correct response, and, when a task like this is given under speeded conditions, most people will make some errors (Baddeley, 1968). This is not just because of the use of abstract letter symbols. For instance, Bishop (1983b) found that normal young people made frequent errors on passive sentences (e.g. "the boy is followed by the girl" or "the boy is not followed by the girl") when required simply to say if a picture (of a boy following a girl, or a girl following a boy) matched the sentence, even though there was no pressure to respond rapidly. No subject was systematically wrong: rather, performance fell to chance levels for the more complex sentence structures, particularly in subjects with relatively low IQ.

Miyake, Carpenter, and Just (1994) presented university students with sentences varying in syntactic complexity, and tested their comprehension of each one with a test sentence. For instance, an easy sentence would be: "the banker hit the doctor and followed the lawyer", and a difficult sentence would be: "the banker the doctor hit followed the lawyer". The subject would then be asked: "did the banker follow the lawyer?" Sentences were presented in written form, one word at a time. The relative difficulty of sentence types was similar to that observed with aphasic patients. Furthermore, error rate was influenced by speed of presentation, with more errors at faster rates of presentation.

Miyake et al. found that centre-embedded sentences (e.g. "the banker the doctor hit followed the lawyer") are especially difficult. In the Test for Reception of Grammar (1989b), the final block consists of four items of this type (see example in Fig. 6.1, below), and only a minority of normal adults get all four items correct, even though there is no time pressure. Note that this type of sentence is widely used in everyday speech (e.g. "the girl I met yesterday is coming over"), but semantic and pragmatic constraints are typically adequate to work out who did what to whom. It is only under test conditions, when the syntax must be decoded to arrive at the correct meaning, that the difficulty of this syntactic construction becomes apparent.

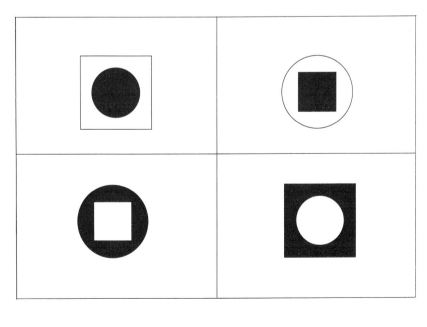

FIG. 6.1   "The circle the square is in is black".

window on top of the stack. The full details of parser operation are too complex to detail here, but to give the reader a sense of how the model operates, a short example of stages of processing is shown in Table 6.1.

Once we appreciate that sentence comprehension occurs on-line as a sentence unfolds, we encounter a new problem. If we don't know how a sentence is going to end, there is often considerable ambiguity about the grammatical structure that is being built. For instance, if we hear "The company awards ..." we do not know whether to parse "awards" as a noun or verb until we listen on and hear what follows:

> The company awards its employees a Christmas bonus
> The company awards for innovation weren't given this year

In many cases where sentences are ambiguous, we remain completely unaware of the ambiguity. For instance, we automatically assign a different syntactic structure (and a different kind of interpretation) to sentences with the same sequence of grammatical elements, as in:

TABLE 6.1

Lexicat Parser: Stages of Processing Involved in Interpreting the Sentence "The farmer fed the duckling"

			Stack			
		4	3	2	1	
Step	Operation		Left Context	Current Item	Lookahead Item	Input Buffer
1						The farmer fed the duckling
2	shift				the NP/N	farmer fed the duckling
3	shift			the NP/N	farmer N	fed the duckling
4	shift		the NP/N	farmer N	fed S/NP\NP	the duckling
5	forward combination			the farmer NP	fed S/NP\NP	the duckling
6	shift		the farmer NP	fed S/NP\NP	the NP/N	duckling
7	backward combination			the farmer fed S/NP	the NP/N	duckling
8	shift		the farmer fed S/NP	the NP/N	duckling N	
9	forward combination		the farmer fed S/NP	the duckling NP		
10	forward combination			the farmer fed the duckling S		
11	halt					

Categorial grammar

Categorial Grammar is a grammatical theory of parsing, particularly suited for specifying how a syntactic representation and its associated logical form are built up incrementally as sentences are encountered. Each word class has a category. For certain word types, e.g. concrete nouns, the category is simply an atomic label (e.g. N = noun). However, others are associated with a complex category which specifies what they must be combined with (i.e. the arguments that they take). For instance, the determiner "the" has the category NP/N. This notation indicates that a determiner is a type of word that will form a NP (noun phrase) if combined with a N (noun). Prepositions have the category PP/NP, indicating that a prepositional phrase (PP) will result from combination of the preposition with a noun phrase. Let us see how this works in practice with a simple example:

determiners = NP/N (e.g. the, this, a, some)
adjectives = N/N (e.g. old, handsome, opaque)
content nouns = N (e.g. man, income, beauty)
proper nouns = NP (e.g. John, Cardiff, Spain)
prepositions = PP/NP (e.g. in, above, under)

Now consider what happens when we encounter the phrase "the old man". We have a sequence of words with the categories NP/N, N/N, N.

A basic rule of application states that two categories can be reduced to a single category if the term on the right hand side of slash for the first item matches (1) a simple category of the next item, or (2) the term on the left-hand side of the slash if the next item is a complex category:

old (N/N) man (N) → old man (N)

Similarly, we can combine the determiner in the same structure:

the (NP/N) old man (N) → the old man (NP)

We can go on to form a prepositional phrase:

to (PP/NP) the old man (NP) → to the old man (PP)

In effect, one performs a kind of algebra, cancelling out common terms on the right-hand side of the first item and the left-hand side of the next. Note that

old (N/N) Mary (NP) *or* the (NP/N) Mary (NP)

cannot be combined. Thus this simple format rejects modification of proper nouns by determiners or adjectives.

The algebraic analogy of cancellation of shared terms can be extended to account for a further rule for combining elements, called composition. This states that a category of the form X/Y can be combined with a category of the form Y/Z to give a category X/Z. An example of composition followed by application, is:

to (PP/NP) the (NP/N) man (N) → to the (PP/N) man (N) → to the man (PP)

Complex categories can also be used to encode the directionality and order of arguments. Generalized Categorial Grammar (Briscoe, 1987) uses categories that look for their arguments in preceding as well as following items, these being denoted by \ rather than /. Thus, as well as a rule that combines X/Y and Y to give X, there is a rule that combines Y and X\Y to give X.

For instance, in the system used by Briscoe, a transitive verb such as "like" has the category S/NP\NP, indicating that a sentence (S) results when it is combined with a preceding NP (subject) and following NP (object), e.g.:

Mary (NP) likes (S/NP\NP) Fido (NP) →
Mary likes (S/NP) Fido (NP) →
Mary likes Fido (S)

See Wood (1993) for a fuller account of categorial grammar.

Joe hit the girl with his umbrella
(the umbrella used as an instrument)
Joe hit the girl with fair hair
(fair hair as a property of the girl)

If we regard grammar as an encapsulated module that has no access to semantic or pragmatic sources of information, then we are forced to assume that the parser keeps its options open and generates a large set of possible syntactic structures, which are then selected between on the basis of further syntactic, semantic, and pragmatic information. However, this would involve a great deal of computation, because there is so much potential for ambiguity in most sentences. It would also mean that processing demands increased dramatically with sentence length, becoming unmanageable for long sentences. This is psychologically implausible, given that we typically have a sense of instantaneous and effortless comprehension of spoken language, regardless of sentence length.

Computational models of natural language understanding typically use semantic and pragmatic sources of information to guide parsing decisions and resolve potential ambiguities as they are encountered (see e.g. Briscoe, 1987). Recent research suggests that people do the same (see *Evidence that visual information can influence on-line grammatical parsing*, opposite).

No doubt because the technical details are hard for nonspecialists to follow, models from computational linguistics have seldom been applied to the study of comprehension disorders (though see Haarman & Kolk, 1991, for an application to adult aphasia). This neglect is unfortunate, because it means that those attempting to explain conditions such as SLI tend to overlook the numerous possible reasons, over and above lack of grammatical competence, that could lead to poor sentence understanding. It is important to appreciate that although parsing places demands on memory, we are not talking just about the kind of short-term phonological memory that was discussed in Chapter 4, which simply involves retaining sequences of verbal material. Indeed, there is ample evidence that memory span, as traditionally assessed, does not have a strong relationship to sentence comprehension (see Carpenter, Miyake, & Just, 1994, for a review). Early work by Hitch and Baddeley (1976) showed that people could understand language surprisingly well while at the same time remembering short sequences of digits, and a case study by Butterworth, Campbell, and Howard (1986) demonstrated that a woman who had a severely limited memory span since childhood nevertheless had good sentence comprehension skills. The critical requirement for comprehension seems to be the ability to retain incoming information while at the same time carrying out cognitive computations: what has been termed working memory (see *Working memory*, p.162).

ON-LINE SENTENCE COMPREHENSION IN SLI

Chapter 5 focused on the problems that some children have in learning grammar. However, the work reviewed earlier suggests that some sentence comprehension problems could reflect processing limitations (e.g. reduced working memory capacity), which would influence the deployment of grammatical knowledge in sentence comprehension. On this view, at least some of the deficits that are seen on comprehension tasks could be indicative of performance rather than competence limitations.

One reason for taking this notion seriously is that the language production data that have been used to document grammatical deficiencies in SLI seldom demonstrate a complete lack of knowledge of grammatical rules. In a study of children's expressive language, Bishop (1994a) concluded that children with SLI do know where and when to apply inflectional endings, but sometimes failed to apply that knowledge when producing utterances under real-time constraints. Similarly, Rice, Wexler, and Cleave (1995) showed that when children marked verb finiteness, they did so correctly; however, children with SLI persisted in treating such marking as optional much longer than did normally developing children. This kind of evidence is compatible with an account that attributes the difficulties experienced by language-impaired children to limited processing capacity in a system that needs to integrate lexical, phonological, and syntactic information on-line in production and comprehension. On this view, it is the on-line processing demands of language comprehension that pose difficulties, rather than a lack of syntactic representations. Leonard's (1989, 1997) surface hypothesis is relevant here. In the original account of this hypothesis, Leonard (1989) stressed the problems that perceptual limitations in SLI might cause in building morphological paradigms (see Chapter 5). However, in more recent writings, Leonard (1997) has modified the surface hypothesis to place more emphasis on the problems that language-impaired children have in processing large amounts of rapid auditory

Evidence that visual information can influence on-line grammatical parsing

Tanenhaus, Spivey-Knowlton, Eberhard, and Sedivy (1995) reported studies that used eye-movement recordings to track a person's mental processes as they carried out instructions to manipulate real objects. They found that nonlinguistic information affected the manner in which linguistic input was structured. They used ambiguous instructions such as "Put the apple on the towel in the box", where "the towel" could specify the location of the apple, or its destination. The visual arrays that they used are schematically represented in Fig. 6.2 with the numbers denoting the order in which eye fixations were made.

When the visual array showed two apples, one on a towel and one on a napkin (set-up A), the subjects would look at both apples immediately after hearing the word "apple". There was no indication that they ever entertained the (wrong) interpretation: "put the apple on the towel", with "towel" as destination,

because they did not look at a second towel that was present in the array. Rather, because there were two potential referents for the word "apple", they treated "on the towel" as a modifier phrase that specified which apple was meant. This pattern of performance contrasted sharply with what was observed when a similar set-up was used, but with just one apple (on a towel) (set-up B). In this situation, the subjects made eye movements from the apple to the second towel on hearing the word "towel", indicating that their initial interpretation was to treat "on the towel" as the destination of the apple.

This study is important in demonstrating that the syntactic structure of a sentence is not computed separately and then combined with other sources of information: to comprehend well, we need to use contextual information to select between possible meanings at the earliest stages of understanding.

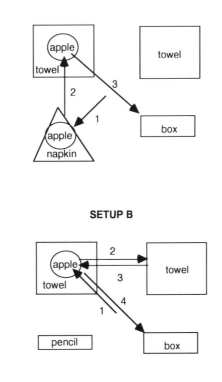

FIG. 6.2

Working memory

Read the following sentences, covering each one up as you read it, and then try to remember the final word of each sentence:

1. When at last his eyes opened, there was no gleam of triumph, no shade of anger.
2. The taxi turned up Michigan Avenue where they had a clear view of the lake.

This "reading span" task was devised by Daneman and Carpenter (1980) with the aim of measuring working memory, i.e. the resources available to a person both for computation and storage in the course of language processing. As Carpenter, Miyake, and Just (1994, p.1075) put it:

> The linearity of language necessitates temporarily storing the intermediate and final products of a reader's or listener's computations as she/he constructs and integrates ideas from the stream of successive words in a text or spoken discourse ... Working memory can be viewed as the pool of operational resources that perform the symbolic computations and thereby generate the intermediate and final products.

On this view, the more resources are consumed by sentence comprehension operations, the less workspace will be available for retaining the final words.

Daneman and Carpenter's working memory task has proved effective in several ways:

- within the normal population, there are substantial individual differences in working memory span;

- working memory span is positively correlated with sentence comprehension. (This was shown in the study by Miyake et al. (1994), reviewed in *Comprehension failure despite adequate grammatical competence* (p.157), as well as in other studies.)

- working memory span has a much closer relationship to reading comprehension level than does traditional memory span;

- working memory span declines as the complexity of the sentences increases, compatible with the notion that complex sentences consume more computational resources.

However, there are some cautions that need to be voiced about the notion of working memory.

1. It is difficult to establish how far one is measuring a cognitive capacity that causes individual differences in comprehension level, and how far one is simply measuring the consequences of such differences. Suppose a child had comprehension difficulties that had nothing to do with memory or processing capacity, but simply arose because the test was not in the child's first language. The process of comprehending written or spoken sentences would be difficult, especially if they were syntactically complex, and it is likely that the child would find it hard to remember material while trying to work out the meaning.

2. If working memory span were measuring some intrinsic capacity of the individual, we might expect to find that it was constant. This has been tested by comparing working memory across different tasks, (e.g. reading span) can be compared with an analogous task involving memory for written numbers which occur in the context of arithmetical sums). There is only weak evidence for a general "working memory capacity" that cuts across different domains (see Carpenter et al., 1994, for a review).

Overall, then, it seems that the working memory span task can provide a useful index of individual differences in sentence processing ability, but it is difficult to be certain which psychological processes it is tapping into; it cannot be assumed that a low score necessarily indexes some intrinsic limitation of general resources, and processes other than memory may be implicated in performance.

It should also be noted that "working memory" is a confusing term which is often used in a more general sense, sometimes being treated as equivalent to "short-term memory".

---

information. Rather than arguing that these children have fundamental limitations of auditory discrimination, he suggests they have a limited capacity language system that cannot cope with rapidly incoming information, and that when the system is stressed, it is phonetically weak information that is most vulnerable. Thus, in effect, he integrates some of Tallal's notions of a temporal processing deficit, with observations about the phonetic characteristics of inflected forms, to explain the disproportionate difficulty that children with SLI have in decoding grammatical morphology.

Leonard (1997, p.251) puts it as follows:

If inflected words were typically heard in one-word sentences separated by pauses, there would be no problem. However, fast on the heels of the inflected word is the next word in the utterance that must be held in working memory and processed, and so on. Thus, processing is pressed from two directions; processing of a first item must be completed before the item fades from memory, and in time for the next item. One of the hallmarks of limited processing capacity is limited speed of processing. Because sufficient processing of one item can't be completed before the next item appears, some material is processed incompletely or not at all.

To date, most of the theorising about performance limitations has focused on language production, and it is sometimes assumed that comprehension should not be affected by processing problems. However, this is misguided. If children comprehend constructions that they cannot produce, on a test that is constructed so that success can only be achieved by using grammatical knowledge, this is indeed evidence for performance rather than competence limitations (see e.g. Connell & Stone, 1992). However, impaired comprehension does not necessarily entail impaired competence. The material reviewed at the start of this chapter demonstrates that even normal adults with excellent language abilities can be induced to make comprehension errors under conditions where they have to process large amounts of complex information in a brief period of time. Furthermore, there is good evidence from normally developing children that accuracy on comprehension tests may be influenced by performance factors. For instance, Labelle (1973) showed that insertion of a pause at a major phrase boundary led to enhanced performance by young children in a sentence comprehension test.

An early study by Tallal (1975) demonstrates the potential importance of performance factors in comprehension deficits. She reported data from a study with the Token Test (de Renzi & Vignolo, 1962), in which the child is presented with a large array of cardboard squares and circles ("tokens") varying in colour, and, in some parts of the test, in size. The task is to carry out commands with a selection of named tokens. Unlike most multiple choice tests of syntactic comprehension, the Token Test places heavy demands on verbal memory (Martin & Feher, 1990). Results from Tallal's study are shown in Table 6.2.

The point underlined by Tallal was that the amount of material to be processed was at least as important as syntactic complexity in determining the errors of children with SLI. For instance, in part II, perfect performance could be achieved even if the child had no syntactic abilities and was simply able to interpret and combine the colour, size, and shape terms. Nevertheless, children with SLI were significantly impaired on this part. Syntax clearly is also important: there are far fewer errors on part III than on part V; both involve the same stimulus array and part V, like part III, consists mainly of instructions involving two tokens, but in addition involves interpretation of function words such as prepositions, negatives and subordinators. (In this regard, Tallal's findings resemble those of Bishop (1979); if the number of critical information words in a sentence is held constant, then grammatical complexity exerts a significant effect.) Furthermore, in part III, even though syntax was not critical for success, the child who had good syntactic skills might have been able to use these to advantage to encode information in memory. In this regard, it would be interesting to compare the Token Test results with a condition where children simply had to respond to a combination of critical words, e.g. square, blue, big, not organised into a syntactic structure. Overall, though, Tallal's study is important in drawing attention to the difficulties that children with SLI have in decoding sentences that contain large amounts of information, even when syntax is kept simple.

Performance-based accounts of language disorders are a relatively new phenomenon, and most of this chapter is speculative; given a dearth of empirical data, it is useful to consider what kinds of data might be informative in distinguishing

TABLE 6.2

Token Test Results with Children with SLI and Age-matched Controls (Data from Tallal, 1975, Fig. 1)

| Part | Sample items | % correct | | SLI error types |
		SLI (n = 12)	Controls (n = 12)	
pretest *	point to a red one; point to a circle; point to a small one	100	100	
I *	point to the red circle	100	100	
II **	point to the small green circle	82	100	mainly on shape
III *	point to the yellow circle and the blue circle; point to the red square and the green circle	70	96	shape and colour
IV **	point to the small white square and the large white circle; point to the large red circle and the small yellow square	43	87	shape, colour, and size
V *	put the red circle on the green square; if there is a black circle, pick up the red square; touch the squares slowly and the circles quickly	49	93	44/131 (34%) were selection of wrong token; others were grammatical; tendency to respond to final part only

* array of 5 large squares and 5 large circles (colours = red, green, blue, yellow, and white);
** array extended to include 5 small squares and 5 small circles, same five colours.

between theories. We can find some clues in the literature on adult aphasiology, where the distinction between explanations in terms of processing vs. representational deficits has been much debated, especially as regards the phenomenon of agrammatism (see, for instance, Fromkin, 1995). Very often the different theoretical accounts are difficult to distinguish empirically; the critical kinds of evidence have more to do with qualitative aspects of performance, rather than whether an impairment is apparent in a particular area of functioning. The following kinds of evidence are relevant when evaluating a performance account of comprehension deficits.

1. Pattern of errors on a specific structure

If a child lacks grammatical competence, then on a given grammatical structure, we should see either random performance arising from guessing, or use of a systematic strategy of using nonsyntactic information (e.g. interpreting the first-named noun phrase as the agent). If we find a pattern of performance that suggests partial knowledge of a grammatical rule, this suggests the limitation is in performance rather than competence. If we look at the detailed pattern of results obtained in studies of grammatical comprehension in SLI, this is the picture that typically emerges: for instance, although Bishop (1982) drew attention to a small subset of children with severe receptive language difficulties who appeared to have no understanding of constructions such as passive or postmodified sentences, most of the children in that study scored above chance levels on such structures while making more errors than control children of the same age. Gopnik (1994a) noted that adults with SLI did not perform randomly on a grammaticality judgement task: they had some awareness of the significance of tense marking, even though overall performance was poor. Even the striking findings of Van der Lely and colleagues (Van der Lely & Harris, 1990; Van der Lely & Stollwerck, 1997) on interpretation of passives or knowledge of Binding Principles reveal a pattern of performance that cannot be completely explained by chance guessing or strategic use of semantic or pragmatic knowledge (see Chapter 5). In short, children with SLI behaved as if they knew something about grammatical principles, but were shaky in applying that knowledge.

2. Profile of performance across different structures

As Gopnik (1994b) has noted, performance accounts which explain the relative difficulty of different grammatical structures in terms of "perceptual salience" or "processing complexity" are in danger of becoming no more than circular redescriptions of the data unless the critical explanatory concepts are made operational. However, if one can use a processing model derived from different data to explain phenomena observed in SLI, one can escape the circularity and make predictions that are independent of the observed data. One such example is Leonard's (1997) use of Lapointe's (1985) model of verb production (see *Lapointe's model of agrammatic errors in verb morphology*, overleaf), which was devised to account for morphological errors in agrammatism. Using this model, Leonard (1997) argued that when inappropriate items are produced, they will be entries in shallower cells than the targets, typically stems rather than inflected forms. In languages such as Italian, which do not permit bare stems, omission of inflections is not predicted; rather a morphologically simple form will tend to

be substituted for a more complex one. This is exactly what is seen in SLI. This model has been used to account for data on morphological production, but it would also predict that in comprehension, only the stem might be accessed when words are being decoded under time pressure.

3. Interaction between syntactic complexity and other language levels

If we assume that the problem is in a limited capacity system which handles several linguistic operations simultaneously, then we should find interaction between language levels; complexity at one level will affect errors at another. For instance, if we restrict ourselves to vocabulary that the child knows, but include some words that are relatively infrequent and others that are common, can we influence the difficulty of a grammatical comprehension test, by influencing the speed of lexical access? Does phonological complexity or word length affect the ability to understand a complex sentence? If we find interactions between language levels, this would be supportive of a processing explanation of comprehension difficulties. To my knowledge, studies of this kind have not been conducted on children with SLI, but they could be illuminating.

Although explicit manipulations of this kind have not been reported in relation to SLI, it has sometimes been noted that when children are learning to write, they make immature errors on grammatical morphology, even though they produce those same morphemes without error in their own speech. Smith-Lock (1991) demonstrated this phenomenon in children with reading difficulties, and my own informal observations suggest it is also characteristic of those with SLI. In effect, it could be argued that before writing is fully automated, the processes of getting words on paper, retrieving spellings, and keeping track of where one is in a sentence all divert attentional resources from grammatical processing. We need studies that explicitly compare the rate of induced errors on grammatical morphemes with other error types in this setting; such evidence as there is does

Lapointe's model of agrammatic errors in verb morphology

Agrammatic aphasia is an acquired neurological disorder in which expressive language is characterised by short, grammatically simplified sentences, so-called "telegraphic speech". However, not all grammatical morphemes are omitted. The verb ending "-ing" is commonly produced by English-speaking patients, and in highly inflected languages, such as Italian, the infinitive form is widely used.

Lapointe (1985) proposed a processing account of agrammatism, in which it was assumed that representations of grammatical morphemes are intact but not always accessible. He noted that grammatical markers associated with verbs express semantic notions (i.e. variations in attitude, voice, aspect, tense, agreement) that can be ordered in terms of their "markedness" or complexity. In producing an utterance, a representation of a sentence frame is constructed, and the specific form of the verb must then be looked up from a verb fragment store. It is assumed that verb fragment stores are organised in columns in terms of the semantic notions they express. Those expressing related notions are grouped together in the same column, and the least complex notions are stored in the most accessible (in Table 6.3, the leftmost) columns. When searching for the correct form of a verb, the search proceeds along the first row until the correct column is reached in terms of attitude, voice, and aspect, and then moves down the rows until a match is obtained on tense and agreement. The further away from the top left-hand corner that a form is stored, the more processing capacity is required to locate it. Lapointe argued that aphasia was associated with reduced processing capacity, and this meant that the search would have to terminate before a match was obtained, and more accessible (less complex) forms would be substituted for less accessible ones. Note that, while in English, this means that there will be a high proportion of bare verb stems (shown in Table 6.3 as V) produced, this is not the case for Italian, where the bare stem is not a legal grammatical form.

seem to support the idea that grammatical morphology is particularly vulnerable when the system is stressed.

4. Task manipulations to affect accuracy

If performance factors prevent the child demonstrating underlying competence, then by manipulating those factors, we should be able to influence accuracy. For instance, if the problem is in rapid access of lexical information, then performance might be improved by slowing down rate of presentation. In a study of children with SLI, McCroskey and Thompson (1973) showed that for younger children, performance on a sentence comprehension task improved significantly when the sentences were presented at a rate of 2.9 syllables per second, compared with 5.0 syllables per second. It would be of interest to do a study comparing the effects of rate manipulations for children with SLI and younger language-matched normal controls, to see whether a fast rate exerts a disproportionately severe effect on the former group.

The most convincing evidence for a performance account of comprehension problems would be if one demonstrated normal levels of competence in children with SLI by altering task demands, e.g. by inserting pauses or slowing the presentation rate. The opposite approach is also possible: i.e. one could look for methods of increasing processing demands to induce a "language-impaired" profile of performance in a normally developing child. This approach has been adopted in the field of adult acquired aphasia: Blackwell and Bates (1995) showed that normal subjects produced an "agrammatic" performance profile if required to perform a secondary task while making grammaticality judgements; they argued from this that grammatical morphemes were selectively vulnerable in receptive processing. The work by Miyake, Carpenter, and Just (1994), reviewed in *Comprehension failure despite adequate grammatical competence* (p.157), provides another example of simulating agrammatic performance in normal adults.

It is important to recognise, however, that predictions from processing accounts are not always straightforward. Consider, for instance, a study by Montgomery (1995) who investigated the effect on comprehension of padding sentences out with redundant verbiage (e.g. "the dirty little boy climbs the great big tall tree" vs. "the little boy climbs the tree"). One could make a case for

TABLE 6.3

Verb Fragment Stores for English and Italian

		←low————————complexity of attitude/voice/aspect————————high→			
English		1	2	3	4
low complexity of tense/agreement	1	V	aux V+ing	aux V+en	aux being V+en
	2	V+s	aux been V+ing	aux been V+en	aux been being V+en
	3	V+ed			
high complexity of tense/agreement	4	aux V+en			
Italian					
low complexity of tense/agreement	1	V+are	aux V+ato	aux V+ato'	aux stato V+ato'
	2	V+a			
	3	V+i			
high complexity of tense/agreement	4	V+o			

arguing that this should help the child with a processing problem, because more time is available for processing the salient words, which occur at longer intervals. On the other hand, it could be argued the processing of the redundant words will divert resources from the salient words, and so comprehension will be impaired. In fact, the latter result was observed in children with SLI. Similar results were reported by Curtiss and Tallal (1991), in a study which contrasted comprehension of sentences that differed in degree of redundancy, but which were designed to have comparable syntactic structure, and conveyed very similar information (see Table 6.4, overleaf). Older children, like normal adults, benefited from redundancy, but children with SLI, like younger language-matched controls did better on the non-redundant sentences. In both these studies, the authors concluded that the data supported the view

that children with SLI have comprehension problems that reflect processing rather than representational deficits, with performance suffering when they have to cope with large amounts of incoming information.

5. Simulation of the effects of performance constraints on comprehension

In addition, we should be able to model the comprehension process and demonstrate that the kinds of errors that are found can be generated by altering one component of the system. In a computer simulation such as Lexicat (see Table 6.1, p.158), slow application of combination rules or slow access of categorial information could lead to decay of material in the input buffer before it had been fully processed. Limited capacity of the stack, or unusually rapid decay of items held on the stack would also lead to failure to compute a correct

TABLE 6.4

Examples of Redundant and Nonredundant Sentence Used by Curtiss and Tallal (1991)

Redundant	Nonredundant
point to the picture of three hats	point to the picture of the hats
the girl who is smiling is pushing the boy	the girl smiling is pushing the boy
the girl who is pushing the boy is smiling	the girl pushing the boy is smiling

interpretation. This would have especially severe effects in processing syntactically complex sentences which contain discontinuous constituents, and which tax the system because incomplete syntactic structures must be held in memory. Of additional interest is the possibility that difficulties in generating a morphosyntactic representation would arise if the listener could not access adequate prosodic, semantic, or pragmatic information to distinguish between two or more interpretations. The possibilities are so numerous that one may start to despair of choosing between them, but the advantage of using a model that has been simulated on a computer is that one can generate testable predictions about the impact of different manipulations on performance. Although such applications have not to date been attempted, in principle, one could use a simulation such as Lexicat to compute the memory load associated with different types of syntactic construction, and one can identify sentences that do or do not require prosodic information for disambiguation.

Computer simulations of comprehension deficits in SLI remain, at present, a goal to strive

towards rather than a reality. However, this approach has been adopted in the related field of acquired aphasia. Haarman and Kolk (1991) used a computer simulation of sentence comprehension to show how slowed processing or rapid decay of transient representations could lead to the kinds of agrammatic comprehension problem seen in some aphasic adults.

We may sum up this chapter by saying that performance accounts of comprehension problems offer a new perspective on SLI, and have the potential to resolve some of the unexplained findings in the field, such as the evidence for partial and probabilistic knowledge of syntax. However, if we are to take this line of argument further, we must specify what it is that is hampering performance. "Processing capacity limitations" are often invoked, but this is a notoriously vague concept. What it tries to capture is the idea that real-life on-line language processing requires that several different types of computation need to be carried out at the same time; when the material to be processed is complex, or when there is time pressure, processing may break down.

7

Understanding discourse: Integrating language and context

There's more to talking than just words.

Humphrey Bogart in *The Barefoot Contessa* (Joseph Mankiewicz, 1954)

OVERVIEW

1. Real-life understanding involves integrating the meaning of language with the environmental context and general knowledge. Children with SLI may be very good at deducing what is probable in a given situation, and so appear much more competent in everyday contexts than in formal tests.

2. Understanding of discourse, i.e. longer stretches of talk beyond the single sentence, involves constructive processing to draw inferences about what has not been directly stated and so to build a mental model of the meaning. Children with SLI seem to be disproportionately poor at building mental models; more so than would be predicted from their comprehension of individual sentences. These deficits can be seen even when discourse is presented in pictorial rather than linguistic form.

3. Information that is not integrated into a mental model is much more fragile and prone to be forgotten, so children with SLI tend to have poor memory for literal as well as inferred meaning of stories they have recently seen or heard.

4. For some children, especially those described as having a "semantic pragmatic disorder", the problem is not just that they don't draw appropriate inferences, but that they sometimes draw the wrong inferences, leading to unexpected and over-literal interpretations. It is suggested that such problems might arise from a failure to engage inhibitory processes that usually serve to suppress unwanted and irrelevant associations.

5. Finally, children with unusual interests and preoccupations may appear to have poor comprehension simply because they are not motivated to process what is being said beyond a shallow level.

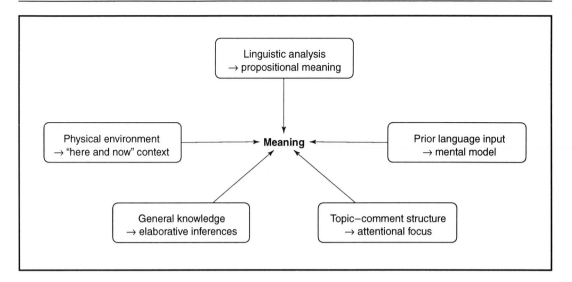

FIG. 7.1   Integration of verbal and nonverbal sources of information in comprehension.

INTRODUCTION

The use of language in context comes under the domain of pragmatics. As shown in Fig. 7.1, the meaning of an utterance may be regarded as jointly determined by its propositional meaning, the context in which it occurs, the background general knowledge that the listener brings to the interpretative process, the focus of linguistic attention, and the mental model that the listener develops as a series of utterances are integrated. Chapters 3 to 6 were concerned with the stages involved in computing a propositional meaning from spoken input. This chapter will focus on the other four sources of information shown in Fig. 7.1. In Chapter 8, we move on to consider another aspect of pragmatics: use of social context.

USE OF CONTEXTUAL CUES TO DECODE LANGUAGE: NORMAL DEVELOPMENT

Cues from the physical environment

For the young child first grappling with the task of decoding language, contextual cues from the physical environment are all-important. The

competent infant shows considerable sensitivity to what message is likely from a given speaker in a given situation. For example, a child who notices mother going into the kitchen can deduce from the context and her questioning tone of voice that she is offering food or drink. Chapman (1978) points out that this is one reason why formal comprehension tests (which are usually designed to minimise the role of contextual cues and general knowledge) may bear only a weak relationship to the child's ability to understand in everyday life, and why there can be considerable mismatch between the level of comprehension reported by a parent (who is interested in whether the child understands the message, and not in whether linguistic or contextual cues are relied upon) and a researcher or clinician (who regards "comprehension" as referring to the understanding of linguistic forms when contextual cues are minimized). She cited an illustrative example from Lewis and Freedle (1973, p.312). The parents of a 13-month-old girl claimed she had excellent language comprehension:

> When handed an apple in the high chair and told "Eat the apple", she bit into it. When handed an apple in her playpen and told "Throw the apple", she threw it. The

skeptical researchers intervened by handing the child an apple in her highchair and requesting "Throw the apple". The child bit into it. Later, as she played in her playpen, she was handed an apple and told "Eat the apple"; she threw it. The basis for her apparent comprehension might be summarized as the strategy, "Do what you usually do in the situation".

If the external environment did not severely constrain the range of possible things that a child might expect to hear, language would be much more difficult to learn. As we saw in Chapter 4, once a few basic words and sentence structures are acquired, the child can use this limited knowledge to "bootstrap" further language learning, by combining information from a partially understood utterance with inferences based on the context. It follows that, if we pit contextual cues against verbal information, we would expect young children to pay more attention to the former, and this is indeed what is found.

In an early study on comprehension, E. Clark (1973) assessed children's understanding of commands containing prepositions (e.g. "put the knife on the table"). It soon became apparent that the actual form of words that was used was the last thing that a child paid attention to. Performance would be excellent if the target sentence corresponded to a likely scenario (e.g. "put the spoon in the cup") but was poor if less probable events were described (e.g. "put the spoon on the cup"). Knowledge of how the objects were typically used would override what was said, and the child would put an object in a container and on an object with a flat supporting surface regardless of the preposition. Strohner and Nelson (1974) reported similar findings with preschoolers who were asked to act out sentences such as "the girl feeds the baby" or "the baby feeds the girl". Three-year-olds acted out the more likely scenario, whereas by five years of age children paid more attention to the syntax.

Awareness of possible response biases is important in interpreting findings on children's comprehension tests. The same sentence may be responded to quite differently depending on

whether the child is required to act out a probable scenario, to carry out a counterintuitive command, or to select from an array of possible interpretations. Grieve, Hoogenraad, and Murray (1977) showed that children demonstrated better understanding of prepositions when presented with three spatial arrangements and asked to find the one to match a sentence, than when they were asked to act out sentences as in the E. Clark (1973) study. Should we therefore prefer multiple choice sentence comprehension tests (e.g. Test of Auditory Comprehension of Language—TACL, Carrow-Woolfolk, 1985; or Test for Reception of Grammar, Bishop, 1989b) to tests that require the child to act out commands, such as the Reynell Developmental Language Scales (Reynell, 1985)? (see *Receptive language assessments*, p.29, for examples). The answer will depend on the purpose of assessment. If the aim is to obtain an index of everyday comprehension, then a test like the Reynell is useful as it allows the child to demonstrate how much is understood in more naturalistic situations where both syntactic and contextual cues may be used. If, however, we are specifically interested in how far the child can use grammatical information, we need a test that was devised to minimise the extent to which contextual cues can help or hinder comprehension, such as TROG. It is possible to devise acting-out tests where contextual biases are minimised: the Token Test (de Renzi & Vignolo, 1962) is an example. However, the lack of bias is achieved by using meaningless materials (shapes), which can make this a tedious task for young children.

General knowledge

Language development has been described as involving a progressive trend towards "decontextualisation". As Givón (1979) has pointed out, at the very start, cultural generic knowledge is not shared between children and adults, but specific knowledge about the immediate environment is. Hence, talk with young children is predominantly about the "here and now" (Keenan & Schieffelin, 1976). However, as they grow older, conversations with them are increasingly about non-observable topics: e.g. what happened in the past, what will happen in the future, feelings and judgements, or

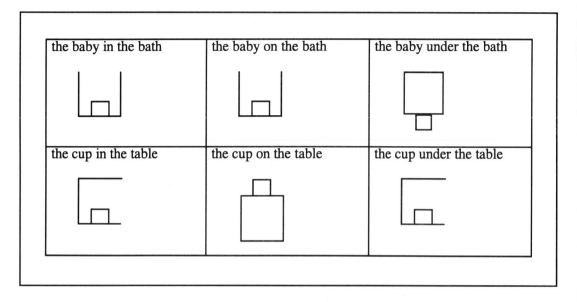

FIG. 7.2   Most frequent responses by two- to four-year-old children when acting out commands with a large and small box, labelled either as baby and bath, or as cup and table (from Grieve et al., 1977). Note that although children show some sensitivity to the target sentence (e.g. they usually respond correctly when asked to "put the baby under the bath"), they are also strongly influenced by the labels given to the boxes, as is evidenced by the different responses to parallel instructions in the top and bottom rows.

abstract ideas. This does not mean that nonlinguistic cues are not used; on the contrary, children continue to make very heavy use of information beyond the words they hear, but the source of this is more likely to include long-term memory as well as the immediate physical environment. This was nicely illustrated in the study on prepositions by Grieve et al. (1977), which was mentioned earlier. In the acting-out condition, the stimuli were a big box and a small box. This experiment showed that children's responses to prepositions could be manipulated simply by altering how the boxes were referred to. When the little box was termed the "baby" and the big box was "the bath", there was a clear tendency to put the little box in the big box; however, when the same objects were labelled as "the chair" and "the table" respectively, then children responded differently to instructions involving "in", "on", or "under" (see Fig. 7.2, above). What these children were doing was using their memorised experience of how things behave to guide their interpretation.

The bulk of experimental evidence shows that when prior knowledge and sentence meaning are placed in conflict, young children start out by placing most reliance on their knowledge of what is probable and how things typically behave, but they gradually give more precedence to the spoken message so that they can correctly interpret even counterintuitive sentences or improbable instructions. However, it would be misleading to conclude that children abandon using one kind of cue to meaning (general knowledge) and start using another (sentence meaning). In everyday communication, general knowledge and the spoken message are seldom in conflict; rather they supplement one another. (Indeed, when they do conflict, this can be a signal that the speaker intends a different meaning from the literal message, as we shall see in Chapter 8.) As Milosky (1992) has pointed out, it is important that general knowledge is not ignored because it provides a vital means of resolving ambiguity. Most words have multiple meanings, and when we take any concatenation of words, the number of possible meanings quickly mushrooms (as was illustrated in *Language ambiguity*, p.13). The problem for the language learner is not to recover *the* meaning of an utterance, but rather to settle on one specific meaning from a host of possibilities. To do this, the child must be able not to ignore background knowledge, but rather to integrate it with the spoken message. Attempts to train computers to understand natural language have emphasised that comprehension would be impossible if we did not integrate the words we hear with our knowledge of what is probable, and of how the world works. As we shall see, some children have a tendency to be "over literal" in their comprehension, suggesting a problem with this integrative process.

General knowledge is used to select among possible meanings for a word. It also plays a major role in enabling a child to go beyond what is directly stated to make elaborative inferences. For example, as noted in Chapter 1, if I say "the fish is on the table" to guests enjoying a pre-dinner drink, they will fill in much unstated information; they will assume the fish is dead, cooked, and on a plate. Note that the kinds of inference that people make based on general knowledge are different from the kinds of logical inference studied by philosophers. Logical inference involves deriving conclusions from premises, and these must be true. So, if I say:

The fish is on the plate. The plate is under the table.

then it must follow that the fish is under the table. In real-world comprehension, however, inferences are seldom of this kind. Rather, they involve interpreting what is said in relation to what is probable in a given situation. For instance, it could be that when they come to the table my guests discover that far from attending to their gastronomic needs, I am showing off my pet Siamese fighting fish which is swimming around in a bowl. However, in this case I could be fairly accused of being obtuse or deliberately provocative. In general, it is safe to make the most probable inference, because competent communicators construct messages in such a way that they leave only the obvious unstated, making explicit mention of things that the listener could not be expected to infer.

Since inferences are based on knowledge of the world, comprehension will depend on the kinds of

experiences and interests that the listener brings to the situation. This is illustrated in a study by Spilich, Vesonder, Chiesi, and Voss (1979), who showed that two groups of people who were matched on reading ability but differed in baseball expertise diverged markedly in their ability to recall a text describing a baseball match. Those with high baseball knowledge showed evidence of having formed a higher order global structure for the story which enabled them to maintain the most important information. If we find that children appear to have difficulty in drawing inferences, we need to ask whether this is because they lack the general knowledge on which inferences depend, or whether there is a more fundamental problem in the inferential process itself.

Attentional focus: Topic and comment

Before reading this section, look at the puzzles posed in *Two puzzles*, below.

We have already noted that speakers tend to omit from an utterance information that can be readily inferred. In addition, the placement of information that is included will typically be arranged so that what is novel is part of the predicate of the sentence and is stressed, whereas the old and familiar information is part of the subject, and is unstressed (Clark & Haviland,

---

Two puzzles

Answer these two questions and then turn to *Answers to two puzzles*, overleaf.

A. How many animals of each kind did Moses take on the ark?

B. There was a tourist flight travelling from Vienna to Barcelona. On the last leg of the journey, it developed engine trouble. Over the Pyrenees, the pilot started to lose control. The plane eventually crashed right on the border. Wreckage was equally strewn in France and Spain. The authorities were trying to decide where to bury the survivors. What is the solution?

Answers to two puzzles

A. The "Moses Illusion" (Erickson & Mattson, 1981).

Most people respond "two". The correct answer is zero. It was Noah, not Moses, who took animals on the ark.

B. Example from Barton and Sanford (1993).

Typical answers to question B are "their relatives should be left to decide" or "they should be buried where they landed". However, it is dead people, rather than survivors who are buried.

These examples illustrate that we do not fully process all the information present in sentences that we hear. In general, we assume the speaker is being co-operative, and we do not expend much effort evaluating whether the presuppositions behind a question are true. Very different results are seen if the incorrect information is the focus of a question, e.g.

> Was it Moses who took two animals of each kind on the ark?

We would also notice the oddity of questions such as:

> How many animals of each sort did Jesus take on the ark?

or

> How many animals of each sort did Noah take on the aeroplane?

Clearly, we do some processing of the information expressed in a presupposition, but this is at a fairly shallow level.

1977). In English, this tends to mean that new material occurs at the end of utterances. When processing a sentence, attention is concentrated on the information in focus; the other information is assumed to be already known and is given much shallower processing, as demonstrated by the Moses illusion and related phenomena.

On the other hand, it would be wrong to suppose that the "topic" information is unimportant. As Gernsbacher (1990) has pointed out, the information that comes first may be regarded as setting up the foundation of a mental structure onto which subsequent information is mapped. In effect, the subject (given) is what is talked about, and the predicate (new) is what is stated about it. If this kind of structure is incompatible with other information, problems can ensue, as was nicely illustrated in an early study by Huttenlocher and Strauss (1968). They showed that the ordering of information in a sentence can dramatically influence performance on "acting out" comprehension tasks, because children are sensitive to the topic-comment structure of the sentence and treat the sentence subject as the item that they should

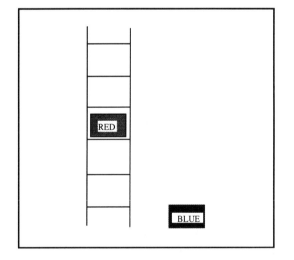

FIG. 7.3 Experimental set-up used by Huttenlocher and Strauss. One block (here, the red block) is fixed on the ladder. The child is given a second block and asked to "make it so that the ___ block is under/on top of the ___ block". Children aged from four to five years are 93% correct when the moveable block is the subject (e.g. "the blue block is under the red block") but only 78% correct when the moveable block is the object (e.g. "the red block is under the blue block").

"do something" with. They asked children to arrange blocks on a ladder (see Fig. 7.3, opposite) so that, for instance, "the red block is under the blue block", and found that for the same sentence, accuracy depended critically on which block was moveable. Children's natural tendency was to pick up and move the block that was first-mentioned (i.e. that denoting the subject), so when given a blue block and told to make it so that "the red block is under the blue block", they had difficulty. In this kind of item, the context provided by the blocks was much harder to map on to the command than when the moveable block was the first named. This kind of example provides further evidence that children's comprehension depends on integrating meaning with context, and is not just a function of knowledge of word meaning and grammatical structure.

The topic-comment structure of a sentence does not just serve to specify an interpretative focus for that sentence. It also plays an important role in ensuring that sequences of sentences can be coherently connected, because the "given"

information points to a connection is with the prior material. This is something that we shall consider further in the next section.

Constructive comprehension beyond the sentence level: Building a mental model

One aspect of context that children become increasingly able to use as they grow older is prior linguistic context. When we have a conversation, or listen to a narrative, we do not simply react to each utterance in isolation. Rather, we build up a representation of situations, events and objects and the relationships between these, effectively summarising all the information from the whole sequence.[1] The surface detail of what has been said gets lost, but the gist is encoded and progressively elaborated with each new utterance (see *Deriving gist from sequences*, below).

How are links formed between successive sentences in a discourse? Haviland and Clark (1974) proposed that the way in which information was represented as "given" or "new" in a sentence, according to whether it was given focus or not,

---

Deriving gist from sequences

Shortly after hearing or reading a story, people are unable to distinguish sentences that were in the story from those that correspond to inferences made from the story (e.g. Johnson, Bransford, & Solomon, 1973). Consider the following short story:

> John was at the beach.
> He trod on some broken glass.
> He had to go to hospital.

After a brief delay, people would accept "He cut his foot on some broken glass" as a sentence that had been in the story. They would, however, reject sentences that drew implausible inferences (e.g. "John broke some glass on the beach").

Another way of demonstrating that people integrate meanings across a sequence of sentences is simply to measure the time people take to read sentences depending on how far they form a coherent sequence.

Myers, Shinjo, and Duffy (1987) presented adults with two-sentence sequences that varied in the extent of causal relatedness, for instance:

High relatedness
(a) Cathy felt very dizzy and fainted at her work.
(b) She was carried unconscious to a hospital.

Moderate relatedness
(a) Cathy worked very hard and became exhausted.
(b) She was carried unconscious to a hospital.

Low relatedness
(a) Cathy had begun working on the new project.
(b) She was carried unconscious to a hospital.

Reading times for the (b) outcomes increased systematically as the sequences became less related. Thus, the time taken to process a sentence is critically dependent on how easy it is to integrate with prior material.

played a crucial role in forming links between the current utterance and what had gone before. When the listener encounters information that is "given", this initiates a search in memory for matching information. For instance, if we hear:

I saw John yesterday.   He looked very tired.

We identify "he" as given information, and look for a suitable referent for this pronoun in memory. We find "John" from the previous sentence, allowing us to form a referential connection between the two utterances. A referential connection, where the same noun phrase is repeated, or a pronoun used to refer back to a previously named entity, is a major way in which connections are formed, but it is not the only one. We have no difficulty, for instance, in comprehending a sequence such as:

Tony drove to London. The car broke down.

Here "the car" cannot be related to any previously mentioned entity, but its existence is readily inferred from the verb "drove".

Bridging inferences that make connections between successive sentences may be far more elaborate than those that are needed simply to establish referential connections.

For instance, if we hear the "John" short story from *Deriving gist from sequences* (p.175) we infer that John was barefoot and he cut his foot, although this was not explicitly stated. If we could not make these inferences, the connections between adjacent utterances would seem opaque.

Early accounts of inferential processing treated language comprehension as the formation of a representation in terms of a set of propositions (see *Propositional and situational models of meanings*, opposite) in a hierarchical relationship to one another. A model developed by Kintsch and van Dijk (1978) proposed that each sentence was represented in propositional format, and a representation of a connected discourse was generated by identifying common elements in subsequent propositions. If no common elements could be found, an inferential process would be initiated, with new propositions, implicit in the

text, being added. The whole set of propositions would then be condensed by deleting or generalising irrelevant or redundant propositions and constructing new inferred propositions that combined information from several utterances. This approach, however, cannot readily account for the richness of the representations that people derive from interpreting language in context. For instance, in the 3-sentence story about John at the beach (*Deriving gist from sequences*, p.175), one could form a connected propositional representation, based on the common referent in all three sentences (John, he, he), but this would not contain the rich additional information necessary to make the text coherent, that John cut his foot. Furthermore, in many instances, there is more than one previously mentioned entity that a pronoun could refer to. Consider:

The teacher scolded the boy
A   He was angry
B   He had spilt some ink

The referent of "he" is ambiguous in both (A) and (B), but general knowledge will bias us to interpret "he" as "the teacher" in (A) and as "the boy" in (B).

It is now generally accepted that at some level meaning must be represented in a format which is more analogous to the real world; a "situation model" or "mental model". Van Dijk (1995) defines a model as a construct in episodic memory that represents the event or situation that a text is about. Thus, rather than an abstract set of interconnected propositions, it is assumed that we generate representations more akin to our memories of experienced events, in their richness, multimodality, subjectivity, and fuzziness. The principal objection to the notion of mental models is simply that the concept is rather vague and hence difficult to incorporate in any formal account of the comprehension process. However, these objections are now being countered by formal implementations of comprehension processes based on mental models (see Glenberg, Kruley, & Langston, 1994).

The ability to interpret successive pieces of information by forming an integrated mental

Propositional and situational models of meaning

Formal semantic theory starts from the notion that, in principle, any declarative sentence can be decomposed into a set of basic meaning elements and the relationship between them. A proposition specifies the relationship between elements and is composed of a predicate and one or more arguments. We encountered arguments in Chapter 5, when discussing the argument structure of verbs (see *Thematic roles and argument structure*, p.123). Arguments correspond to the elements that enter into a relationship, and the predicate denotes the relationship that obtains. Any kind of relationship between elements can be depicted as one or more propositions, as illustrated in the following examples:

Hilary is tired	Tired (Hilary)
Elisabeth eats	Eats (Elisabeth)
Karen is a gardener	Gardener (Karen)
Rik drives the car	Drives (Rik, car)
Linda is in the car	In (Linda, car)
Sally gives Ruth an apple	Give (Sally, Ruth, apple)

More complicated sentences contain several propositions, sometimes conjoined but more often in a hierarchy, e.g. in this example, we number each component proposition and then show the relationships between the whole utterance.

The excitable scientist attacked the speaker during the seminar

P1 = Excitable (scientist)
P2 = Attacked (P1, speaker)
P3 = During (P2, seminar)
During (Attacked (excitable (scientist), speaker), seminar)

Propositional notation resembles algebra, and can be used to express functions with the arguments unspecified, e.g.:

Attacked (X, Y)

Propositional representations have been especially popular in theories of discourse, where the problem of establishing coherence in a text is seen as that of identifying common terms in successive propositions, allowing a higher-order summary proposition to be formed, just as one might solve a series of algebraic equations by deleting and combining terms. However, despite their elegant simplicity, there are a number of problems with propositional representations. In the first place, much natural language does not readily lend itself to a propositional notation, and this kind of system can run into difficulties when confronted with real-life utterances. Second, there is ample evidence that people are aware of much richer meanings than are embodied in a propositional representation. For instance, if one merely formed a propositional representation of the "the fish is on the table"

on (fish, table)

one would anticipate the kind of scenario depicted in Fig. 7.4, rather than incorporating information relevant to a meal, such as tablecloth, plate, cutlery, and a cooked fish.

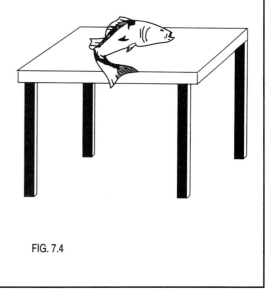

FIG. 7.4

model is not something that has been much studied by developmentalists. There is a small literature on children's developing expressive ability to produce narratives that are both cohesive and coherent (Kemper & Edwards, 1986) (see *Cohesion and coherence*, overleaf). Karmiloff-Smith (1985) showed that when children are asked to describe a story shown in a series of pictures presented one at a time, four- and five-year-olds tend to use pronouns to refer to something visible in the picture, with their output being largely driven by each stimulus picture as it appears. By six to seven years of age, pronouns are used anaphorically, i.e. to refer back to something already mentioned in the text, but discourse relations are expressed in a very rigid manner. By eight to nine years, the child is able to express discourse relations in a more flexible fashion.

There is also work with older schoolchildren looking at appreciation of structure in written stories; for instance, van den Broek (1989) showed that 11-year-olds were more adept at appreciating connections that extended across story episodes, whereas 8-year-olds focused more on within-episode connections. However, we know much less about children's understanding of spoken dis-course, particularly in more naturalistic settings, the most important of which is in conversation. The conversational context adds a new dimension to discourse comprehension, in that it requires two individuals to collaborate in establishing and developing a topic (Keenan & Schieffelin, 1976). This involves appreciation of the social role of language (see Chapter 8) as well as the ability to integrate the current utterance with someone else's prior discourse. Research on conversations with children has not looked systematically at how mental models are developed and used, but observational studies suggest that children whose productive language is at the one- or two-word stage have a limited attention span that precludes extended development of a discourse topic.

Cohesion and coherence

A series of utterances—either a narrative by one speaker, or a conversation with contributions from two participants—is cohesive in so far as the same entities are referred to in successive utterances, using pronouns such as "him" or "her", or expressions containing a definite article, such as "the man". For instance, here is a short extract from a story retold by a language-impaired child, with all the instances where something is referred back to highlighted.

> bernard walked down 'stair
> and **he** saw a 'monster
> got little 'horns
> and **he** say why you here my 'garden.
> **he** said oh I will gobble you 'up
> and **he** gobbled **bernard** 'up
> and **he** have a little bit on **bernard** 'shoe
> and dad reading the 'paper
> and **the monster** ate **his** 'shoe

The use of pronouns, proper names, and definite reference ("he") links the content of each utterance to what has gone before. Note, however, that this child's control of cohesion is far from perfect, and the listener has to use general knowledge to work out which character is being referred to by "he" in some of these utterances.

Coherence refers to the extent to which a text forms an integrated unit. Gernsbacher (1990) proposes four sources of coherence:

- referential coherence: consistency in who or what is being talked about
- temporal coherence: consistency in when the events occur
- locational coherence: consistency in where the events occur
- causal coherence: consistency in why these events occur.

A text may be coherent without being cohesive. For instance, the sequence:

> John drove to London
> the car broke down

is not cohesive, in that there is no prior referent for "the car", but it is coherent.

Conversely, simply repeating common material in adjacent sentences does not make a text coherent, as in this example:

> I live near the river.
> The river is full of weeds.
> Dandelions are yellow weeds.
> Jane has a yellow hat.

Each sentence has a common word with the prior sentence, but there is no coherence.

Furthermore, at this stage, children are easily distracted by events in the immediate physical environment (Keenan & Schieffelin, 1976). At four years of age most children still have some difficulty in taking prior context into account. Thus, in answering a question, they may respond simply to whatever has immediately gone before, without relating this to the global topic set up by the prior conversation. The ability to build up mental structures on the basis of longer stretches of talk probably depends both on increasing powers of memory and attention, and also on developing general knowledge that provides a suitable framework into which the information can be slotted and which allows appropriate inferences to be drawn about what is not directly stated. By concentrating on talk about things and events in the current environment, young children may give an impression of conversational sophistication that evaporates as soon as they are required to discuss past or future happenings. The difference is that talk of the past or future requires that they generate a mental model to use as a frame of reference instead of the externally present environment. The ability to use a mental representation of a situation to "stand in place" of the real world is a major cognitive achievement, but the way in which this develops and is used in spoken language comprehension has barely been studied in normally developing children, let alone in those with SLI.

INTEGRATION OF DIFFERENT SOURCES OF MEANING BY CHILDREN WITH SLI

Comparatively little work has been done on use of contextual cues in comprehension by children with SLI. Van der Lely and Dewart (1986) applied a method that had originally been used in a study by Tager-Flusberg (1981). The child is asked to act out commands using small toys, with the test sentences being systematically varied in terms of both grammatical complexity and "semantic bias".[2] Tager-Flusberg had previously shown that children with autism showed some sensitivity to word order but were less likely than other children to use a

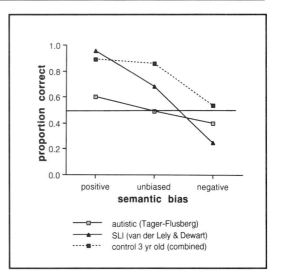

FIG. 7.5   Results from studies by Tager-Flusberg (1981) and Van der Lely and Dewart (1986) using identical test sentences. The graph shows the proportion of reversible active sentences acted out correctly by children with autism, children with SLI, and normal three-year-olds (data from both studies combined). The control children are matched to the clinical groups in terms of receptive vocabulary. The horizontal line corresponds to chance level performance.

"probable event" strategy, i.e. their responses were typically not influenced by the fact that some commands described probable scenarios and others were improbable. Van der Lely and Dewart, using the same materials, found just the opposite trend in children with SLI. These children showed little sensitivity to word order, but were highly sensitive to semantic bias, so much so that they performed below chance on items with negative semantic bias, above chance on those with positive semantic bias, and around chance on unbiased items (see Fig. 7.5, above). On the unbiased and negatively biased items their performance fell below that of younger normal children who had been matched on receptive language level. This study suggests that children with SLI place unusually heavy reliance on nonsyntactic cues to meaning, and are poor at using syntactic information to arrive at an interpretation.

This is exactly what one might expect if one accepts the kind of theory put forward in Chapter 5, that attributes comprehension problems in SLI as primarily due to syntactic deficiencies in an otherwise normally developing child.

Prior linguistic context: Inferencing and comprehension of discourse in SLI

As we have seen, context encompasses the prior discourse as well as environmental context. If a limited processing capacity restricts the amount of information the child can integrate, then discourse should provide a particularly taxing challenge to the child with SLI. Research in the 1980s addressed this issue, and generally confirmed this expectation. Merritt and Liles (1987) conducted a study comparing language-impaired and age-matched control children on tasks of story generation, story retelling, and story comprehension. Comprehension of factual details from the stories was similar in the two groups, but the language-impaired children did more poorly on questions concerned with causal relationships that had not been directly stated. The authors concluded that the problems that language impaired children have in processing narratives do not simply reflect poor memory, but nor do they seem due to limitations in understanding component sentences.   In both story generation and story retelling, the language-impaired children produced fewer complete story episodes, in some cases producing loosely connected initiating events combined with irrelevant information. The story generation task, in particular, places no demands on the child's comprehension. All that is involved is production of a coherent narrative from a story stem beginning. Nevertheless, in this situation, the children with SLI had evident difficulties. Such a finding provides the first suggestive evidence that problems with discourse may not be simply reducible to secondary effects of more fundamental limitations of sentence interpretation.

Another way of addressing this issue is to see whether, on discourse comprehension tasks, children with SLI resemble younger children of similar comprehension level. Ellis Weismer (1985) compared inferential skills in story comprehension in three groups of children: those with SLI, an age-matched control group, and another group of younger children matched on raw scores on a receptive language test. Children were presented with three-item verbal or pictorial sequences and

then asked questions about these, half of which required them to recall premises that had been shown or stated, and half which required them to make an inference. Ellis Weismer found that children with SLI were poor on this task relative to age-matched controls, but they did not differ from younger normally developing children matched on comprehension level. Similar results were reported by Crais and Chapman (1987) in a study in which children were given literal and inferential questions about short stories that were presented orally. In contrast to the Merritt and Liles (1987) study, neither of these researchers found any evidence of a selective problem with inferences in children with SLI. Rather, it seemed as if ability to answer both inferential and non-inferential questions was a function of overall comprehension level as assessed by multiple choice tests.

The picture was further complicated by a study by Bishop and Adams (1992), which obtained rather different results. Children with SLI and controls of similar and younger ages were asked both factual and inferential questions about stories they had heard or seen as a series of pictures (see Table 7.1, p.181, and Fig. 7.6, p.182, for sample story and questions). In common with Ellis Weismer and Crais and Chapman, Bishop and Adams found that children with SLI were impaired on story comprehension, regardless of whether questions involved recall of overtly presented detail (literal questions), or whether an inference had to be drawn. However, in this study the impairment in story comprehension for children with SLI was still evident when raw score from the Test for Reception of Grammar (Bishop, 1989b) was partialled out in an analysis of covariance. Thus it seemed that the problems in story comprehension could not simply be attributed to difficulties in understanding grammatical structure. Bishop and Adams suggested two possible methodological reasons why this study found disproportionate difficulty with story comprehension vs. sentence comprehension, while others had not; first, the statistical power of their study was stronger because the sample size was relatively large, and second, the sentence comprehension tests used in other studies had a lower ceiling.

TABLE 7.1

Sample Story and Questions from Bishop and Adams' (1992) Study

Andrew was skating on the ice, wrapped up in his woolly hat, gloves, and scarf. He skated to the middle of the pond where the ice was thin. Andrew cried out when the ice gave way under his weight and he crashed through it. A man rushed quickly to rescue him, pulling him out by both arms. When he got home, Andrew got wrapped up in a blanket and sat down by the fire, holding a hot cup of tea.

Questions:

literal

1. What was Andrew doing at the start of the story?

2. What was he wearing on his head?

5. Did he skate to the middle of the pond or to the edge?

7. What did Andrew do when the ice gave way?

9. Who rescued Andrew?

11. Where did Andrew sit when he got back?

12. What was he holding?

inferential

3. Why was Andrew all wrapped up when he went skating?

4. Why wasn't he wearing ordinary shoes?

6. Did Andrew know that the ice was thin?

8. Why did Andrew cry out?

10. How did the man know that something was wrong?

13. Why was Andrew sitting by the fire when he got home?

14. How do you think Andrew felt when he got back?

The corresponding pictures for the pictorial version of the same story are shown in Fig. 7.6, p.182.

Perhaps the most surprising result from these studies was the finding that children with SLI were poor at story comprehension even when the stories were presented pictorially. Both Ellis Weismer (1985), and Bishop and Adams (1992), found that children with SLI did just as poorly for stories presented as a series of pictures as they did for orally presented stories. It had been anticipated that these children would have normal understanding of stories if there was no verbal input to be processed. These results, then, provide evidence that children with SLI have difficulty in integrating sequentially presented information, and these processing limitations extend beyond situations where language is overtly implicated.

In their study, Bishop and Adams drew a distinction between two subgroups of children with SLI. On the basis of clinical descriptions, they identified a subset of children who fitted the picture of "semantic-pragmatic disorder" (Bishop & Rosenbloom, 1987; Rapin & Allen, 1983). One characteristic of such children is that they are prone to give "over-literal" answers to questions that indicate that they have understood what an utterance literally means, but failed to take the prior linguistic context into account (see *Examples of*

FIG. 7.6   Materials used by Bishop and Adams (1992) for pictorial presentation of the same story as shown in Table 7.1. The pictures (original size 12 cm x 8.5 cm, in colour) were mounted in a small photograph album and shown one at a time. No verbal input was given except to introduce the names of principal characters (e.g. "This is Andrew"). (Original artwork by Catherine Adams.)

responses that fail to take prior context into account, opposite). Semantic-pragmatic disorder will be discussed in much more detail in Chapter 8, but for the present, the important fact to note is that Bishop and Adams predicted that these children would have comprehension problems that were different in kind from those of other children, with selective problems in answering questions

that required them to draw an inference. Results gave little support to that interpretation. It was true that children with a diagnosis of semantic-pragmatic disorder did do more poorly than other children with SLI on this task, but the difference was a matter of degree rather than a sharp division. Furthermore, overall, children had just as much difficulty with answering questions that simply

Examples of responses that fail to take prior context into account

In each of the following examples, the final question–answer pair looks adequate only if the preceding context is ignored.
(A = adult; C = child)

Example A
A   do you like ice cream?
C   yes.
A   what are your favourite flavours?
C   hamburger..., fish n chips...

Example B
A   are there any other times when you have parties?
C   no.
A   what about at Christmas?
C   it snows.

Example C
A   so when did you have your party?
C   on Saturday
A   was it good?
C   yeah.
A   and what did you have to eat?
C   cornflakes.
A   cornflakes?
     when did you have cornflakes?
C   this morning.

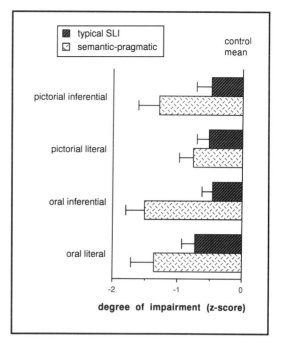

FIG. 7.7   Impairment on story comprehension task by children with semantic-pragmatic disorder vs. children with typical SLI. Scores are expressed as z-scores relative to the control group, so the more negative a score, the more severe the impairment. Error bars show standard errors. The semantic-pragmatic group do significantly more poorly than the typical SLI group, but there is no main effect of mode of presentation (oral vs. pictorial) or question type (literal vs. inferential), and no interaction with group.

required them to recall a factual detail as they had done with questions that involved making an inference (see Fig. 7.7, above).

There are intriguing parallels between the findings from studies of SLI and results from research studies concerned with individual differences in children's *reading* comprehension. Oakhill and her colleagues have conducted a series of studies on "less skilled comprehenders" (see Oakhill, 1994; Yuill & Oakhill, 1991 for reviews). These children were not diagnosed as cases of SLI: they were identified from within normal class-rooms on the basis of having unusually poor reading comprehension despite obtaining normal scores on measures of reading accuracy and single word decoding. However, in a series of studies Oakhill and her colleagues have demonstrated that

the comprehension problems of these children extend to spoken and pictorial stories, suggesting that their difficulties are similar to those of children with SLI. *Examples of studies on use of context by children with poor reading comprehension*, over-leaf, illustrates some of the methods that Oakhill and colleagues used to demonstrate that less-skilled comprehenders draw fewer inferences when processing written or spoken material, and are less likely to integrate meaning across utterances.

An important point to emerge from these studies is that two children may appear identical in terms of their superficial processing of written language; they may perform normally if asked to read sentences aloud, or recall the exact words they have heard, and yet they may differ quite radically in the

Examples of studies on use of context by children with poor reading comprehension

Inference generation: Oakhill (1982)
Child hears eight three-sentence stories, e.g.:

> The car crashed into the bus
> The bus was near the crossroads
> The car skidded on the ice

Then, after a brief interval, sentences are presented for recognition. These include original sentences plus two types of foil, semantically congruous and incongruous. Results are shown in Fig. 7.8

Conclusion: skilled comprehenders are more likely to form a constructive memory representation from a set of related utterances.

Instantiation: Oakhill (1983)
Children are presented with spoken sentences such as:

> the insect stung the boy

and then, immediately after further instructions, they are given "clue words" to help in recall.

Skilled and less skilled comprehenders did not differ (around 30–40% recall) when the clue was a general term such as "insect". However, skilled comprehenders showed considerable benefit, and less skilled comprehenders no benefit at all, if given an instantiated term (i.e. contextual interpretation of the clue word), e.g. "bee".

Skilled comprehenders did, however, remember the precise wording as well as other children.

Conclusion: groups differ in the extent to which they make use of context and specific knowledge when comprehending spoken material.

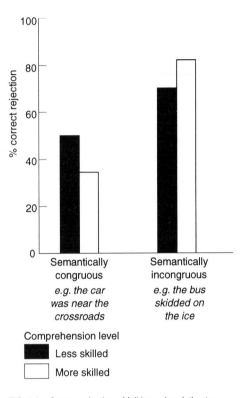

FIG. 7.8   Correct rejection of foil items in relation to reading comprehension level (based on Oakhill, 1982). If more congruous than incongruous foils are accepted, this is evidence that the child engaged in constructive processing, and congruous semantic information was inferred.

deeper processing that they engage in. Furthermore, a child who does not engage in constructive processing will have difficulty not only in answering questions that involve inference, but also in remembering the basic details of a story. In doing the work that is needed to integrate incoming information into a mental model, one converts the information into a more permanent form: the surface detail is lost, but the gist remains. In view of such findings, we can see that it is rather unrealistic to expect children to do poorly on inferential questions while remaining unimpaired on literal questions: quite simply, if you do not draw inferences, you will not form a long-lasting representation of the text as a whole, so ability to answer all types of question will suffer.

Underlying causes of problems with constructive comprehension in SLI

Downstream effects of early perceptual problems: The processing "bottleneck". The literature on written language comprehension suggests alternative explanations for problems that some children have with constructive comprehension. In work on children's reading problems, it has been suggested that inferential processing may suffer when limited resources are overstretched by problems in decoding written words. If the child has to devote a great deal of attention to extracting meaning from individual words, then reading proceeds slowly and effortfully and one can have "lower level processing bottlenecks" (Perfetti, 1994) that lead to problems in higher level comprehension. One can see parallels here with some of the debates that were reviewed in earlier chapters: for instance, it could be argued that problems in auditory processing in SLI could make basic word and sentence decoding effortful and so divert attention from higher level interpretative processes.

This is an attractive hypothesis, as it would allow us to treat the inferential problems of children with SLI as secondary to more basic deficits and so explain impairments at different stages of comprehension in terms of a single common mechanism, but, as we have seen, studies of children with SLI have been inconsistent. Both Ellis Weismer (1985) and Crais and Chapman (1987) found that discourse comprehension was in line with sentence comprehension, whereas Bishop and Adams (1992) found disproportionate difficulties in story comprehension. The literature on children with poor reading comprehension is also inconsistent. Stothard and Hulme (1992) found a close link between level of reading comprehension and performance on an oral test of sentence comprehension, TROG, whereas Yuill and Oakhill (1991) found that less skilled comprehenders had inferential problems that were out of keeping with their sentence comprehension abilities, as assessed on TROG. It is unclear whether different results reflect differences in the samples of children that were studied, or whether the length of text or number of inferences was the critical factor.

One result which is hard to account for by a "bottleneck" account is the finding that discourse comprehension in children with SLI is poor for pictorial as well as for verbally presented stories (Bishop & Adams, 1992; Ellis Weismer, 1985). This would seem to rule out difficulties with early

stages of processing oral or written input as the whole explanation for inferential problems. This is an important conclusion: studies of story comprehension reveal difficulties in understanding discourse that are not simply reducible to problems earlier on in the chain of auditory language comprehension.

Processing capacity limitations. Kintsch and van Dijk (1978) drew attention to the fact that the building of a mental model imposes demands on memory. They proposed a model (of adult comprehension) in which each new sentence that is encountered is decomposed into propositions, and referential connections are then made with propositions that were derived from prior material. It is assumed that limitations of processing capacity mean that only some of the propositions from the prior cycle can remain activated in a short-term buffer while a new sentence is processed. Propositions that are connected to many other propositions are activated in many cycles; these correspond to events, people, or objects that may be regarded as in central focus. Propositions with few connections correspond to peripheral detail and will have low levels of activation and become increasingly inaccessible. In line with this view, Miller and Kintsch (1980) found that propositions from a text with many referential connections were the most likely to be remembered.

This model was derived from work on processing of written texts by adults. However, it is of interest in relation to SLI in view of suggestions that "processing capacity limitations" are implicated in this condition (see e.g. Johnston, 1991). If children with SLI are able to retain a smaller set of activated propositions, one would predict that the number of referential links necessary to ensure retention of information would be greater than for normally developing children. Furthermore, even well-connected propositions might be lost if incidental detail intervened. Experimental tests of such predictions have not, to my knowledge, been carried out in SLI.

Failure to suppress irrelevant information. Kintsch (1994) noted that if we assume that people use their general knowledge to make sense of what they read or hear, then we have to consider how they select which information is important. Why are we not reminded of irrelevant, contextually inappropriate things? For instance, in the short "John at the beach" story (*Deriving gist from sequences*, p.175) one would expect all kinds of information to be mobilised: "beach" would activate associations of sand, sea, holidays, seashells, swimsuits, paddling; "broken glass" would activate ideas of bottles, drinks, windows, danger; "hospital" would activate ideas of illness, doctors, nurses, ambulances, beds, and so on. How are we able to select, from this welter of information, that which is relevant to make cohesive links between sentences?

The reality of this problem has been demonstrated in experimental studies on adults showing that during sentence processing a great deal of associated information is activated when a word is encountered. Related concepts are activated even if they relate to an irrelevant meaning of a word, e.g. if we encounter the word "bank" in a story about financial institutions, the concept of "river" as well as "money" will be activated. A method for studying this process is described in *Studying enhancement and suppression of activation*, opposite.

What determines which information is retained, and which is rejected? The mental model set up by the prior context plays a critical role. A plausible scenario is that items in long-term memory are automatically retrieved if they are linked to the text, but only remain activated if they can be integrated with the global text context. According to this view, activation of irrelevant information simply decays away because it cannot be integrated with prior information.

A more radical proposal has been put forward by Gernsbacher (1990) in the context of her Structure Building Framework. Although she does not use the term "mental model", her approach has much in common with those that do. She proposes that a mental structure is built up as meaningful material is encountered, and this is represented in memory cells. These cells transmit processing signals that enhance the activation of other cells with related meaning, and suppress activation of unrelated material. When new material is encountered, all related meanings are auto-

matically activated. However, memory cells in the existing mental structure act rapidly to suppress irrelevant meanings. Thus the inhibition of unwanted meanings does not just involve passive decay, but a more active process. Gernsbacher suggests that we are unaware of the activation of irrelevant meanings because their suppression is usually so rapid.

The distinction between passive (decay) and active (inhibition) accounts may seem an esoteric issue of interest only to theoretical psycholinguists, but it does have implications for our understanding of children with comprehension problems. Gernsbacher has argued that people who are relatively poor at comprehending stories are able to make connections between elements of a text, but they are poor at suppressing the irrelevant associations. It is important to stress that the people studied by Gernsbacher were adults and they did not have SLI. They were selected from large samples of college students or air force recruits screened on a battery of comprehension tests. They did not differ from other adults on measures of short-term memory, but they did do relatively poorly when asked questions about stories that they had just heard, read, or seen depicted in a series of drawings. In an experiment by Gernsbacher, Varner, and Faust (1990) these less-skilled comprehenders were compared with more-skilled comprehenders on a task where they read short sentences presented on a computer screen one word at a time, and then had to judge if a test word did or did not match the meaning of the sentence. For instance, on one trial, the subject would read:

He dug with the shovel

and then would see either a related word (e.g. GARDEN—correct response YES), or an unrelated word (e.g. ACE—correct response NO). On half the trials, the last word in the sentence was ambiguous, e.g.:

He dug with the spade

In such a sentence, the test word ACE should again be rejected, as it is unrelated in meaning of the sentence. However, ACE and SPADE do have

Studying enhancement and suppression of activation

The time course of activation of concepts can be studied by an ingenious use of a method widely used in experimental psycholinguistics, the lexical decision task. In lexical decision, the subject is simply presented with a written letter string and must judge if it is a real word or not. The assumption behind this method is that reaction time (RT) of correct decisions will reflect the extent to which the concept expressed by the test word is activated; when the letter string denotes an activated concept the decision will be faster.

To investigate activation of concepts during sentence processing, the subject is presented with a spoken sentence, which is interrupted at a specific point by a lexical decision task. It is reliably found that if the letter string corresponds to a word related in meaning to the spoken word that was just heard, then subjects respond faster and more accurately than if it is an unrelated word. For instance, if the subject hears

"Pam was diagnosed by a quack ..." and the written word DOCTOR is then presented, the decision that this is a word is made faster than if the unrelated word BUTTER is presented. The difference in lexical decision RT for related and unrelated words is used as a measure of the extent to which the activation of the concept is enhanced by the presentation of the spoken sentence. A counterintuitive result obtained using this method is that, provided the lexical decision task is given immediately on hearing the relevant word (e.g. quack), irrelevant as well as relevant meanings are activated. Thus, the response to DUCK as well as that to DOCTOR is speeded. If, however, the lexical decision task is given a few syllables later, only the relevant meaning, DOCTOR is enhanced. A review of the literature using this method is given by Gernsbacher (1990).

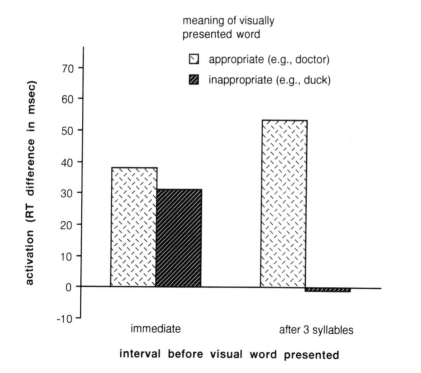

FIG. 7.9   Data from Swinney (1979), experiment 2. Activation time is the difference in lexical decision RT for a word with a related (relevant or irrelevant) meaning to an ambiguous target word, minus the RT for a word of unrelated meaning.

associated meanings in the context of playing cards. What is typically seen is a slowing in the time taken to make this judgement for a sentence such as containing an ambiguous word (e.g. "spade"), relative to a sentence containing a neutral word (e.g. "shovel"), which indicates that the irrelevant meaning has been activated. To quantify the amount of activation of an irrelevant concept, we can compare the reaction time (RT) to reject a word such as ACE in ambiguous vs. neutral contexts. Data from Gernsbacher et al. (1990) are shown in Fig. 7.10.

It is apparent that the amount of activation of irrelevant meanings is similar for skilled and less-skilled comprehenders when the test word is presented immediately after reading the sentence, but differs if a delay of 850msec is imposed between sentence reading and test. In the less-skilled comprehenders, the irrelevant meaning remains activated.

Gernsbacher (1990, p.203) reviewed other experimental data that supported her conclusion that "a critical characteristic of less-skilled

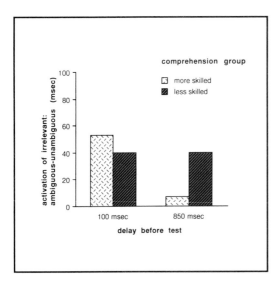

comprehenders is their inefficiency in suppressing inappropriate or irrelevant information while they are comprehending both linguistic and non-linguistic information". Furthermore, she showed that less skilled comprehenders showed normal priming, i.e. they obtained at least as much benefit as other people when judging that a related word matched a prior context. She concluded there was nothing wrong with their ability to activate relevant information from a context; the problem is in suppressing the irrelevant associations.

Could we extend Gernsbacher's framework to incorporate children with SLI, by proposing that they have similar difficulties in suppressing irrelevant information but to a more marked degree? There are several features of Gernsbacher's framework that make this an attractive proposal.

First, the model could explain the disproportionate problems that children with SLI have in answering questions about narratives, compared with comprehension of isolated sentences (e.g. Bishop & Adams, 1992). According to the Structure Building Framework, every time a person encounters information that cannot readily be integrated with an existing mental structure, there is a shift to develop a new structure. In normal comprehension, this can be demonstrated in the course of a story as one episode is completed and a new one is started. Gernsbacher argued that persistent activation of irrelevant meanings prevents new information from being integrated into an existing structure, and will instead encourage the development of a series of unrelated structures. The result is that the individual who does not suppress irrelevant meanings will build mental structures that are "bulkier, less cohesive and less accessible" than those of other people (p.213).

Second, the Structure Building Framework makes very specific predictions about comprehension of nonverbal sequences. In her investigations of individual differences in comprehension, Gernsbacher (1990) demonstrated high correlations between comprehension of spoken stories, written narratives, and pictorial story sequences. She argued that the processes described in the Structure Building Model are not

FIG. 7.10   Data from Gernsbacher et al. (1990), experiment 4, showing the time course of activation of irrelevant associated concepts in more skilled and less skilled comprehenders (adult subjects). Activation is estimated from the difference in lexical decision RT for an ambiguous word (with an associated but irrelevant meaning, e.g. "spade") minus the RT for an unambiguous (and unrelated) word (e.g. "shovel").

Examples of "topic shift" and "topic drift"

"Topic shift" is identified when a person produces an utterance on a different global topic to what has gone before. Usually, a speaker who changes topic, prepares the listener for this (e.g. by using specific phrases such as "by the way" or "incidentally"); if no warning of the topic shift is given, this disrupts coherence and makes the narrative or conversation appear bizarre. Unmarked topic shift is very unusual in the conversations of school-aged children, whether normally developing or language impaired. It is, however, observed in the talk of children with a diagnosis of early onset schizophrenia. The following examples are taken from the corpus of conversations of children with semantic-pragmatic disorder, by Bishop and Adams (1989). (A = adult; C = child)

Example A

A   tell me what's going on in that picture? (shows picture of boy in bed being examined by a doctor with a stethoscope)
C   this picture?
A   mhm.
C   he's looking at his tummy.
A   yes.
    and why has that doctor come?
C   to see if he's sick or something.
A   yes
    and have you been sick like that?
C   that's there.
    he has been sick.
    but what about people fall in wat-
    what about lakes?
A   what about the lakes?
C   lakes and rivers.
A   well we're not talking about lakes and rivers, are we. we're talking about that boy.

Bishop and Adams (1989) noted that although topic shift was very rare in their conversational samples, it was more common to see "topic drift", identified when an utterance has some relation to the preceding talk, but does not pick up on the global topic that has been set up in the preceding turns. These do not give such a

striking impression of oddity as cases of topic shift, but one typically sees that the conversational partner is somewhat thrown by what the child has said, and may pause or request clarification. In the following examples the adult's contribution after a topic drift is shown to illustrate the effect on the listener. (Examples A, B, and C, were produced by three different children.)

Example B

A   (produces a photograph showing a child's birthday party, with cake and candles) what's going on there?
C   it's someone's birthday
    something could be dangerous, you know, like a fire from the candles
A   do you think so? (surprised)
    do you think that's a bit dangerous?

Example C

A   and where do you live now?
C   rhyl.
A   rhyl.
    right.
    have you been to the pleasure beach there?
C   er, yeah!
    two times!
A   what do you think of it?
C   great.
A   and how about the beach itself?
    have you been on that?
    in the sand?
C   er, mm yes.
    and I also been to another seaside in South Shields.
A   that's near Newcastle isn't it?
C   mmh.
A   is that near where you used to live then?
C   yeah.
    and we also had the in Newcastle some Metro.
A   (1.5 sec pause)
    a Metro.
C   yeah.
A   an underground railway system?

specific to oral and written language, and that limitations in these processes will lead to weak comprehension regardless of the mode of presentation. The findings of poor comprehension of pictorial sequences by children with SLI, described previously, make sense if we assume that

the processes of Structure Building are deficient in these children.

Finally, the notion of lack of suppression of irrelevant associations could make sense of some phenomena that are hard to account for in other ways. Bishop and Adams (1989) found that children with semantic-pragmatic disorder were characterised by "topic drift", i.e. the production of utterances that do have some relation to the prior conversation, but which move off in an unexpected direction, perhaps picking up on an incidental detail. Although these types of response were not common, they were seen in the transcripts of 8- to 12-year-old children with semantic-pragmatic disorder, and virtually never encountered in conversations with normally developing children of the same age. They are of considerable interest because it is hard to pin down exactly what it is about them that gives an impression of oddity. A few examples are shown in *Examples of "topic shift" and "topic drift"*, previous page. An account in terms of failure to suppress irrelevant meanings meshes well with this kind of observation, because one can see that if irrelevant information is activated, it could form the basis for tangential or irrelevant inferences. This evidence is unsystematic and unquantified, but suggests a more experimental study of processes of suppression in such children would be well worth undertaking. Furthermore, the more bizarre and abrupt topic shifts seen in the utterances of distractible children with a diagnosis of early-onset schizophrenia (see Caplan, Foy, Asarnow, & Sherman, 1990) might correspond to a more extreme version of the same phenomenon.

Lack of knowledge base/unusual interests. We have noted already how the inferences that people draw from texts is a function of how much they know about the subject matter. In addition, it seems trivially obvious that people are more likely to process information that they find interesting. Attempts have, in fact, been made to study "interestingness": Kintsch (1980) drew a distinction between emotional interest (dependent on how far the subject matter aroused emotions such as fear, excitement or sorrow), and cognitive interest, which is a function of how far the text deals with information already known to the individual (we are less interested in things we know already, or things we know nothing about), how far it is predictable, and whether it hangs together coherently. In general, there seems no reason to

believe that children with SLI have unusual interests, but an exception may be children with the clinical picture of semantic-pragmatic disorder, who have some features in common with pervasive developmental disorder (i.e. autistic disorder or Asperger's syndrome) (Bishop, 1989a). These latter disorders are characterised by on the one hand a relative lack of concern for or understanding of the emotions of others, and on the other hand unusual and sometimes obsessional interests. When children like this do poorly on tasks such as remembering or retelling narratives, or keeping track of the topic of a conversation, we need to take seriously the possibility that we might be seeing shallow processing of material that has little intrinsic interest for them. If this is the explanation, we should see much better evidence of children's inferential powers when materials are designed to mirror their specific interests. Furthermore, some cases of "topic drift", as illustrated in *Examples of "topic shift" and "topic drift"* (previous page), may arise not because of any general difficulty in suppressing irrelevant information, but rather because certain favoured topics are highly primed, and will be introduced into the conversation when an opportunity presents itself. Thus, what we may be seeing is the child using fairly advanced inferential powers to forge links between prior conversation and the favoured topic.

Implications for intervention

Can problems with using context in comprehension be overcome? Some cause for optimism comes from studies of remedial approaches to reading comprehension problems. We have already noted that there are some similarities between the problems that children with SLI have in drawing inferences from discourse, and the difficulties of "less skilled comprehenders" studied by researchers working on children's literacy. There is good evidence that improvements can be made to children's understanding of written texts, by training them to engage in less superficial processing of what they read. For instance, Yuill and Joscelyne (1988) gave children short texts such as this:

Tommy was lying down looking at a reading book. The room was full of steam. Suddenly Tommy got some soap in his eye. He reached wildly for the towel. Then he heard a splash. Oh no! What would he tell his teacher? He would have to buy a new one. Tommy rubbed his eye and it soon felt better.

After reading the text, the child was given a "puzzle":

Where was Tommy, and what happened to the book?

In early stages of training, children are given clues and helped to use them, e.g. they might be asked to work out where Tommy was from the information:

lying down
steam
soap

towel
splash

However, as training proceeds, they are asked to find their own clues from a new puzzle story.

Another example comes from Brown, Palincsar, and Armbruster (1984), who trained children several times a week to read a section of text, and think of a question that might be asked about it. The teacher helped guide the child to a suitable answer if necessary. The difficulty that some children experience with this task is illustrated by the extract in Table 7.2. The child tends to repeat verbatim stretches of text and has difficulty paraphrasing it. The same child was able spontaneously to generate appropriate questions by day 15.

To take one final example, Oakhill and Patel (1991) showed children pictures representing sequences of events in a story that they read, and then asked them to imagine the pictures in their minds when answering inferential questions about the story. After this training, they were encouraged

TABLE 7.2

Extract from Teaching Session in Study by Brown et al. (1984)

Day 4 (T = Teacher; C = Child)

T:	Think of a question to ask about that paragraph
C:	–
T:	What's this paragraph about?
C:	Spinner's mate How do spinner's mate …
T:	Good, keep going
C:	How do spinner's mate is small than … How am I going to say that?
T:	Take your time with it. You want to ask a question about spinner's mate and what he does, beginning with the word "How"
C:	How do they spend most of his time sitting?
T:	You're very close The question would be "How does spinner's mate spend most of his time?" Now you ask it
C:	How does spinner's mate spend most of his time?

to generate their own mental images without any pictorial support.

Oakhill (1994) provides a review of these and related methods. These approaches have been demonstrated to be effective in promoting understanding of written material in poor comprehenders: and, in principle, there is no reason why such approaches should not be adapted to facilitate comprehension of oral language. It would seem well worth extending such methods to children with SLI.

CONCLUSIONS

We can see that "context" covers a wide range of extralinguistic influences on interpretation. The earliest form of context used by children developing language is the environmental setting. Children with SLI, like normally developing children, appear to place heavy reliance on the environment to give them cues so they can interpret language even if they do not fully understand all the words. A second aspect of context is background general knowledge that gives the child expectations of what is probable. This too seems to be a valuable source of information for children with SLI who may have problems understanding the verbal message.

One skill that develops as children grow older is the ability to use language as its own context, by developing mental representations of meaning from incoming language, which are then used as a basis for interpreting what follows. Rather than relying on what is externally present, or what is already known, children learn to treat verbal input as the basis for forming mental representations that can act like external stimuli by providing structure and expectations that guide interpretation. Very young children appear to not use verbal context at all; by three to four years of age, they are able to use the immediately prior verbal context, but seem unable to integrate long series of sentences into a coherent model. However, by around six years of age, most children do seem able to develop a structured mental model from narratives or conversations extending over several sentences.

For children with SLI, this seems to be an area of particular difficulty, and it is intriguing to consider why this should be so. We know already, from the work reviewed in preceding chapters, that SLI is associated with problems in processing oral language at the level of word or sentence. We need therefore to consider whether the comprehension difficulties with discourse are logically connected. The "low level processing bottleneck" explanation regards discourse difficulties as secondary to more basic comprehension deficits at the level of word or sentence. Because discourse involves taxing the comprehension system with large amounts of verbal material, it could be argued that any problems at a lower level will be magnified in discourse comprehension tasks, especially if one sentence follows rapidly after another. One reason why children with SLI do more poorly on story comprehension tasks than would be predicted from their performance on sentence comprehension may be that the sentence comprehension task gives them time to work out a response, so even if they have problems in comprehending, they can overcome these by devoting extra resources to interpretation. However, as sentence follows sentence, interpretation will fall behind, with problems accumulating as the story progresses. The principal objection to this line of explanation is that similar difficulties are seen with pictorial as with oral presentation of stories. By presenting stories as pictures, one should by-pass any basic problems with understanding of phonology, semantics, or grammar, and yet difficulties with discourse remain. The only way one could retain the notion of "low level" explanations for discourse problems would be by assuming that adequate pictorial story interpretation does involve some kind of verbal encoding of the material, and that children with SLI are poor at mobilising their limited language resources for this task.

An alternative line of explanation maintains that the problems in discourse comprehension are not secondary to problems in word and sentence processing, but have a common origin. A good candidate for a general deficit that would lead to problems at all levels is some general limitation of processing capacity, that means that children with SLI have a smaller "workspace" for retaining and manipulating material during comprehension. We have already seen, in Chapter 6, how limitations in a memory buffer could lead to problems in parsing complex sentences; perhaps the same buffer is implicated in maintaining active representations of discourse propositions, so that children with SLI retain fewer relevant propositions in memory, and have problems retaining crucial propositions if less relevant material intervenes. Although this type of explanation has the benefit of simplicity, by proposing that a single limitation of memory workspace leads to problems in maintaining representations at different levels, it may be oversimplistic. There is, as yet, no evidence that the same storage buffer is implicated in parsing as in constructing a mental model from discourse.

Another line of explanation considered here was that the discourse comprehension problems of children with SLI might arise from similar processes as have been proposed to account for individual differences in comprehension in the normal range. Gernsbacher's studies, demonstrating inadequate suppression of irrelevant meanings, offer a novel perspective on comprehension problems, and some of the experimental methods that she has used would, in principle, be applicable to children with SLI. This, then, is an approach that is testable and makes clear predictions. Its main drawback is that it is hard to integrate it with the other accounts of SLI and to extend this account to explain deficits at the level of phonology and syntax.

A final point to note is that there may be quite wide individual variation in the severity of discourse comprehension problems seen in children with SLI. We have discussed the possibility that there is a subgroup of children, those with semantic-pragmatic disorder, for whom discourse problems seem particularly pronounced. Although experimental data on story comprehension do not separate this group from other cases of SLI as cleanly as might be hoped, more qualitative observations suggest that inadequate suppression of irrelevant information might be a

particular problem in this subgroup. It is also important to bear in mind that some of these children have unusual interests, and that failure to construct a complex representation of what is heard might reflect unusual motivation rather than lack of ability. Quite simply, the content of stories or conversation may be perceived by them as irrelevant to their current concerns. Yet another possibility, to be discussed in Chapter 8, is that discourse difficulties may be particularly apparent for some children when the social context needs to be taken into account.

FOOTNOTES

1. In pragmatics, a connected sequence of utterances or sentences is referred to as a discourse or text. Both terms may be used for spoken or written language, although there is a tendency to identify discourse with spoken language and text with written language.

2. Most studies in this area, including this one, conflate two variables under "semantic bias". The term "negative semantic bias" is used for sentences that describe improbable scenarios, e.g. "the baby feeds the mother". However, in some cases these are not just improbable, they also contravene the selection restrictions on the verb. For instance, in the Van der Lely and Dewart study, one sentence with "negative semantic bias" was "the hat wears the dog". "Wear" requires an animate subject and an article of clothing as object; to act out this sentence correctly requires that the child ignore these constraints and employs imaginative powers of interpretation. To that extent, it could be argued that the child who acts out the reversed interpretation is not showing lack of sophistication in syntax, but is rather giving more weight to the information in the verb than to the information conveyed by word order when these are in conflict.

8

Understanding intended meaning: Social aspects of comprehension

When the eyes say one thing; and the tongue another, a practised man relies on the language of the first.

Emerson's *Conduct of Life* (1898).

OVERVIEW

1. Understanding of a speaker's communicative intention is the ultimate goal in comprehension, and involves going beyond the literal propositional meaning of an utterance.
2. Those interested in the philosophy of language have tended to treat this pragmatic aspect of comprehension as a final step in the process of understanding, which follows decoding of literal meaning. However, studies of children suggest the converse: they are able to infer a great deal about the communicative intentions of others long before they can interpret the literal meaning of words and sentences.

3. Pragmatic competence requires an awareness of other people's beliefs, desires, and knowledge. This is termed having a "theory of mind".
4. A fully developed theory of mind requires not only that the child has the cognitive capacity to build complex mental representations of other people's attitudes to propositions ("metarepresentations"), but also that he or she is exposed to sufficient examples of social contexts and behaviours to learn how people react in different situations. In addition, a major source of information about mental states comes from paralinguistic cues such as facial expression and tone of voice. These are attended to and interpreted by children from the earliest stages of development.

5. Impairment in the social aspects of understanding is a cardinal feature of autistic disorder. Children with this disorder are impaired on nonverbal as well as verbal communication and demonstrate great difficulties with tasks designed to assess theory of mind.

6. The literature on social understanding in children with SLI gives a rather confusing mixed picture. Although in general they do not have the kinds of pragmatic impairment seen in autism, some children do have deficits in social communication.

7. Three explanations for impaired social communication in SLI will be considered. The first maintains that general information processing limitations make it difficult for children to integrate verbal information over time. This kind of account can explain why children with SLI tend to do poorly on experimental communication tasks with a high information load. Children who fail such tasks don't necessarily have difficulty in working out what the listener does and does not know; rather they are overwhelmed by the need to hold a large amount of information in mind while formulating or interpreting a message. A similar account might explain why some children have difficulty in maintaining a topical thread during conversations.

8. In addition, there are several studies that point to the adverse social consequences of having SLI. Children with poor communication skills tend to be neglected and rejected by their peers, and this diminishes their opportunities to learn age-appropriate skills in social interaction.

9. For a small subset of children with SLI, there appear to be more fundamental pragmatic difficulties that are not just the consequence of information processing limitations or poor social learning. Rather, such children, who correspond to those in the clinical category of "semantic-pragmatic disorder", seem to have social impairments similar to those seen in autistic disorder, but milder in degree. Such children may have impoverished or inaccurate representations of other people's mental states.

INTRODUCTION

A critical point in the comprehension process is reached when the listener understands not just what the speaker said, but what was meant. This is a complex skill that can fail even in competent adults: Shakespearean plays and TV soap operas alike are replete with examples of how people can misunderstand one another's meaning. Inferring another person's communicative intention is one aspect of the more general process of using context to disambiguate potentially ambiguous messages, as discussed in Chapter 7, and is an aspect of comprehension that comes clearly under the domain of pragmatics. However, whereas Chapter 7 focused on children's ability to use general knowledge, environmental context, and prior discourse as sources of information about meaning, in this chapter we focus on how the social context is used to interpret messages. There are good reasons for treating nonsocial and social aspects of context separately, even though both are implicated in pragmatics. In the physical, nonsocial world, our understanding of such notions as causality is based very much on what is physically observable. A ball will knock over a milk bottle if it is travelling towards it with a certain speed and makes contact with it. The likelihood of the milk bottle smashing is a function of the fragility of the glass, the distance it falls, and the type of surface that it lands on, whether soft or hard. All these contingencies depend on physical relationships that are directly observable. This contrasts sharply with understanding of relationships in the social world. Whether a person moves or remains stationary is not simply a function of whether something bumps into them: animate beings can move under their own volition. They can influence and be influenced by events from a distance, as when a crying baby summons its mother. Among the critical factors that determine how a person behaves in a given environmental context are plans, beliefs, preferences, and memories, none of which is directly observable. Emotions, which are a major determinant of behaviour, do have physical correlates, but these can be subtle and hard to read. It might be supposed that the covert nature of causal influences in the social world would make the development of social understanding much more difficult than the development of physical understanding, but this appears not to be the case: if anything, understanding of social causality precedes understanding of physical causality (Gelman & Spelke, 1981; Hoffman, 1981). Developmental data support the notion that these domains of understanding are processed quite differently, raising the interesting possibility that in some individuals, either as the result of a developmental disorder, or after localised brain damage, one might see selective impairment of one type of understanding, nonsocial or social, with the other left intact.

Indirect speech acts

Examples of messages where the literal and intended meaning are discrepant are shown in Table 8.1, below. These are known as indirect speech acts, because the communicative intention is not the same as the logical, propositional meaning. For instance, "yes" or "no" would not be an appropriate answer to the first three examples.

Some of these utterance types are so common that it is reasonable to suppose that they have acquired a specific meaning through social convention: for instance, in English, an utterance starting "Could you ..." is much more likely to be a request that an action be carried out than an enquiry about whether the listener is capable of doing an action. However, there are many other instances where there is a host of plausible communicative intentions that could be expressed by the same utterance, and the speaker's meaning cannot be recovered simply by formulaic interpretation of a sentence frame. The sentence "the fish is on the table" from Chapter 1 is a clear example. This could be a warning (if the cat had just come in), an invitation to eat, an indirect command to clean the table, and so on. The problem in comprehending speaker's intentions is not just that a literal meaning sometimes conflicts with an intended meaning, but rather that we have to select a single interpretation of an utterance that could potentially be interpreted in many different ways.

An influential theory was proposed by Grice (1975) to explain how it is that we are able to understand what a speaker intends. This maintains that listeners recover the intended meaning by making some basic assumptions about the co-operativeness of a conversational partner, namely that he or she is:

TABLE 8.1

Examples of Indirect Speech Acts

Command/request with grammatical form of question

- could you please stop talking?
- do you mind opening the window?

Complaint with grammatical form of question

- don't you ever listen?

Invitation with grammatical form of statement

- I don't suppose you'd like to come to the shops with me.

Invitation with grammatical form of command

- do have some cake.

Warning with grammatical form of statement

- video camera surveillance is in operation on these premises.

- attempting to be as informative as possible, while giving neither too much nor too little information (maxim of quantity);
- attempting to be truthful (maxim of quality);
- attempting to be relevant (maxim of relation);
- attempting to be brief and clear (maxim of manner).

Grice noted that if a speaker appears to be clearly flouting one of these maxims (e.g. by saying "what a lovely day!" when it is raining) we treat this as a deliberate attempt to create a specific effect, rather than a lie. In this case, irony would be intended. Thus by combining an analysis of the context of an utterance, with awareness of its literal meaning, and making some basic assumptions about the co-operative nature of a conversational partner, it is argued that one can derive basic rules for interpreting utterances.

Understanding of literal meaning vs. understanding of intention: Developmental trends

Many linguistic and philosophical accounts of pragmatics treat understanding of the social significance of communication as a final step in a chain of understanding, assuming that we first decode words, put them together in sentences, and only then compute the intended meaning (by using Gricean maxims or some alternative process). Gibbs (1994) questioned this view, noting that reaction time data do not support the idea that people first of all compute the literal meaning of an utterance: we can interpret some kinds of figurative utterance just as fast as literal meanings. And viewed from a developmental perspective, the Gricean conceptualisation has serious problems, because it implies that children would only be able fully to understand intended meaning after they had learned enough to decode literal meanings. Givón (1979) challenged the notion that extraction of intended meaning occurs after decoding of literal meaning, arguing rather that the child is thrown into the world with an urgent need to communicate but no shared mode of communication. He proposed that the only solution is for the child to adopt an entirely pragmatic mode of early communication, relying heavily on the immediate

context as a means of conveying intentions. As language is learned, there is a gradual transition to a syntactic mode of communication, which enables the child to engage in communication about events outside the "here and now" context. But, far from pragmatics following syntax, Givón argues that a pragmatic mode is the earliest and most rudimentary form of communication, and one that is not supplanted by the development of syntactic skills, but which remains with us throughout life. More recently Locke (1993) has marshalled evidence to support the position that spoken language is a late manifestation of human social communication, that appears only after the young child has already developed an impressive range of nonverbal communicative strategies. Far from being primary, spoken language seems a supplementary system that is added to an already thriving communicative process. Ervin-Tripp (1981) demonstrated just how much can be understood about communicative intentions without decoding the spoken words in a message. In her study, people were asked to judge from videos of natural interactions which speech act was likely to occur next. Accuracy of their judgements was well above chance level, confirming that much of what is said is predictable on the basis of what had gone before and the surrounding contextual cues. Her study also challenged the view of communication as predominantly consisting of information exchange. Much of what is said serves to influence social relations, to orient the attention of the listener, or to add specification to what is already known. Ervin-Tripp concluded that understanding starts from context and requires minimal interpretative work; the "literal interpretation" may not be considered at all in some situations.

Shatz (1978) took a similar stance, noting that if understanding proceeded by first computing a literal meaning and then looking for possible mismatch with the context, this would make the understanding of indirect speech acts an enormously difficult task for young children with limited cognitive skills. Yet children as young as two years are able to respond equally well to literal requests for action such as "Shut the door" and indirect directives like "Can you shut the door". Shatz examined children's responses to different kinds of utterances in a range of contexts. The sentence types used in her study are illustrated in Table 8.2, below.

The interest was in whether the children treated an utterance as a directive, and hence responded with an action, or if they treated it as a request for information, to which a "yes" or "no" response would be appropriate. Young children tended to treat all these sentence types as requests for action, responding by putting the ball in the truck, rather than behaving as if asked for information. Shatz explained these findings by proposing that children use a primitive action strategy when responding to language, obeying the simple rule: "Act out or act on what can be identified from the speech stream".

Shatz's account suggests that children have a bias to interpret utterances as commands, but context clearly plays a part in whether they do so. Abbeduto, Davies, and Furman (1988) noted that children as young as five years old (and older intellectually impaired people of similar mental age) took into account the plausibility of an utterance being a question, in terms of whether the "answer" was obvious. In real life, people don't request information they already have. On this view, "can you stand up" is more likely to be treated as a command than as a request for information, but "can you roll your tongue" could be a request for information. Reeder and Wakefield (1987) directly manipulated context in a study in which children were asked to paraphrase the meaning of a puppet "speaker" who uttered sentences such as "Would you like to play on the bike". This sentence is ambiguous in terms of communicative intent: it could be a request, equivalent to "I want you to play on the bike", in which case a response such as "okay" would be appropriate; it could be an offer, equivalent to "I'll let you play on the bike", in which case a response such as "thanks" would be appropriate; or it could be a question, equivalent to "Do you want to play on the bike", in which case "yes" or "no" would be a suitable answer. Reeder and Wakefield noted that the physical arrangement of speaker, listener, and plaything (bike) made one or other interpretation more plausible (see Fig. 8.1, p.200), and they found that children as young as three years of age were significantly above chance in selecting an interpretation that was suited to the context. Furthermore, while four-year-olds did less well when presented with truncated or distorted utterances, three-year-olds seemed unaffected by these manipulations, and seemed happy to base their judgement on partial verbal information combined with contextual cues.

The developmental primacy of intentional meaning was demonstrated in a very different kind of task by Beal and Flavell (1984). They studied four- to five-year-old children using a paradigm that has a long tradition in research on communicative competence, the referential comm-unication paradigm (see *Referential communica-tion*, p.201). A doll gave a message that could be either ambiguous or unambiguous (e.g. "the black one" would be an ambiguous message in the context of the array in *Referential communication*, (p.201); "the white one" would be unambiguous). Children's ability to recognise ambiguity was

TABLE 8.2

Test Sentences* Used by Shatz (1978)

Fit the ball in the truck

Can you fit the ball in the truck?

Can the ball fit in the truck?

The ball fits in the truck

May you fit the ball in the truck?

* These sentences were embedded among a set of filler sentences so that children did not treat them as repetitions of the same intended meaning.

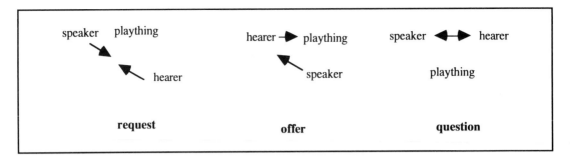

FIG. 8.1   Physical arrangements of speaker, hearer, and plaything used in the study by Reeder and Wakefield (1987) to study contextual influences on children's interpretations of utterances such as "Would you like to play on the bike". Arrows depict direction of gaze.

assessed by asking them whether they knew what the doll wanted, or whether they had to guess. Under standard conditions, these young children showed some ability to identify ambiguous messages. However, if the examiner told them in advance which item the doll meant, and then asked them to judge the adequacy of the message, they were quite unable to appreciate ambiguity. It was as if the child was focused on understanding what the speaker meant, and, once this was achieved, it was difficult to appreciate what had actually been said.

Beyond co-operation and situational context: The need for a "theory of mind"

Gricean theory has a further difficulty in that it proposes general principles for interpreting utterances in context, but does not explain how we are able to interpret the same utterance in the same context in different ways depending on the speaker. One major source of information that is critically important in inferring a speaker's intention in making an utterance is knowledge of that person's mental state: this includes both what the person does and does not know, and their emotional attitude. Consider this example from Gibbs (1994):

Joe: Are you going to the big dance tonight?
Sue: Didn't you hear that Billy Smith will be there?

Gricean principles will allow us to infer that Sue's response is an indirect speech act, in that she is not literally expecting a "yes" or "no" answer

from Joe. However, to uncover what she means to say, we need to go beyond general communicative principles to take into account specific information about the speaker's mental state. She could mean "yes" or "no", depending on her attitude to Billy Smith. Thus, in order to understand children's pragmatic competence, we need to know how they develop the ability to do what Baron-Cohen (1995) has called "mindreading".

For many years, people accepted Piaget's (1929) claim that young children are essentially "egocentric" and unaware that others have a different mental perspective from themselves. However, this was seriously challenged by a seminal study by Wimmer and Perner (1983). These authors devised an ingenious task for evaluating the child's ability to appreciate another person's false belief (see Fig. 8.3, p.202). They found that below the age of about three and a half, children do not succeed in this task, but maintain instead that Sally will look for the marble in the box, where they know it really is, rather than in the basket where she last saw it hidden. However, by four years of age, most children can do the task. Ability to recognise a false belief is seen as clear evidence of "theory of mind", i.e. the ability to deduce other people's mental states, even if these are different from one's own.

How do children develop this intricate skill? We shall consider three factors that contribute to developing a theory of mind: complexity of mental representations, nonverbal communicative skill, and social learning.

Referential communication

Glucksberg and Krauss (1967) pointed out that in order to communicate effectively, the child must not only learn to understand and produce words and sentences, they must also use contextual information to select what to talk about. This involves understanding what the listener needs to be told and what is already known. To study the development of these skills in an experimental setting, they developed a referential communication paradigm which has since been very widely used. Essentially, this involves giving children an array of items, and requiring that they describe one item so that a listener can identify it. Items have shared attributes, so success on the task depends on the child's ability to identify the critical information that uniquely specifies the target item. In a modification of this procedure, investigators have also assessed how well children can evaluate the adequacy of messages given by others. For instance, Beal and Flavell (1984) presented children with picture arrays such as that shown in Fig. 8.2.

Suppose I want you to pick out the left-most item. "The black one" or "the round one" would be an inadequate message in this context. However, if it was the middle item that was to be selected, then "the white one" would be sufficient.

Research using this technique has demonstrated that four-year-old children are very poor at both producing and evaluating messages. They tend to give insufficient information to identify one item uniquely. The interpretation of this finding, however, has been the subject of much debate. Originally, it was thought that poor performance reflected the child's inability to appreciate another's point of view; thus, when formulating a message, children would know which item was intended and be unable to put themselves in the position of a listener who was ignorant of this information. However, later work has demonstrated that the cognitive complexity of the task affects performance. The child needs to analyse which dimensions are salient and integrate this information while formulating a message. This may overwhelm the information processing capacity of a young child.

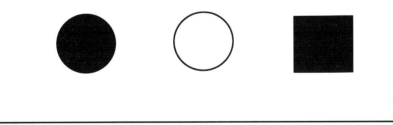

FIG. 8.2

Complex mental representations. Over the past decade, there has been a proliferation of studies on theory of mind, with research focusing predominantly on two related issues: first, what kinds of mental representation are implicated, and second, how early in development does theory of mind appear. There has been a great deal of debate about these issues, but there is general agreement that in order to appreciate another person's mental state, the child must be able to form a kind of mental representation that is rather different from the representations that are used when thinking about physical objects or events, i.e. a metarepresentation (see *Metarepresentation*, p.203). Ability to form mental representations of complex propositions

marks a crucial step in cognitive development that enables the child to think about notions that were previously unthinkable. It follows, then, that difficulty with forming these complex mental representations could be a factor affecting a child's social comprehension.

Researchers have therefore been keen to trace the development of mental representation and social cognition, to try to identify the point at which children show evidence of theory of mind. However, there is tremendous variability, depending on the specific task that is used (e.g. Chandler, Fritz, & Hala, 1989; Flavell, Flavell, Green, & Moses, 1990). For the theoreticians, this variation reflects "noise", and the quest remains to devise better and better tasks to

FIG. 8.3 Baron-Cohen, Leslie and Frith's (1985) version of the classic false belief task, originally devised by Wimmer and Perner (1983). (Reprinted from Frith, 1989.)

Metarepresentation

In order to be able to refer to absent entities or to contemplate imaginary events, we must have the ability to form mental representations. Suppose I show you a picture of a cat playing with a ball of string, and later on, after removing the picture, I remind you of it and ask you to remember it. You will have no difficulty in generating an image corresponding to what was previously seen. This is what has been termed a primary representation (see Fig. 8.4).

FIG 8.4   A primary representation.

Now suppose that after showing you the picture, I point to the back of it and ask you to think of what is depicted on the other side. As before, you generate a mental representation of the cat with its ball of string. However, unbeknownst to you, I have substituted a picture of a rabbit eating lettuce. My mental representation of what is on the card will differ from yours (see Fig. 8.5).

However, I am aware of your false belief, and I can also form a representation of your mental representation. This is what most theorists mean by a metarepresentation. This contains the embedded representation of the cat playing with the ball of string.

FIG 8.5   Different mental representation.

The cognitive complexity involved in representing another person's mental state is far greater than that implicated in forming a primary representation. In effect, it involves representing the relationship between an agent and a proposition. To detect whether the agent's belief is true or false, one also needs to compare their mental state with one's own.

Leslie and Thaiss (1992) argued that the ability to represent other people's mental states depends on the operation of a specialised brain module. The evidence for this is that one can see sharp dissociations between a child's ability to perform the standard theory of mind task, illustrated in Fig. 8.3, opposite, and ability to do a closely similar task that does not involve mental states (i.e. understanding that a photograph will depict reality as it existed when the photograph was taken, and will not be affected if the photographed scene subsequently changes).

This is a necessarily simplified account of a highly complex and controversial topic. See Perner (1991) and Leslie and Roth (1993), for contrasting accounts of the developmental aspects of metarepresentation.

FIG. 8.6   A metarepresentation.

minimise the role of such nuisance "performance" factors, and hence to study theory of mind in as pure a form as possible. However, an alternative stance one could take is to argue that there is no "pure" test of theory of mind, only tasks that assess awareness of others' mental states in specific contexts, and that the extent to which a given context can help or hinder the child's demonstration of a theory of mind is itself of some interest, especially for those concerned with individual differences.[1] One thing the research in this field has demonstrated is that a child who possesses a capacity for metarepresentation may not necessarily show appreciation of others' mental states on a specific experimental task. Thus, we need to go further to ask what information is used by children when deducing another's mental state, how far "mindreading" is facilitated by exposure to specific experiences, and how far easy computation and automatic access of mental state information depends on other cognitive attainments.

Ability to interpret transient visual and vocal cues.   Facial expressions and body language offer cues to the speaker's attentional focus, sincerity, engagement in a conversation, and emotional state. Thus, if we say "did you see the game last night?" and receive a blank look in return, we recognise a need to back-track and clarify what is being talked about. Vocal cues are also important: prosodic features such as pauses and intonation enable us to estimate a speaker's knowledge about, commitment to, and confidence in what they are saying (Brennan & Williams, 1995). The role of these paralinguistic factors has been largely ignored in treatments of pragmatics by philosophers, who appear to regard them as optional ornamentation in the communicative process. One suspects that this attitude arises because they base arguments on abstract, decontextualised, written examples. After all, I do not need to see or hear Dorothy Parker to appreciate her intended, non-literal, meaning in her poem *Comment*[2]:

Oh, life is a glorious cycle of song,
A medley of extemporanea;
And love is a thing that can never go wrong,
And I am Marie of Roumania.

This demonstrates that meaning can be inferred on the basis of the words, context, and general knowledge alone, without using any other cues. However, this does not mean that nonverbal communication plays only a marginal role in the development of intentional understanding. Once language has been learned, we may be able to rely on partial information to interpret it, but it is questionable whether it could be learned in the first place if we had no ability to process paralinguistic cues.

Most of the work that looks at prelinguistic communication in infants has concentrated on how children use nonverbal means to express intentions, but, from our perspective, interest focuses more on how far the child can infer other people's intentions when ability to understand the words that they say is nonexistent or rudimentary. Long before children can understand literal meanings of complex sentences, they use nonverbal cues to interpret communicative behaviour of the people around them. Locke (1993) reviewed research showing that sensitivity to vocal tone starts to develop before the child is born. The ability to make broad distinctions between facial expressions can be demonstrated in infants as young as five months of age (see review by Oster, 1981), and by around ten months of age, many infants actively monitor the facial expression of a familiar adult when confronted with an uncertain situation (such as an unfamiliar adult or novel toy), and will decide whether to approach or retreat on the basis of their emotional expression (Klinnert, Campos, Sorce, Emde, & Svejda, 1983). This phenomenon of "social referencing" provides ample evidence that facial expressions are not just discriminated by preverbal infants, but are interpreted in terms of their affective and communicative significance. And after language has been learned, nonverbal behaviours, facial expression, and prosodic variation remain as salient communicative cues that can override the verbal message. Consider the examples shown in Fig. 8.7, where the facial expression and verbal message do not correspond. Most people assume that the speakers are being insincere, sarcastic, or joking in such cases, and trust their facial expressions much more than what they say.

FIG. 8.7 Examples of discrepancy between verbal message and facial expression. Consider which of the three reactions you would prefer to receive.

There has been some interest in tracking children's developing ability to use and integrate different channels of communication when interpreting the emotional significance of messages, but the findings have been rather inconsistent, perhaps because it is not possible to equate visual, vocal, and verbal channels on the same scale, so results may reflect the salience of particular speakers and stimuli used in a given experiment. Furthermore, experiments have varied in the extent to which they use naturalistic stimuli (e.g. videos) or static images, and how under-standing is assessed, whether by verbal report or some other means. However, what is clear is that children as young as four or five years of age can accurately interpret emotional tone from visual, vocal, and verbal channels (Bugental, Kaswan, Love, & Fox, 1970).

It is instructive to turn to the literature on autistic disorder when considering how the development of social communication might depend on the ability to read such characteristics as facial expression or tone of voice. Problems in interpreting such nonverbal cues are common in children with autism, especially when we consider the ability to distinguish facial expressions depicting complex emotions such as pride or shame. These difficulties seem to reflect basic impairments of affective contact with other people that are evident from infancy, well before a capacity for metarepresentation and theory of mind can be demonstrated (see reviews by Hobson, 1993; Mundy, Sigman, & Kasari, 1993). Given that transient paralinguistic cues provide powerful evidence about a speaker's communicative intentions, we can see that problems in reading them would have a seriously disruptive effect on social communication, especially when the deficit is not restricted just to one modality, but affects interpretation of vocal as well as visual cues. Faces provide cues to attentional focus as well as emotional state. Baron-Cohen and Ring (1994) noted that direction of gaze provides information about the attentional focus of another person, allowing a child to detect whether there is a shared focus of attention, and/or which object is another person's goal. They argued that children with autism are able to tell whether another person's eyes are directed at them, but unable to read eye-direction in terms of mental states such as goal or desire.

Opportunities for social learning.   A competent communicator needs to go beyond a general ability to infer mental states by analogy to one's own reactions, to develop a more sensitive differen-tiation between individuals, so that one can appreciate the need to phrase one's message, or interpret another's message, differently depending on whom one is talking with.

To some extent, this can be achieved by using social stereotypes, i.e. generalisations based on observable characteristics of the individual. Age, gender, race, form of dress, and type of accent are all factors which affect our expectations of how other people think and behave, and which may influence how we interpret what they say. These factors will determine not only a person's emotional attitude to a verbal interaction, but also what knowledge they are likely to share with another person. So, if I am walking around Cambridge and a stranger approaches me and asks where they can buy a paper, I am likely to reply differently depending on whether they appear to be a local person or a foreign tourist, in terms of the quantity of detail that I supply.

Where we have previous experience of another person, we have knowledge of how they have behaved in a range of other situations, which makes our predictions about their mental state more accurate. For instance, among our colleagues we will know of some individuals who are ready to take offence and others who have a remarkably thick skin. We also can use our awareness of that person's past history to deduce what knowledge they have in common with us, and so what aspects of a conversational topic need to be explicitly mentioned and which can be tacitly assumed as common knowledge. Person-specific knowledge may also be critical in interpreting indirect speech acts. In the earlier example from Gibbs (1994, p.200), if we know that Sue is smitten with Billy Smith, we will interpret this as a "yes"; if we know she hates him venomously, then we will interpret it as "no".

Rather little work has been done on children's ability to communicate differentially according to the partner's characteristics, although Shatz and Gelman (1973) showed that by four years of age children use simplified speech when addressing younger children. If, as argued previously, effective interpersonal communication depends not just on the ability to represent another person's mental state, but also to appreciate when and how this might differ from one's own mental state, then one might expect social learning to play a part in the development of theory of mind: the more people one interacts with, the more sensitive one might be to differences between them in terms of beliefs, thoughts, and emotions. Perner, Ruffman, and Leekam (1994) proposed that development of social cognition does depend on experience of others with different views and perspectives. They showed that family size was a significant predictor of performance on theory of mind tasks at three to four years of age: single children did less well than those with siblings. They interpreted this in line with work by Dunn (1988) showing that sibling conflict frequently prompts mothers to talk to their children about feeling states, and note that this evidence for social learning effects contradicts the notion that theory of mind simply depends on the maturation of an innate cognitive module. Cultural factors might also be implicated in facilitating the child's ability to appreciate the content of others' minds. For instance, the Japanese place high value on an empathic style of communication that is indirect, and regard it as undesirable to state anything that could be inferred. In effect, this calls for a very highly developed theory of mind. Clancy (1986) described how mothers ensure that their children develop the necessary skills by overt "empathy training". Specifically, she noted (p.233):

> Given the Japanese emphasis on indirection and avoidance of imposing on others, it is important to be able to anticipate the needs of others, so that they will not be forced to make a direct request. One might well wonder how Japanese children learn to "read

the minds" of other people in this way. Judging from the present transcripts, the answer seems rather simple: their mothers tell them directly what other people are thinking and feeling in various situations.

The importance of social cognition for communication

This overview emphasises that effective communication involves integrating formal linguistic knowledge with more general social understanding. A person who lacked the ability to appreciate what other people were thinking, to recognise differences between communicative needs of different types of people, to read nonverbal cues to meaning, or to learn the normative behaviours of the local culture, would have problems in comprehending what people meant, even though there might be no difficulty in understanding the propositional content of what had been said. An analysis of comprehension problems is therefore incomplete unless it encompasses the role of social understanding.

SOCIAL COMMUNICATION IN CHILDREN WITH SLI: RESEARCH FINDINGS

The classical textbook view of SLI is that it involves an isolated deficit in language acquisition occurring in the context of otherwise normal development. It is assumed that the difficulties are restricted to phonology, grammar, and/or vocabulary, and there is no fundamental problem with social aspects of communication. Indeed, it is sometimes suggested that children with SLI may use their well-developed social cognitive skills to compensate for their more basic linguistic deficiencies. As Miller (1991, p.6) puts it:

> Children with language disorders evidence strengths in conversation skills. They are purposeful and responsive; however communication is limited by their mastery of grammatical form.

According to this view, we should not expect children with SLI to have any undue difficulty in understanding another person's meaning. Just like the young normally developing child, we would expect them to gain a good idea of a speaker's intention on the basis of contextual cues and social understanding, which is then supplemented with whatever information they can understand from a verbal utterance.

When pragmatics was first investigated in the context of SLI, several studies gave results broadly in agreement with this view; most of the emphasis was on the types of communicative act produced by language-impaired children, and it was found that they used language to express the same communicative intentions as other children, and generally showed pragmatic skills that were at least as good as younger children of similar language level (see review by Fey & Leonard, 1983). However, as research has progressed, there has been a growing body of work that casts doubt on such a clearcut position. Especially when looking at children's understanding, there is evidence that those with SLI may have difficulties that are not readily explained in terms of limited ability to understand literal meaning or formulate utterances.

Intended vs. literal meaning. An early study that considered pragmatic aspects of comprehension was carried out by Shatz, Shulman, and Bernstein (1980), who studied a group of five- to six-year-old language-impaired children using the same methods as in the earlier study of normally developing children by Shatz (1978) (see Table 8.2, p.199). The children were impaired on both expressive and receptive language. No IQ data were presented, and their MLUs ranged from 1.5 to 4.0. These children were even more likely than normally developing two-year-olds to adopt a simple action strategy when interpreting utterances directed to them. More than three-quarters of the test sentences elicited meaningful responses, and 98% of these were action responses (i.e. the child put the ball in the truck). In a further study, Shatz et al. (1980) went on to compare how children's interpretations were influenced by the context in which sentences were presented, by contrasting two different settings, as shown in Table 8.3, below.

The first point made by Shatz et al. was that language-impaired children were not over-literal in their interpretation; had they been so, we would have expected them to have interpreted the test sentence as a request for information, regardless of context. Second, language impaired children clearly differentiated between these two contexts. In the "directive" setting, they produced 78% of appropriate action responses, 8% informing responses, and 14% of "other" responses. In the "information eliciting" condition they produced 38% action responses, 33% informing responses,

---

TABLE 8.3

Test Sentences Used by Shatz et al. (1980) to Investigate the Effect of a Biasing Context on Utterance Interpretation

	Condition where introductory sentence biases child to interpret test sentence as a directive	*Condition where introductory sentence biases child to interpret test sentence as information eliciting*
Introductory setting sentences	come and get the telephone push the button find the "one" ring the bell	who talks on the telephone in your house? can Mommy talk on the telephone? can Daddy talk on the telephone? can (sibling or pet) talk on the telephone? can a dolly talk on the telephone?
Test sentence	can you talk on the telephone?	can you talk on the telephone?
Anticipated response	child picks up telephone and talks into it	child says "yes" or "no"

and 29% "other" responses. Overall, their response profile was similar to that seen in normally developing two-year-olds studied by Shatz (1978). However, they were less consistent in their responses to informational sequences, and tended to treat these as requests for action.

Responsiveness in conversation. Fey and Leonard (1983) reviewed studies of conversational participation in children with SLI. Results were highly inconsistent, and they suggested that some of the variability might be explained in terms of the child's level of comprehension; those with comprehension deficit would have greater difficulty taking part in conversations. They also commented on the variability seen within the SLI population, and pointed out that studies that focus solely on group characteristics may be misleading.

Rosinski-McClendon and Newhoff (1987) studied a group of four- to five-year-old language-impaired children, comparing them with younger normal children matched on language ability. Children with major comprehension problems were excluded from the study. Nevertheless, they concluded that the language-impaired children were less responsive than the normally developing children; the problem was not so much that they remained silent, but rather that they gave inappropriate responses.

Referential communication. Bishop and Adams (1991) administered a referential communication task to language-impaired children. Although the task requires the child to formulate an utterance (when describing a target item), it can also be regarded as a measure of social comprehension insofar as optimal performance depends on the ability to recognise precisely what information the listener needs to be given, and what can be assumed to be mutual knowledge.

A sample of the materials used by Bishop and Adams is shown in Fig. 8.8. The child was presented with eight cards, showing scenes that varied on three orthogonal dimensions. A star was stuck on the back of one card, and the child's task was to find this card when the adult was not looking, and then describe that picture un-ambiguously so the adult could locate it. Thus, the

child had to appreciate that the adult did not share the same knowledge about the identity of the card, and needed to be told about all three salient dimensions. Information provided by the child was coded as relevant (i.e. concerning a critical dimension), redundant (i.e. perfectly correlated with a critical dimension so not informative once that dimension had already been mentioned), or irrelevant (not discriminating because it applied to all pictures). So, for instance, in the example shown in Fig. 8.8, if the child said "It's a black and white cat with whiskers and a tail", the information "cat" and "black and white" would be credited as relevant, "whiskers" as redundant, and "tail" as irrelevant. The overall finding from this study was that children with SLI were poor at the task compared to age-matched controls, and often failed to provide sufficient relevant information. We were confident that this was not just because of inadequate vocabulary to describe the appropriate dimensions, because we gave children a post-test in which critical words that they had failed to produce were elicited. For instance, if the child gave the response as before, failing to give information about whether the tail was straight or curly, two cats, one with a straight tail and one with a curly tail, would be shown to the child who would be asked to say how they differed. Most children had no difficulty in finding the words to describe the critical dimensions when they were explicitly contrasted in this fashion.

Paralinguistic communication
Another indirect source of evidence for poor social cognition comes from analysis of paralinguistic aspects of communication. Quite simply, if problems in comprehending or producing oral language are the only source of communicative difficulty, then we would expect the child to show normal use and understanding of paralinguistic cues. Insofar as nonverbal as well as verbal communication is impaired, this suggests that there is a broader underlying problem with social communication that cannot be attributed to difficulties with oral language.

As noted earlier, abnormalities of nonverbal communication are seen in autistic disorder. This can be observed in young children, who fail to

FIG. 8.8   Example of a test array used by Bishop and Adams (1991) in a referential communication task. The pictures (original size 12 × 9 cm, in colour) are arrayed in front of the child. The child looks under each picture while the adult hides her eyes, to locate the item with a star. The task is then to describe this picture so that the adult can find it immediately. (Original artwork by Catherine Adams.)

demonstrate shared attention through the use of mutual gaze, and who use gestures predominantly in an instrumental fashion, to get a desired object, rather than in a social fashion, to communicate a shared interest. It is noteworthy that studies investigating nonverbal communication in autism sometimes use children with SLI as a control group, who are assumed to have impairments restricted to the domain of spoken language. For instance, Landry and Loveland (1988) found a much wider range and greater severity of both verbal and nonverbal communicative impairments in autistic children than in those with receptive-expressive language impairments, even though the groups were matched on an assessment of receptive and expressive language skills. The language-impaired children, with a mean age of five years, were very similar to two-year-old normally developing children of similar language level. However, some level of impairment, relative to normally developing children, is sometimes reported in those with SLI, especially where the child has poor verbal comprehension (Thal, Tobias, & Morrison, 1991).

Courtright and Courtright (1983) assessed how well children could match a photographed expression with the emotional tone of voice in which a standard utterance ("Would you please bring that to me") was uttered. Children with language impairments did more poorly than control children. Interestingly, Courtright and Courtright did not interpret their results as indicating any basic impairment of socio-emotional development in children with SLI, but rather suggested that poor interpretation of prosody might result from the kinds of problems in processing rapidly changing auditory information described by Tallal and her colleagues (see Chapter 3). However, they did not directly examine the relationship between prosodic impairment and auditory perception, and the background information given about the children is not sufficient to tell whether the two groups were adequately matched in terms of nonverbal ability, or whether any of the children had pragmatic difficulties in everyday communication. Also, no control task was used, so we cannot therefore be certain whether the deficit was in identifying the vocal emotion, or simply in

attending to the task demands. Nevertheless, their suggestion underlines the complex interactions that might exist between the different levels of processing outlined in Chapter 1, by raising the possibility that an auditory perceptual deficit could affect pragmatic function by its impact on interpretation of prosody.

SOCIAL COMMUNICATION IN CHILDREN WITH SLI: THEORETICAL ACCOUNTS

The evidence we have reviewed poses some challenges to the traditional view of SLI as affecting mastery of spoken language while leaving social communication intact. In this section, we shall review three broad classes of explanation that have been put forward to account for such findings. According to the first, limited information processing capacity is responsible both for the child's language learning difficulties and for the problems observed in tests of social communication. The second account maintains that children with SLI have limited opportunities for social learning because they tend to be rejected by other people, especially their peer group. Finally, a third line of explanation proposes that some children with SLI have primary deficits in the domain of social cognition, and so in effect their communication is compromised by impairments extending beyond oral language.

A. Impairment of information processing

The first possibility to consider is that the deficits that are seen in communication in SLI do not reflect any basic social impairment, but they reflect more general and nonspecific cognitive limitations to do with working memory and processing capacity. This is illustrated as model A in Fig. 8.9, overleaf. This notion will be familiar from earlier chapters, where it has been invoked to account for a very wide range of linguistic deficits. In particular, in Chapter 7, it was suggested that children might have difficulties in integrating meanings from a series of sentences to build a coherent narrative. Clearly, if the child had that kind of general problem in building representations of meaning,

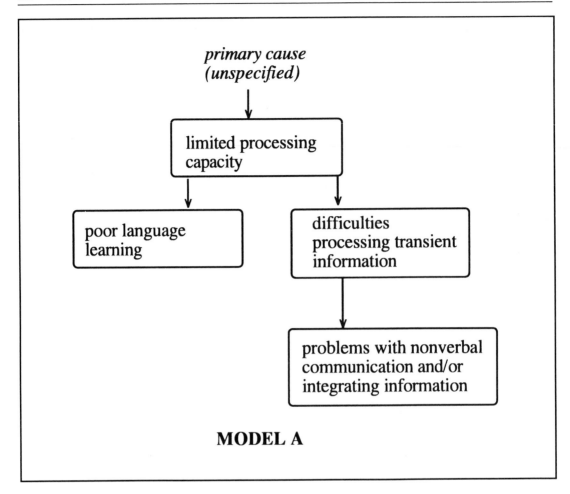

FIG. 8.9   Model A: general cognitive limitations affect performance on tests of social communication skills.

this would affect some forms of social interaction. To be a skilled conversationalist, for instance, one needs to keep track of utterances over time, and build a mental model that integrates contributions from all the participants.

This kind of explanation has been proposed to account for several of the findings reviewed in the previous section. In their study of comprehension of indirect utterances (see Table 8.3, p.208) Shatz et al. (1980, p.304) concluded that children with SLI "have difficulty processing multiple input sentences across time and inferring conversational cohesiveness among them ... Although they demonstrated some ability to take prior linguistic context into account, it does appear that it was

difficult for them to do so". This would explain why they were less influenced by a biasing prior context than normally developing children.

Bishop and Adams (1991) noted that referential communication tasks are cognitively complex, and require children to analyse an array of pictures, determine which dimensions are salient, and hold this information in mind while formulating an appropriate message. These information-processing demands of the task might be at least as critical in determining success or failure as the need to infer the listener's mental state (see e.g. Ammon, 1981, for an analysis of the role of general intellectual capacity and cognitive style in referential communication tasks). This explanation of poor performance by children with SLI in the Bishop and Adams study seemed especially plausible because performance did not relate to how children performed in a conversational setting; some children who were poor at giving optimally informative responses in conversation did the referential communication task without difficulty, whereas others who seemed normal in conversation had great difficulty with the experimental task.

B. Inadequate opportunity for social learning

A second line of explanation maintains that the social communicative deficits arise as secondary consequences of the distorted social experiences that children have if they have primary language limitations. If the child is rejected or neglected by others of the same age, then it could be that a vicious spiral develops, such that the child ceases to seek out opportunities for social interaction, and gains increasingly less experience of how others think and feel, as shown in model B (Fig. 8.10).

There is ample evidence of adverse social consequences of having a language impairment. In her review of this area, Gallagher (1993) noted that peer acceptance is related to the ability to adjust a message to the listener's needs, to initiate conversation, to ask appropriate questions, to contribute to ongoing conversation and to communicate intentions clearly. Other studies have

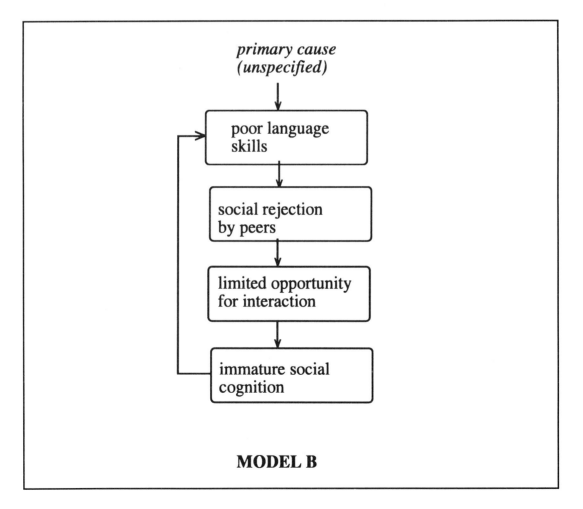

MODEL B

FIG. 8.10   Model B: communication difficulties lead to decreased opportunities for social learning.

stressed the importance of conversational skills to peer acceptance even in children as young as three or four years (Kemple, Speranza, & Hazen, 1992). It follows that children with limited language abilities are at high risk of peer rejection. This has been demonstrated in a preschool setting by Rice, Sell, and Hadley (1991), who showed that even before they start school, children are sensitive to the communicative status of other children and will cease to make social overtures to those who have limited language abilities.

One problem for those advocating a social learning explanation is that it is difficult to rule out alternative explanations that maintain that the reason the child is rejected by peers is because of some fundamental impairment in social cognition (see model C later), rather than because verbal communication is compromised. One way of disentangling causal mechanisms is by contrasting children whose language is limited for different reasons. Rice et al. (1991) did this and found that children who spoke a foreign language also had problems with acceptance by preschool peers, a finding that offers strong support to the view that it is how the child communicates rather than any intrinsic social limitations that determine other children's reactions.

Nevertheless, there is mounting evidence that social difficulties in language-impaired children cannot be totally reduced to secondary consequences of peer reactions to language limitations. Next we will consider studies looking at individual variation within the language-impaired population which show that scores on language tests do not necessarily predict success in social communication. We will also review evidence that some children with language impairments are also limited in their ability to use and interpret nonverbal cues to meaning. Since facility in nonverbal communication typically predates language learning, one might expect that language-impaired children should be unimpaired in this channel of communication, and might indeed rely on it more heavily than do other children. Evidence such as this leads us to consider the third line of explanation, that of a primary impairment in social communication in a subset of children with SLI.

C. Impairment of social cognition

Impaired development of social cognition is nowadays regarded as a hallmark feature of autistic disorder. Research on theory of mind in autism was initiated with the publication of a seminal paper by Baron-Cohen et al. in 1985. Baron-Cohen et al. used a simple task based on the original Wimmer and Perner procedure (see Fig. 8.3, p.202) and showed that children with autism had a striking deficit on this task. This finding on its own is perhaps not so remarkable. After all, most children with autism are intellectually impaired and perform at a low level on a wide range of cognitive tests. However, Baron-Cohen et al. were able to show that other, nonautistic children, with comparable levels of intellectual impairment, could do the theory of mind task just as well as normally developing children of a similar mental level. Since this paper was published, there has been a proliferation of research studies on theory of mind in autism, and it is now widely accepted that difficulty in understanding the mental state of others is a core deficit in autistic disorder that can be demonstrated using a range of different methods (Baron-Cohen, 1993). Lack of "theory of mind" could explain not only the social impairments seen in autism, but also some of the peculiarities of language use (Frith, 1989).

Could, then, a similar kind of deficit be implicated in SLI? This kind of explanation, depicted in model C (Fig. 8.11, p.216), would run counter to the assumptions embodied in contemporary classification systems (e.g. *ICD-10* and *DSM-IV*), which make a sharp differentiation between autistic disorder and SLI. *DSM-IV* draws a distinction between specific developmental disorders (such as SLI), where a single domain of functioning is impaired, and pervasive developmental disorders (PDD), of which autistic disorder is the prototypical example (see *Diagnostic criteria for autistic disorder*, opposite), where a wider range of functions, including social understanding, are abnormal. Most textbooks of child psychiatry devote some space to discussing the differential diagnosis of autistic disorder and SLI, noting that only in the former disorder does one see broad impairments of social communication that go beyond difficulty in formulating or understanding

Diagnostic criteria for autistic disorder: Based on *DSM-IV*
(American Psychiatric Association, 1994)

A total of six (or more) items from (1), (2), and (3), with at least two from (1), and one each from (2) and (3). Delay or abnormal functioning must be present with onset prior to three years in at least one of the following areas: (1) social interaction, (2) language as used in social communication, and (3) symbolic or imaginative play*.

1. Qualitative impairment of social interaction, as manifested by at least two of:
   (a) marked impairment in the use of multiple nonverbal behaviours such as eye-to-eye gaze, facial expression, body postures, and gestures to regulate social interaction;
   (b) failure to develop peer relationships appropriate to developmental level;
   (c) a lack of spontaneous seeking to share enjoyment, interests, or achievements with other people;
   (d) lack of social or emotional reciprocity.

2. Qualitative impairments in communication as manifested by at least one of the following:
   (a) delay in, or total lack of, the development of spoken language (not accompanied by an attempt to compensate through alternative modes of communication such as gesture or mime);

   (b) in individuals with adequate speech, marked impairment in the ability to initiate or sustain a conversation with others;
   (c) stereotyped and repetitive use of language or idiosyncratic language;
   (d) lack of varied, spontaneous make-believe play, or social imitative play appropriate to developmental level.

3. Restricted repetitive and stereotyped patterns of behaviour, interests and activities, as manifested by at least one of the following:
   (a) encompassing preoccupation with one or more stereotyped and restricted patterns of interest that is abnormal either in intensity or focus;
   (b) apparently inflexible adherence to specific, nonfunctional routines or rituals;
   (c) stereotyped and repetitive motor mannerisms (e.g. hand or finger flapping or twisting, or complex whole-body movements);
   (d) persistent preoccupation with parts of objects.

*Children who meet diagnostic criteria for Rett's Disorder or Childhood Disintegrative Disorder are excluded.

---

spoken language. In general, the distinction is borne out in clinical practice, and a classically autistic child does look quite different from a typical case of SLI. However, there are children who do not fall neatly into one or the other category, because they do appear to have undue difficulty with the social aspects of communication, and show some autistic-like behavioural oddities, but their problems are much less pervasive and severe than those seen in autistic children.[3] In general, these correspond to those children whose language disorder is of the semantic-pragmatic subtype. Thus, even if we do not think hypothesis C is a plausible account for the majority of children with SLI, we need to consider whether there might be a subset whose communication problems are compounded by autistic-like difficulties with social cognition.

SEMANTIC-PRAGMATIC DISORDER: CLINICAL ACCOUNTS

The concept of "semantic-pragmatic disorder" was introduced in Chapter 2. Several independent experts in the field of language disorder have suggested that it makes sense to identify a subset of children for whom difficulties at the pragmatic level seem a major problem. Rapin and Allen (1983), for instance, described "semantic-pragmatic syndrome" in language-impaired children who did not meet criteria for autism. The principal language characteristics of this disorder are summarised in Table 8.4, overleaf.

Rapin and Allen (1987) noted that the communication difficulties of children with semantic-pragmatic disorder were more apparent

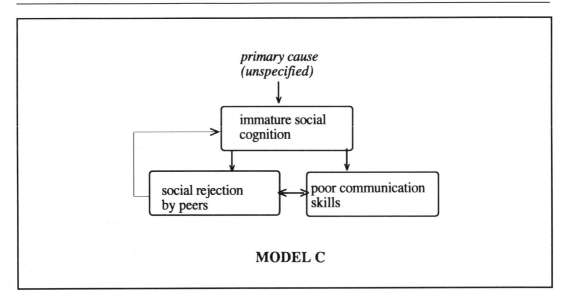

FIG. 8.11   Model C: problems in communication are secondary to impaired social cognition.

in continuous discourse than at the level of producing or understanding single utterances. Furthermore, they described features that seem unusual rather than just immature; a tendency to talk a great deal without really communicating much, to give tangential answers to questions, and to change topic unexpectedly. Several case studies have been reported describing children with these sorts of characteristics: Blank, Gessner, and Esposito (1979); Conti-Ramsden and Gunn (1986); Fujiki and Brinton (1991); McTear (1985).

These papers provided valuable insights, but the problem remains that identification of the language features of interest tends to be rather subjective, and it is unclear how far a specific syndrome is being described, as opposed to sporadic unusual clusters of symptoms.

It is difficult to validate the existence of a semantic-pragmatic subgroup, or to compare it with autistic disorder, because we lack suitable instruments for assessing the critical language characteristics described in clinical accounts.

TABLE 8.4

Features Mentioned in the Original Account of "Semantic-Pragmatic Syndrome" by Rapin and Allen (1983)

- very fluent expressive language
- utterances are syntactically well-formed and phonologically intact
- language is often not really communicative
- impairment in the ability to encode meaning relevant to the conversational situation
- striking inability to engage in communicative discourse
- short phrases and individual words are comprehended
- comprehension of connected discourse is impaired
- questions frequently answered with seemingly irrelevant responses
- young children may echo what is said to them

Three approaches have been used in research on this topic: (1) experimental studies using specially constructed tests of language and social communication, (2) observational studies of conversational behaviour, and (3) checklist ratings of children's behaviour. The last part of this chapter will review evidence from all three areas to consider how far the notion of semantic-pragmatic disorder is a valid one, whether children with the language characteristics shown in Table 8.4 tend to have autistic clinical features, and how far their communication difficulties are related to impairments of social cognition.

Experimental studies

Theory of mind.   An obvious place to start is with the theory of mind task that has been so extensively investigated in autism. Deficits on this task are regarded as such a hallmark of autistic disorder, that one immediately wants to ask whether similar deficits are seen in some children with SLI. Leslie and Frith (1988) contrasted theory of mind skills in language-impaired and autistic children and reported that the children with SLI performed at ceiling, but they did not subclassify the SLI group, so it is unclear whether any children with semantic-pragmatic disorder were included. A theory of mind test was given to 18 of the children who took part in the study by Bishop and Adams (1992), but the results were inconclusive and the data have not previously been published. We followed the procedure adopted by Baron-Cohen et al. (1985), but, to keep the vocabulary as simple as possible, we substituted an inverted cup and a box as hiding places, and a ball as the hidden object. Because we were concerned that children with SLI might fail because they did not understand the language used in the test sentences, we added additional questions to check their knowledge. As well as being asked "where will Sally look for her ball?", we asked whether each doll knew where the ball was, and where each of them *thought* it was. Data are shown in Table 8.5. The children with SLI were of normal nonverbal intelligence and aged from 8 to 12 years, well above the age at which theory of

mind tasks are usually passed. The sample included five children who, on the basis of conversational characteristics, were regarded as having semantic-pragmatic disorder. Only one of these five children fulfilled the usual criteria for passing theory of mind, compared with 9 of the 13 children with more typical SLI. However, closer scrutiny of the data makes one wary of interpreting this as showing theory of mind deficits in those with semantic-pragmatic disorder. First, two of the children with semantic-pragmatic disorder (compared to one in the typical SLI group) failed the "reality" question, which is given at the end of the test to ensure that the child understands where the ball actually is. In such cases, responses to the "false belief" question cannot be interpreted. Second, in the combined typical SLI and semantic-pragmatic subgroups, all but one of the children who failed the critical first false belief question (Q1) went on to pass the subsequent questions. Note that these questions tap the same knowledge about the mental states of the protagonists.

It is not clear why Q1 should have proved more difficult than the other questions. It could be that the use of "will" to refer to future time is problematic for children with language difficulties, who have difficulty in imagining events beyond the "here and now". Or the verb "look for" might be confused with "find" in children with semantic difficulties. These results are far from conclusive, but they suggest that children with SLI, including those with semantic-pragmatic disorder, can appreciate another's false belief, provided they are questioned about this using simple language. However, no direct comparison has been made between a semantic-pragmatic group and an autistic group using the same test materials. Also, the ability to pass an elementary false belief task does not necessarily entail that the child will always correctly infer another person's mental state. Most of the evidence that children with semantic-pragmatic disorder are prone to misunderstand other people's beliefs, knowledge, or intentions is circumstantial, and comes from analysis of communicative problems in naturalistic situations, as we shall see later.

TABLE 8.5

Unpublished Data on a Theory of Mind Task Administered to a Subset of Children with SLI Who Took Part in the Study by Bishop and Adams (1992)

ID	group*	M	R	Q1	Q2	Q3	Q4	Q5	FB
m05	s	✓	✓	A	✓	✓	✓	✓	no
m06	s	✓	✓	dk	✓	✓	✓	✓	no
j06	s	✓	✗						—
n10	s	✓	✗						—
j09	s	✓	✓	✓	✓	✓	✓	✓	yes
m04	t	✓	✓	B	✓	✓	✓	✓	no
j01	t	✓	✓	✓	✓	✓	✓	✓	yes
n07	t	✓	✓	✓	✓	✓	✓	✓	yes
m03	t	✓	✓	✓	✓	✓	✓	✓	yes
m01	t	✓	✓	✓	✓	✓	✓	✓	yes
j03	t	✓	✓	C	✓	✓	✓	D	no
n09	t	✓	✓	✓	✓	✓	✓	✓	yes
n01	t	✓	✓	✓	✓	✓	✓	✓	yes
j07	t	✓	✗						—
n11	t	✓	✓	✓	✓	✓	✓	✓	yes
n06	t	✓	✓	✗	✓	✓	✓	✓	no
n02	t	✓	✓	✓	✓	✓	✓	✓	yes
n12	t	✓	✓	✓	✓	✓	✓	✓	yes

*group: s = semantic–pragmatic; t = typical SLI.

M(emory question): Where was the ball at the beginning? (cup)
R(eality question): Where is the ball really? (box)

False belief questions:

> Q1: Where will Sally look for the ball? (cup)
> Q2: Does Sally know where the ball is? (no)
> Q3: Does Anne know where the ball is? (yes)
> Q4: Where does Sally think the ball is? (cup)
> Q5: Where does Anne think the ball is? (box)

FB: Child meets criteria for passing false belief, i.e. passes questions R, M, Q1:

> A: "Sally"
> B: "look for it"
> C: "have to look for it everywhere"
> D: "someone got it"

Language understanding and production. Two experimental studies by Bishop and Adams (1991, 1992) were designed with the aim of developing measures that would highlight the qualitative distinctions between children with the clinical picture of semantic-pragmatic disorder and other language-impaired children. However, neither study was particularly successful in this regard: the problem was not so much that the tests were insensitive, but rather that they were less specific than had been hoped, and revealed unexpected problems in children with more typical SLI as well as in those with semantic-pragmatic disorder. The study of inferential comprehension by Bishop and Adams (1992), which is described more fully in Chapter 7, looked at comprehension of stories which were presented in pictorial as well as oral form. To our surprise, we found that problems in comprehending pictorial stories were a general feature of all language-impaired children; we had expected that only those with semantic-pragmatic disorder might be impaired. Although comprehension scores were lower overall on this test for children with semantic-pragmatic disorder, the difference between this group and those with more typical SLI was more a matter of degree than a qualitative one.

The referential communication task used by Bishop and Adams (1991) is described earlier. Once again, the task revealed difficulties in children with SLI, but it did not neatly divide the semantic-pragmatic group from those with more typical SLI. In particular, children who provided irrelevant detail in conversation, or who were vague and unclear did not show these characteristics in the referential communication task. We were forced to conclude that the referential communication task was not a good way of assessing children's ability to infer the listener's communicative needs, and that information processing demands might be a more critical determinant of performance. To explain why some children who seemed insensitive to the listener's needs in conversation coped well with the referential communication task, we noted that, compared to natural conversation, the task was highly concrete and rule-governed. The structure provided by the experimental set-up might be especially helpful to children who had difficulty in keeping track of the topic of conversation. The picture array defined what was going to be talked about and remained present as a visible prompt.

To date, we have failed to produce an experimental test that can be used to identify cases of "semantic-pragmatic disorder". One possibility is that the structure and concrete setting provided by experimental tasks helps children compensate for underlying problems in using contextual cues. In keeping with this view, we have found that investigations of conversational behaviour are more useful in throwing light on the characteristics of children with this clinical profile.

Conversational behaviour

Adams and Bishop (1989) studied a group of children with SLI, most of whom were attending special residential schools, who were subdivided according to the judgements of their teachers or therapists into those who did or did not have the characteristics of semantic-pragmatic disorder, as described in clinical accounts. Conversational data was gathered in a semi-structured situation, where specific topics were introduced with photographs, which were used to prompt the children to talk about their own experiences. The aim was to have a relatively natural conversation, rather than the kind of teaching/therapeutic interaction where the adult asks questions to which the answers are already known. We applied a method of discourse analysis developed by Coulthard (1977), in which utterances are coded as (1) initiations, (2) responses, or (3) follow-ups, depending on whether they (a) set up an expectation of a response, (b) respond to what has gone before, or (c) acknowledge what has gone before. We found that the semantic-pragmatic group tended to be characterised by an unusually high rate of initiations. This was of interest in view of the fact that the clinical accounts described these children as "verbose". It seemed that it was not so much how much the child said, as the extent to which the child took the conversational lead, that led to this impression.

In a later small-scale study, Bishop et al. (1994) looked more closely at a subgroup of children with semantic-pragmatic disorder who had specifically been selected on the basis that they were judged by their teachers to be "verbose". One possible explanation for this behaviour was that the children were poor at discriminating between what was appropriate behaviour with an unfamiliar adult as opposed to, say, a family member. Most normally developing children are relatively restrained when interviewed by an unfamiliar adult, and, although they may talk readily, they tend to let the adult take the conversational lead. However, we would anticipate that they would behave differently in an informal setting with friends or family. We therefore compared conversational behaviour of our semantic-pragmatic group and a control group of children in relation to the conversational setting and familiarity of the partner. We found that both groups of children behaved differently in these different situations, initiating more when the partner was familiar and the setting was more informal (i.e. toy play). The high rate of initiations of the semantic-pragmatic group which led to the impression of "verbosity" was even more pronounced when we moved away from the setting of an interview with an unfamiliar adult. The conclusion we drew was that children with semantic-pragmatic disorder do differentiate bet-ween social partners and communicative settings, so their high rate of initiations cannot be seen as reflecting poor social discrimination. Rather, it seemed to reflect some general lack of inhibition.

Using data from the original larger con-versational study, Bishop and Adams (1989) went on to try to pinpoint what factors gave the impression of oddity in some conversations. Transcriptions were scrutinised for indications of "inappropriacy", where the smooth flow of conversation broke down. Utterances that were just grammatically immature would not be marked— the aim was to identify utterances that were odd or unexpected. This is not as easy as it might sound; almost any utterance can be made sense of with hindsight and a degree of imagination. It was therefore necessary to establish that the "inappropriacy" was not just in the mind of the rater, and so we spent some time doing independent ratings of conversations, and then discussing the sections that had been coded as "inappropriate", in

order to achieve reasonable agreement between independent raters as to how frequent in-appropriate child utterances were. The overall index of percentage of inappropriate utterances in the conversation was significantly higher for those with semantic-pragmatic disorder than for other children. A post hoc classification of instances of inappropriacy was then developed. Some of the categories are hard to account for in terms of basic linguistic limitations, and seem rather to reflect difficulties in appreciating the partner's communicative needs or intentions. For instance, children with SLI would sometimes give over-literal responses, which did not take the context into account. Some examples are shown in Table 8.6, opposite.

It must be stressed, however, that these were not common, and they were also seen in younger normally-developing children. Other types of response were, however, seldom seen in normally developing children of any age, but were relatively frequent in children with semantic-pragmatic disorder. These included the categories of "too much information" and "too little information" (see Table 8.7, overleaf). One might have anticipated that children would tend to cluster into those giving too much information and those giving too little, but in fact the two categories tended to co-occur. This suggested that for some children there was a problem in matching the message to the conversational partner, sometimes providing unnecessary detail and sometimes omitting crucial information. It seems plausible that this might arise because the child was poor at judging what the other person did or did not know. Note, however, that these problems are fairly subtle, and, even in the most extreme cases, the majority of child utterances were "appropriate". No child produced contributions that were totally bizarre, and the "inappropriate" utterances usually led to just a temporary "glitch" in the conversation, rather than a sense of total disruption. The important point is that raters who were trained to identify such glitches could achieve reasonable agreement as to when they occurred, and this measure did differentiate a subgroup of children who, on clinical grounds, were regarded as having pragmatic difficulties.

TABLE 8.6

Examples of Over-literal Responses

Misreads communicative intention

A:	Can you tell me about your party?
C:	Yes (with no sign of continuing)

Fail to use prior context

A:	How did you get to your holiday in Campomar?
C:	By car
A:	By car Who drove you?
C:	And aeroplane of course, aeroplane
A:	A plane So it's not in England?
C:	No
A:	Where is it?
C:	Campomar

Wrong meaning of homonym

	(C is shivering and complaining of cold)
A:	I thought you said you were hardy?
C:	No, I wasn't I was Jones

Wrong meaning of homonym

	(at end of long and tiring session)
A:	Can you stand to do some more?
C:	(stands up)

The evidence from conversational data is indirect, but it offers tentative support to the notion that some children may have pragmatic difficulties that are associated with subtle impairments of social cognition.

Checklist ratings

One of the frustrations for anyone wishing to study semantic-pragmatic disorder is the lack of objective and reliable criteria for diagnosing this type of problem. Many of the behaviours listed in Table 8.4, (p.216) are hard to rate reliably, and may be difficult to elicit in a clinical assessment. Bishop (in press) reported preliminary data from a checklist devised to address this issue. Checklists of pupil behaviour were completed by teachers and speech-language pathologists working at special schools for children with SLI. Checklist items were divided into those assessing language form, those assessing content and use (including many of the characteristics described in Table 8.4, p.216), and those assessing nonlinguistic autistic features. Inter-rater reliability of some items was disappointingly low, but it was nevertheless possible

TABLE 8.7

Examples of Too Much or Too Little Information Provided to Conversational Partner

Too little information: Inappropriate presupposition

A: So what did you do when you were sick?

C: I can't remember
            I did though when I was run over by a car

(elliptical form "did" does not refer back to previously mentioned verb)

Too little information: Unestablished referent

A: What did you do on your holiday?

C: Splash him at the sunsplash

(unclear who "him" refers to)

Too little information: Logical step omitted

C: My brother was feeling sick on Monday

A: mm

C: And I took my trouser off

A: uhhuh
            Why did you take your trousers off?

C: He was sick on my trouser

(initially the connection between the child's utterances is unclear, although he is able to make a link when explicitly questioned)

Too much information: Unnecessary assertion/denial

C: My dad got a new car

A: mm

C: The exhaust wasn't rusty

A: mm

C: And the silencer hadn't dropped off

(negation is usually only used to deny a state of affairs that has been assumed to be the case)

Too much information: Excessive elaboration

A: Have you ever been ill?

C: Yes ... on February the first nineteen ninety four

Too much information: Unnecessary reiteration

A: Where did you have your operation?

C: Kings Medical Centre
            You been there?

A: Yes

C: Yeah
            I been there to have my operation

A: uhhuh

C: Had my operation there

to combine sets of items into composite scales with adequate reliability. When this was done, it emerged that there was a significant correlation between autistic features and low scores on the content/use scale. However, the profiles of individual children were very mixed. Some were characterised by abnormal nonverbal communication; others by poor peer relation ships; others by restricted interests.

Is semantic-pragmatic disorder on a continuum with autistic disorder?

The evidence available to date suggests that language-impaired children with the clinical characteristics of "semantic-pragmatic disorder" may be rather different from other children with SLI, perhaps having more in common with children with high-functioning autism.

This conclusion remains tentative, and many issues remain to be settled. The lack of clearcut diagnostic criteria make it difficult to do research on semantic-pragmatic disorder. Little is known about the natural history of the disorder, other than anecdotal reports suggesting quite dramatic changes in language characteristics with age (Bishop & Rosenbloom, 1987). It remains unclear how far we are describing a qualitatively distinct subgroup of children, or whether there is heterogeneity even within this subgroup. It has not been established that semantic difficulties invariably accompany the kinds of pragmatic problems described in this chapter, and this has led to the term "semantic-pragmatic disorder" being criticised as misleading.[4] The diagnostic category descibed by Rapin and Allen has been useful in focusing the attention of researchers on pragmatic difficulties in language-impaired children, but, in the final analysis, we may need to take a more dimensional approach, which regards impairments of social functioning and impairments of basic language skills as independent problems which co-occur at above chance levels, perhaps because adjacent brain areas are implicated (see Bishop, 1989a; in press).

CONCLUSIONS

In this chapter, three models accounting for a link between language impairment and poor social interaction have been considered. They are not easy to distinguish, because they all predict similar patterns of correlation. However, differentiating between them is important when we consider intervention with these children. Should we focus on improving the child's basic language skills, extend our focus to nonverbal communication, work on social skills, or train the child on theory of mind tasks? The work reviewed in this chapter suggests that the answer is likely to vary from child to child. What is plain is that it is dangerous to assume that a child with SLI has adequate skills in the domains of social cognition and nonverbal communication which can be used to compensate for the oral language difficulties. This is true in some cases, but some children need help in learning about social interaction, even when no spoken language is involved. All too often, the educational options open to the child are either a placement where there is support from a speech-language therapist, or a setting specialised in the education of autistic children, where staff have expertise in working to improve the social functioning of the children. For many children with language impairments, some mixture of the two would be optimal.

FOOTNOTES

1. Of course, this is not to say that we should take any putative "theory of mind" test at face value; there are bound to be situations when a test cannot be regarded as a valid test of theory of mind, because task requirements or instructions are not understood by the child, or because it is possible to succeed by adopting a strategy that requires no real understanding. However, it seems fruitless to search for a pure, context-free test of theory of mind. All tests must occur in some context, and this will influence the results.

2. *Comment* by Dorothy Parker, copyright 1926, © renewed 1954 by Dorothy Parker, from *The Portable Dorothy Parker*, Introduction by Brendan Gill. Used by permission of Gerald Duckworth & Company Limited, and Viking Penguin, a division of Penguin Books USA Inc.

3. *DSM-IV* introduced the category of Pervasive Developmental Disorder Not Otherwise Specified (PDDNOS) for cases which do not meet criteria for autistic disorder but where there is "severe and pervasive impairment in the development of reciprocal social interaction, verbal and nonverbal communication skills or the developmental of stereotyped behaviour, interests and activities", including cases where there is late age at onset, or "atypical" or "subthreshold" symptomatology. Little space in *DSM-IV* is devoted to this diagnosis, which is apparently viewed as a rare "default" diagnosis to be applied only when criteria for other disorders are not met. It is, however, becoming increasingly popular as a label for children with autistic-like disorders, including some with semantic-pragmatic disorder. See Bishop (in press) for more discussion of the relationship between PDDNOS and semantic-pragmatic disorder.

4. In my current work, I use the term "pragmatic language impairment" (PLI).

9

Modularity and interaction in language development and disorders

i never think at all when i write
nobody can do two things at the same time
and do them well

Don Marquis (1961), *Archy's Life of Mehitabel*

THE MODULAR APPROACH TO SLI

Imagine that a group of 10 people decide to set up a co-operative enterprise manufacturing toy cars, and that they had available 10 rooms arranged down a corridor in which they could work. They might decide to have one person in each room, each building an entire car from start to finish. This, however, could be slow and inefficient, because each worker would need to learn many skills, and the rooms would have to contain the whole range of components involved in manufacture. It might be difficult to keep track of which stage of assembly was currently under way.

Suppose instead it was decided to set up a production line where each worker specialises in one step of the production process, such as putting on wheels, spraying the car body, or putting the product in a box, with a different operation carried out in each room of the factory. Each room would be stocked just with the necessary components, and so there would be less time spent locating the materials that were needed. A conveyer belt could link the rooms, and deliver each car to the next worker when it was ready for the next operation. Each worker could become highly specialised and skilled in a relatively short space of time, especially if they selected the job that best matched their aptitude. This seems like a much more efficient way to organise the workforce, and indeed, the advantages of production lines are well known in industry.

However, the production line does have its drawbacks. The pace of work in each room would be determined by the rate at which part assembled cars were provided by the worker from the previous room. Thus, workers at a late stage in production might be overwhelmed with too much work, or sit idly by waiting for new input. To some extent, this might be ameliorated by having workers free to communicate, so they could know when to slow down or speed up. However, this would distract workers from their dedicated tasks. The problem could be compounded if an emergency, such as an epidemic or transport strike, led to some workers being absent. Production could grind to a halt altogether because a critical stage was not carried out. In contrast, the more flexible set-up, where each worker can carry out all operations, is less vulnerable to loss of workers.

This analogy captures the distinction between modular and nonmodular brain systems. A module can be likened to a stage in processing in a production line. According to Fodor (1983), many aspects of human language processing are modular in nature, i.e. they operate as stages in a processing chain that are largely independent of one another. Fodor reasoned that it would make biological and evolutionary sense for compartmentalised brain regions to be specialised for performing certain kinds of operation; by remaining largely autonomous and hence immune from the influence of other cognitive processes, these modules could operate quickly and efficiently. Fodor's list of defining features for a brain module is given in Table 9.1, opposite, together with the corresponding characteristics of a mythical production line.

If a system is modular, we can deduce which operations are carried out by separate modules by examining patterns of impairment after brain damage. To continue our analogy for a while, suppose we do not know how the factory is organised, but when there is a shortage of workers, we notice that some cars are coming off the production line missing all four wheels, whereas others are coming off complete but unpainted. We can conclude that there are normally separate workers responsible for adding wheels and for painting the car, and that these processes do not in any way depend on one another. On the other hand, if we find some cars are missing only front wheels, while others are missing only back wheels, then we might deduce that there are separate workers responsible for adding front or back wheels. The analogy here is with the neuropsychological logic

of double dissociation, whereby we look for patients who show mirror image patterns of deficits, in order to identify aspects of functioning which are logically independent of one another, i.e. putative modules.

The field of cognitive neuropsychology is concerned with studying neurological patients with the aim of throwing light on normal cognitive processes. A focal brain lesion can have a strikingly selective effect on a specific aspect of language functioning. The greatest impact of cognitive neuropsychology comes not from large studies of groups of patients, but rather from detailed single case studies of patients who demonstrate dissociations between cognitive impairments. The rationale adopted by those in this field is that even a single case who shows the ability to perform operation X but is unable to do Y can demonstrate that Y does not depend on X. One of the most famous examples is illustrated in *GR: A man whose reading errors challenged a whole theory* (p.228). This case, of a dyslexic man GR, had a pattern of deficit that was impossible to explain in terms of contemporary models of reading, and so forced those working in basic psycholinguistics to alter how they conceptualised the stages of information processing involved in reading. Another famous example is the patient, KF, studied by Shallice and Warrington (1970), who presented with impaired short-term memory but preserved long-term memory, and so challenged models that assumed that material had first to be held in a short-term store before being transferred to long-term memory. These examples illustrate how dissociations are theoretically informative, because even a single person who shows a dissociation between two impairments is sufficient to demonstrate a lack of logical dependence between them. This has led some cognitive neuropsychologists to go so far as to argue that individual case studies are the only valid way of proceeding if one's aim is to use neuropsychological data as evidence for building a model of the cognitive system (Caramazza, 1986).

Cognitive neuropsychology is growing in popularity as an approach to the study of developmental as well as acquired disorders (Temple, 1997). The information processing

TABLE 9.1

Properties of Modules Compared with a Production Line

Fodor's (1983) characterisation of properties of a module	Production line analogy
Domain specificity Systems constrained in terms of the range of information they can access	Each worker specialised to perform operations using a limited range of components
Mandatory processing No voluntary control over whether relevant input is processed	The workers do not make decisions about whether or not to do the job; they carry it out whenever a new car appears on the conveyor belt
Limited central access to intermediate representations Information which must have been processed is not available to conscious awareness	A quality controller evaluates the final product without knowing much about the nature or number of the operations involved in its construction
Speed Complex information processing (as in language comprehension) takes place remarkably quickly	Workers do their tasks rapidly and repetitively
Information encapsulation Information from higher levels is not fed back to lower ones (e.g. no top-down processing occurs)	Workers pass on their completed work as soon as it is ready, without receiving any feedback about how later stages of production are progressing
Shallow output A module computes only a very limited range of representations	Workers are skilled to carry out just one step in the production chain
Fixed neural architecture A circumscribed brain region is dedicated to the function of a module	A different job is done in each room
Characteristic breakdown pattern Focal brain injury can cause selective deficits in one area of functioning that cannot be explained in terms of some general loss of capacity	If a worker is absent, others do not step in to take over the job; we can identify which worker was missing by the specific faults seen in the final product
Characteristic pace and sequencing in development Developmental course of a modular function is highly dependent on maturation of endogenous systems, and insensitive to environmental influences	Differences in skill of workers carrying out various operations are largely due to how they are initially selected, with each being given a job suited to his or her particular talents

models derived from the study of adults provide a useful framework for understanding the levels of representation that need to be investigated, and attention has been drawn to developmental analogues of some acquired disorders, such as prosopagnosia (Young & Ellis, 1992), subtypes of reading impairment (Castles & Coltheart, 1993), or dyscalculia (Temple, 1992).

We might imagine that the methods of cognitive neuropsychology should be particularly

GR: A man whose reading errors challenged a whole theory

Figure 9.1 shows a plausible model of reading that was popular in the early 1960s.

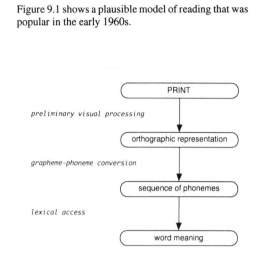

FIG. 9.1

According to this model, written words are understood by first recoding them into phonological form, and then using the same processes as are involved in speech recognition to access lexical representations.

In 1966, Marshall and Newcombe reported a patient, GR, who as a result of a gunshot wound became severely aphasic and dyslexic. The most striking and consistent feature of his language impairment was the occurrence of semantic errors, whereby words were misread as other words related in meaning, for instance:

antique → vase
canary → parrot
gnome → pixie

At the same time, GR found it impossible to read nonwords, such as "wux", or "dup", indicating an inability to carry out grapheme–phoneme conversion. Now, it can be seen from the model above that if grapheme–phoneme conversion fails, then understanding of written meaning should be impossible, yet GR understands a great deal of what he reads, despite often having no notion of the correct phonological form. This type of observation, contributed to the development of dual-route models of reading, in which lexical access could either be achieved directly from orthographic input (the "direct" route), or indirectly by translating graphemes into phonemes and then identifying a matching phonological string in the mental lexicon, as shown in Fig. 9.2, below.

GR is seen as having damage to the indirect, grapheme–phoneme conversion route. He could still use the direct route from orthography to meaning, but would not always contact the exact lexical representation that was required.

For more detailed treatment of patterns of dyslexia see Coltheart, Patterson, and Marshall (1980) and Patterson, Marshall, and Coltheart (1985).

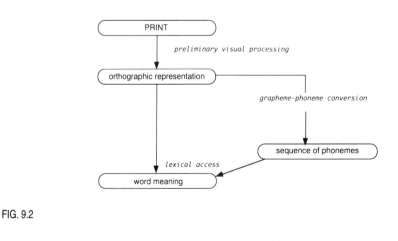

FIG. 9.2

well-suited for studying SLI. After all, Fodor (1983) regarded language input systems as quintessentially modular, and SLI is typically defined on the basis of a dissociation between language development and nonverbal ability. The existence of other conditions where general IQ is impaired while language is relatively normal provides the other half of the double dissociation (see *Good language despite general ability*, p.33), and offers evidence for the independence of language learning from other aspects of cognitive development. Problems, however, arise when we try to take the modularity concept a step further and look for modules within the language system. If we try to do this, we become acutely aware of two difficulties. First, an analytical framework based on autonomous modules is not at all well suited for analysing impairments within a developing system. Second, even if we restrict consideration to the static, adult state, then the cognitive neuropsychology approach can be something of a straitjacket, forcing us to focus on representational deficits and to neglect processing accounts of cognitive impairment.

Static rather than developmental models

In a developmental disorder, where the pattern of impairment may change over time, dissociations between cognitive abilities may be misleading. A good example is the study by Bernstein and Stark (1985), which was reviewed in Chapter 3 (p.68). In this study, a group of language-impaired children who were originally studied by Tallal and colleagues were followed up several years later and readministered Tallal's repetition test. The original deficit in discriminating tone pairs at short inter-stimulus intervals could no longer be seen; children with SLI did as well as control children on tasks involving tone pairs. Thus at this age, we have a dissociation between intact auditory discrimination, and impaired comprehension of sentences. Following conventional logic, we might conclude that the persisting language deficit in these children was not caused by any auditory difficulty. Yet we know from the earlier studies, that several years previously the same children had marked impairments of auditory processing. This raises the possibility that a slow-maturing auditory

perceptual system might leave a lasting legacy of language impairment, even after ceiling levels of auditory discrimination had been reached.

A simulation of this situation is shown in Fig. 9.3 (overleaf), which contrasts outcomes of five groups of children with differing levels of auditory discrimination in the preschool years. The simulation specifies that vocabulary learning is a direct function of auditory discrimination. We can see that by age six, the auditory discrimination deficit in the poorest group has resolved. However, there is no instantaneous catch-up of vocabulary, and so a deficit in this area will still be found. A cognitive neuropsychologist looking only at the six-year-old data might conclude that the child's language deficits arose from a primary impairment of a module concerned with vocabulary learning, and was not due to any auditory processing problem. However, the longitudinal data would tell a very different story.

The more longitudinal studies are carried out in the field of SLI, the more evidence mounts for a changing profile of language impairments with age, highlighting the dangers of basing a model of underlying processes solely on cross-sectional data.

Focus on bottom-up processing

Very often, when dealing with a developmental disorder, the problem is not so much one of identifying a dissociation, as in trying to account for a complex pattern of associated impairments. In such a case it might seem reasonable to search for the earliest stage of processing at which impairment could be seen. For instance, suppose a child has weak vocabulary, poor understanding of syntax, and poor ability to discriminate between speech sounds. If we accept Fodor's proposition that processing of language input is handled by an informationally encapsulated modular system, where processing is strictly bottom-up (depicted in simplified form in Fig. 9.4, p.231), then we could conclude that the speech discrimination deficit reflects impairment to an earlier stage of processing than the vocabulary or syntactic difficulties, and hence should be regarded as the primary deficit which influences all subsequent stages of processing.

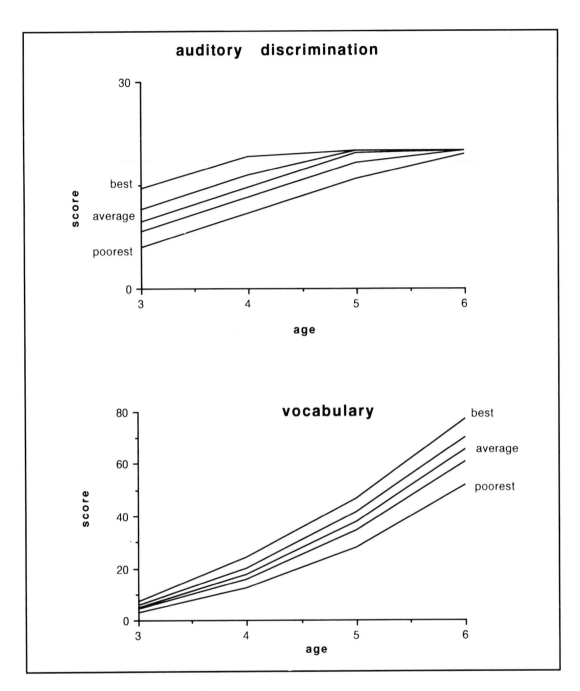

FIG. 9.3 Simulated data showing separation of subgroups of children at different ages on measures of auditory discrimination and vocabulary. The simulation took as a starting point a normal distribution of auditory discrimination ability. Auditory discrimination (AD) increases linearly with age (i) until an upper limit of 20 is reached; ($AD_i = AD_{i-1} + 5$). Vocabulary is a joint function of auditory discrimination at the same age and vocabulary level at the previous age; ($VO_i = AD_i \times 0.75 + VO_{i-1} \times 1.33$). Thus, no basic differences in vocabulary learning level are assumed, other than those depending on auditory discrimination skill. Note that whereas at early ages, the five groups of children are differentiated on auditory discrimination but not on vocabulary, by six years of age the position has reversed. The early deficit in auditory discrimination leaves a lasting legacy on vocabulary level, long after those with poor auditory discrimination have "caught up".

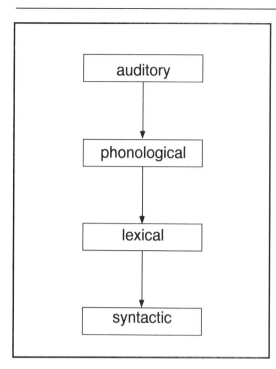

FIG. 9.4   A simplified "bottom-up" modular model of the early stages of comprehension.

However, the evidence reviewed in preceding chapters showed that a model such as that shown in Fig. 9.4 is far too simple, because it ignores developmental interactions between language levels (Crystal, 1987), and in particular fails to take into account the role of top-down influences. A more realistic model is shown in Fig. 9.5.

Consider, for instance, the path shown feeding back from syntax to lexicon. As we noted in Chapter 4, children's word learning is facilitated by "syntactic bootstrapping"; i.e. knowledge of the grammatical context in which a novel word occurs helps establish its meaning. The child who has poor syntactic skills will have reduced access to this important source of information about word meaning, and so vocabulary learning would be retarded. Next consider the path back from lexicon to phonological processing. In Chapter 4 we also noted how lexical development influences the development of a phonological system. When vocabulary is small, the child might be able to operate effectively by representing phonological information in the lexicon in the form of

"templates" or syllable-sized units. Increase in vocabulary size is one of the factors that has been postulated as motivating a restructuring of the child's phonological system, so that the phoneme rather than the syllable is the processing unit. Furthermore, we know that ability to remember novel strings of phonemes is influenced by their wordlikeness (Gathercole et al., 1991), and the correlation between vocabulary level and phonological short-term memory is likely to reflect bi-directional influences. These are just a few examples of top-down influences that have been shown to operate in the course of development. Overall, the Fodorian notion of a module that operates entirely in bottom-up mode might be a reasonable characterisation of the stable state that is achieved in the adult when language is fully learned (although this is debatable—see Marslen-Wilson & Tyler, 1987); however, it provides an unrealistic model of processing in the child who is developing language, where there is ample

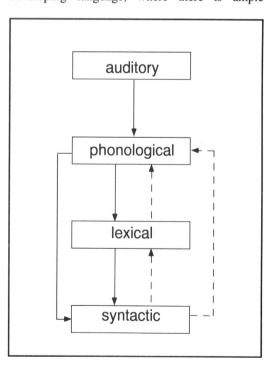

FIG. 9.5   A more realistic model, showing interactions between levels of processing in the development of comprehension. "Top-down" information flow is shown as dashed lines.

evidence of top-down influences on earlier stages of processing.

This creates serious difficulties in establishing direction of causation when deficits are found in children with developmental difficulties. Consider our hypothetical child who does poorly on auditory discrimination, vocabulary, and syntactic comprehension tests. When asked to distinguish between minimal pairs such as "bear" and "pear", the child does much more poorly than other children of the same age. However, it may be that the child is less familiar with the vocabulary items, so that many of the test items are effectively treated as nonsense words. Nonsense words are usually harder to discriminate than real words. Thus the child's weak vocabulary could exert a top-down influence on performance on the discrimination task. And weak vocabulary could itself be a consequence of lack of syntactic knowledge, which would prevent the child from learning new word meanings by syntactic bootstrapping. In brief, it is not valid to assume that we can identify primary causes by locating the earliest point in the language comprehension chain at which a deficit can be seen.

Problems in interpreting differential deficit

Another tack one might adopt is to look for evidence of differential deficit. Even if a child has a whole host of impairments, they may differ in terms of severity, giving clues as to which deficit is the primary one. For instance, we can match children with SLI with a younger normally developing control group in terms of some index of language level, and hope to show that the two groups are different on test X, but comparable on a control task Y. There are, however, methodological difficulties inherent in this approach, which are often overlooked. These concern psychometric characteristics of tests, especially item difficulty and item reliability. Most researchers are aware of interpretative problems created by floor and ceiling effects. For instance, in Fig. 9.6 (opposite), the control and SLI groups differ significantly on test X but not on test Y, but we would be wary of assuming that there was differential deficit in X because performance on Y is near ceiling for both groups, and hence by choosing too easy a test we may have masked a real difference between groups.

Chapman and Chapman (1973) pointed out that, even when group performance is off floor or ceiling, differences in the relative difficulty of items in two tests can lead to spurious "dissociations", and they recommended that researchers attempt to match the difficulty level of tasks that are to be compared, and use items that give good discrimination within a control group wherever possible. They also illustrated the extent to which test reliability can influence the size of differences in scores between two groups. Figure 9.7 shows real data from multiple choice analogies tests obtained by these authors from 49 people with schizophrenia and 206 normal controls. From within the same test, they selected items to form a high reliability (X) and a low reliability (Y) version. Only the more reliable test showed a significant deficit in the group with schizophrenia. The point emphasised by Chapman and Chapman is that the two tests were selected to be equivalent both in terms of item content and in terms of overall difficulty in the control group. It is clearly the difference in test reliability that is responsible for the differential deficit of the schizophrenic group. Yet, if X and Y had different types of content, we might easily have been misled into assuming that the people with schizophrenia had a selective deficit in carrying out the cognitive operations involved in test X. In general, the demonstration of differential deficit is less of a problem if our control task (Y) is a well-standardised psychometric instrument, because it is then reasonable to suppose that Y is at least as discriminating and reliable as an experimental test (X), and so if we find that people who are matched on Y perform differently on X, it is unlikely that this is because Y is less sensitive. However, where both X and Y are assessed by experimental tasks, Chapman and Chapman recommended that researchers match the tasks on discriminating power and reliability, in order to have confidence in interpreting dissociations.

In classic cognitive neuropsychology, these kinds of difficulty are implicitly recognised by those who stress the particular importance of double dissociations for informing theory. In short, if we have two patients who show the opposite patterns of deficit, with one selectively impaired on

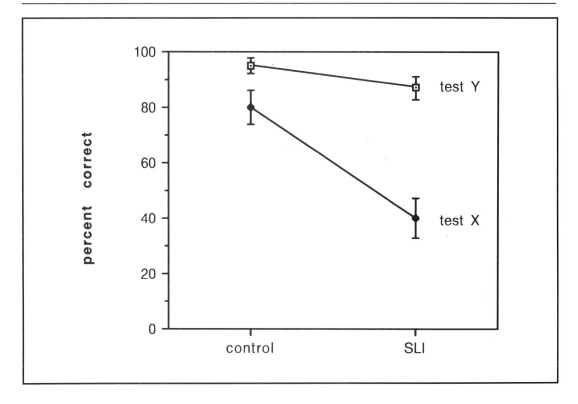

FIG. 9.6   Differential deficit complicated by a ceiling effect (fictitious data).

X and the other selectively impaired on Y, then it would seem that we are in a stronger position to conclude X and Y are independent faculties, and to reject any simple explanation in terms of "general" task factors, such as test reliability or difficulty. Even here, however, some awareness of psychometric principles is needed. Bates, Appelbaum, and Allard (1991) noted that some dissociations between measures can be expected by chance alone (this being particularly likely when test reliability is low, and when reliance is placed on data from a single case).

Focus on dissociations rather than associations

The emphasis that cognitive neuropsychology places on studying dissociations is rooted in the fact that the aim of the enterprise is to elucidate normal cognitive architecture. The fact that patients with striking patterns of dissociation are the exception rather than the rule is irrelevant, if one's aim is to build a model of cognition, rather than to document the difficulties of neuropsychological patients. However, these concerns do not apply to those studying SLI, where the primary goal of the enterprise is to understand the disorder itself. Rare but theoretically informative cases are to be welcomed when they are found, but for the majority of children, we see a constellation of associated deficits which we need to explore.

If our aim is to advance understanding of SLI, we need group data to establish which patterns of deficit reliably co-occur, which are chance associations, and whether scores are evenly depressed on a range of tests, or whether distinctive profiles can be reliably detected.

Developmental disorders tend to be characterised by complex patterns of deficit rather than the very selective difficulties seen in some adults with acquired lesions. In the developing child, an impairment at an early stage of processing would affect all the processes downstream of that stage. In this regard, children are different from adults, where it is possible to have damage affecting an

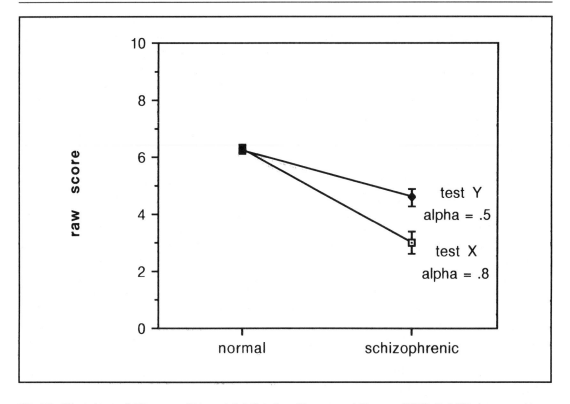

FIG. 9.7   Effect of test reliability on sensitivity to deficit. Data from Chapman and Chapman (1973). Reliability is assessed in terms of coefficient alpha, a measure of how well individual items correlate with the test total (i.e. internal consistency).

early stage of processing, without later stages being affected. Saffran, Marin, and Yeni-Komshian (1976), for instance, described a patient with "word deafness" who was quite unable to do any tasks requiring perceptual analysis at the phonemic level. Although he could not understand spoken language, semantic and syntactic processes remained intact in his expressive speech. Furthermore, he could understand written language. Contrast this with the case of a child who, from the earliest stage of language acquisition, has a problem in decoding speech sounds. A disruption at this stage of processing would lead to impairment at all subsequent levels, because the systems that would normally be responsible for vocabulary learning and mastery of grammar will not receive adequate input. In such a case, we would expect to see a very different profile of impairment in the child compared to the adult. In particular, we would expect the child to have difficulty in learning to read, because the necessary

substrate of spoken language skills would not be acquired.

To take another example, we know that in adults a brain lesion can severely impair phonological short-term memory, without any obvious effects on comprehension or speech production (Vallar & Baddeley, 1984). However, learning of new vocabulary is impaired (Baddeley et al., 1988). In an adult, whose vocabulary is already established, this may be just a minor inconvenience. However, in a child who is still learning language, the consequences would be much more serious. In short, for the child who is still developing language, a selective impairment at an early stage of processing will have repercussions throughout all subsequent stages of processing. The fact that children are especially likely to have associated deficits is not a coincidence; it is inevitable, given the interdependence of different stages of processing upon one another in the course of development.

Assumption that modality of deficit and nature of errors relate to primary underlying cause

In an adult with an acquired disorder, we can gain a good picture of the stage of processing that is affected by comparing tasks that involve similar representations in different input modalities, or by looking at the nature of errors. On the surface, it seems very reasonable to assume that similar logic applies to developmental disorders. However, as was discussed in Chapter 5, the case is less clearcut than it may seem. For instance, those who are arguing against an auditory deficit account of SLI have emphasised that language difficulties in these children depend more on grammatical character-istics of language than on perceptual salience. Within a language (and indeed within the same child), the same word ending, such as "-s", may be produced and perceived differently depending on whether it functions as a plural, a possessive, or the final phoneme in a word such as "horse". Also, the same grammatical errors of both production and comprehension may be evident in written as well as spoken language (e.g. Bishop, 1982; Cromer, 1978). Authors such as Gopnik and Crago (1991) have regarded such findings as evidence against auditory deficit accounts of SLI. The assumption is that, if the problem were simply that /s/ were hard to perceive, processing of all forms of /s/ should be impaired, and if auditory discrimination is the basis of the disorder, then much better performance should be observed with visual presentation. However, this type of assumption is unsafe. Low-level general impairments of perceptual or cognitive systems can lead to unexpected patterns of deficit, both because of compensatory mechanisms on the one hand, and because of interactions between different components of a developing system on the other. If we take the extreme case of children with profound congenital hearing loss, on tests of grammatical com-prehension of English, they performed very differently on items that simply required under-standing of content words, and on those that involved appreciating the significance of contrasts signalled by morphological endings, function words, and word order, regardless of whether or not these were perceptually salient (Bishop, 1982,

1983a). Furthermore, presentation of sentences in a written form did very little to overcome these problems. Indeed, it was noted that there were some deaf children who could read aloud every word in a sentence such as "the boy is not running" or "the man is pushed by the elephant" but still selected the picture of a boy running and the man pushing the elephant. When confronted with complex syntactic constructions, deaf children did not just guess at random, but rather adopted systematic strategies which sometimes led to below-chance performance. Even those children with facility in a native sign language had major difficulties in decoding the syntax of English—presumably because the surface forms used in oral languages to mark grammatical functions (i.e. word order and morphological endings) are not well-suited to processing in the visual modality, where simultaneous rather than sequential grammatical processes are the rule. Thus, hearing loss did not simply lead to slowing of language acquisition, nor did it lead to a predictable pattern of grammatical impairment affecting only non-salient morphemes. In fact, the distinctive response patterns seen in hearing-impaired children were remarkably similar to those seen in hearing children who had been diagnosed as having receptive language disorders. The crucial points emphasised by these studies of deaf children are that a general nonlinguistic impairment in auditory perception early in development can (1) have a disproportionately severe impact on the ability to produce and comprehend certain grammatical components of oral language (with different effects on grammatical morphology and vocabulary) and (2) affect written as well as spoken forms of an oral language. Note that this pattern of findings is totally different from what one would see if a hearing loss was acquired in adulthood, after proficiency in oral language had developed. Hearing loss does not just disrupt the input to specific parts of the language system; if acquired early in life, it alters the entire course of oral language development.

It must be stressed that I am not suggesting that SLI is caused by hearing loss. Rather, the point is that it is dangerous to imagine that we can predict on a priori grounds what pattern of language impairment would result if the child had a nonspecific cognitive or perceptual deficit that affected language learning, e.g. a disorder of auditory perception such as has been proposed by Tallal (1976) or a limitation of phonological short-term memory as mooted by Gathercole and Baddeley (1990a). The impact of a primary perceptual problem can be felt across the whole language system.

Exactly the same arguments apply when one comes to look at the profile of language performance. It is sometimes assumed that if a child has an uneven pattern of grammatical difficulties that does not resemble that of a normal child at any stage of development, that this must indicate some primary linguistic deficit. This is wrong. Nonlinguistic deficits can affect the pattern as well as the timing of language learning; the impact of hearing loss on oral language acquisition once again provides a clear example. An unusual and distinctive pattern of grammatical difficulty in a child does not in itself constitute evidence for a biological defect in a grammatical module.

Emphasis on representational rather than processing deficits

The quote at the start of this chapter captures the notion of a "processing" deficit, i.e. there is some overall processing capacity which must be divided between different operations. Processes that can be carried out successfully on their own may break down when the child has to do several things simultaneously. The notion is forcefully illustrated in the case of Archy, the poetic cockroach whose quotation heads this chapter. One can understand why the business of getting words on paper consumes most of Archy's cognitive resources, when one appreciates that he types by banging his head against the keys of a typewriter (hence the absence of capitalisation).

Accounts of SLI as a processing deficit have been mentioned at several points in this book. In Chapter 3, we reviewed Tallal's theory which maintains that children can discriminate speech sounds, but that they have difficulty doing so when having to handle large amounts of information rapidly. The notion of processing resurfaced in Chapter 6, where we contrasted theories that regard

grammatical deficits in SLI as performance limitations that were seen when the language processing system was put under pressure, against those which maintained that there was defective competence, with inability to generate certain kinds of representation.

Models with the box-and-arrows architecture of Fig. 9.4 or Fig. 9.5 (p.231) are useful for describing representational deficits, but are not well suited to characterise processing deficits. Reliance on such models has, no doubt, played a part in the relative neglect of processing accounts of language disorders in adult neuropsychology, despite evidence that the comprehension of aphasic patients could be influenced by factors unrelated to linguistic content, such as rate of presentation (e.g. Albert & Bear, 1974). More recently, some cognitive neuropsychologists have attempted to incorporate processing factors in models of language impairment (e.g. Haarman & Kolk, 1991), but, in general, the tendency is still to look for explanations in terms of deficient linguistic representations.

In Chapters 5 and 6, we noted the controversy in the field of SLI between those who assume that syntactic deficits reflect a lack of linguistic knowledge, and those who proposed explanations in terms of limited processing capacity. In many respects, those in the "competence" camp adopt a stance that sits very well with a cognitive neuropsychology perspective, whereas for those in the "performance" camp, the modular models of cognitive neuropsychology cannot capture adequately the interactions between language levels that lead to trade-offs when processing capacity is put under pressure.

The debate between representation vs. processing accounts is often heated, with positions so polarised as to make it appear as if there is no common ground. This division has probably arisen because the two perspectives have their roots in very different academic traditions. The representational position comes from the Chomskyan tradition, where "grammar" is regarded as a formal device for generating grammatical sentences of a language, and the aim is to characterise grammatical knowledge in static terms. This is assumed to be part of our innate mental ability, i.e.

language competence, embodied in a specialised brain module. It is recognised that in everyday life, our ability to deploy this knowledge may be influenced by factors outside the module —variations in memory, attention, motivation and so on: what Fodor would refer to as "central processes". However, many linguists regard these influences on language performance as relatively uninteresting—the main aim is to characterise language competence.

The processing position has been adopted by those who are concerned with building artificial systems that simulate real-time comprehension. For these computational linguists, limitations in attentional capacity, memory, and motor programming are regarded as fundamental constraints that shape the form that languages take. This approach may be characterised as functional rather than formal: the aim is to explain grammar in terms of natural constraints on language processing, rather than to regard grammar as something entirely independent or autonomous, whose characteristics can only be accounted for by appealing to innateness (see Briscoe, 1987).

The conflict between these different approaches to grammar is reflected in explanations of language disorders. Those with a background in Chomskyan linguistics have a particular interest in the notion that morphosyntactic impairments in children with SLI reflect impairment of an innate grammatical module; in consequence, the child lacks some of the specialised knowledge crucial for grammatical acquisition, despite normal cognitive development in all other areas. Researchers such as Clahsen (1989), Gopnik and Crago (1991), and Van der Lely (1994) exemplify this kind of approach.

The contrasting, functionalist or processing approach favours explanations of SLI which do not presuppose the existence of innate grammatical knowledge. Learning of grammar is seen as being dependent on general cognitive processes of perception, recognition, attention, classification, memory retrieval, and planning, and it is in one or more of these processes that the basis for morpho-syntactic impairments in SLI is sought. Tallal and colleagues (e.g. Tallal, Miller, & Fitch,

1993), Gathercole and Baddeley (1990a), Chapman (1992), and Johnston (1994) favour this class of explanation.

Because representational accounts maintain that grammatical knowledge is defective, they cannot readily account for cases where a child shows partial mastery of a grammatical structure, i.e. performance that is above chance but still defective. Nevertheless, such evidence does not disprove a representational account. One can always argue that the observed behaviour arises from the use of atypical strategies (see e.g. p.134 for Gopnik's (1990) explanation of why children with SLI are able to perform accurately on comprehension tasks testing knowledge of plural "-s"). Processing theories, on the other hand, anticipate that the child's ability to do grammatical tasks will vary depending on task demands. Although acquisition of grammatical knowledge is bound to be delayed, learning is assumed to take place slowly, but deployment of learned knowledge may still be problematic. If one can demonstrate that children's errors reflect failure to use grammatical knowledge rather than total lack of rule-based knowledge, this supports a processing account, although the onus is then on the theorist to test further predictions about how manipulation of task demands might influence performance.

Notions of limited processing capacity have been justly criticised for being vague, but they do make testable predictions that children's ability to produce and comprehend language will depend not just on the nature and complexity of specific grammatical forms, but also on the overall processing demands placed on the child. They steer us away from looking only at the grammatical aspects of language, and draw attention to the trade-offs that may exist between different levels of processing (Masterson & Kamhi, 1992); and to the effects of variables such as speech rate on linguistic processing (Ellis Weismer & Hesketh, 1993). Processing accounts predict that we may be able to manipulate level of performance with particular sentence structures by changing the processing demands of a task. If so, this would not only further our theoretical understanding of SLI, but would also have implications for intervention.

Modules as hard-wired innate systems

Fodor's definition of a module (Table 9.1, p.227) includes a number of different features that are logically separable. He proposes that if a cognitive process has the characteristics of domain-specificity and information encapsulation, then it is likely to be an evolutionary adaptation with an innate biological basis. Those postulating modular explanations of SLI have emphasised the mounting evidence, from both pedigree and twin studies, that SLI has a genetic basis, and in some cases may even be caused by a single defective gene (Bishop et al., 1995; Gopnik & Crago, 1991; Hurst et al., 1990; Tomblin & Buckwalter, 1994). On the basis of such evidence, Gopnik and Crago (1991) made the tentative proposal that a single gene might control mechanisms responsible for learning morphological paradigms. However, accounts of this work in secondary sources have made more extravagant claims, not only over-exaggerating the selectivity of the morphological deficit (cf. Vargha-Khadem et al., 1995), but also treating the genetic etiology of SLI as evidence for an innate grammatical module. For instance, Gazzaniga (1992, p.81) stated "Mutations to one gene can cause a deficit in one grammatical dimension of a language without affecting others" and Jackendoff (1993, p.116) argued that:

> These results strongly suggest that the impairment is genetic, and that it specifically affects the ability to construct a mental grammar, leaving other cognitive abilities intact. In order for this to be possible, there must be at least one gene that is responsible for a special-purpose mental endowment for language acquisition. The part of Universal Grammar having to do with acquiring inflectional endings must not be a general-purpose learning strategy.

The danger of this logic may be illustrated with a simple analogy between the ability to walk and the ability to talk. Like language, walking is a "species universal", i.e. common to all normal humans but not seen in other primates, which develops without overt instruction in a wide range of environmental circumstances. The ability to walk upright across an uneven terrain involves astonishingly complex co-ordination of motor and proprioceptive systems. No other primate shares this skill, yet all normal humans master it without specific instruction within the first few years of life, regardless of whether their local environment is a desert plain, a rainforest, a snowy mountainside, or a Western city. Attempts to build bipedal robots have met with some success, but the end results still fall far short of a typical three-year-old's competence. However, just as with language, some unfortunate individuals have a specific single-gene disorder—muscular dystrophy—that selectively interferes with this ability. But nobody supposes that because a single genetic mutation can cause muscular dystrophy there is a "gene for walking". It is apparent that walking depends on integrity of a wide range of underlying systems, involving muscles, nerves, and central control processes that regulate balance, proprioception, and motor planning. Muscular dystrophy has a specific effect on just one of these systems—the muscles—but this is sufficient to make walking difficult or impossible.

Those favouring processing accounts of SLI would argue that just the same can be said for language. The path from gene to behaviour is an immensely complex one, and there are many possible explanations for SLI. Genes associated with SLI may operate by disturbing the development of those brain areas concerned with processing or retaining transient auditory stimuli, for instance. Fodor argued that functions which met the first few criteria for modularity outlined in Table 9.1 were likely to be "hard-wired" and innate, so that they could function rapidly and reliably without requiring a prolonged learning period. However, models of developmental processes suggest a very different story, whereby "modularity", in the sense of a domain-specific and informationally encapsulated system, emerges with experience (see Elman et al., 1996; Tucker & Hirsh-Pasek, 1993). The distinction between "automatic" and "controlled" processes, which maps closely onto Fodor's modular/central processes distinction, seems more a function of practice and experience than of task domain. Indeed, some highly automatic processes involve artificial tasks that could not plausibly be regarded as innate, e.g. piano playing or bicycle riding.

Nor does localisation of a function in a particular brain region imply innateness. There is plentiful evidence from acquired dyslexia that the brain regions involved in reading are highly localised and specialised, but reading is a relatively late arrival on the stage of world history and the majority of the world's population do not read and write. Cerebral specialisation depends as much on specific experiences as on pre-wiring.

The fact, then, that in adults, certain aspects of language processing have the characteristics of modularity—domain specificity, information encapsulation, and localisation—tells us nothing about whether the brain is innately set up for this type of processing, and the finding of a genetic basis of SLI is compatible with a deficit in an innate grammatical module, but it is not evidence for such an account.

BEYOND COGNITIVE NEUROPSYCHOLOGY: STUDYING INTERACTION AND CHANGE IN LANGUAGE IMPAIRMENTS

Given the difficulties encountered when trying to apply the traditional methods of cognitive neuropsychology to a developmental disorder, what are the alternative approaches one can adopt? The traditional kind of study, where children with SLI are compared with a control group on one or more language tests, is usually a useful first step in trying to elucidate the nature of SLI, but it is unlikely to resolve questions about primacy of specific cognitive deficits. Striking dissociations are rare in children, and, even when they occur, their interpretation is often ambiguous because of changing patterns of impairment with age. Associations between deficits are even more difficult to interpret, because they could reflect bottom-up influences on high level processes, top-down influences on low-level processes, or it could be that the deficits are causally unconnected, but tend to co-occur because they are mediated by adjacent brain areas. This does not mean that we should abandon attempts at furthering our understanding of psycholinguistic processes in SLI, only that we need to recognise that converging evidence from different methodologies will be needed. To conclude this

chapter, a brief overview of different methods is offered for researchers to consider.

Language-age matched controls. One of the commonest strategies used in the study of SLI is to compare a language-impaired group with a younger control group matched on some index of "language age". The rationale for this approach is that it should give us some indication of whether a specific impairment on a test, X, is disproportionate to the child's language level. If not, it could be argued that poor performance on X is simply a consequence of low language skills, rather than being of primary importance in causing the language difficulties. However, if children with SLI do even more poorly than language-matched controls, this indicates that we can't just dismiss the deficit as secondary.

There are several difficulties inherent in this approach. First, it is an exceedingly conservative method. A lack of difference between groups does not tell us much except that the impairment could be a secondary one. Since the children with SLI are older than the control group, they are likely to be more advanced in general cognitive development, have better attention, and better ability to develop strategies for doing an experimental task, and these could counteract any effect of underlying impairment. Second, as noted in Chapter 2 (see *Age equivalent scores*, p.28), "age equivalent" scores can vary substantially from one test to another, and it can be difficult to know which language test children should be matched on. Third, the psychometric issues involved in looking for differential deficit (mentioned earlier) are critical in this kind of design, but are often ignored.

Comparison with other groups with known level of impairment. When considering the impact of relatively peripheral impairments on language development, i.e. those affecting sensory or motor processes, useful insights can be obtained by studying children suffering conditions known to affect these. Bishop's (1982, 1983a) studies of comprehension of English grammar in children with hearing impairment provide one example. Contrary to expectation, these studies revealed a distinctive pattern of grammatical difficulties, cutting across input modality, in such children, and thus offered indirect supporting evidence to those who would argue that an early auditory impairment can distort acquisition of oral syntax. Another example comes from studies of children who are dysarthric or anarthric, i.e. who find oral speech difficult or impossible because of impairments of motor control. These children allow one to address questions such as how far articulatory coding plays a role in memory or phonological segmentation (e.g. Bishop & Robson, 1989a,b), and whether experience of producing language is critical for the development of understanding (Bishop et al., 1990). In general, these studies have revealed surprising intact abilities in domains of phonological and syntactic processing in children who cannot produce clear speech, and they therefore make us less ready to assume that comprehension difficulties in children with SLI are due to their expressive limitations.

Experimental studies on "trade-offs" and capacity limitations. A growing interest in processing accounts of language development and disorders encourages us to do more studies using a within-subjects design, where the goal is to see how various experimental manipulations affect the child's ability to understand, as opposed to the more traditional between-subjects studies, where two or more groups are compared. Methods include varying such factors as rate of presentation, background noise, prosody, and so on, on children's understanding, as well as those that vary within the same task difficulty at different levels of processing, e.g. phonology, semantics, and syntax. A nice feature of such studies is the potential they have for providing results that are useful in intervention, by specifying which parameters make it easier or more difficult for children to process language.

Longitudinal studies. The potential importance of longitudinal studies for addressing causal questions has already been emphasised. Such methods have not been widely used in the study of SLI, and application of sophisticated statistical modelling (see, for instance, Magnusson, Bergman, Rudinger, & Törestad, 1989, for examples) has barely been attempted. Never-

theless, even with a fairly simple methodological approach, longitudinal studies can be invaluable in helping clarify the direction of causal relationships in normal development (e.g. Gathercole et al., 1992), for highlighting the role that early impairments may play in causing later deficits (e.g. Bernstein & Stark, 1985) and for throwing light on questions of classification (see e.g. Bishop & Edmundson, 1987a).

Modelling the learning process and simulating effects of impairment at a given stage. Exciting new developments in dynamic systems theory (Thelen & Smith, 1993) and connectionist modelling (Elman et al., 1996) are making it possible to think in terms of computer models of developmental change, in contrast to previous computational approaches that were based on static, information-processing systems. These have the potential to let us see how the nature of representations change as an organism interacts with its environment, and how fluctuations either in the biological substrate or in the input it receives may affect developing language processes.

Intervention studies. The ultimate test of a hypothesis is through experimental manipulation. If one believes one has identified the primary process that is implicated in SLI, then by ameliorating that deficit, one should be able to show beneficial effects on other aspects of language development. Although applications to intervention are frequently cited by researchers as justification for doing experimental studies, all too often the link with clinical practice is never made. It is time for researchers to recognise that intervention studies are not just an optional, applied adjunct to experimental work, but that they provide the best method available for evaluating hypotheses and unconfounding correlated factors. Intervention studies, such as the methods for sharpening discrimination of rapid auditory stimuli mentioned at the end of Chapter 3, the experimental vocabulary training work reviewed in Chapter 4, and the morphological learning studies described in Chapter 5, are still very new, but they generate excitement precisely because they allow us to test causal theories directly, and to monitor the process of comprehension development as it occurs.

References

Abbeduto, L., Davies, B., & Furman, L. (1988). The development of speech act comprehension in mentally retarded individuals and nonretarded children. *Child Development, 59*, 1460–1472.

Adams, A.-M., & Gathercole, S.E. (1995). Phonological working memory and speech production in preschool children. *Journal of Speech and Hearing Research, 38*, 403–414.

Aitchison, J. (1972). Mini-malapropisms. *British Journal of Disorders of Communication, 7*, 38–43.

Akshoomoff, N., Courchesne, E., Yeung-Courchesne, R., & Costello, J. (1989). Brainstem auditory evoked potentials in receptive developmental language disorder. *Brain and Language, 37*, 409–418.

Albert, M.L., & Bear, D. (1974). Time to understand: A case study of word deafness with reference to the role of time in auditory comprehension. *Brain, 97*, 373–384.

American Psychiatric Association. (1994). *Diagnostic and statistical manual of mental disorders, 4th ed. (DSM-IV)*. Washington, DC: American Psychiatric Association.

Ammon, P. (1981). Communication skills and communicative competence: A neo-Piagetian process-structural view. In W.P. Dickson (Ed.), *Children's oral communication skills*. New York: Academic Press.

Anglin, J.M. (1993). Vocabulary development: A morphological analysis. *Monographs of the Society for Research in Child Development, 238*, 1–165.

Aram, D.M., & Nation, J.E. (1975). Patterns of language behaviour in children with developmental language disorders. *Journal of Speech and Hearing Research, 18*, 229–241.

Arnold, D., Balkan, L., Humphreys, R.L., Meijer, S., & Sadler, L. (1994). *Machine translation: An introductory guide*. Oxford: NCC Blackwell.

Aslin, R.N., Pisoni, D.B., & Jusczyk, P. (1983). Auditory development and speech perception in infancy. In M.M. Haith & J.J. Campos (Eds.), *Infancy and the biology of development*. (Carmichael's manual of child psychology, 4th ed, Vol. 2). New York: Wiley.

Atkinson, M. (1992). *Children's syntax: an introduction to principles and parameters theory*. Oxford: Blackwell.

Baddeley, A.D. (1968). A 3 min reasoning test based on grammatical transformation. *Psychonomic science, 10*, 341–342.

Baddeley, A.D., & Hitch, G.J. (1974). Working memory. In G. Bower (Ed.), *Recent advances in learning and motivation*. New York: Academic Press.

Baddeley, A., Papagno, C., & Vallar, G. (1988). When long-term learning depends on short-term storage. *Journal of Memory and Language, 27*, 586–595.

Baker, L., & Cantwell, D.P. (1982). Psychiatric disorder in children with different types of communication disorder. *Journal of Communication Disorders, 15*, 113–126.

Bamford, J., & Saunders, E. (1985). *Hearing impairment, auditory perception and language disability*. London: Edward Arnold.

Barisnikov, K., Van der Linden, M., & Poncelet, M. (1996). Acquisition of new words and phonological working memory in Williams syndrome: A case study. *Neurocase, 2*, 395–404.

Baron-Cohen, S. (1993). From attention-goal psychology to belief-desire psychology: The development of a theory of mind and its dysfunction. In S. Baron-Cohen, H. Tager-Flusberg, & D.J. Cohen (Eds.), *Understanding other minds: Perspectives from autism*. Oxford: Oxford University Press.

Baron-Cohen, S. (1995). *Mindblindness*. Cambridge, MA: MIT Press, Bradford Books.

Baron-Cohen, S., Baldwin, D.A., & Crowson, M. (1997). Do children with autism use the Speaker's Direction of Gaze (SDG) strategy to crack the code of language? *Child Development, 68*, 48–57.

Baron-Cohen, S., Leslie, A.M., & Frith, U. (1985). Does the autistic child have a "theory of mind"? *Cognition, 21*, 37–46.

Baron-Cohen, S., & Ring, H. (1994). A model of the mindreading system: Neuropsychological and neurobiological perspectives. In C. Lewis & P. Mitchell (Eds.), *Children's early understanding of mind: Origins and development*. Hove: Lawrence Erlbaum Associates Ltd.

Barton, D., Miller, R., & Macken, M.A. (1980). Do children treat clusters as one unit or two? *Papers and Reports on Child Language Development, 18*, 93–137.

Barton, S.B., & Sanford, A.J. (1993). A case study of anomaly detection: Shallow semantic processing and cohesion establishment. *Memory and Cognition, 21*, 477–487.

Bates, E. (1993). Commentary: Comprehension and production in early language development. *Monographs of the Society for Research in Child Development, 233*, 222–242.

Bates, E., Appelbaum, M., & Allard, L. (1991). Statistical constraints on the use of single cases in neuropsychological research. *Brain and Language, 40*, 295–329.

Bates, E., Bretherton, I., & Snyder, L. (1988). *From first words to grammar: Individual differences and dissociable mechanisms*. Cambridge: Cambridge University Press.

Bates, E., & MacWhinney, B. (1989). Functionalism and the competition model. In B. MacWhinney & E. Bates (Eds.), *The crosslinguistic study of sentence processing. Cambridge: Cambridge University Press*.

Beal, C.R., & Flavell, J.H. (1984). Development of the ability to distinguish communicative intention and literal message meaning. *Child Development, 55*, 920–928.

Beitchman, J.H., Nair, R., Clegg, M., Ferguson, B., & Patel, P.G. (1986). Prevalence of psychiatric disorders in children with speech and language disorders. *Journal of the American Academy of Child and Adolescent Psychiatry, 25*, 528–535.

Bellaire, S., Plante, E., & Swisher, L. (1994). Bound morpheme skills in the oral language of school-age, language-impaired children. *Journal of Communication Disorders, 27*, 265–279.

Bellugi, U., Marks, S., Bihrle, A., & Sabo, H. (1988). Dissociation between language and cognitive functions in Williams syndrome. In D. Bishop & K. Mogford (Eds.), *Language development in exceptional circumstances*. Edinburgh: Churchill Livingstone.

Bellugi, U., van Hoek, K., Lillo-Martin, D., & O'Grady, L. (1988). The acquisition of syntax and space in young deaf signers. In D. Bishop & K. Mogford (Eds.), *Language development in exceptional circumstances*. Edinburgh: Churchill Livingstone.

Berko, J.B. (1958). The child's learning of English morphology. *Word, 14*, 150–177.

Berndt, R.S., Basili, A., & Caramazza, A. (1987). Dissociation of functions in a case of transcortical sensory aphasia. *Cognitive Neuropsychology, 4*, 79–107.

Bernstein, L.E., & Stark, R.E. (1985). Speech perception development in language-impaired children: A 4-year follow-up study. *Journal of Speech and Hearing Research, 50*, 21–30.

Bird, J., & Bishop, D.V.M. (1992). Perception and awareness of phonemes in phonologically impaired children. *European Journal of Disorders of Communication, 27*, 289–311.

Bird, J., Bishop, D.V.M., & Freeman, N. (1995). Phonological awareness and literacy development in children with expressive phonological impairments. *Journal of Speech and Hearing Research, 38*, 446–462.

Bishop, D.V.M. (1979). Comprehension in developmental language disorders. *Developmental Medicine and Child Neurology, 21*, 225–238.

Bishop, D.V.M. (1982). Comprehension of spoken, written, and signed sentences in childhood language disorders. *Journal of Child Psychology and Psychiatry, 23*, 1–20.

Bishop, D.V.M. (1983a). Comprehension of English syntax by profoundly deaf children. *Journal of Child Psychology and Psychiatry, 24*, 415–434.

Bishop, D.V.M. (1983b). Linguistic impairment after left hemidecortication for infantile hemiplegia? A reappraisal. *Quarterly Journal of Experimental Psychology, 35A*, 199–207.

Bishop, D.V.M. (1987a). The causes of specific developmental language disorder ("developmental dysphasia"). *Journal of Child Psychology and Psychiatry, 28*, 1–8.

Bishop, D.V.M. (1987b). The concept of comprehension in language disorder. *Proceedings of the First International Symposium on Specific Speech and Language Disorders in Children.* London: Association for All Speech Impaired Children.

Bishop, D.V.M. (1988a). Can the right hemisphere mediate language as well as the left? A critical review of recent research. *Cognitive Neuropsychology, 5*, 353–367.

Bishop, D.V.M. (1988b). Language development after focal brain damage. In D.V.M. Bishop & K. Mogford (Eds.), *Language development in exceptional circumstances.* Edinburgh: Churchill Livingstone.

Bishop, D.V.M. (1989a). Autism, Asperger's syndrome and semantic-pragmatic disorder: Where are the boundaries? *British Journal of Disorders of Communication, 24*, 107–121.

Bishop, D.V.M. (1989b). *Test for reception of grammar* (2nd ed.). University of Manchester: The Author, Age and Cognitive Performance Research Centre.

Bishop, D.V.M. (1989c). Quantitative aspects of specific developmental language disorders. In T. Munsat (Ed.), *Quantification of neurological deficit.* Boston, MA: Butterworths.

Bishop, D.V.M. (1990). *Handedness and developmental disorder.* Oxford: Blackwell Scientific and Philadelphia: J.B. Lippincott.

Bishop, D.V.M. (1992). The underlying nature of specific language impairment. *Journal of Child Psychology and Psychiatry, 33*, 1–64.

Bishop, D.V.M. (1994a). Grammatical errors in specific language impairment: Competence or performance limitation? *Applied Psycholinguistics, 15*, 507–549.

Bishop, D.V.M. (1994b). Is specific language impairment a valid diagnostic category? Genetic and psycholinguistic evidence. *Philosophical Transactions of the Royal Society, B, 346*, 105–111.

Bishop, D.V.M. (1997). Pre- and perinatal hazards and family background in children with specific language impairments: A study of twins. *Brain and Language, 56*, 1–26.

Bishop, D.V.M. (in press). What's so special about Asperger syndrome? The need for further exploration of the borderlands of autism. In A. Klin, F. R. Volkmar, & S. S. Sparrow (Eds.), *Asperger syndrome.* New York: Guilford Press.

Bishop, D.V.M., & Adams, C. (1989). Conversational characteristics of children with semantic-pragmatic disorder: II. What features lead to a judgement of inappropriacy? *British Journal of Disorders of Communication, 24*, 241–263.

Bishop, D.V.M., & Adams, C. (1990). A prospective study of the relationship between specific language impairment, phonological disorders and reading retardation. *Journal of Child Psychology and Psychiatry, 31*, 1027–1050.

Bishop, D.V.M., & Adams, C. (1991). What do referential communication tasks measure? A study of children with specific language impairment. *Applied Psycholinguistics, 12*, 199–215.

Bishop, D.V.M., & Adams, C. (1992). Comprehension problems in children with specific language impairment: Literal and inferential meaning. *Journal of Speech and Hearing Research, 35*, 119–129.

Bishop, D.V.M., Byers-Brown, B., & Robson, J. (1990). The relationship between phoneme discrimination, speech production and language comprehension in cerebral-palsied individuals. *Journal of Speech and Hearing Research, 33*, 210–219.

Bishop, D.V.M., & Edmundson, A. (1986). Is otitis media a major cause of specific developmental language disorders? *British Journal of Disorders of Communication, 21*, 321–338.

Bishop, D.V.M., & Edmundson, A. (1987a). Language-impaired four-year-olds: Distinguishing transient from persistent impairment. *Journal of Speech and Hearing Disorders, 52*, 156–173.

Bishop, D.V.M., & Edmundson, A. (1987b). Specific language impairment as a maturational lag: Evidence from longitudinal data on language and motor development. *Developmental Medicine and Child Neurology, 29*, 442–459.

Bishop, D.V.M., Hartley, J., & Weir, F. (1994). Why and when do some language impaired children seem talkative? *Journal of Autism and Developmental Disorders, 24*, 177–197.

Bishop, D.V.M., North, T., & Donlan, C. (1995). Genetic basis of specific language impairment: Evidence from a twin study. *Developmental Medicine and Child Neurology, 37*, 56–71.

Bishop, D.V.M., North, T., & Donlan, C. (1996). Nonword repetition as a behavioural marker for inherited language impairment: Evidence from a twin study. *Journal of Child Psychology and Psychiatry, 37*, 391–403.

Bishop, D.V.M., & Robson, J. (1989a). Accurate nonword spelling despite congenital inability to speak: Phoneme-grapheme conversion does not require subvocal articulation. *British Journal of Psychology, 80*, 1–13.

Bishop, D.V.M., & Robson, J. (1989b). Unimpaired short-term memory and rhyme judgement in congenitally speechless individuals: Implications for the notion of "articulatory coding". *Quarterly Journal of Experimental Psychology, 41A*, 123–140.

Bishop, D.V.M., & Rosenbloom, L. (1987). Classification of childhood language disorders. In W. Yule & M. Rutter (Eds.), *Language development and disorders. Clinics in Developmental Medicine* (double issue). London: MacKeith Press.

Blackwell, A., & Bates, E. (1995). Inducing agrammatic profiles in normals: Evidence for the selective vulnerability of morphology under cognitive resource limitation. *Journal of Cognitive Neuroscience, 7*, 228–257.

Blank, M., Gessner, M., & Esposito, A. (1979). Language without communication: A case study. *Journal of Child Language, 6*, 329–352.

Bloom, L., Hood, L., & Lightbown, P. (1974). Imitation in language development: If, when, and why? *Cognitive Psychology, 6*, 380–420.

Boehm, A.E. (1971). *Boehm Test of Basic Concepts—Preschool.* San Antonio, TX: Psychological Corporation.

Borden, G.J., Harris, K.S., & Raphael, L.J. (1994). *Speech science primer: Physiology, acoustics, and perception of speech* (3rd ed.). Baltimore, PA: Williams & Wilkins.

Bradbury, M. (1986). *Why come to Slaka?* London: Arrow Books.

Brennan, S.E., & Williams, M. (1995). The feeling of another's knowing: Prosody and filled pauses as cues to listeners about the metacognitive states of speakers. *Journal of Memory and Language, 34*, 383–398.

Briscoe, E.J. (1987). *Modelling human speech comprehension: A computational approach.* Chichester: Ellis Horwood.

Brown, A.L., Palincsar, A.S., & Armbruster, B.B. (1984). Instructing comprehension-fostering activities in interactive learning situations. In H. Mandl, N.L. Stein, & T. Trabasso (Eds.), *Learning and comprehension of text.* Hillsdale, NJ: Lawrence Erlbaum Associates Inc.

Brown, R. (1957). Linguistic determinism and parts of speech. *Journal of Abnormal and Social Psychology, 55*, 1–5.

Brown, R. (1973). *A first language.* Cambridge, MA: Harvard University Press.

Brown, R., & McNeill, D. (1966). The "tip of the tongue" phenomenon. *Journal of Verbal Learning and Verbal Behavior, 5*, 325–337.

Bryant, P., & Bradley, L. (1985). *Children's reading problems.* Oxford: Blackwell.

Bryden, M.P., McManus, I.C., & Bulman-Fleming, M.B. (1994). Evaluating the empirical support for the Geschwind-Behan-Galaburda model of cerebral lateralization. *Brain and Cognition, 26*, 103–167.

Bugental, D.E., Kaswan, J.W., Love, L.R., & Fox, M.N. (1970). Child versus adult perception of evaluative messages in verbal, vocal and visual channels. *Developmental Psychology, 2*, 367–375.

Butterworth, B., Campbell, R., & Howard, D. (1986). The uses of short-term memory: A case study. *Quarterly Journal of Experimental Psychology, 38*, 705–737.

Caplan, R., Foy, J.G., Asarnow, R.F., & Sherman, T.L. (1990). Information processing deficits of children with formal thought disorder. *Psychiatry Research, 31*, 169–177.

Caramazza, A. (1986). On drawing inferences about the structure of normal cognitive systems from the analysis of patterns of impaired performance: The case for single-patient studies. *Brain and Cognition, 5*, 41–66.

Caramazza, A., Berndt, R.S., & Basili, A.G. (1983). The selective impairment of phonological processing: A case study. *Brain and Language, 18*, 128–174.

Carey, S. (1978). The child as word learner. In M. Halle, J. Bresnan, & G. A. Miller (Eds.), *Linguistic theory and psychological reality.* Cambridge, MA: MIT Press.

Carpenter, P.A., Miyake, A., & Just, M.A. (1994). Working memory constraints in comprehension: Evidence from individual differences, aphasia, and aging. In M.A. Gernsbacher (Ed.), *Handbook of psycholinguistics.* San Diego, CA: Academic Press.

Carrow, E. (1975). *Test for auditory comprehension of language.* Austin, TX: Learning Concepts.

Carrow-Woolfolk, E. (1985). *Test of Auditory Comprehension for Language—Revised* (TACL-R). Allen, TX: DLM Teaching Resources.

Castles, A., & Coltheart, M. (1993). Varieties of developmental dyslexia. *Cognition, 47*, 149–180.

Chandler, M., Fritz, A.S., & Hala, S. (1989). Small-scale deceit: Deception as a marker of two- three- and four-year-olds' early theories of mind. *Child Development, 60*, 1263–1277.

Chapman, L.J., & Chapman, J.P. (1973). Problems in the measurement of cognitive deficit. *Psychological Bulletin, 79*, 380–385.

Chapman, R.S. (1978). Comprehension strategies in children. In J. F. Kavanagh & W. Strange (Eds.), *Speech and language in laboratory, school, and clinic.* Cambridge, MA: MIT Press.

Chapman, R. (1981). Computing mean length of utterance in morphemes. In J. F. Miller (Ed.), *Assessing language production in children*. London: Edward Arnold.

Chapman, R.S. (1992). *Processes in language acquisition and disorders*. St Louis: Mosby Year Book.

Chapman, R.S., Streim, N.W., Crais, E.R., Salmon, D., Strand, E.A., & Negri, N.A. (1992). Child talk: Assumptions of a developmental process model for early language learning. In R.S. Chapman (Ed.), *Processes in language acquisition and disorders*. St Louis, MO: Mosby Year Book.

Charles-Luce, J., & Luce, P.A. (1990). Similarity neighborhoods of words in young children's lexicons. *Journal of Child Language, 17*, 205–215.

Chien, Y.-C., & Wexler, K. (1990). Children's knowledge of locality conditions in binding as evidence for the modularity of syntax and pragmatics. *Language Acquisition, 1*, 225–295.

Choi, S., & Bowerman, M. (1991). Learning to express motion events in English and Korean: The influence of language-specific lexicalization patterns. *Cognition, 41*, 83–121.

Chomsky, N. (1976). *Reflections on language*. London: Temple Smith.

Chomsky, N. (1980). *Rules and representations*. Oxford: Blackwell.

Chomsky, N. (1981). *Lectures on government and binding*. Dordrecht, Netherlands: Foris.

Clahsen, H. (1989). The grammatical characterization of developmental dysphasia. *Linguistics, 27*, 897–920.

Clahsen, H., Rothweiler, M., Woest, A., & Marcus, G. (1992). Regular and irregular inflection in the acquisition of German noun plurals. *Cognition, 45*, 225–255.

Clancy, P. (1986). The acquisition of communicative style in Japanese. In B. B. Schieffelin & E. Ochs (Eds.), *Language acquisition and socialization across cultures*. Cambridge: Cambridge University Press.

Clark, E.V. (1973). Non-linguistic strategies and the acquisition of word meanings. *Cognition, 2*, 161–182.

Clark, H.H. (1973). The language-as-fixed-effect fallacy: A critique of language statistics in psychological research. *Journal of Verbal Learning and Verbal Behavior, 12*, 335–359.

Clark, H.H., & Haviland, S.E. (1977). Comprehension and the given-new contract. In R.O. Freedle (Ed.), *Discourse production and comprehension*. Norwood, NJ: Ablex.

Cohen, M., Campbell, R., & Yaghmai, F. (1989). Neuropathological abnormalities in developmental dysphasia. *Annals of Neurology, 25*, 567–570.

Cohen, N.J., Davine, M., & Meloche-Kelly, M. (1989). Prevalence of unsuspected language disorders in a child psychiatric population. *Journal of the American Academy of Child and Adolescent Psychiatry, 28*, 107–111.

Cole, K.N., Dale, P.S., & Mills, P.E. (1992). Stability of the intelligence quotient–language quotient relation: Is discrepancy modeling based on a myth? *American Journal on Mental Retardation, 97*, 131–143.

Coltheart, M. (1987). Functional architecture of the language processing system. In M. Coltheart, G. Sartori, & R. Job (Eds.), *The cognitive neuropsychology of language*. Hove: Lawrence Erlbaum Associates Ltd.

Coltheart, M., Patterson, K.E., & Marshall, J.C. (1980). *Deep dyslexia*. London: Routledge & Kegan Paul.

Connell, P.J., & Stone, C.A. (1992). Morpheme learning of children with specific language impairment under controlled instructional conditions. *Journal of Speech and Hearing Research, 35*, 844–852.

Conti-Ramsden, G., & Gunn, M. (1986). The development of conversational disability: A case study. *British Journal of Disorders of Communication, 21*, 339–352.

Cook, V.J. (1988). *Chomsky's universal grammar*. Oxford: Blackwell.

Cooper, F.S., Liberman, A.M., & Borst, J.M. (1951). The interconversion of audible and visible patterns as a basis for research in the perception of speech. *Proceedings of the National Academy of Sciences, 37*, 318–325.

Coulthard, M. (1977). *An introduction to discourse analysis*. London: Longman.

Courtright, J.A., & Courtright, I.C. (1983). The perception of nonverbal vocal cues of emotional meaning by language-disordered and normal children. *Journal of Speech and Hearing Research, 26*, 412–417.

Crais, E.R., & Chapman, R.S. (1987). Story recall and inferencing skills in language/learning disabled and nondisabled children. *Journal of Speech and Hearing Disorders, 52*, 50–55.

Cromer, R.F. (1978). The basis of childhood dysphasia: A linguistic approach. In M. A. Wyke (Ed.), *Developmental dysphasia*. London: Academic Press.

Cromer, R.F. (1983). Hierarchical planning disability in the drawings and constructions of a special group of severely aphasic children. *Brain and Cognition, 2*, 144–164.

Cromer, R. (1994). A case study of dissociations between language and cognition. In H. Tager-Flusberg (Ed.), *Constraints on language acquisition: Studies of atypical children*. Hove: Lawrence Erlbaum Associates Ltd.

Crystal, D. (1987). Towards a "bucket" theory of language disability taking account of interaction between linguistic levels. *Clinical Linguistics and Phonetics, 1*, 7–22.

Curtiss, S., & Tallal, P. (1991). On the nature of the impairment in language-impaired children. In J. Miller (Ed.), *Research on child language disorders: A decade of progress*. Austin, TX: Pro Ed.

Cutler, A. (1994). Segmentation problems, rhythmic solutions. *Lingua, 92*, 81–104.

Cutting, J.E., & Pisoni, D.B. (1978). An information processing approach to speech perception. In J. F. Kavanagh & W. Strange (Eds.), *Speech and language in the laboratory, school, and clinic*. Cambridge, MA: MIT Press.

Dall'Oglio, A.M., Bates, E., Volterra, V., Di Capua, M., & Pezzini, G. (1994). Early cognition, communication and language in children with focal brain injury. *Developmental Medicine and Child Neurology, 36*, 1076–1098.

Daneman, M., & Carpenter, P.A. (1980). Individual differences in working memory and reading. *Journal of Verbal Learning and Verbal Behavior, 19*, 450–466.

Daw, N.W. (1995). *Visual development*. New York: Plenum Press.

Dawkins, R. (1982). *The extended phenotype*. Oxford: Oxford University Press.

De Renzi, E., & Vignolo, L. A. (1962). The Token Test: A sensitive test to detect receptive disturbances in aphasics. *Brain, 85*, 665–678.

Denes, G., Balliello, S., Volterra, V., & Pellegrini, A. (1986). Oral and written language in a case of childhood phonemic deafness. *Brain and Language, 29*, 252–267.

Deonna, T. (1993). Annotation: Cognitive and behavioural correlates of epileptic activity in children. *Journal of Child Psychology and Psychiatry, 34*, 611–620.

Disimoni, F. (1978). *The Token Test for Children*. Chicago: Riverside Publishing.

Dollaghan, C.A., Biber, M.E., & Campbell, T.F. (1993). Constituent effects in a nonsense word repetition task. *Journal of Speech and Hearing Research, 36*, 1051–1054.

Dollaghan, C.A., Biber, M.E., & Campbell, T.F. (1995). Lexical influences on nonword repetition. *Applied Psycholinguistics, 16*, 211–222.

Donlan, C., Bishop, D.V.M., & Hitch, G.J. (in press). Magnitude comparisons by children with specific language impairments: Evidence of unimpaired symbolic processing. *European Journal of Disorders of Communication*.

Dunn, J. (1988). *The beginnings of social understanding*. Oxford: Blackwell.

Dunn, L.M. (1965). *The Peabody Picture Vocabulary Test*. Circle Pines, MN: American Guidance Service, Inc.

Dunn, L.M., & Dunn, L.M. (1981). *The Peabody Picture Vocabulary Test—Revised*. Circle Pines, MN: American Guidance Service Inc.

Dunn, L.M., Dunn, L.M., Whetton, C., & Pintilie, D. (1982). *British Picture Vocabulary Scale*. Windsor: NFER-Nelson Publishing Co.

Eimas, P.D., Siqueland, E.R., Jusczyk, P., & Vigorito, J. (1971). Speech perception in infants. *Science, 171*, 303–306.

Eisenson, J. (1968). Developmental dysphasia (dyslogia): A postulation of a unitary concept of the disorder. *Cortex, 4*, 184–200.

Eisenson, J. (1972). *Aphasia in children*. New York: Harper & Row.

Elliott, C., Murray, D.J., & Pearson, L.S. (1983). *British Ability Scales*. Windsor: NFER-Nelson.

Elliott, L.L., & Hammer, M.A. (1988). Longitudinal changes in auditory discrimination in normal children and children with language-learning problems. *Journal of Speech and Hearing Disorders, 53*, 467–474.

Elliott, L.L., & Hammer, M.A. (1993). Fine grained auditory discrimination: Factor structures. *Journal of Speech and Hearing Research, 93*, 396–409.

Elliott, L.L., Hammer, M.A., & Scholl, M.E. (1989). Fine-grained auditory discrimination in normal children and children with language-learning problems. *Journal of Speech and Hearing Research, 32*, 112–119.

Ellis, R., & Wells, G. (1980). Enabling factors in adult-child discourse. *First Language, 1*, 46–62.

Ellis Weismer, S. (1985). Constructive comprehension abilities exhibited by language-disordered children. *Journal of Speech and Hearing Research, 28*, 175–184.

Ellis Weismer, S., & Hesketh, L.J. (1993). The influence of prosodic and gestural cues on novel word acquisition by children with specific language impairment. *Journal of Speech and Hearing Research, 36*, 1013–1025.

Elman, J., Bates, E., Johnson, M.H., Karmiloff-Smith, A., Parisi, D., & Plunkett, K. (1996). *Rethinking innateness: A connectionist perspective on development.* Cambridge, MA: MIT Press.

Elman, J.L. (1992). Grammatical structure and distributed representations. In S. Davis (Ed.), *Connectionism: Theory and practice.* New York: Oxford University Press.

Emerson, R.W. (1898). *The conduct of life.* Boston, MA: Houghton Mifflin Co.

Erickson, T.D., & Mattson, M.E. (1981). From words to meaning: A semantic illusion. *Journal of Verbal Learning and Verbal Behavior, 20,* 540–551.

Ervin-Tripp, S. (1981). How to make and understand a request. In H. Parret, M. Sbisa, & J. Verschueren (Eds.), *Possibilities and limitations of pragmatics.* Amsterdam: Benjamins.

Evans, E.F. (1992). Auditory processing of complex sounds: An overview. In R.P. Carlyon, C.J. Darwin, & I J. Russell (Eds.), *Processing of complex sounds by the auditory system.* Oxford: Clarendon Press.

Ewing, A.W.G. (1967). *Aphasia in children.* (Facsimile reprint of 1930 ed.) New York: Hafner.

Fey, M.E., & Leonard, L.B. (1983). Pragmatic skills of children with specific language impairment. In T.M. Gallagher & C.A. Prutting (Eds.), *Pragmatic assessment and intervention issues in language.* San Diego, CA: College-Hill.

Fey, M.E., Long, S.E., & Cleave, P.L. (1994). Reconsideration of IQ criteria in the definition of specific language impairment. In R. Watkins & M. Rice (Eds.), *Specific language impairments in children.* Baltimore, MD: Paul H. Brookes.

Fischel, J.E., Whitehurst, G.J., Caulfield, M.B., & Debaryshe, B. (1989). Language growth in children with expressive language delay. *Pediatrics, 83,* 218–227.

Fisher, C., Hall, D.G., Rakowitz, S., & Gleitman, L. (1994). When it is better to receive than to give: Syntactic and conceptual constraints on vocabulary growth. *Lingua, 92,* 333–375.

Flavell, J.H., Flavell, E.R., Green, F.L., & Moses, L.J. (1990). Young children's understanding of fact beliefs versus value beliefs. *Child Development, 61,* 915–928.

Fleming, D.E., Anderson, R.H., Rhees, R.W., Kinghorn, E., & Bakaitis, J. (1986). Effects of prenatal stress on sexually dimorphic asymmetries in the cerebral cortex of the male rat. *Brain Research Bulletin, 16,* 395–398.

Fodor, J.A. (1983). *The modularity of mind.* Cambridge, MA: Bradford Books.

Fried-Oken, M. (1987). Qualitative examination of children's naming skills through test adaptations. *Language, Speech and Hearing Services in the Schools, 18,* 206–216.

Friel-Patti, S., Finitzo-Hieber, T., Conti, G., & Clinton Brown, K. (1982). Language delay in infants associated with middle ear disease and mild, fluctuating hearing impairment. *Pediatric Infectious Disease, 1,* 104–109.

Frith, U. (1989). A new look at language and communication in autism. *British Journal of Disorders of Communication, 24,* 123–150.

Fromkin, V., & Rodman, R. (1978). *An introduction to language.* New York: Holt, Rinehart & Winston.

Fromkin, V.A. (1995). Linguistic representation and processing: Analyses of agrammatism. *Brain and Language, 50*(1), 1–134.

Frumkin, B., & Rapin, I. (1980). Perception of vowels and consonant-vowels of varying duration in language-impaired children. *Neuropsychologia, 18,* 443–454.

Fujiki, M., & Brinton, B. (1991). The verbal non-communicator: A case study. *Language, Speech, and Hearing Services in Schools, 22,* 322–333.

Fundudis, T., Koluin, I., & Garside, R. (1979). *Speech retarded and deaf children: Their psychological development.* London: Academic Press.

Galaburda, A., Corsiglia, J., Rosen, G.D., & Sherman, G.F. (1987). Planum temporale asymmetry: Reappraisal since Geschwind and Levitsky. *Neuropsychologia, 25,* 853–868.

Galaburda, A.M., Sherman, G.F., Rosen, G.D., Aboitiz, F., & Geschwind, N. (1985). Developmental dyslexia: Four consecutive cases with cortical anomalies. *Annals of Neurology, 18,* 222–233.

Gallagher, T.M. (1993). Language skill and the development of social competence in school-age children. *Language, Speech and Hearing Services in the Schools, 24,* 199–205.

Gardner, H., & Zurif, E. (1975). BEE but not BE: Oral reading of single words in aphasia and alexia. *Neuropsychologia, 13,* 181–190.

Garnham, A. (1985). *Psycholinguistics: Central topics.* London: Methuen.

Gathercole, S.E. (1995). Is nonword repetition a test of phonological working memory or long-term knowledge? It all depends on the nonwords. *Memory and Cognition, 23,* 83–94.

Gathercole, S.E., & Adams, A. (1993). Phonological working memory in very young children. *Developmental Psychology, 29,* 770–778.

Gathercole, S.E., & Baddeley, A.D. (1989). Evaluation of the role of phonological STM in the development of vocabulary in children: A longitudinal study. *Journal of Memory and Language, 28*, 200–213.

Gathercole, S.E., & Baddeley, A.D. (1990a). Phonological memory deficits in language disordered children: Is there a causal connection? *Journal of Memory and Language, 29*, 336–360.

Gathercole, S.E., & Baddeley, A.D. (1990b). The role of phonological memory in vocabulary acquisition: A study of young children learning new names. *British Journal of Psychology, 81*, 439–454.

Gathercole, S.E., Willis, C., Baddeley, A.D., & Emslie, H. (1994). The children's test of nonword repetition: A test of phonological working memory. *Memory, 2*, 103–127.

Gathercole, S.E., Willis, C., Emslie, H., & Baddeley, A.D. (1991). The influences of syllables and wordlikeness on children's repetition of nonwords. *Applied Psycholinguistics, 12*, 349–367.

Gathercole, S.E., Willis, C., Emslie, H., & Baddeley, A.D. (1992). Phonological memory and vocabulary development during the early school years: A longitudinal study. *Developmental Psychology, 28*, 887–898.

Gelman, R., & Spelke, E. (1981). The development of thoughts about animate and inanimate objects: Implications for research on social cognition. In J.H. Flavell & L. Ross (Eds.), *Social cognitive development: Frontiers and possible futures*. Cambridge: Cambridge University Press.

German, D.J. (1982). Word-finding substitutions in children with learning disabilities. *Language, Speech, and Hearing Services in Schools, 13*, 223–230.

Gernsbacher, M.A. (1990). *Language comprehension as structure building*. Hillsdale, NJ: Lawrence Erlbaum Associates Inc.

Gernsbacher, M.A., Varner, K.R., & Faust, M.E. (1990). Investigating differences in general comprehension skill. *Journal of Experimental Psychology: Learning, Memory, and Cognition, 16*, 430–445.

Geschwind, N. (1983). Genetics: Fate, change, and environmental control. In C.L. Ludlow & J.A. Cooper (Eds.), *Genetic aspects of speech and language disorders*. New York: Academic Press.

Geschwind, N., & Galaburda, A. (1987). *Cerebral lateralization: Biological mechanisms, associations and pathology*. Cambridge, MA: MIT Press.

Gibbs, R.W. (1994). Figurative thought and figurative language. In M. A. Gernsbacher (Ed.), *Handbook of psycholinguistics*. San Diego, CA: Academic Press.

Gilhooly, K.J., & Green, A.J.K. (1988). The use of memory by experts and novices. In A.M. Colley & J.M. Beech (Eds.), *Cognition and action in skilled behaviour*. Amsterdam, Netherlands: North-Holland.

Gillam, R.B., Cowan, N., & Day, L.S. (1995). Sequential memory in children with and without language impairment. *Journal of Speech and Hearing Research, 38*, 393–402.

Givón, T. (1979). *On understanding grammar*. New York: Academic Press.

Gleitman, L.R. (1994). Words words words. *Philosophical Transactions of the Royal Society, B, 346*, 71–77.

Gleitman, L.R., & Wanner, E. (1982). Language acquisition: The state of the state of the art. In E. Wanner & L.R. Gleitman (Eds.), *Language acquisition: The state of the art*. New York: Cambridge University Press.

Glenberg, A.M., Kruley, P., & Langston, W.E. (1994). Analogical processes in comprehension: Simulation of a mental model. In M.A. Gernsbacher (Ed.), *Handbook of psycholinguistics*. San Diego, CA: Academic Press.

Glucksberg, S., & Krauss, R.M. (1967). What do people say after they have learned to talk? Studies of the development of referential communication. *Merrill-Palmer Quarterly, 13*, 309–316.

Goad, H., & Rebellati, C. (1994). Pluralization in familial language impairment. In J. Matthews (Ed.), *Linguistic aspects of familial language impairment*. Special Issue of the McGill Working Papers in Linguistics, Vol. 10. Montréal, Canada: McGill University.

Goldman, R.W., Fristoe, M., & Woodcock, R.W. (1970). *Goldman-Fristoe-Woodcock test of auditory discrimination*. Circle Pines, MN: American Guidance Service.

Golinkoff, R.M., Hirsh-Pasek, K., Cauley, K.M., & Gordon, L. (1987). The eyes have it: Lexical and syntactic comprehension in a new paradigm. *Journal of Child Language, 14*, 23–45.

Gopnik, M. (1990). Feature blindness: A case study. *Language Acquisition, 1*, 139–164.

Gopnik, M. (1994a). Impairments of tense in a familial language disorder. *Journal of Neurolinguistics, 8*, 109–133.

Gopnik, M. (1994b). The perceptual processing hypothesis revisited. In J. Matthews (Ed.), *Linguistic aspects of familial language impairment*. Special Issue of the McGill Working Papers in Linguistics, Vol. 10. Montréal, Canada: McGill University.

Gopnik, M., & Crago, M. (1991). Familial aggregation of a developmental language disorder. *Cognition, 39,* 1–50.

Grice, H.P. (1975). Logic and conversation. In P. Cole & J. L. Morgan (Eds.), *Syntax and semantics.* New York: Academic Press.

Grieve, R., Hoogenraad, R., & Murray, D. (1977). On the young child's use of lexis and syntax in understanding locative instructions. *Cognition, 5,* 235–250.

Grillon, C., Akshoomoff, N., & Courchesne, E. (1989). Brain-stem and middle latency auditory evoked potentials in autism and developmental language disorder. *Journal of Autism and Developmental Disorders, 19,* 255–269.

Grimshaw, J., & Pinker , S. (1989). Positive and negative evidence in language acquisition. *Brain and Behavioral Sciences, 12,* 341.

Grimshaw, J., & Rosen, S.T. (1990). Knowledge and obedience: The developmental status of the binding theory. *Linguistic Inquiry, 21,* 187–222.

Haarman, H.J., & Kolk, H.H.J. (1991). A computer model of the temporal course of agrammatic sentence understanding: The effects of variation in severity and sentence complexity. *Cognitive Science, 15,* 49–87.

Haegeman, L. (1994). *Introduction to government and binding theory* (2nd ed.). Oxford: Blackwell.

Harcherik, D.F., Cohen, D.J., Ort, S., Paul, R., Shaywitz, B.A., Volkmar, F.R., Rothman, S.L.G., & Leckman, J.F. (1985). Computed tomographic brain scanning in four neuropsychiatric disorders of childhood. *American Journal of Psychiatry, 142,* 731–734.

Hardy-Brown, K., & Plomin, R. (1985). Infant communicative development: Evidence from adoptive and biological families for genetic and environmental influences on rate differences. *Developmental Psychology, 21,* 378–385.

Harris, M. (1992). *Language experience and early language development: From input to uptake.* Hove: Lawrence Erlbaum Associates Ltd.

Harris, M., Jones, D., Brookes, S., & Grant, J. (1986). Relations between the non-verbal context of maternal speech and rate of language development. *British Journal of Developmental Psychology, 4,* 261–268.

Hart, B., & Risley, T.R. (1992). American parenting of language-learning children: Persisting differences in family-child interactions observed in natural home environments. *Developmental Psychology, 28,* 1096–1105.

Haviland, S.E., & Clark, H.H. (1974). What's new? Acquiring new information as a process in comprehension. *Journal of Verbal Learning and Verbal Behavior, 13,* 512–521.

Hier, D.B., Yoon, W.B., Mohr, J.P., Price, T.R., & Wolf, P.A. (1994). Gender and aphasia in the Stroke Data Bank. *Brain and Language, 47,* 155–167.

Hitch, G.J., & Baddeley, A.D. (1976). Verbal reasoning and working memory. *Quarterly Journal of Experimental Psychology, 28,* 603–621.

Hobson, P. (1993). Understanding persons: The role of affect. In S. Baron-Cohen, H. Tager-Flusberg, & D.J. Cohen (Eds.), *Understanding other minds: Perspectives from autism.* Oxford: Oxford University Press.

Hoffman, M.L. (1981). Perspectives on the difference between understanding people and understanding things: The role of affect. In J.H. Flavell & L. Ross (Eds.), *Social cognitive development: Frontiers and possible futures.* Cambridge: Cambridge University Press.

Holm, V.A., & Kunze, L.H. (1969). Effect of chronic otitis media on language and speech development. *Pediatrics, 43,* 833–839.

Hurst, J.A., Baraitser, M., Auger, E., Graham, F., & Norell, S. (1990). An extended family with a dominantly inherited speech disorder. *Developmental Medicine and Child Neurology, 32,* 352–355.

Huttenlocher, J., Haight, W., Bryk, A., Seltzer, M., & Lyons, T. (1991). Early vocabulary growth: Relation to language input and gender. *Developmental Psychology, 27,* 236–248.

Huttenlocher, J., & Strauss, S. (1968). Comprehension and a statement's relation to the situation that it describes. *Journal of Verbal Learning and Verbal Behavior, 7,* 300–304.

Hyams, N. (1986). *Language acquisition and the theory of parameters.* Dordrecht, Holland: Reidel.

Jackendoff, R. (1993). *Patterns in the mind.* Hemel Hempstead: Harvester Wheatsheaf.

Jacobson, M. (1991). *Developmental neurobiology* (3rd ed.). New York: Plenum Press.

James, W. (1893). *The principles of psychology* (Vol. I). New York: Holt.

Jernigan, T., Hesselink, J.R., Sowell, E., & Tallal, P. (1991). Cerebral structure on magnetic resonance imaging in language- and learning-impaired children. *Archives of Neurology, 48,* 539–545.

Johnson, M.K., Bransford, J.D., & Solomon, S.K. (1973). Memory for tacit implications of sentences. *Journal of Experimental Psychology, 98,* 203–205.

Johnston, J. (1994). Cognitive abilities of children with language impairment. In R. Watkins & M. Rice (Eds.), *Specific language impairments in children*. Baltimore, MD: Paul H. Brookes.

Johnston, J.L. (1991). Questions about cognition in children with specific language impairment. In J.F. Miller (Ed.), *Research on child language disorder: A decade of progress*. Austin, TX: Pro-Ed.

Johnston, R.B., Stark, R.E., Mellits, E.D., & Tallal, P. (1981). Neurological status of language-impaired and normal children. *Annals of Neurology, 10*, 159–163.

Jusczyk, P. (1986). Toward a model of the development of speech perception. In J.S. Perkell & D.H. Klatt (Eds.), *Invariance and variability in speech processes*. Hillsdale, NJ: Lawrence Erlbaum Associates Inc.

Jusczyk, P.W. (1994). Infant speech perception and the development of the mental lexicon. In J.C. Goodman & H.C. Nusbaum (Eds.), *The development of speech perception: The transition from speech sounds to spoken words*. Cambridge, MA: MIT Press.

Jusczyk, P.W. (1995). Language acquisition: Speech sounds and the beginning of phonology. In J.L. Miller & P.D. Eimas (Eds.), *Speech, language and communication. Handbook of perception and cognition (2nd. ed.), Vol.11*. San Diego, CA: Academic Press.

Kail, R., Hale, C.A., Leonard, L.B., & Nippold, M. (1984). Lexical storage and retrieval in language-impaired children. *Applied Psycholinguistics , 5* , 37–49.

Kamhi, A., Ward, M.F., & Mills, E.A. (1995). Hierarchical planning abilities in children with specific language impairments. *Journal of Speech and Hearing Research, 38*, 1108–1116.

Kamhi, A.G., & Catts, H.W. (1986). Toward an understanding of developmental language and reading disorders. *Journal of Speech and Hearing Disorders , 51*, 337–347.

Kamhi, A.G., Catts, H.W., Mauer, D., Apel, K., & Gentry, B.F. (1988). Phonological and spatial processing abilities in language- and reading-impaired children. *Journal of Speech and Hearing Disorders, 53*, 316–327.

Kaplan, G.J., Fleshman, J.K., Bender, T.R., Baum, C., & Clark, C.S. (1973). Long term effects of otitis media: A ten year cohort study of Alaskan Eskimo children. *Pediatrics, 52*, 577–585.

Karmiloff-Smith, A. (1985). Language and cognitive processes from a developmental perspective. *Language and Cognitive Processes, 1*, 61–85.

Karmiloff-Smith, A. (1992). *Beyond modularity: A developmental perspective on cognitive science*. Cambridge, MA: MIT Press.

Katz, W.F., Curtiss, S., & Tallal, P. (1992). Rapid automatized naming and gesture by normal and language-impaired children. *Brain and Language, 43*, 623–641.

Kay, R.H., & Matthews, D.R. (1972). On the existence in human auditory pathways of channels selectively tuned to the modulation present in frequency-modulated tones. *Journal of Physiology, 225*, 657–677.

Keenan, E.O., & Schieffelin, B. (1976). Topic as a discourse notion: A study of topic in the conversations of children and adults. In C. N. Li (Ed.), *Subject and topic*. New York: Academic Press.

Kemper, S., & Edwards, L.L. (1986). Children's expression of causality and their construction of narratives. *Topics in Language Disorders, 7*, 11–20.

Kemple, K., Speranza, H., & Hazen, N. (1992). Cohesive discourse and peer acceptance: longitudinal relation in the preschool years. *Merrill-Palmer Quarterly, 38*, 364–381.

King, A.J., & Moore, D.R. (1991). Plasticity of auditory maps in the brain. *Trends in the Neurological Sciences, 14*, 31–37.

Kintsch, W. (1980). Learning from text levels of comprehension or why anyone would read a story anyway. *Poetics, 9*, 87–98.

Kintsch, W. (1994). The psychology of discourse processing. In M.A. Gernsbacher (Ed.), *Handbook of psycholinguistics*. San Diego, CA: Academic Press.

Kintsch, W., & van Dijk, T.A. (1978). Toward a model of discourse comprehension and production. *Psychological Review, 85*, 363–394.

Kirk, S.A., McCarthy, J.J., & Kirk, W.D. (1968). *Illinois test of psycholinguistic abilities* (Rev. ed.). Urbana, IL: University of Illinois Press.

Klatt, D.H. (1980). Speech perception: A model of acoustic-phonetic analysis and lexical access. In R.A. Cole (Ed.), *Perception and production of fluent speech*. Hillsdale, NJ: Lawrence Erlbaum Associates Inc.

Klinnert, M.D., Campos, J.J., Sorce, J.F., Emde, R.N., & Svejda, M. (1983). Emotions as behavior regulators: Social referencing in infancy. In R. Plutchik & H. Kellerman (Eds.), *Emotion: Theory research and experience: Vol. 2. Emotions in early development*. New York: Academic Press.

Kluender, K.R. (1994). Speech perception as a tractable problem in cognitive science. In M.A. Gernsbacher (Ed.), *Handbook of psycholinguistics*. San Diego, CA: Academic Press.

Kraus, N., McGee, T., Carrell, T.D., & Sharma, A. (1995). Neurophysiologic bases of speech discrimination. *Ear and Hearing, 16*, 19–37.

Kraus, N., McGee, T.J., Carrell, T.D., Zecker, S.G., Nicol, T.G., & Koch, D.B. (1996). Auditory neurophysiologic responses and discrimination deficits in children with learning problems. *Science, 273*, 971–973.

Kuhl, P. (1980). Perceptual constancy for speech-sound categories in early infancy. In G.H. Yeni-Komshian & J.F. Kavanagh (Eds.), *Child phonology: Vol. 2. Perception.* New York: Academic Press.

Kuhl, P. (1982). Speech perception: An overview of current issues. In N.J. Lass, L.V. McReynolds, J.L. Northern, & D.E. Yoder (Eds.), *Speech, language, and hearing: Vol. 1. Normal processes.* Philadelphia, PA: W. B. Saunders.

Labelle, J.L. (1973). Sentence comprehension in two age groups of children as related to pause position or the absence of pauses. *Journal of Speech and Hearing Research, 16*, 231–237.

Ladefoged, P. (1993). *A course in phonetics* (3rd ed.). Fort Worth, TX: Harcourt Brace Jovanovich.

Landau, B., & Gleitman, L. (1985). *Language and experience: Evidence from the blind child.* Cambridge, MA: Harvard University Press.

Landau, W.M., & Kleffner, F.R. (1957). Syndrome of acquired aphasia with convulsive disorder in children. *Neurology, 7*, 523–530.

Landry, S., & Loveland, K. (1988). Communication behaviors in autism and developmental language delay. *Journal of Child Psychology and Psychiatry, 29*, 621–634.

Lapointe, S.G. (1985). A theory of verb form use in the speech of agrammatic aphasics. *Brain and Language, 24*, 100–155.

Lee, L. (1971). *Northwestern Syntax Screening Test.* Evanston, IL: Northwestern University Press.

Lee, L.L. (1974). *Developmental sentence analysis.* Evanston, IL: Northwestern University Press.

Leiter, R.G., & Arthur, G. (1955). *Leiter International Performance Scale.* New York: C. H. Stoelting.

Leonard, L. (1989). Language learnability and specific language impairment in children. *Applied Psycholinguistics, 10*, 179–202.

Leonard, L., Schwartz, R., Folger, M., Newhoff, M., & Wilcox, M. (1979). Children's imitations of lexical items. *Child Development, 59*, 19–27.

Leonard, L., Schwartz, R., Morris, B., & Chapman, K. (1981). Factors influencing early lexical acquisition lexical orientation and phonological composition. *Child Development, 52*, 882–887.

Leonard, L.B. (1979). Language impairment in children. *Merrill-Palmer Quarterly, 25*, 205–232.

Leonard, L.B. (1997). *Children with specific language impairment.* Cambridge, MA: MIT Press.

Leonard, L.B., Bortolini, U., Caselli, M.C., McGregor, K.K., & Sabbadini, L. (1992). Morphological deficits in children with specific language impairment: The status of features in the underlying grammar. *Language Acquisition, 2*, 151–179.

Leonard, L.B., & Eyer, J.A. (1996). Deficits of grammatical morphology in children with specific language impairment and their implications for notions of bootstrapping. In J.L. Morgan & K. Demuth (Eds.), *Signal to syntax: Bootstrapping from speech to grammar in early acquisition.* Mahwah, NJ: Lawrence Erlbaum Associates Inc.

Leonard, L.B., McGregor, K.K., & Allen, G.D. (1992). Grammatical morphology and speech perception in children with specific language impairment. *Journal of Speech and Hearing Research, 35*, 1076–1085.

Leonard, L.B., Nippold, M.A., Kail, R., & Hale, C.A. (1983). Picture naming in language-impaired children. *Journal of Speech and Hearing Research, 26*, 609–615.

Leonard, L.B., Sabbadini, L., Leonard, J S., & Volterra, V. (1987). Specific language impairment in children: a cross-linguistic study. *Brain and Language, 32*, 233–252.

Leonard, L.B., Sabbadini, L., Volterra, V., & Leonard, J.S. (1988). Some influences on the grammar of English- and Italian-speaking children with specific language impairment. *Applied Psycholinguistics, 9*, 39–57.

Leonard, L.B., & Schwartz, R.G. (1985). Early linguistic development of children with specific language impairment. In K.E. Nelson (Ed.), *Children's language: Vol. 5.* Hillsdale, NJ: Lawrence Erlbaum Associates Inc.

Leonard, L.B., Schwartz, R.G., Chapman, K., Rowan, L.E., Prelock, P.A., Terrell, B., Weiss, A.L., & Messick, C. (1982). Early lexical acquisition in children with specific language impairment. *Journal of Speech and Hearing Research, 25*, 554–564.

Leslie, A., & Frith, U. (1988). Autistic children's knowledge of seeing, knowing and believing. *British Journal of Developmental Psychology, 6*, 315–324.

Leslie, A., & Roth, D. (1993). What autism teaches us about metarepresentation. In S. Baron-Cohen, H. Tager-Flusberg, & D.J. Cohen (Eds.), *Understanding other minds: Perspectives from autism.* Oxford: Oxford University Press.

Leslie, A.M., & Thaiss, L. (1992). Domain specificity in conceptual development: Neuropsychological evidence from autism. *Cognition, 43*, 225–251.

Lewis, B., & Freebairn, L. (1992). Residual effects of preschool phonology disorders in grade school, adolescence, and adulthood. *Journal of Speech and Hearing Research, 35*, 819–831.

Lewis, B.A., & Thompson, L.A. (1992). A study of developmental speech and language disorders in twins. *Journal of Speech and Hearing Research, 35*, 1086–1094.

Lewis, C., Hitch, G.J., & Walker, P. (1994). The prevalence of specific arithmetic difficulties and specific reading difficulties in 9- to 10-year-old boys and girls. *Journal of Child Psychology and Psychiatry, 35*, 283–292.

Lewis, M., & Freedle, R. (1973). Mother-infant dyad: The cradle of meaning. In P. Pliner, L. Krames, & T. Alloway (Eds.), *Communication and affect*. New York: Academic Press.

Liberman, A.M., Cooper, F.S., Shankweiler, D., & Studdert-Kennedy, M. (1967). Perception of the speech code. *Psychological Review, 74*, 431–461.

Liberman, A.M., Mattingly, I.G., & Turvey, M.T. (1972). Language codes and memory codes. In A. W. Melton & E. Martin (Eds.), *Coding processes in human memory*. New York: Winston.

Liberman, I.Y., Shankweiler, D., Fischer, F.W., & Carter, B. (1974). Explicit syllable and phoneme segmentation in the young child. *Journal of Experimental Child Psychology, 18*, 201–212.

Liberman, I.Y., Shankweiler, D., & Liberman, A.M. (1989). The alphabetic principle and learning to read. In D. Shankweiler & I.Y. Liberman (Eds.), *Phonology and reading disability: Solving the reading puzzle*. Ann Arbor, MI: University of Michigan Press.

Liles, B.Z., Shulman, M.D., & Bartlett, S. (1977). Judgements of grammaticality by normal and language-disordered children. *Journal of Speech and Hearing Disorders, 42*, 199–209.

Lincoln, A.J., Dickstein, P., Courchesne, E., Elmasian, R., & Tallal, P. (1992). Auditory processing abilities in non-retarded adolescents and young adults with developmental receptive language disorder and autism. *Brain and Language, 43*, 613–622.

Linebarger, M., Schwartz, M., & Saffran, E. (1983). Sensitivity to grammatical structure in so-called agrammatic aphasics. *Cognition, 3*, 361–392.

Lively, S.E., Pisoni, D.B., & Goldinger, S.D. (1994). Spoken word recognition: Research and theory. In M.A. Gernsbacher (Ed.), *Handbook of psycholinguistics*. San Diego, CA: Academic Press.

Locke, J.L. (1980). The inference of speech perception in the phonologically disordered child: Parts I and II. *Journal of Speech and Hearing Research, 45*, 431–468.

Locke, J.L. (1988). The sound shape of early lexical representations. In M. D. Smith & J. L. Locke (Eds.), *The emergent lexicon: The child's development of a linguistic vocabulary*. San Diego, CA: Academic Press.

Locke, J.L. (1993). *The child's path to spoken language*. Cambridge, MA: Harvard University Press.

Lous, J., & Fiellau-Nikolajsen, M. (1984). A 5-year prospective case-control study of the influence of early otitis media with effusion on reading achievement. *International Journal of Pediatric Otorhinolaryngology, 8*, 19–30.

Lowe, A.D., & Campbell, R.A. (1965). Temporal discrimination in aphasoid and normal children. *Journal of Speech and Hearing Research, 8*, 313–314.

Lyon, G., & Gadisseux, J. (1991). Structural abnormalities of the brain in developmental disorders. In M. Rutter & P. Casaer (Eds.), *Biological risk factors for psychosocial disorders*. Cambridge: Cambridge University Press.

Magnusson, D., Bergman, L.R., Rudinger, G., & Törestad, B. (1989). *Problems and methods in longitudinal research: Stability and change*. Cambridge: Cambridge University Press.

Markman, E.M. (1990). Constraints children place on word meanings. *Cognitive Science, 14*, 57–77.

Marquis, D. (1961). *Archy's life of Mehitabel*. London: Faber & Faber.

Marshall, J.C., & Newcombe, F. (1966). Syntactic and semantic errors in paralexia. *Neuropsychologia, 4*, 169–176.

Marslen-Wilson, W.D., & Tyler, L.K. (1980). The temporal structure of spoken language understanding. *Cognition, 8*, 1–71.

Marslen-Wilson, W., & Tyler, L.K. (1987). Against modularity. In J.L. Garfield (Ed.), *Modularity in knowledge representation and natural-language understanding*. Cambridge, MA: MIT Press.

Marslen-Wilson, W., & Warren, P. (1994). Levels of perceptual representation and process in lexical access: Words, phonemes, and features. *Psychological Review, 101*, 653–675.

Martin, R.C., & Feher, E. (1990). The consequences of reduced memory span for the comprehension of semantic vs. syntactic information. *Brain and Language, 38*, 1–20.

Mason, S.M., & Mellor, D.H. (1984). Brain-stem middle latency and late cortical evoked potentials in children with speech and language disorders. *Electroencephalography and Clinical Neurology, 59*, 297–309.

Massaro, D.W. (1994). Psychological aspects of speech perception: Implications for research and theory. In M.A. Gernsbacher (Ed.), *Handbook of psycholinguistics*. San Diego, CA: Academic Press.

Masterson, J.J., & Kamhi, A.G. (1992). Linguistic trade-offs in school-age children with and without language disorders. *Journal of Speech and Hearing Research, 35*, 1064–1075.

Matthei, E.H. (1981). Children's interpretation of sentences containing reciprocals. In S. Tavakolian (Ed.), *Language acquisition and linguistic theory.* Cambridge, MA: MIT Press.

Mauner, G., Fromkin, V.A., & Cornell, T.L. (1993). Comprehension and acceptability judgements in agrammatism: Disruptions in the syntax of referential dependency. *Brain and Language, 45*, 340–370.

McCarthy, D. (1972). *McCarthy Scales of Children's Abilities*. New York: Psychological Corporation.

McCauley, R.J., & Swisher, L. (1984a). Psychometric review of language and articulation tests for preschool children. *Journal of Speech and Hearing Disorders, 49*, 34–42.

McCauley, R.J., & Swisher, L. (1984b). Use and misuse of norm-referenced tests in clinical assessment: A hypothetical case. *Journal of Speech and Hearing Disorders, 49*, 338–348.

McClelland, J.L., & Elman, J.L. (1986). Interactive processes in speech perception: The TRACE model. In J.L. McClelland, D.E. Rumelhart, & The PDP Research Group (Eds.), *Parallel distributed processing*. Cambridge, MA: MIT Press.

McCroskey, R.L., & Thompson, N.W. (1973). Comprehension of rate controlled speech by children with specific learning disabilities. *Journal of Learning Disabilities, 6*, 621–628.

McKee, D. (1980). *Not now, Bernard*. London: Arrow Books.

McNicol, D. (1972). *A primer of signal detection theory*. London: Allen & Unwin.

McReynolds, L.V. (1966). Operant conditioning for investigating speech sound discrimination in aphasic children. *Journal of Speech and Hearing Research, 9*, 519–528.

McTear, M. (1985). Pragmatic disorders: A case study of conversational disability. *British Journal of Disorders of Communication, 20*, 119–128.

Merritt, D.D., & Liles, B.Z. (1987). Story grammar ability in children with and without language disorder: Story generation, story retelling, and story comprehension. *Journal of Speech and Hearing Research, 30*, 539–552.

Merzenich, M.M., Jenkins, W.M., Johnston, P., Schreiner, C., Miller, S.L., & Tallal, P. (1996). Temporal processing deficits of language-learning impaired children ameliorated by training. *Science, 271*, 77–81.

Michas, I.C., & Henry, L.A. (1994). The link between phonological memory and vocabulary acquisition. *British Journal of Developmental Psychology, 12*, 147–163.

Michel, G.F., & Moore, C.L. (1995). *Developmental psychobiology*. Cambridge, MA: MIT Press.

Miller, J. (1991). Research on language disorders in children: A progress report. In J. Miller (Ed.), *Research on child language disorders*. Austin, TX: Pro-Ed.

Miller, J., & Paul, R. (1995). *The clinical assessment of language comprehension*. Baltimore, MD: Paul H. Brookes.

Miller, J.R., & Kintsch, W. (1980). Readability and recall of short prose passages: A theoretical analysis. *Journal of Experimental Psychology: Human Learning and Memory, 6*, 335–354.

Mills, D.L., Coffey-Corina, S.A., & Neville, H.J. (1993). Language acquisition and cerebral specialization in 20-month-old infants. *Journal of Cognitive Neuroscience, 5*, 317–334.

Milner, B., & Teuber, H.-L. (1968). Alterations of perception and memory in man: Reflections on method. In L. Weiskrantz (Ed.), *Analysis of behavioral change*. New York: Harper & Row.

Milosky, L.M. (1992). Children listening: The role of world knowledge in comprehension. In R. Chapman (Ed.), *Processes in language acquisition and disorders*. St Louis, MO: Mosby Year Book.

Mitchell, D.C. (1994). Sentence parsing. In M. A. Gernsbacher (Ed.), *Handbook of psycholinguistics*. San Diego, CA: Academic Press.

Miyake, A., Carpenter, P.A., & Just, M.A. (1994). A capacity approach to syntactic comprehension disorders: Making normal adults perform like aphasic patients. *Cognitive Neuropsychology, 11*, 671–717.

Mody, M., Studdert-Kennedy, M., & Brady, S. (1997). Speech perception deficits in poor readers: Auditory processing or phonological coding? *Journal of Experimental Child Psychology, 64*, 199–231.

Moffitt, A.R. (1971). Consonant cue perception by twenty- to twenty-four-week-old infants. *Child Development, 42*, 717–731.

Mogford, K., & Bishop, D. (1988). Five questions about language development considered in the light of exceptional circumstances. In D. Bishop & K. Mogford (Eds.), *Language development in exceptional circumstances*. Edinburgh: Churchill Livingstone.

Molfese, D. (1990). Auditory evoked responses recorded from 16-month-old human infants to words they did and did not know. *Brain and Language, 38*, 345–363.

Montgomery, J.W. (1995). Sentence comprehension in children with specific language impairment: The role of phonological working memory. *Journal of Speech and Hearing Research , 38 ,* 189–199.

Montgomery, J.W., Scudder, R.R., & Moore, C. (1990). Language-impaired children's real time comprehension of spoken language. *Applied Psycholinguistics, 11*, 273–290.

Moore, D.R. (1990). Effects of early auditory experience on development of binaural pathways in the brain. *Seminars in Perinatology, 14*, 294–298.

Morehead, D.M., & Ingram, D. (1976). The development of base syntax in normal and linguistically deviant children. In D.M. Morehead & A.E. Morehead (Eds.), *Normal and deficient child language*. Baltimore, PA: University Park Press.

Morgan, J., Meier, R.P., & Newport, E.L. (1987). Structural packaging in the input to language learning: Contributions of prosodic and morphological marking of phrases to the acquisition of language. *Cognitive Psychology, 19*, 498–550.

Morley, M.E. (1972). *The development and disorders of speech in childhood*. Edinburgh: Churchill Livingstone.

Morton, J. (1969). Interaction of information in word recognition. *Psychological Review, 76*, 165–178.

Morton, J., & Johnson, M.H. (1991). CONSPEC and CONLERN: A two-process theory of infant face recognition. *Psychological Review, 98*, 164–181.

Moyer, R.S., & Landauer, T. (1967). Time required for judgements of numerical inequality. *Nature, 215*, 1519–1520.

Mundy, P., Sigman, M., & Kasari, C. (1993). The theory of mind and joint-attention deficits in autism. In S. Baron-Cohen, H. Tager-Flusberg, & D.J. Cohen (Eds.), *Understanding other minds: Perspectives from autism*. Oxford: Oxford University Press.

Murray, L., Hipwell, A., Hooper, R., Stein, A., & Cooper, P. (1996). The cognitive development of 5-year-old children of postnatally depressed mothers. *Journal of Child Psychology and Psychiatry, 37*, 927–935.

Murray, L., Kempton, C., Woolgar, M., & Hooper, R. (1993). Depressed mothers' speech to their infants and its relation to infant gender and cognitive development. *Journal of Child Psychology and Psychiatry, 34*, 1083–1102.

Myers, J.L., Shinjo, M., & Duffy, S.A. (1987). Degree of causal relatedness and memory. *Journal of Verbal Learning and Verbal Behavior, 26*, 453–465.

Naigles, L.G., & Kako, E.T. (1993). First contact in verb acquisition: Defining a role for syntax. *Child Development, 64*, 1665–1687.

Neligan, G.A., & Prudham, D. (1969). Norms for four standard developmental milestones by sex, social, class, and place in family. *Developmental Medicine and Child Neurology, 11*, 413.

Neville, H.J., Coffey, S.A., Holcomb, P.J., & Tallal, P. (1993). The neurobiology of sensory and language processing in language-impaired children. *Journal of Cognitive Neuroscience, 5*, 235–253.

Nygaard, L.C., & Pisoni, D.B. (1995). Speech perception: New directions in research and theory. In J. L. Miller & P. D. Eimas (Eds.), *Speech, language, and communication: Handbook of perception and cognition* (2nd ed.). San Diego, CA: Academic Press.

O'Hara, M., & Johnston, J. (1997). Syntactic bootstrapping in children with specific language impairment. *European Journal of Disorders of Communication, 32*, 147–163.

Oakhill, J. (1982). Constructive processes in skilled and less skilled comprehenders' memory for sentences. *British Journal of Psychology, 73*, 13–20.

Oakhill, J. (1983). Instantiation in skilled and less skilled comprehenders. *Quarterly Journal of Experimental Psychology, 35A*, 441–450.

Oakhill, J. (1994). Individual differences in children's text comprehension. In M. A. Gernsbacher (Ed.), *Handbook of psycholinguistics*. San Diego, CA: Academic Press.

Oakhill, J., & Patel, S. (1991). Can imagery training help children who have comprehension problems? *Journal of Research in Reading, 14*, 106–115.

Oetting, J.B., Rice, M.L., & Swank, L.K. (1995). Quick incidental learning (QUIL) of words by school-age children with and without SLI. *Journal of Speech and Hearing Research, 38*, 434–445.

Oster, H. (1981). "Recognition" of emotional expression in infancy. In M. E. Lamb & L. R. Sherrod (Eds.), *Infant social cognition*. Hillsdale, NJ: Lawrence Erlbaum Associates Inc.

Parsons, T. (1995). Thematic relations and arguments. *Linguistic Inquiry, 26*, 635–662.

Patterson, K.E., Marshall, J.C., & Coltheart, M. (1985). *Surface dyslexia: Neuropsychological and cognitive studies of phonological reading.* Hove: Lawrence Erlbaum Associates Ltd.

Paul, R. (1996). Clinical implications of the natural history of slow expressive language development. *American Journal of Speech Language Pathology, 5,* 5–21.

Perfetti, C. (1994). Psycholinguistics and reading ability. In M. A. Gernsbacher (Ed.), *Handbook of psycholinguistics.* San Diego, CA: Academic Press.

Perner, J. (1991). *Understanding the representational mind.* Cambridge, MA: MIT Press.

Perner, J., Ruffman, T., & Leekam, S.R. (1994). Theory of mind is contagious: You catch it from your sibs. *Child Development, 65,* 1228–1238.

Peters, S.A.F., Grievink, E.H., van Bon, W.H.J., & Schilder, A.G.M. (1994). The effects of early bilateral otitis media with effusion on educational attainment: A prospective cohort study. *Journal of Learning Disabilities, 27,* 111–121.

Piaget, J. (1929). *The child's conception of the world.* London: Granada Publishing Ltd.

Piaget, J. (1970). Piaget's theory. In P. H. Mussen (Ed.), *Carmichael's manual of child psychology* (Vol. 1). New York: John Wiley.

Pine, J. (1995). Variation in vocabulary development as a function of birth order. *Child Development, 66,* 272–281.

Pinker, S. (1984). *Language learnability and language development.* Cambridge, MA: Harvard University Press.

Pinker, S. (1991). Rules of language. *Science, 253,* 530–535.

Pinker, S. (1994). *The language instinct: The new science of language and mind.* London: Penguin Books.

Pinker, S., & Mehler, J. (Eds.). (1988). Connectionism and symbol systems: Special issue of *Cognition, 28,* 1–2. The Hague, Netherlands: Elsevier.

Pinker, S., & Prince, A. (1988). On language and connectionism: Analysis of a parallel distributed processing model of language acquisition. *Cognition, 28,* 73–193.

Plante, E., Swisher, L., Vance, R., & Rapcsak, S. (1991). MRI findings in boys with specific language impairment. *Brain and Language, 41,* 52–66.

Plunkett, K., & Marchman, V. (1993). From rote learning to system building: Acquiring verb morphology in children and connectionist nets. *Cognition, 48,* 21–69.

Poizner, H., Klima, E.S., & Bellugi, U. (1987). *What the hands reveal about the brain.* Cambridge, MA: MIT Press.

Portoian-Shuhaiber, S., & Cullinan, T.R. (1984). Middle ear disease assessed by impedance in primary school children in South London. *Lancet, 1,* 1111–1112.

Powell, R., & Bishop, D.V.M. (1992). Clumsiness and perceptual problems in children with specific language impairment. *Developmental Medicine and Child Neurology, 34,* 755–765.

Puckering, C., & Rutter, M. (1987). Environmental influences on language development. In W. Yule, & M. Rutter (Eds.), *Language development and disorders.* London: MacKeith Press.

Quigley, S. P., Power, D.J., & Steinkamp, M.W. (1977). The language structure of deaf children. *Volta Review, 79,* 73–84.

Quine, W.V.O. (1960). *Word and object.* Cambridge, MA: MIT Press.

Radford, A. (1988). *Transformational grammar: A first course.* Cambridge: Cambridge University Press.

Ramer, A. (1976). The function of imitation in child language. *Journal of Speech and Hearing Research, 19,* 700–717.

Rapin, I. (1982). *Children with brain dysfunction.* New York: Raven Press.

Rapin, I., & Allen, D. (1983). Developmental language disorders: Nosologic considerations. In U. Kirk (Ed.), *Neuropsychology of language, reading, and spelling.* New York: Academic Press.

Rapin, I., & Allen, D. (1987). Developmental dysphasia and autism in pre-school children: Characteristics and subtypes. *Proceedings of the first international symposium on specific speech and language disorders in children.* London: Association for All Speech Impaired Children.

Rapin, I., Mattis, S., & Rowan, A.J. (1977). Verbal auditory agnosia in children. *Developmental Medicine and Child Neurology, 19,* 192–207.

Raven, J.C., Court, J.H., & Raven, J. (1986). *Raven's Progressive Matrices and Raven's Coloured Matrices.* London: H.K. Lewis.

Reeder, K., & Wakefield, J. (1987). The development of young children's speech act comprehension: How much language is necessary? *Applied Psycholinguistics, 8,* 1–18.

Reynell, J. (1985). *Reynell Developmental Language Scales* (2nd rev. ed.). Windsor: NFER-Nelson.

Reznick, J.S. (1990). Visual preference as a test of infant word comprehension. *Applied Psycholinguistics, 11,* 145–166.

Rice, M.L., Buhr, J., & Oetting, J.B. (1992). Specific-language-impaired children's quick incidental learning of words: the effect of a pause. *Journal of Speech and Hearing Research, 35,* 1040–1048.

Rice, M.L., & Oetting, J.B. (1993). Morphological deficits of children with SLI: Evaluation of number marking and agreement. *Journal of Speech and Hearing Research, 36*, 1249–1257.

Rice, M.L., Oetting, J.B., Marquis, J., Bode, J., & Pae, S. (1994). Frequency of input effects on word comprehension of children with specific language impairment. *Journal of Speech and Hearing Research, 37*, 106–122.

Rice, M.L., Sell, M.A., & Hadley, P.A. (1991). Social interactions of speech and language impaired children. *Journal of Speech and Hearing Research, 34*, 1299–1307.

Rice, M.L., Wexler, K., & Cleave, P.L. (1995). Specific language impairment as a period of extended optional infinitive. *Journal of Speech and Hearing Research, 38*, 850–863.

Roberts, J.E., Sanyal, M.A., Burchinal, M.R., Collier, A.M., Ramey, C.T., & Henderson, F.W. (1986). Otitis media in early childhood and its relationship to later verbal and academic performance. *Pediatrics, 78*, 423–430.

Robinson, R.J. (1987). Introduction and overview. *Proceedings of the first international symposium on specific speech and language disorders in children.* London: Association for All Speech Impaired Children.

Robinson, R.J. (1991). Causes and associations of severe and persistent specific speech and language disorders in children. *Developmental Medicine and Child Neurology, 33*, 943–962.

Rodgon, M., & Kurdek, L. (1977). Vocal and gestural imitation in children under two years old. *Journal of Genetic Psychology, 131*, 115–123.

Rolf, J., Masten, A.S., Cicchetti, D., Nuechterlein, K.H., & Weintraub, S. (Eds.). (1990). *Risk and protective factors in the development of psychopathology.* Cambridge: Cambridge University Press.

Roncagliolo, M., Benitez, J., & Perez, M. (1994). Auditory brainstem responses of children with developmental language disorders. *Developmental Medicine and Child Neurology, 36*, 26–33.

Rosenberger, P.B., & Hier, D.B. (1980). Cerebral asymmetry and verbal intellectual deficits. *Annals of Neurology, 8*, 300–304.

Rosenzweig, M.R. (1966). Environmental complexity, cerebral change, and behavior. *American Psychologist, 21*, 321–332.

Rosinski-McClendon, M.K., & Newhoff, M. (1987). Conversational responsiveness and assertiveness in language-impaired children. *Language, Speech and Hearing Services in Schools, 18*, 53–62.

Ruben, R.J. (1986). Unsolved issues around critical periods with emphasis on clinical application. *Acta Otolaryngologica (Suppl.), 429*, 61–64.

Ruben, R.J., & Rapin, I. (1980). Plasticity of the developing auditory system. *Annals of Otology, Rhonology, and Laryngology, 89*, 303–311.

Rumelhart, D.E., & McClelland, J.L. (1986). On learning the past tenses of English verbs. In J.L. McClelland, D.E. Rumelhart, & The PDP Research Group (Eds.), *Parallel distributed processing.* Cambridge, MA: MIT Press.

Rust, J. (1996). *The Wechsler Objective Language Dimensions.* London: Psychological Corporation.

Rust, J., Golombok, S., & Trickey, G. (1993). *Wechsler Objective Reading Dimensions.* Sidcup: Psychological Corporation.

Rutter, M. (1991). Nature, nurture and psychopathology: A new look at an old topic. *Development and Psychopathology, 3*, 125–136.

Rutter, M., Tizard, J., & Whitmore, K. (Eds.). (1970). *Education, health and behaviour.* London: Longman.

Sachs, J., Bard, B., & Johnson, M. (1981). Language learning with restricted input: Case studies of two hearing children of deaf parents. *Applied Psycholinguistics, 2*, 33–54.

Saffran, E.M., Marin, O.S. M., & Yeni-Komshian, G.H. (1976). An analysis of speech perception in word deafness. *Brain and Language, 3*, 209–228.

Schiff-Myers, N. (1988). Hearing children of deaf parents. In D. Bishop & K. Mogford (Eds.), *Language development in exceptional circumstances.* Edinburgh: Churchill Livingstone.

Schwartz, M., Saffran, E.M., & Marin, O.S.M. (1980). The word order problem in agrammatism: I. Comprehension. *Brain and Language, 10*, 249–262.

Schwartz, R., & Leonard, L. (1982). Do children pick and choose? An examination of phonological selection and avoidance in early lexical acquisition. *Journal of Child Language, 9*, 319–336.

Seidenberg, M.S. (1992). Connectionism without tears. In S. Davis (Ed.), *Connectionism: Theory and practice.* Oxford: Oxford University Press.

Semel, E.M., Wiig, E.H., & Secord, W. (1980). *Clinical Evaluation of Language Fundamentals—Revised.* San Antonio, TX: Psychological Corporation.

Seymour, C.M., Baran, J.A., & Peaper, R.E. (1981). Auditory discrimination: Evaluation and intervention. In N.J. Lass (Ed.), *Speech and Language* (Vol. 6). New York/London: Academic Press.

Shallice, T. (1988). *From neuropsychology to mental structure.* Cambridge: Cambridge University Press.

Shallice, T., & Warrington, E.K. (1970). Independent functioning of verbal memory stores: A neuropsychological study. *Quarterly Journal of Experimental Psychology, 22,* 261–273.

Sharp, D., Hay, D.F., Pawlby, S., Schmücker, G., Allen, H., & Kumar, R. (1995). The impact of postnatal depression on boys' intellectual development. *Journal of Child Psychology and Psychiatry, 36,* 1315–1336.

Shatz, M. (1978). On the development of communicative understandings: An early strategy for interpreting and responding to messages. *Cognitive Psychology, 10,* 217–301.

Shatz, M., & Gelman, R. (1973). The development of communication skills: Modifications in the speech of young children as a function of listener. *Monographs of the Society for Research in Child Development, 5,* 1–38.

Shatz, M., Shulman, M.A., & Bernstein, D.K. (1980). The responses of language disordered children to indirect directives in varying contexts. *Applied Psycholinguistics, 1,* 295–306.

Shaywitz, S.E., Shaywitz, B.A., Fletcher, J.M., & Escobar, M.D. (1990). Prevalence of reading disability in boys and girls. *Journal of the American Medical Association, 264,* 998–1002.

Siegel, L.S. (1982). Reproductive, perinatal, and environmental factors as predictors of the cognitive and language development of preterm and full-term infants. *Child Development, 53,* 963–973.

Siegel, L.S., Lees, A., Allan, L., & Bolton, B. (1981). Non-verbal assessment of Piagetian concepts in preschool children with impaired language development. *Educational Psychology, 2,* 153–158.

Skinner, B.F. (1957). *Verbal behavior.* New York: Appleton-Century-Crofts.

Skuse, D.H. (1988). Extreme deprivation in early childhood. In D.V.M. Bishop & K. Mogford (Eds.), *Language development in exceptional circumstances.* Edinburgh: Churchill Livingstone.

Smith, N., & Tsimpli, I.-M. (1995). *The mind of a savant: Language learning and modularity.* Oxford: Blackwell.

Smith-Lock, K.M. (1991). Errors of inflection in the writing of normal and poor readers. *Language and Speech, 34,* 341–350.

Snijders, J.T., & Snijders Oomen, N. (1959). *Non-verbal intelligence test.* Groningen, Netherlands: J. B. Walters.

Snow, C. (1989). Imitativeness: A trait or a skill? In G. E. Speidel & K.E. Nelson (Eds.), *The many faces of imitation in language learning.* New York: Springer Verlag.

Snowling, M., Chiat, S., & Hulme, C. (1991). Words, nonwords and phonological processes: Some comments on Gathercole, Willis, Emslie, and Baddeley. *Applied Psycholinguistics, 12,* 369–373.

Sparks, S.N. (1984). *Birth defects and speech-language disorders.* San Diego, CA: College-Hill Press.

Spelke, E.S., Breinlinger, K., & Macomber, J. (1992). Origins of knowledge. *Psychological Review, 99,* 605–632.

Spilich, G.J., Vesonder, G.T., Chiesi, H.L., & Voss, J.F. (1979). Text processing of domain-related information for individuals with high and low domain knowledge. *Journal of Verbal Learning and Verbal Behavior, 18,* 275–290.

Stark, R.E., & Montgomery, J.W. (1995). Sentence processing in language impaired children under conditions of filtering and time compression. *Applied Psycholinguistics, 16,* 137–154.

Stark, R.E., & Tallal, P. (1981a). Perceptual and motor deficits in language impaired children. In R. W. Keith (Ed.), *Central auditory and language disorders in children.* San Diego, CA: College-Hill Press.

Stark, R.E., & Tallal, P. (1981b). Selection of children with specific language deficits. *Journal of Speech and Hearing Disorders, 46,* 114–122.

Stark, R.E., & Tallal, P. (1988). *Language, speech and reading disorders in children.* Boston: Little, Brown & Co.

Stefanatos, G.A., Green, G.G.R., & Ratcliff, G.G. (1989). Neurophysiological evidence of auditory channel anomalies in developmental dysphasia. *Archives of Neurology, 46,* 871–875.

Stevens, K.N., & Blumstein, S.E. (1981). The search for invariant acoustic correlates of phonetic features. In P.D. Eimas & J.L. Miller (Eds.), *Perspectives on the study of speech.* Hillsdale, NJ: Lawrence Erlbaum Associates Inc.

Stevenson, J., Richman, N., & Graham, P. (1985). Behaviour problems and language abilities at 3 years and behavioural deviance at 8 years. *Journal of Child Psychology and Psychiatry, 26,* 215–230.

Stothard, S.E., & Hulme, C. (1992). Reading comprehension difficulties in children: The role of language comprehension and working memory skills. *Reading and Writing, 4,* 245–256.

Strohner, H., & Nelson, K. (1974). The young child's development of sentence comprehension: Influence of event probability, nonverbal context, syntactic form and strategies. *Child Development, 45,* 567–576.

Studdert-Kennedy, M., & Mody, M. (1995). Auditory temporal perception deficits in the reading-impaired: A critical review of the evidence. *Psychonomic Bulletin and Review, 2,* 508–514.

Sussman, J.E. (1993). Perception of formant transition cues to place of articulation in children with language impairments. *Journal of Speech and Hearing Research, 36*, 1286–1299.

Swinney, D.A. (1979). Lexical access during sentence comprehension: (Re)consideration of context effects. *Journal of Verbal Learning and Verbal Behavior, 18*, 645–659.

Tabachnick, B.G., & Fidell, L.S. (1989). *Using multivariate statistics* (2nd ed.). New York: Harper Collins.

Tager-Flusberg, H. (1981). Sentence comprehension in autistic children. *Applied Psycholinguistics, 2*, 5–24.

Tallal, P. (1975). Perceptual and linguistic factors in the language impairment of developmental dysphasics: An experimental investigation with the Token test. *Cortex, 11*, 196–205.

Tallal, P. (1976). Rapid auditory processing in normal and disordered language development. *Journal of Speech and Hearing Research, 19*, 561–571.

Tallal, P. (1990). Fine-grained discrimination deficits in language-learning impaired children are specific neither to the auditory modality nor to speech perception. *Journal of Speech and Hearing Research, 33*, 616–621.

Tallal, P., Miller, S.L., Bedi, G., Byma, G., Wang, X., Najarajan, S.S., Schreiner, C., Jenkins, W.M., & Merzenich, M.M. (1996). Language comprehension in language-learning impaired children improved with acoustically modified speech. *Science, 271*, 81–84.

Tallal, P., Miller, S., & Fitch, R.H. (1993). Neurobiological basis of speech: A case for the pre-eminence of temporal processing. In P. Tallal, A.M. Galaburda, R.R. Llinas, & C. von Euler (Eds.), *Annals of the New York Academy of Sciences: Temporal information processing in the nervous system*. New York: New York Academy of Sciences.

Tallal, P., & Piercy, M. (1973a). Defects of non-verbal auditory perception in children with developmental aphasia. *Nature, 241*, 468–469.

Tallal, P., & Piercy, M. (1973b). Developmental aphasia: Impaired rate of nonverbal processing as a function of sensory modality. *Neuropsychologia, 11*, 389–398.

Tallal, P., & Piercy, M. (1974). Developmental aphasia: Rate of auditory processing and selective impairment of consonant perception. *Neuropsychologia, 12*, 83–93.

Tallal, P., & Piercy, M. (1975). Developmental aphasia: The perception of brief vowels and extended stop consonants. *Neuropsychologia, 13*, 69–74.

Tallal, P., & Stark, R.E. (1981). Speech acoustic-cue discrimination abilities of normally developing and language-impaired children. *Journal of the Acoustical Society of America, 69*, 568–574.

Tallal, P., Stark, R., & Curtiss, B. (1976). Relation between speech perception and speech production in children with developmental dysphasia. *Brain and Language, 3*, 305–317.

Tallal, P., Stark, R.E., Kallman, C., & Mellits, D. (1980). Perceptual constancy for phonemic categories: A developmental study with normal and language impaired children. *Applied Psycholinguistics, 1*, 49–64.

Tallal, P., Stark, R., Kallman, C., & Mellits, D. (1981). A re-examination of some nonverbal perceptual abilities of language-impaired and normal children as a function of age and sensory modality. *Journal of Speech and Hearing Research, 24*, 351–357.

Tanenhaus, M.K., Spivey-Knowlton, M.J., Eberhard, J.M., & Sedivy, J.C. (1995). Integration of visual and linguistic information in spoken language comprehension. *Science, 268*, 1632–1634.

Temple, C. (1997). Developmental cognitive neuropsychology. *Journal of Child Psychology and Psychiatry, 38*, 27–52.

Temple, C.M. (1992). Developmental dyscalculia. In S.J. Segalowitz & I. Rapin (Eds.), *Handbook of neuropsychology: Vol. 7, Section 10: Child neuropsychology, Pt. 2*. Amsterdam: Elsevier Science.

Templin, M.C. (1957). *Certain language skills in children*. Minnesota, MN: University of Minnesota Press.

Templin, M.C., & Darley, F. (1960). *The Templin-Darley Test of Articulation*. Iowa City, IA: Bureau of Educational Research, University of Iowa.

Thal, D.J., Tobias, S., & Morrison, D. (1991). Language and gesture in late talkers: A one-year follow-up. *Journal of Speech and Hearing Research, 34*, 604–612.

Thelen, E., & Smith, L.B. (1993). *A dynamic systems approach to the development of cognition and action*. Cambridge, MA: MIT Press.

Thibodeau, L.M., & Sussman, H.M. (1979). Performance on a test of categorical perception of speech in normal and communication disordered children. *Journal of Phonetics, 7*, 375–391.

Tomblin, J.B., Abbas, P.J., Records, N.L., & Brenneman, L.M. (1995). Auditory evoked responses to frequency-modulated tones in children with specific language impairment. *Journal of Speech and Hearing Research, 38*, 387–392.

Tomblin, J.B., & Buckwalter, P.R. (1994). Studies of genetics of specific language impairment. In R. Watkins & M. Rice (Eds.), *Specific language impairments in children*. Baltimore, MD: Paul H. Brookes.

Tomblin, J.B., Freese, P.R., & Records, N.L. (1992). Diagnosing specific language impairment in adults for the purpose of pedigree analysis. *Journal of Speech and Hearing Research, 35*, 832–843.

Tomblin, J.B., Hardy, J.C., & Hein, H.A. (1991). Predicting poor communication status in preschool children using risk factors present at birth. *Journal of Speech and Hearing Research, 34*, 1096–1105.

Treiman, R. (1985). Onsets and rimes as units of spoken syllables: Evidence from children. *Journal of Experimental Child Psychology, 39*, 161–181.

Treiman, R., & Zukowski, A. (1991). Levels of phonological awareness. In S.A. Brady & D.P. Shankweiler (Eds.), *Phonological processes in literacy*. Hillsdale, NJ: Lawrence Erlbaum Associates Inc.

Tucker, M., & Hirsh-Pasek, K. (1993). Systems and language: Implications for acquisition. In L.B. Smith & E. Thelen (Eds.), *A dynamic systems approach to development: Applications*. Cambridge, MA: MIT Press.

Ullman, M., & Gopnik, M. (1994). The production of inflectional morphology in hereditary specific language impairment. In J. Matthews (Ed.), *Linguistic aspects of familial language impairment*. Special Issue of the McGill Working Papers in Linguistics (Vol. 10). Montréal, Canada: McGill University.

Vallar, G., & Baddeley, A.D. (1984). Phonological short-term store, phonological processing and sentence comprehension: A neuropsychological case study. *Cognitive Neuropsychology, 1*, 121–141.

Vallar, G., & Baddeley, A.D. (1984b). Fractionation of working memory: Neuropsychological evidence for a phonological short-term store. *Journal of Verbal Learning and Verbal Behavior, 23*, 151–161.

Vallar, G., & Papagno, C. (1993). Preserved vocabulary acquisition in Down's syndrome: The role of phonological short-term memory. *Cortex, 29*, 467–483.

Van den Broek, P.W. (1989). Causal reasoning and inference making in judging the importance of story statements. *Child Development, 60*, 286–297.

Van der Lely, H.K.J. (1990). *Sentence comprehension processes in specifically language impaired children*. Unpublished PhD thesis, Birkbeck College, University of London, London.

Van der Lely, H.K.J. (1994). Canonical linking rules forward versus reverse linking in normally developing and specifically language-impaired children. *Cognition, 51*, 29–72.

Van der Lely, H.K.J. (1996a). Specifically language impaired and normally developing children: Verbal passive vs. adjectival passive sentence interpretation. *Lingua, 98*, 243–272.

Van der Lely, H.K.J. (1996b). Language modularity and grammatical specific language impairment in children. In M. Aldridge (Ed.), *Child language*. Clevedon, Avon: Multilingual Matters Limited.

Van der Lely, H.K.J., & Dewart, H. (1986). Sentence comprehension strategies in specifically language impaired children. *British Journal of Disorders of Communication, 21*, 291–306.

Van der Lely, H.K.J., & Harris, M. (1990). Comprehension of reversible sentences in specifically language impaired children. *Journal of Speech and Hearing Research, 55*, 101–117.

Van der Lely, H.K.J., & Howard, D. (1993). Children with specific language impairment: Linguistic impairment or short-term memory deficit? *Journal of Speech and Hearing Research, 36*, 1193–1207.

Van der Lely, H.K.J., & Stollwerck, L. (1997). Binding theory and grammatical specific language impairment in children. *Cognition, 62*, 245–290.

Van Dijk, T.A. (1995). On macrostructures, mental models and other inventions: A brief personal history of the Kintsch-van Dijk theory. In C.A. Weaver, S. Mannes, & C.R. Fletcher (Eds.), *Discourse comprehension: Essays in honor of Walter Kintsch*. Hillsdale, NJ: Lawrence Erlbaum Associates Inc.

Vargha-Khadem, F., Watkins, K., Alcock, K., Fletcher, P., & Passingham, R. (1995). Praxic and nonverbal cognitive deficits in a large family with a genetically transmitted speech and language disorder. *Proceedings of the National Academy of Sciences, 92*, 930–933.

Veneziano, E. (1988). Vocal-verbal interaction and the construction of early lexical knowledge. In M. D. Smith & J. L. Locke (Eds.), *The emergent lexicon*. San Diego, CA: Academic Press.

Walley, A.C. (1993). The role of vocabulary development in children's spoken word recognition and segmentation ability. *Developmental Review, 13*, 286–350.

Warrington, E.K., & McCarthy, R.A. (1987). Categories of knowledge: Further fractionations and an attempted integration. *Brain, 110*, 1273–1296.

Waterson, N. (1971). Child phonology: A prosodic view. *Journal of Linguistics, 7*, 179–211.

Watkins, R., & Rice, M. (1991). Verb particle and preposition acquisition in language-impaired preschoolers. *Journal of Speech and Hearing Research, 34*, 1130–1141.

Wechsler, D. (1992). *Wechsler Intelligence Scale for Children* (3rd ed.). London: Psychological Corporation.

Weller, A., Glaubman, H., Yehuda, S., Caspy, T., & Ben-Uria, Y. (1988). Acute and repeated gestational stress affect offspring learning and activity in rats. *Physiology and Behavior, 43*, 139–143.

Wellman, H.M. (1977). Tip of the tongue and feeling of knowing experiences: A developmental study of memory monitoring. *Child Development, 48*, 13–21.

Wells, G. (1979). *Language development in the preschool years*. Cambridge: Cambridge University Press.

Wepman, J.M. (1973). *Auditory discrimination test*. Chicago, IL: Language Research Associates.

Whitehurst, G.J. (1997). Language processes in context: Language learning in children reared in poverty. In L.B. Adamson & M.A. Romski (Eds.), *Communication and language acquisition*. Baltimore, MD: Brookes.

Whitehurst, G.J., & Fischel, J.E. (1994). Early developmental language delay: What, if anything, should the clinician do about it? *Journal of Child Psychology and Psychiatry, 35*, 613–648.

Wightman, F., & Allen, P. (1992). Individual differences in auditory capability among preschool children. In L.A. Werner & E.W. Rubel (Eds.), *Developmental psychoacoustics*. Washington, DC: American Psychological Association.

Wightman, F., Allen, P., Dolan, T., Kistler, D., & Jamieson, D. (1989). Temporal resolution in children. *Child Development, 60*, 611–624.

Wiig, E., Semel, E.M., & Nystrom, L.A. (1982). Comparison of rapid naming abilities in language-learning-disabled and academically achieving eight-year-olds. *Language, Speech and Hearing Services in the Schools, 13*, 11–23.

Wilcox, J., & Tobin, H. (1974). Linguistic performance of hard-of-hearing and normal-hearing children. *Journal of Speech and Hearing Research, 17*, 286–293.

Wilson, B.C., & Risucci, D.A. (1986). A model for clinical-quantitative classification generation 1: Application to language disordered preschool children. *Brain and Language, 27*, 281–310.

Wimmer, H., Landerl, K., Linortner, R., & Hummer, P. (1991). The relationship of phonemic awareness to reading acquisition: More consequence than precondition but still important. *Cognition, 40*, 219–249.

Wimmer, H., & Perner, J. (1983). Beliefs about beliefs: Representation and constraining function of wrong beliefs in young children's understanding of deception. *Cognition, 13*, 103–128.

Wolfus, B., Moscovitch, M., & Kinsbourne, M. (1980). Subgroups of developmental language impairment. *Brain and Language, 10*, 152–171.

Wood, M.M. (1993). *Categorial grammars*. London: Routledge.

Woodhouse, W., Bailey, A., Rutter, M., Bolton, P., Baird, G., & Le Couteur, A. (1996). Head circumference in autism and other pervasive developmental disorders. *Journal of Child Psychology and Psychiatry, 37*, 665–671.

World Health Organization. (1992). *The ICD-10 classification for mental and behavioural disorders: Clinical descriptions and diagnostic guidelines*. Geneva, Switzerland: WHO.

World Health Organization. (1993). *The ICD-10 classification for mental and behavioural disorders: Diagnostic criteria for research*. Geneva, Switzerland: WHO.

Worster-Drought, C., & Allen, I.M. (1929). Congenital auditory imperception (congenital word-deafness): With report of a case. *Journal of Neurology and Psychopathology, 10*, 193–208.

Wyke, M.A., & Asso, D. (1979). Perception and memory for spatial relations in children with developmental dysphasia. *Neuropsychologia, 17*, 231–239.

Young, A.W., & Ellis, H.D. (1992). Visual perception. In S.J. Segalowitz & I. Rapin (Eds.), *Handbook of Neuropsychology: Vol. 7, Section 10: Child Neuropsychology, Pt. 2*. Amsterdam, The Netherlands: Elsevier Science.

Yuill, N., & Joscelyne, T. (1988). Effect of organizational cues and strategies on good and poor comprehenders' story understanding. *Journal of Educational Psychology, 80*, 152–158.

Yuill, N., & Oakhill, J. (1991). *Children's problems in text comprehension*. Cambridge: Cambridge University Press.

Yule, W. (1987). Psychological assessment. In W. Yule & M. Rutter (Eds.), *Language development and disorders. Clinics in developmental medicine* (double issue). London: MacKeith Press.

Zangwill, O.L. (1978). The concept of developmental dysphasia. In M.A. Wyke (Ed.), *Developmental dysphasia*. London: Academic Press.

Author Index

Subject Index